GRAMMAR FOR WRITING

ELEMENTS of SUCCESS

ANNE M. EDIGER

JENNI CURRIE SANTAMARIA

RANDEE FALK

OXFORD
UNIVERSITY PRESS

SHAPING learning TOGETHER

We would like to thank the following class for piloting *Elements of Success*:

ABC Adult School, Cerritos, CA
Teacher: Jenni Santamaria
Students: Gabriela A. Marquez Aguilar, Yijung Chen, Laura Gomez, Terry Hahn, EunKyung Lee, Subin Lee, Sunmin Lee, Jane Leelachat, Lilia Nunezuribe, Gina Olivar, Young Park, Seol Hee Seok, Kwang Mi Song

---

During the development of *Elements of Success*, we spoke with teachers and professionals who are passionate about teaching grammar. Their feedback led us to create *Elements of Success: Grammar for Language Learning*, a course that solves teaching challenges by presenting grammar clearly, simply, and completely. We would like to acknowledge the advice of teachers from

USA • BRAZIL • CANADA • COSTA RICA • GUATEMALA • IRAN • JAPAN • MEXICO • OMAN • RUSSIA SAUDI ARABIA • SOUTH KOREA • TUNISIA • TURKEY • UKRAINE • THE UNITED ARAB EMIRATES

Mehmet Abi, Mentese Anatolian High School, Turkey; **Alena Acker**, EC New York, NY; **Anna-Marie Aldaz**, Doña Ana Community College, NM; **Diana Allen**, Oakton Community College, IL; **Marjorie Allen**, Harper College, IL; **Mark Alves**, Montgomery College, Rockville, MD; **Kelly Arce**, College of Lake County, IL; **Irma Arencibia**, Union City Adult Learning Center, NJ; **Arlys Arnold**, University of Minnesota, MN; **Marcia Arthur**, Renton Technical College, WA; **Alexander Astor**, Hostos Community College, NY; **Chris Atkins**, CHICLE Language Institute, NC; **Karin Avila-John**, University of Dayton, OH; **Ümmet Aydan**, Karabuk University, Iran; **Fabiana Azurmendi**; **John Baker**, Wayne State University, MI; **Sepehr Bamdadnia**; **Terry Barakat**, Missouri State University, MO; **Marie Bareille**, Borough of Manhattan Community College, NY; **Eileen Barlow**, SUNY Albany, NY; **Denise Barnes**, Madison English as a Second Language School, WI; **Kitty Barrera**, University of Houston, TX; **Denise Barsotti**, EID Training Solutions, FL; **Maria Bauer**, El Camino College; **Christine Bauer-Ramazani**, Saint Michael's College, VT; **Julie Baumgartner**, Washington State University, WA; **Jamie Beaton**, Boston University, MA; **Gena Bennett**, Cornerstone University, NE; **Linda Berendsen**, Oakton Community College, IL; **Carol Berteotti**; **Grace Bishop**, Houston Community College, TX; **Perrin Blackman**, University of Kansas, KS; **Mara Blake-Ward**, Drexel University English Language Center, PA; **Melissa Bloom**, ELS; **Alexander Bochkov**, ELS, WA; **Marcel Bolintiam**, University of Colorado, CO; **Nancy Boyer**, Golden West College, CA; **T. Bredl**, The New School, NY; **Rosemarie Brefeld**, University of Missouri, MO; **Leticia Brereton**, Kingsborough Community College, NY; **Deborah Brooks**, Laney College, CA; **Kevin Brown**, Irvine Community College, CA; **Rachel Brown**, Center for Literacy, NY; **Tracey Brown**, Parkland College, IL; **Crystal Brunelli**, Tokyo Jogakkan Middle and High School, Japan; **Tom Burger**, Harris County Department of Education, TX; **Thom Burns**, Tokyo English Specialists College, Japan; **Caralyn Bushey**, Maryland English Institute, MD; **Gül Büyü**, Ankara University, Turkey; **Scott Callaway**, Community Family Centers, TX; **Adele Camus**, George Mason University, VA; **Nigel Caplan**, University of Delaware, DE; **Nathan Carr**, California State University, CA; **Christina Cavage**, Savannah College of Art and Design, GA; **Neslihan Çelik**, Özdemir Sabancı Emirgan Anatolian High School, Turkey; **Shelley Cetin**, Kansas City Kansas Community College, KS; **Hoi Yuen Chan**, University of Wyoming, WY; **Esther Chase**, Berwyn Public Library, IL; **Suzidilara Çınar**, Yıldırım Beyazıt University, Turkey; **Diane Cirino**, SUNY Suffolk, NY; **Cara Codney**, Emporia State University, KS; **Catherine Coleman**, Irvine Valley College, CA; **Jenelle Collins**, Washington High School, AZ; **Greg Conner**, Orange Coast Community College, CA; **Ewelina Cope**, The Language Company, PA; **Jorge Cordon**, Colegio Montessori, Guatemala; **Kathy Cornman**, University of Michigan, MI; **Barry Costa**, Castro Valley Adult and Career Education, CA; **Cathy Costa**, Edmonds Community College, WA; **Julia Cote**, Houston Community College NE, TX; **Eileen Cotter**, Montgomery College, MD; **Winnie Cragg**, Mukogawa Fort Wright Institute, WA; **Douglas Craig**, Diplomatic Language Services, VA; **Elizabeth Craig**, Savannah College of Art and Design, GA; **Ann Telfair Cramer**, Florida State College at Jacksonville, FL; **R. M. Crocker**, Plano Independent School District, TX; **Virginia Cu**, Queens Adult Learning Center, CT; **Marc L. Cummings**, Jefferson Community and Technical College, KY; **Roberta Cummings**, Trinidad Correctional Facility, CO; **David Dahnke**, Lone Star College-North Harris, TX; **Debra Daise**, University of Denver, CO; **L. Dalgish**, Concordia College, NY; **Kristen Danek**, North Carolina State University, NC; **April Darnell**, University of Dayton, OH; **Ella Datsenko**, Ohio University, OH; **Heather Davis**, OISE Boston, MA; **Megan Davis**, Embassy English, NY; **Jeanne de Simon**, University of West Florida, FL; **Renee Delatizky**, Boston University, MA; **Sonia Delgadillo**, Sierra Community College, NY; **Holly DeLong**, Ohio University, OH; **Gözde Burcu Demirkul**, Orkunoglu College, Turkey; **Stella L. Dennis**, Longfellow Middle School, NY; **Mary Diamond**, Auburn University, AL; **Emily Dibala**, Bucks County Community College, PA; **Cynthia Dieckmann**, West Chester East High School, PA; **Michelle DiGiorno**, Richland College, TX; **Luciana Diniz**, Portland Community College, OR; **Özgür Dirik**, Yıldız Technical University, Turkey; **Marta O. Dmytrenko-Arab**, Wayne State University, MI; **Margie Domingo**, Intergenerational Learning Community, CO; **Kellie Draheim**, Hongik University, South Korea; **Ilke Buyuk Duman**, Sehir University, Turkey; **Jennifer Eick-Magan**, Prairie State College, IL; **Juliet Emanuel**, Borough of Manhattan Community College, NY; **David Emery**, Kaplan International Center, CA; **Patricia Emery**, Jefferson County Literacy Council, WI; **Eva Engelhard**, Kaplan International Center, WA; **Nancey Epperson**, Harry S. Truman College, IL; **Ken Estep**, Mentor Language Institute, CA; **Cindy Etter**, University of Washington, WA; **Rhoda Fagerland**, St. Cloud State University, MN; **Anrisa Fannin**, Diablo Valley College, CA; **Marie Farnsworth**, Union Public Schools, OK; **Jim Fenton**, Bluegrass Community Technical College, KY; **Lynn Filazzola**, Nassau BOCES Adult Learning Center, NY; **Christine Finck**, Stennis Language Lab; **Mary Fischer**, Texas Intensive English Program, TX; **Mark Fisher**, Lone Star College, TX; **Celeste Flowers**, University of Central Arkansas, AR; **Elizabeth Foss**, Washtenaw Community College, MI; **Jean Francis**, University of Missouri, MO; **Jacqueline Fredericks**, West Contra Costa Adult Education, CA; **Patricia Gairaud**, San Jose City College, CA; **Patricia Gallo**, Delaware Technical Community College, DE; **Beverly Gandall**, Coastline Community College, CA; **Alberto Garrido**, The Community College of Baltimore County, MD; **Debbie Garza**, Park University, MO; **Karen Gelender**, Castro Valley Adult and Career Education, CA; **Ronald Gentry**, Suenos Compartidos, Mexico; **Kathie Madden Gerecke**, North Shore Community College, MA; **Jeanne Gibson**, Colorado State University, CO; **A. Elizabeth Gilfillan**, Houston Community College, TX; **Melanie Gobert**, The Higher Colleges of Technology, UAE; **Ellen Goldman**, West Valley College, CA; **Jo Golub**, Houston Community College, TX; **Maria Renata Gonzalez**, Colegio Montessori, Guatemala; **Elisabeth Goodwin**, Pima Community College, AZ; **John Graney**, Santa Fe College, FL; **Karina Greene**, CUNY in the Heights, NY; **Katherine Gregorio**, CASA de Maryland, MD; **Claudia Gronsbell**, La Escuelita, NY; **Yvonne Groseil**, Hunter College, NY; **Christine Guro**, University of Hawaii, HI; **Alejandra Gutierrez**, Hartnell College, CA; **Eugene Guza**, North Orange County Community College District, CA; **Mary Beth Haan**, El Paso Community College, TX; **Elizabeth Haga**, State College of Florida, FL; **Saeede Haghi**, Ozyegin University, Turkey; **Laura Halvorson**, Lorain County Community College, OH; **Nancy Hamadou**, Pima Community College, AZ; **Kerri Hamberg**, Brookline Community and Adult Education, MA; **Katia Hameg**, L'Envol Des Langues, Québec, Canada; **Sunsook Han**, King Abdulaziz University, Saudi Arabia; **Aniko Harrier**, Valencia College, FL; **James M. Harris**, University of Texas-Pan American, TX; **Susan Haskins-Doloff**, Pratt Institute, NY; **Olcay Havalan**, Bursa Anadolu Erkek Lisesi, Turkey; **Marla Heath**, Sacred Heart University, CT; **Jean Hendrickson**, SUNY Stony Brook, NY; **Tracy Henninger-Willey**, Lane Community College, OR; **Emily Herrick**,

Contents

3 | Expanding and Condensing Information

ACADEMIC AND PROFESSIONAL FUNCTION Building reasearch skills

4 | Making Comparisons

ACADEMIC AND PROFESSIONAL FUNCTION Developing powers of independent reasoning

5 | Softening and Strengthening Statements

ACADEMIC AND PROFESSIONAL FUNCTION Preparing for professional practice

Vocabulary Endnotes

Resources

Index

1 Narrating and Describing

What happens is of little significance compared with the stories we tell ourselves about what happens. Events matter little; only stories of events affect us.

—RABIH ALAMEDDINE, NOVELIST (1959–)

Talk about It What does the quotation above mean? Do you agree or disagree?

WARM-UP

A | Read the paragraphs and answer the questions with *A* or *B*.

1. Which paragraph primarily tells a story? ____

2. Which paragraph primarily describes something, without telling a story? ____

A	**B**
Cornelius Vanderbilt was born on Staten Island, New York in 1794. At the age of 16, he started a business as a boatman[1], repaying his parents for the cost of his boat within a year. In the early nineteenth century, Vanderbilt immediately saw the great advantage of steam power. During his long and active career, he built and owned more than 100 steamboats[2] and ships, and never lost one in an accident. In the 1860s, he turned his attention to railroads. According to various stories of Vanderbilt's career, all difficulties seemed to disappear at his magic touch. He had great willpower and a strong, healthy frame. Not surprisingly, he became a leader among men.	Yosemite National Park's **747,956** acres[3] are home to hundreds of **wildlife** species and thousands of plants. Designated a World Heritage Site in 1984, Yosemite is **famous** for its **spectacular** rocks, countless[4] waterfalls, clear streams, and giant sequoia trees. Two **wild** and beautiful rivers, the Tuolumne and Merced, begin in the park and flow west to the Central Valley. From about late May through October or November, visitors can make the **one-hour** drive up to Glacier Point. The views from Glacier Point and along the nearby Panorama Trail are **breathtaking**.

B | Answer these questions about the paragraphs above.

1. Which paragraph is primarily in the past? Why did the writer choose the past time frame?

2. Which paragraph is primarily in the present? Why did the writer choose the present time frame?

3. Circle the words and phrases in paragraph A that tell when something happened.

4. In paragraph B, underline the nouns (or noun phrases) that the **bold** adjectives or describing nouns describe.

   a. Which of these adjectives or describing nouns come before the noun they describe?

   b. Which adjectives come after the noun they describe?

[1] See page V-2 for the Vocabulary Endnotes for this unit.

1.1 Overview of Narration and Description

A

NARRATION

1 It was late on a sunny afternoon, I remember, after secretaries and students **had disappeared** from our building, that he **stuck** his head nervously through my open door. I **looked** up just as he **knocked**, and he **was** already **walking** quickly to my desk.

2 When the lunch bell rings, the children file down the stairs into the dining hall. They spend 45 minutes eating lunch and talking at the long tables, until the bell calls them back to class. When afternoon classes are finished, they are allowed one hour of free time before dinner.

3 Neither of us spoke **[a] during the meal [b] that night.** We split the check and drove back to the apartment. We were **[c] still** silent **[d] as we walked across the bridge to our apartment.** We decided to watch a couple of movies **[e] before going to bed. [f] After our third one**, I decided to go to bed.

Writers use **narration** to tell a story or describe a series of events, usually in chronological (time) order.

Many written narrations describe events that happened in the past and use primarily **past verb forms**, as in **1**.

Some narrations describe events that occur regularly or are generally true. They use primarily **present verb forms**, as in **2**.

Narrations often refer to time using:

- **prepositional phrases**, as in **3a** and **3f**
- **noun phrases** that function as adverbs, as in **3b**
- **adverbs** or adverb phrases, as in **3c**
- **adverb clauses**, as in **3d**
- **reduced adverb clauses**, as in **3e**

B

DESCRIPTION

4 Wes walked through the **city** market, passing tables covered with **fresh** flowers and **enormous** piles of **colorful** fruit.

        adverb   adjective   adjective *to-* infinitive

5 Some contracts are **extremely complex** and **difficult to interpret.**
            — adjective phrases —

6 Krista nodded to everyone but avoided conversation. **Anxious [a] to see Myrna**, she walked straight to the back room, where she found her asleep on a sofa. She gently tapped Myrna's shoulder, **worried [b] that a sudden movement would frighten her.** But Myrna was too deeply asleep to be **afraid [c] of anything.**

Writers use **description** to talk about how people, places, things, and/or ideas look, sound, or seem. Descriptive details make writing vivid and interesting.

One way to add descriptive details is with **adjectives** and **describing nouns**, as in **4**, or **adjective phrases**, as in **5**. An adjective phrase may contain one or more adjectives + other structures which add information to the adjective(s), as in **5**.

We can use adjectives and adjective phrases before nouns, as in **4**, or after *be* or other linking verbs, as in **5**.

We can follow some **adjectives** with:

- **to- infinitive forms**, as in **6a**
- *that* clauses, as in **6b**
- **prepositional phrases**, as in **6c**

GO ONLINE For more practice with present and past verb forms, go to the Online Practice.

1 | Noticing Narration and Description Read the story. Then answer the questions on page 5.

1.1 A–B

○ ○ ○

A Good Habit After All

My father is a man of routines and habits. Every morning he rises early and goes to the kitchen for an hour of coffee, news, and a crossword[5]. When the coffee is done, the news absorbed, and the crossword completed, he takes out his famous "to-do" list—a leather-bound calendar with a replaceable paper insert[6]—and reviews his tasks for the day. At the end of every year, he adds the insert to a drawer filled with years and years of them, each one containing page after page of his careful lists—"Call insurance company, buy bread, clean the patio." Some items are crossed out. Items that are not crossed out appear on the following day, again and again until at last they are checked off.

Before Dad retired, the list-making took place at his office. I was unaware of it until one day I went to work with him for some reason that I can't remember now. I must have been about 13 years old. The first to arrive, we walked through the empty office to his desk at the back. He brought in a rolling chair for me to sit in, settled himself at his clean, uncluttered[7] desk, and then pulled out the leather-bound book—identical to the one he uses now. "Today I'll begin with this," he said, indicating the top item, "because it's the first thing on the list." To my restless[8] young mind, the office was like a prison and the to-do list was a sign of a depressing, overly controlled existence. I was certain that Dad's list represented everything I was determined to avoid as an adult—a life without spontaneity[9] or freedom, a life lived according to plan.

But here it is some 30 years later, and every morning I'm at the table with my coffee, contemplating[10] a list of the day's reminders[11] on my phone, just like Dad. My life doesn't feel too controlled or lacking in spontaneity. Time has taught me that the list is not a prison, but rather the opposite. All those obligations written down, organized, and waiting to be checked off give me control over my day. They free me from the anxiety that I may be forgetting something and give me the space I need to be creative and spontaneous. I have no doubt that, like Dad, I'll be making lists even when I have far fewer obligations to occupy me each day.

QUESTIONS

1. In your own words, describe the writer's father. How did the narrator's view of him change over time?

2. Which paragraph (1, 2, or 3) does *not* focus on narration? (It doesn't tell about a series of events.) _____

   a. What is the purpose of this paragraph? _____

   b. Is the paragraph mostly in present or past time? _____

3. Which paragraph contains past narration? _____ Present narration? _____

4. Find these adjectives in the story in Activity 1. Complete the chart. Then add a third adjective, describing noun, or adjective phrase.

Adjective (phrase) or describing noun	Paragraph	Noun or pronoun it describes	Is the adjective before or after the noun or pronoun? (Write *before* or *after*.)
famous	1		
creative	3		

5. Find these adjectives in paragraph 2. What kind of structure follows them? Write *prepositional phrase, to- infinitive,* or *that clause.*

   a. unaware _____   c. determined _____

   b. certain _____

6. The following words, phrases, and clauses from paragraph 1 refer to time. Label each one as an adverb (*A*), an adverb clause (*AC*), a noun phrase (*NP*), or a prepositional phrase (*PP*).

   a. every morning _____   d. when the coffee is done _____

   b. early _____   e. until at last they are checked off _____

   c. for an hour _____

1.2 Narrating in Present and Past Time Frames

When we write, we often choose a particular time frame (usually the present or the past). Within each time frame, certain verb forms are common. The verbs in this chart represent some of the common choices we make in present and past time frames, both in active and in passive sentences.

A

PRESENT AND FUTURE TIME FRAMES

ACTIVE

1 She **begins** her day with coffee at home and then another cup on the way to work. After she **has spent** a couple of hours answering emails and working at her desk, she **heads** over to the break room to make a fresh pot. While she **is waiting** for the pot to fill, several co-workers usually **come** in, attracted by the smell of the coffee. If she **isn't** too busy, she**'ll stay** in the break room to chat while she **drinks** that third cup.

PASSIVE

2 In the best emergency-response systems, a caller's location **is** automatically **displayed** when he or she calls in. An operator determines the nature of the emergency and then contacts the closest appropriate service. Operators must be prepared to provide instructions to people who **have been injured** or are suffering from a huge variety of medical emergencies.

In present time frames, as in **1 – 2**, most of the verbs are usually in the **simple present**, which can describe habitual actions or general truths. We may also use:

- the **present perfect** to describe things that happened before the time of the story
- the **present progressive** to describe ongoing or changing states or situations
- the **future** with *will* or *be going to* + **main verb** to describe things that happen after the time of the story

Remember: In **active** sentences, the subject performs the action. Most sentences are active. In **passive** sentences, the subject receives the action. Writers often use the passive to focus on what happened rather than on who did something.

For more information on verb forms, see the Resources, pages R5–R8. For more information on passive and active sentences, see pages R12–R16.

B

PAST TIME FRAMES

ACTIVE

3 Many of the Irish who **entered** the United States at that time **had received** letters telling them that it **was becoming** more and more difficult to find land. But they **came** anyway, not realizing that their future **was going to lie** in the industrial cities.

PASSIVE

4 The police arrived and asked some brief questions. We **were** then **taken** to the Chippenham police station. There I **was questioned** about what I had seen, while my son **was being interviewed** in another room. I told them everything I knew. My son **was permitted** to leave, but I **was held** overnight at the police station. I **had** never **been arrested** before, and the experience was extremely frightening.

In past time frames, as in **3 – 4**, most of the verbs are usually in the **simple past**, which describes completed actions. We may also use:

- the **past perfect** to describe things that happened before the time of the story, often background information
- the **past progressive** to describe actions that were in progress at the time of the story
- *was / were* + *going to* + *verb* or *would* + *verb* to describe things occurring after the time of the story (a kind of future-in-the-past)

GO ONLINE For more practice with verb forms and with passive and active sentences, go to the Online Practice.

2 | Noticing Verb Forms Check (✓) all of the different verb forms that you find in each passage. Underline one example of each form that you check. `1.2 A–B`

TIME FRAMES AND DIFFERENT TYPES OF NARRATION

1. They <u>didn't see</u> a single person as they ran through the tiny village, which consisted of[12] a pharmacy, a souvenir shop, and a butcher. They jogged back to the castle where they showered and changed. At 7:30 they went down to dinner and were seated at a table by a large window overlooking the garden. The rain had stopped, and the night was peaceful.

- [✓] simple past active
- [ ] simple past passive
- [ ] past perfect active
- [ ] past perfect passive
- [ ] past progressive active
- [ ] past progressive passive

2. I come in at about 4. I clock in[13] and start setting up for the evening—you know, pull out the rugs, fill the sugar containers, cut some lemons—basically do everything that hasn't been done already. At 9:30 we open and the people start coming in. While I'm greeting them and showing them to their seats, the busser[14] pours water and fills breadbaskets to take to the tables.

- [ ] simple present active
- [ ] simple present passive
- [ ] present perfect active
- [ ] present perfect passive
- [ ] present progressive active
- [ ] present progressive passive

3. The World Wide Web is used by so many people nowadays that it's hard to believe it didn't exist 30 years ago. Its inventor is an English computer scientist named Tim Berners-Lee. It was never surprising that Berners-Lee became a pioneer[15] in computing. Before his birth, his parents had worked on the first commercially built computer, and Berners-Lee developed an interest in electronics at an early age. After he graduated from college with a degree in physics, he began working on software design. Eventually, he ended up at the European Organization for Nuclear Research (CERN). While he was working at CERN, Berners-Lee designed and built the World Wide Web. The first website was put online at CERN on August 6, 1991. Berners-Lee has been active in the development of the Web ever since.

- [ ] simple present active
- [ ] simple present passive
- [ ] present perfect active
- [ ] present perfect passive
- [ ] present progressive active
- [ ] present progressive passive
- [ ] simple past active
- [ ] simple past passive
- [ ] past perfect active
- [ ] past perfect passive
- [ ] past progressive active
- [ ] past progressive passive

Tim Berners-Lee

Think about It What type of narration is each of the passages above? Write the number of each passage next to the word that describes it. Explain your answer.

fiction ____

biography ____

spoken narration ____

3 | Using a Present Time Frame Choose a verb from the box to complete each sentence. Use present verb forms. (Different forms are possible.) You may not use all of the verbs. `1.2 A`

DESCRIBING ROUTINES

1. Ms. Tully is pleased with her new job, which provides health insurance, sick days, and paid vacations. She appreciates the Cooperative's training program, which she says taught her not only how to identify many diseases but also what to do if a patient _____ *has* _____ a heart attack, stroke, or seizure[16]. For three years, she _____ Carolyn McNeil, a 44-year-old former nurse who suffered a stroke that paralyzed[17] her right side. Ms. McNeil also has seizures. On a typical day, Ms. Tully _____ and cleans, and she feeds Ms. McNeil's cat. She _____ to interpret Ms. McNeil's gestures[18] when she has a seizure.

cook
have
learn
take
take care of

2. She is a single mother who _____ to make ends meet as a movie director, working mainly for Jordanian television. She _____ by her son's teachers, who _____ that Omar is a troublemaker[19], talking back to teachers and making rude comments in class. On a typical day, Omar _____ home early—the ride to school takes an hour and a half by bus—in order to have time to meet friends at a park near the school or to play basketball, which he _____. He arrives home late in the afternoon, and after he _____ dinner, has to help his mother around the house.

call (often)
complain
eat
leave
love
struggle
take

3. As a newer lawyer she worked seven days a week, but in the past ten years she _____ to six. She usually _____ Saturdays off to spend with family and _____ into the office on Sundays. The work, while no longer new, _____ satisfying. "I _____ fortunate to be working where I can be proud of what I'm doing every day," she _____. Saturdays _____ a time for reflection and relaxation, for sitting on the patio of her family's home, near a pot of orange-red roses that belonged to her late grandmother.

be
cut back
feel
go
remain
say
take

4. Every morning, Alberto _____ at 5:45 and _____ to the corner of Shallowford Road and Bufford Highway in Atlanta, Georgia where he often _____ several hours to be picked up for short-term jobs. Once a week, he walks three miles to a remittances[20] center to send his savings to his wife Isaura, who stayed behind in El Salvador with their four children. He _____ almost all of his wages to feed his family and educate his children. These remittances _____ Isaura to start a small street business selling pupusas (a type of stuffed tortilla) in front of a factory. She _____ able to begin working on her own immigration paperwork.

allow
be
be (also)
get up
send
wait
walk

Think about It The passages above are written primarily in a present time frame, but three of them contain some past verb forms. Circle the past verb forms in these passages. Why did the writer choose the past for those verbs?

Think about It Look at the verbs you wrote above and compare answers with other students. Was more than one verb form possible in some sentences? What other form could you have used?

4 | Using a Past Time Frame Underline the correct form of the verbs in parentheses. **1.2 B**

the *Titanic*

1. That morning the *Titanic*'s wireless operator (received / was receiving) an ice warning from the *Caronia* at 9 a.m. This was the first of eight warnings regarding ice that the *Titanic* would receive that day; all along the North Atlantic shipping lanes, ships (were encountering / encounter) a large belt of ice. This was not surprising news, for it (is / had been) a bad season for ice in the North Atlantic. A warm winter (had caused / has caused) numerous icebergs to break off from the coast of Greenland. Only a few days earlier, a collision with ice (had knocked / was knocking) two holes in the steamer[21] *Niagara,* but the ship had managed to reach New York.

2. The *Paquet Real* arrived at Capetown in 1818 with 171 slaves on board. The journey should have taken only about 60 days, but it took 71. By the time the ship (has reached / reached) Capetown, she* (ran / had run) out of food, and (has been / had been) damaged by storms. The ship's arrival (was / had been) a problem for the British authorities, then in command of the Cape. Britain (had outlawed[22] / was outlawing) the slave trade in 1808, and Britain's colonies[23] were not allowed to give assistance to slavers.

3. Families began moving into Jefferson County after the territory (was opened / has opened) for settlement[24] in 1819. By 1825 hundreds of people (had taken / have taken) advantage of government-owned lands good for growing cotton. They were part of the land rush[25] that rapidly (filled / has filled) the Red Hills region, which lies on the border of Georgia and Florida.

4. In 1805, Lewis and Clark and the Nez Perce Indians (met / were meeting) near the lower Snake River. This encounter was the beginning of a steady wave of non-Native immigrants entering Nez Perce territory in search of both land and riches. By 1813 the Nez Perce (have traded / were trading) furs with the North West Company on the upper Columbia River.

*Ships, and sometimes other vehicles, are often referred to as *she*.

Think about It The passages above are written primarily in a past time frame, but the third passage contains one present verb form. Circle that verb. Why did the writer choose this form?

5 | Usage Note: The Habitual Past with *Used to* and *Would* Read the note. Then do Activities 6 and 7.

We can use *used to* + the **base form of a verb** or *would* + the **base form of a verb** to emphasize that past actions were habitual.

1 We **used to meet** in the park on Sundays.

2 Charles **used to be** a good friend of mine.

3 She **used to take** the train to Oxford on her days off. She **would walk** the streets to discover the town. At noon she **would get** herself a sandwich and a cup of coffee. Then she **would visit** one of the libraries, and from there she **would go** to one of the parks if the weather was good.

Used to + the **base form of a verb** can describe habitual past actions, as in **1**. It can also describe habitual states that are no longer true, as in **2**.

Would + the **base form of a verb** can describe habitual past actions. Before using *would*, it is necessary to establish the past time frame. In **3**, the first verb, *used to take*, makes the past time frame of the paragraph clear. The verb forms with *would* then describe the specific actions that took place.

WARNING! *Would* is not usually used to describe past states.

✗ When I was a child, we **would have** a small yellow car.

WARNING! The habitual past is not the only way we use *would* for describing the past.

4 Every morning, my father would go out early to take care of the animals. (habitual past)

5 He woke up early, knowing that the animals would be hungry. (future in the past)

6 | Noticing the Habitual Past Underline *would* + the main verb used for the habitual past. Circle the verb that first establishes the time frame for each passage. `1.2 B`

WOULD IN PAST NARRATIVES

1. The students participating in the study (attended) the Tutoring Center twice a week. The tutors <u>would go</u> through each homework problem with the students and make sure that they understood the whole procedure.

2. On spring break, the girls got up early every morning to run on the beach. Carol would run for an hour or so, and when she got back, she and her friends would lie on the beach all day. Carol never ate breakfast and ate very little for lunch. For dinner, they went out to eat at a different restaurant every night, but she would always order a salad and eat half of it, at most. She didn't think that her eating behavior was unusual, and her friends never commented on it. Later she would realize that she had developed an eating disorder[26].

3. My discovery about Cathy came as an accident. She normally complained that reading was boring as I was helping her to pick a new book to read. I would suggest a book and Cathy would reject it. One day I suggested *Little Women* and told her a little bit about the book. After that, she came into class each day and asked, "Can we just read today?" When a half hour had passed, I would ask the students if they were ready to stop reading. After we started *Little Women*, Cathy would always beg to keep reading. Even though this change in attitude toward reading appeared to be an accident with Cathy, I have seen similar reading breakthroughs in several other students.

4. Our usual procedure for catching the rats was to place traps at the tunnel openings and then dig into the mound[27], capturing the animals as they raced away in panic. We would follow a tunnel from the central part of the mound to the trap we had placed at the exit. As each tunnel was opened and cleared, we would move on to the next.

5. Bethe started reading at the age of four and began writing in capital letters at about the same age. Very soon after mastering the art of handwriting, he began filling large numbers of little booklets with stories. His mode of writing was distinctive[28]: he would write one line from left to right and the next line from right to left.

6. With $2,000 of his own hard-earned wages and no helper, Grote Reber built a bowl-shaped antenna 31 feet in diameter[29] in his backyard in the suburbs. For nearly a decade he listened for and tracked radio signals from outer space, rushing home each night from his job in Chicago, 30 miles away. Upon reaching his home in the evening he would sleep for a few hours. Then he would awaken and become a backyard radio astronomer[30] from midnight to 6 a.m. Eventually his work would become well known and the new field of radio astronomy would be born.

Think about It In the narratives above, which examples of *would* + the base form of a verb are not used for the habitual past?

7 | Using the Habitual Past Edit this blog entry by changing some of the simple past forms to the habitual past. Use your judgment to decide when to emphasize the habitual past. (Different answers are possible.) `1.2 B`

Aunt Eloise

When I think about my childhood, the person who first comes to mind is

used to call

my Aunt Eloise. My sisters and I ~~called~~ her Eloista. She was more than our

nanny[31]. My parents were hard-working people. They didn't have time to

take care of us, so my aunt came to our house every morning. She brought

newly baked bread for breakfast. She helped us get ready to go to school.

She prepared my lunchbox and sometimes even helped me with my hair.

We came back from school to her delicious food. Nobody could cook like

she did. She was famous for her tasty roast beef and an Italian soup called

minestrone. We had a kitten in our yard, and Aunt Eloista fed her leftover[32]

bits of the wonderful meals she cooked.

Think about It Which simple past verbs in the paragraph above cannot be changed to *would* + the base form of a verb? Why?

8 | Usage Note: The Historical Present Read the note. Then do Activity 9.

> Writers sometimes use present verb forms to narrate past events. We call this use the **historical present**. The historical present is often used to make a story from the past seem more immediate and exciting.
>
> It**'s** past noon by the time he **enters** the city, exhausted and hungry. His feet **are aching** from the long walk. The sun **has burned** off the early morning fog, and as he **wanders** around in the fine, 60-degree weather, Brick **is** happy to discover that the place **has not changed**. He **will not regret** this journey.

9 | Noticing the Historical Present Underline the present verb forms in this excerpt. `1.2 A`

From Fiction

They walked in silence. Cale looked up at the sky. The stars were beginning to appear overhead and the moon was climbing. He thought it was about 9:00. After an hour had passed, he stopped and found a rock to sit on near the side of the road. As David looked for his own place to rest, he finally spoke: "So you won't believe what happened today."

Cale didn't respond. He had been expecting this.

"I saw Matthew. About 10:00 this morning, he just knocks on my door. So what can I do? I invite him in. He tells me about the work that he's been doing lately. As if nothing has changed. The whole time I'm thinking, 'Why are you here?'"

F Y I

The historical present is generally considered informal and is most common in fiction and conversation.

Think about It The passage in Activity 9 contains two narrations, one in the past and one in the present. Why do you think the writer changed to present narration?

Think about It Find the future verb form in the story in Activity 9. Why did the writer use this form?

10 | Using Verb Forms Read this short excerpt from *The Kite Runner*, a novel by Khaled Hosseini. Complete the sentences with the correct form of the verb in parentheses. `1.2 A–B`

The Kite Runner* (excerpt 1)
by Khaled Hosseini

The next morning, as he brewed[33] black tea for breakfast, Hassan told me

he _____ a dream. "We were at Ghargha Lake, you, me, Father,
(1. had)

Agha sahib, Rahim Khan, and thousands of other people," he said. "It was

warm and sunny, and the lake _____ clear like a mirror. But no
(2. be)

one was swimming because they said a monster had come to the lake.

It _____ at the bottom, waiting."
(3. swim)

   He poured me a cup and _____ sugar, blew on it a few
(4. add)

times. Put it before me. "So everyone is scared to get in the water, and

suddenly you kick off your shoes, Amir agha, and _____ your shirt. 'There's no monster,'
(5. take off)

you say. 'I _____ you all.' And before anyone can stop you, you _____ into
(6. show)   (7. dive)

the water, start swimming away. I follow you in and we're both swimming."

   "But you can't swim."

   Hassan laughed. "It's a dream, Amir agha, you can do anything. Anyway, everyone is screaming,

'Get out! Get out!' But we just swim in the cold water. We make it way out to the middle of the

lake and we stop swimming. We _____ toward the shore and wave to the people.
(8. turn)

They _____ small like ants, but we can hear them clapping. They see now. There is
(9. look)

no monster, just water. They change the name of the lake after that, and _____ it the
(10. call)

'Lake of Amir and Hassan, Sultans of Kabul,' and we get to charge people money for swimming in it."

   "So what does it mean?" I said.

   He coated my naan[34] with marmalade[35], and _____ it on a plate. "I don't know.
(11. place)

I _____ you could tell me."
(12. hope)

*In *The Kite Runner*, Khaled Hosseini tells the story of a privileged young boy named Amir growing up in Afghanistan during a time of
political turmoil. You will read a second excerpt from *The Kite Runner* on page 20.

Think about It In the excerpt above, where does the writer change to the historical present? Why?

1.3 Time Adverbials

A

1 They **now** had tools that they had **never** had **before**.

2 The disease **almost always** appeared **quite early** in life.

3 Participants were asked how often they had behaved **a certain way** during the previous week.

4 The lights were out **all night**, but the power was restored **the following day**.

5 Students had brought up this topic **on several other occasions**.

6 She hurried off, returning **in a few moments** with a glass of water.

In a narration, writers often use **adverbials** to signal time relationships. Time adverbials can tell us *when, how often,* or *for how long.*

Time adverbials can be:

- adverbs or adverb phrases, as in **1** and **2**
- noun phrases functioning as adverbials, as in **3** and **4**
- prepositional phrases, as in **5** and **6**
- adverb clauses (discussed in Chart 1.4)

For more information on adverbials, see the Resources, pages R-33 and R-36.

B

7 We showed them four pictures, three of which they recognized **almost immediately**.

8 The rare cactus was seen in 1938, **then** lost from view, and **later** rediscovered in 1947.

9 The public's knowledge of health information has increased **since that time**.

10 **Several years after the tornado**, many of the buildings were still under construction.

Adverbs and adverb phrases can appear in many different places in a sentence, including after a verb, as in **7**, and before a verb, as in **8**.

Longer adverbials usually appear at the end of a main clause, as in **9**.

Writers sometimes place time adverbials before a main clause, as in **10**. In this case, the adverbial is normally followed by a comma.

GO ONLINE For more practice with adverbs and adverbials, go to the Online Practice.

11 | Noticing Time Adverbials Underline the time adverbials in each passage. `1.3 A`

AROUND THE WORLD

1. For much of post-colonial history, Mayan communities have been encouraged to give up their traditions. Now, however, Mayan culture has been given a rebirth[36] in this region of Mexico.

2. Jadav Payeng has been planting trees in northeastern India for the past three decades. His efforts have already resulted in an impressive forest.

3. Three large elephants approached our vehicle and stopped less than 12 feet away. Unfortunately, during this time I was too afraid to take a picture, convinced that if the elephants heard the click of my camera, they would run away. I regretted not having captured the scene for hours afterward.

4. On the morning of June 8, 1924, George Mallory and Andrew Irvine started up the summit[37] of Mount Everest. They were last seen alive at 12:50 p.m. by their companion Noel Odell, who saw them momentarily[38] through the clouds that had gathered on the mountain. No one knows what happened after that. Mallory's body and some of his gear were finally located in 1999, but his camera was never found, so whether he reached the summit or not is still unknown.

5. There's no better place to be on a warm August night in Helsinki. We did our best to try as many different foods as we could, but it was difficult with only one day at the festival. The reality is that to sample all of the good food there, you really need to arrive at the festival on day 1 and stay for all three days.

6. We left the city first thing in the morning and pulled into our camp just after sunset. We dropped off our bags and immediately jumped into a small motorboat to look along the riverbanks for wildlife.

7. I had high expectations of the food in Ethiopia. Years ago, I was fortunate enough to be introduced to Ethiopian food in Washington, D.C. The flavors and communal[39] style of eating were like nothing I had experienced before.

FYI

Putting a time adverbial before the main clause helps the reader understand the time frame of the actions that follow.

Think about It Label each time adverbial you underlined in Activity 11 as an adverb (*A*), a noun phrase (*NP*), or a prepositional phrase (*PP*).

12 | Using Time Adverbials Choose four or more time adverbials from the box to add to each passage. (Different answers are possible.) `1.3 A–B`

IMPORTANT TEACHERS

Georgia Landon

again	eventually	in my first year of high school	often
always	frequently	in the years that followed	

The teacher who made the greatest difference in my life was Georgia Landon. She taught
in my first year of high school
the beginning algebra class. I had hated math and considered myself bad at it. Just hearing the

word *algebra* scared me, but Ms. Landon had a way of making the mysterious subject funny and

non-threatening. She gave the people in the word problems silly names, and she told jokes that

young people could relate to[40]. Her classroom was filled with the sound of laughter. But her

wonderful sense of humor wasn't even her best quality. Even more importantly, Ms. Landon

was organized, patient, and kind. She explained everything so clearly and wrote so neatly on

the board that I lost my fear, and algebra became quite easy for me. And for the students who

struggled more, she found ways to explain and explain without boring the rest of us. I took as

many classes from Ms. Landon as I could. You don't meet teachers, or other people, with that

combination of intelligence, humor, and kindness.

Anne Sullivan

around seven years later	as a baby	at 18 years old	in 1880
until Anne's death in 1936	at first	from that moment on	

Helen Keller was born. She suffered an illness that left her unable to see, hear, or speak.

Anne Sullivan began working with Helen, teaching her language by using her fingers to

spell words into Helen's hand. The method wasn't successful, but one day Helen made

the connection between the water that was flowing over her hand and the

word *water* being spelled into her palm[41]. She began to acquire language at a

rapid pace. Helen entered a school to prepare for college, and Anne Sullivan

stayed by her side, reading the books Helen needed to study and spelling

the information into Helen's hand. Teacher and student stayed together.

Helen lived to be 80 years old. She wrote many books and became famous,

and Anne Sullivan was remembered as one of history's great teachers.

Helen Keller and Anne Sullivan

Think about It Compare your sentences in Activity 12 with a partner. If you made different choices, do they both make sense? Could you place the adverbials you chose in a different part of the sentence?

Talk about It Tell your partner about an important teacher in your life. Listen to your partner speak, and write down any time adverbials you hear.

Write about It Write a short paragraph about an important teacher in your life. Use two different types of time adverbials. See Activity 12, passage 1 for an example.

1.4 Adverb Clauses and Reduced Adverb Clauses of Time

A

Along with other kinds of adverbials, we can use **adverb clauses**, as in **1 – 2**, to signal time relationships in narration. Each adverb clause begins with a **subordinator**.

We usually place the adverb clause after the main clause, as in **1**. Writers sometimes put the adverb clause before the main clause, as in **2**. We usually use a comma (,) after an adverb clause that comes before a main clause.

main clause	adverb clause

1 | All students' papers were photocopied | **before** they were graded by the course teaching assistant.

adverb clause	main clause	

2 | **By the time** the war ended, | average salaries had dropped by more than half. | Returning soldiers found that they were unable to support their families.

Time clauses at the beginning of a sentence often introduce a time frame or a change in time (such as from general to specific). This placement helps establish the time frame for the sentences that follow.

COMMON TIME SUBORDINATORS					
as	after	every time	before	until	(ever) since
just as	as soon as	whenever	by the time		
when	(just / right / immediately) after				
while	once				

For more information on adverb clauses of time, see the Resources, page R-38.

B

COMPARE

3a **Some of the workers** have not had a job **since they left the factory.** (adverb clause with subject *they*)

3b **Some of the workers** have not had a job **since leaving the factory.** (reduced adverb clause)

4a **While he was looking** for a way to reduce the use of chemicals on fruit trees, Glenn developed a new way to protect against insects.

4b **While looking** for a way to reduce the use of chemicals on fruit trees, Glenn developed a new way to protect against insects.

5a William Herschel was an eighteenth-century musician who became an astronomer for Britain's King George III **after he discovered the planet Uranus.**

5b William Herschel was an eighteenth-century musician who became an astronomer for Britain's King George III **after discovering the planet Uranus.**

6a **After he was hired,** he put in long, 15-hour days.

6b **After being hired,** he put in long, 15-hour days.

7 X After working hard all day, the sofa is very comfortable. (The sofa didn't work hard all day.)

We can **reduce adverb clauses of time** when the **subject** of the main clause and the subject of the adverb clause are the same, as in **3a – 3b**.

There are a few ways to reduce an adverb clause:
- When the adverb clause has a form of *be*, drop the subject and *be*, as in **4b**.
- When the adverb clause has a verb other than *be*, drop the subject plus any helping verbs and change the main verb to its *-ing* form, as in **3b** and **5b**.
- When the adverb clause is passive, drop the subject and change the form of *be* to *being*, as in **6b**.

We can reduce adverb clauses of time with these subordinators:

after	before	when	while	(ever) since	until

WARNING! The subject of the reduced clause should be the same as the subject of the main clause. (Notice the error in **7**.)

For more information on reduced adverb clauses, see the Resources, page R-40.

GO ONLINE For more practice with adverb clauses, go to the Online Practice.

13 | Noticing Adverb Clauses of Time Circle the subordinators in each passage and underline the adverb clauses and reduced adverb clauses of time. `1.4 A–B`

DESCRIBING ACTION

1. (After) we hooked the fish, I jumped in and searched for clues as to why it was there in the first place. Sure enough, (when) I dove down in the area where the fish was hooked, I saw a school of them swimming around a line of algae[42].

2. Several passengers and crew members jumped into the cold water and swam to shore while others climbed on ropes to the rocks below. Nareen Fauled, from South Africa, ran to the top of the ship and hurried into a lifeboat[43], but as the ship tilted[44] to its side, the lifeboat was suspended[45] for nearly 45 minutes in midair.

3. He has been trying out new things since leaving his native Wales to find a teaching job in London in 1938. He ended up in the Territorial Army and eventually became an officer. After retiring from the Army in his late 60s, he and his wife Aileen traveled extensively. In his 80s, he decided to learn about computers.

4. Olya came to Moscow when she was 17 to study for a year at the city's main construction trade institute and then began working at various building sites for the state. After lifting boxes and plastering[46] walls all day, she searches the stores for affordable children's clothes. For the last six months she has been looking for a jacket for her youngest daughter.

5. Now, most of the men were relaxing in the warm sunshine with a glass of lemonade at hand. Several were fishing for that night's supper, but most simply sat and had a laugh with the other sailors. Jess had even brought out his guitar and was playing a simple tune while the girls, with their sleeves rolled up and their hair tied back, scrubbed[47] the deck dutifully.

Think about It Discuss these questions with a partner.

1. Which adverb clauses and reduced adverb clauses above come after the main clause? Which come before?

2. Which adverb clauses are reduced?

Write about It Rewrite the reduced adverb clauses you identified above as full adverb clauses.

_____

_____

_____

Write about It Choose ten of the time subordinators from Chart 1.4. Use each one in a sentence about something you did in the past. Share your sentences with a partner.

1. *As soon as I arrived in Rio, I began looking for an apartment in my old neighborhood.*

14 | Using Reduced Adverb Clauses of Time Underline the adverb clauses of time. Rewrite them as reduced adverb clauses. [1.4 B]

BIOGRAPHIES

after discovering Matisse and Picasso

1. Lam was attracted to modernism[48], and <u>after he discovered Matisse and Picasso</u>, he began to experiment with geometrical forms.

2. Filling empty days while he was waiting for responses to job applications, Shaw bought a ticket to the British Museum and spent most weekdays at a desk in the reading room.

3. Miyazaki worked in animation for over 15 years before he directed his first big film.

4. Clifton was active in the wider world of science, but he had published only one scientific article since he had arrived at Oxford.

5. Smith returned to New York City in 1880 and worked as a maid[49] until she met her husband in 1885.

6. While she was working as a nurse at a military hospital in Texas, McKenzie discovered her interest in psychology.

7. Doctors released Mandela after they examined him and found that there was nothing seriously wrong with him.

Hayao Miyazaki

8. Wilgus taught at Mount Vernon College in the late 1960s and early 1970s and then worked for the Montgomery County school system until she retired in 1981.

9. Since he joined the university faculty[50], Cohen has authored[51] or co-authored over 120 papers.

10. A few days before she went to Mono Lake, Wolfe met with a journalist to discuss her work.

1.5 Adverbial -ing Clauses

A

1 **Arriving in Guadeloupe during the economic downturn of the mid-1990s, Leslie** was never able to find work for more than a few days per week.
(Leslie arrived in Guadeloupe. Leslie could not easily find work.)

2 **Researchers** set up an experiment, **creating and placing their own stone tools in the wet ground.**
(Researchers set up an experiment. These researchers created the stone tools.)

Sometimes we use reduced **adverbial -ing clauses** without a subordinator. They can come before the main clause, as in **1**, or after the main clause, as in **2**. As with reduced adverb clauses, the implied **subject** of a reduced adverbial -ing clause should be the same as the subject of the main clause.

These -ing clauses add detail to sentences. They generally refer to an action that occurred around the same time as or before the action in the main clause. They are often clauses of time or reason.

These clauses are normally separated from main clauses with a comma.

GRAMMAR TERM: Reduced adverbial -ing clauses without a subordinator are also called **adverbial participles**.

B

3 **Having traveled extensively,** she bases her books on geographical fact and the customs of the people about whom she writes.
(She has traveled extensively. Now she writes books.)

4 **Having been diagnosed with mental illness,** she was placed in an institution.
(She had been diagnosed with mental illness. As a result, she was placed in an institution.)

Sometimes -ing clauses use **having** + a **past participle**, as in **3**. These clauses describe an action that was completed before the action in the main clause. They can be used in a present time frame, as in **3**, or in a past time frame, as in **4**.

These clauses can also be passive, using **having** + **been** + a **past participle**, as in **4**.

15 | Noticing Adverbial *-ing* Clauses Underline the adverbial *-ing* clauses in each passage. `1.5 A–B`

ADDING DETAILS

1. Lamar also helped organize the first Agricultural Fair in 1855 and served as a committee member in subsequent years. In 1855, he took another shot at politics, <u>running for the state legislature on the American Party ticket</u>.

2. Caton was denied entry to Mexico and kept under guard for more than two months until he was sent back to Jamaica. <u>Believing that he would never be able to accomplish his mission</u>, he returned to England permanently in January 1740.

3. Within a week, Feldman called to offer me the position as teacher associate. <u>Having written virtually nothing beyond college term papers</u>, I questioned his wisdom in selecting me for the position, but I agreed to join the project, and in the summer of 1966, I traveled to Dartmouth to do so. <u>Showing great confidence</u>, I arranged a one-year leave of absence from my school district, put my furniture in storage, and headed for an adventure in the New Social Studies.

4. In Boston, prisoner-soldiers permitted to work on area farms sometimes chose not to return to their camp, <u>preferring to live on the farms</u>. Some of them married farmers' daughters. Others made their way to British-occupied New York, where they rejoined the British Army. Many escapees wandered the countryside, <u>looking for work</u>.

5. We were up before daylight on the 2nd of July and everything we needed was packed up to go. Every man had written his last letter home and was anxiously awaiting the start to the train, which was to carry us to Port Tampa. Half an hour's ride brought us to our transport. The next morning we started, <u>having been delayed several hours by a break in the machinery</u>.

Think about It Answer these questions about the passages above.

1. Which of the underlined clauses describe action(s) that happened around the same time as the action in the main clause?

2. Which describe action(s) that were completed before the action in the main clause?

3. What is the subject of each *-ing* clause?

4. Which of the *-ing* clauses express a time relationship? Which provide a reason?

16 | Using Adverbial *-ing* Clauses Choose an *-ing* clause from the box to add to each passage. (Different answers are possible.) `1.5 A`

FROM FICTION

1. As she held the child with one hand and reached for her suitcase from the carousel[52] with the other, someone said, "Please, allow me." The warm voice belonged to the man standing next to her. Kate turned toward the voice. The man smiled. *, reaching for the bag* She inspected[53] the suitcase briefly and saw that it was not hers.

arriving home
calling to ask about the schedule
holding his homework under his chin
ignoring the applause as he took his seat at the grand piano
reaching for the bag
realizing that she'd forgotten to reset her alarm
seeing the direction of Carl's attention
seeming eager to have our visit over and done with
turning left and right many times
waking to a nice, warm afternoon

2. My mom and I went to Disney World for spring break. The first night, we used GPS to get directions from our hotel to an Italian restaurant. We followed the directions for about 20 minutes before arriving at the restaurant.

3. She quickly changed clothes and then made herself some tea.

4. He took advantage of the light and spent an hour at his easel[54]. Then he ate half a chicken sandwich, took a hot shower, and left for the station.

5. Dylan pulled the door open and stepped into the empty apartment. He had been alone a lot since his parents got divorced.

6. He was watching a large bird that was picking at the ground behind her as it searched for insects among the fallen leaves. She waved an arm to shoo[55] the bird away. "Look at me," she said.

7. As he ended the first call, his other line clicked. It was Remy, one of the producers, he was sure.

8. At last the house lights dimmed[56]. The audience fell silent. A tall man strode[57] across the stage.

9. Fran took us to the kitchen table. She'd lost weight. Her hair had thinned and her brown eyes looked dull and lifeless.

10. She glanced[58] at the clock and groaned. She pulled herself up and sat for a moment with her feet resting on the cold floor.

RESEARCH SAYS...

Adverbial -*ing* clauses are far more common in descriptive writing than in other kinds of writing, and they are very rare in speaking.

CORPUS

Think about It Answer these questions about the passages in Activity 16.

1. What do you think the time relationship is between each main clause and the -*ing* clause you added?
2. Underline the additional adverb clauses of time in Activity 16. Circle the other time adverbials.

Write about It Add an adverbial -*ing* clause to the beginning of two of these sentences and to the end of the other two. Then share your work with a partner.

1. I opened the door slowly

   I opened the door slowly, hoping that the room was empty.

2. I walked into the classroom
3. I answered the phone
4. I closed my eyes

17 | Using Adverbial *Having* + Past Participle Clauses Combine the sentences, changing the sentence in parentheses to an adverbial *having* + past participle clause. `1.5 B`

SENTENCES FROM HISTORICAL NARRATIVES

1. (They had come from rocky, barren[59] areas.) The newcomers highly prized the fertile[60] soil of their new home.

   Having come from rocky, barren areas, the newcomers highly prized the fertile soil of their new home.

2. (It had just negotiated[61] a peace treaty[62] in the war against the French and Spanish.) The British government decided to reduce its forces in North America.

3. (It had controlled inflation and reduced its debt.) Brazil weathered[63] the 2008 financial crisis better than most countries did.

4. Between the censuses[64] of 1980 and 1991, the population of Belize increased by 44,000 (30.3 percent). (It had grown at an average annual rate of 2.4 percent.)

5. (He had worked as an oil ministry[65] official in London from 1980 to 1985.) He had valuable experience with energy policy.

6. The traditional clothing designs were known to extend back through generations. (They had been worn by the grandmothers and great-grandmothers of the women in the village.)

7. (They had spent some 50 percent of government revenue[66] on the war effort for four full years.) The major European nations were left with gigantic debts.

8. (She had just won the battle for women's suffrage[67] in New York.) Whitehouse was ready to accept a new challenge.

9. (It had been cleaned before its journey.) The sculpture glowed[68] under the lights.

10. The majority of the Anishinaabe people were left impoverished[69]. (They had lost access to their land and resources.)

11. (It has driven the economy into the ground.) The government desperately needs foreign investment, loans, and aid[70].

Think about It Which of the adverbial clauses you wrote in Activity 17 are passive?

18 | Reading Read another excerpt from *The Kite Runner*. Then do the tasks below and on page 21.

The Kite Runner* (excerpt 2)
by Khaled Hosseini

By three o'clock that afternoon, tufts[71] of clouds had drifted[72] in and the sun had slipped behind them. Shadows started to lengthen. The spectators on the roofs bundled up[73] in scarves and thick coats. We were down to a half dozen and I was still flying. My legs ached and my neck was stiff. But with each defeated kite, hope grew in my heart. My eyes kept returning to a blue kite that had been wreaking havoc[74] for the last hour.

"How many has he cut?" I asked.

"I counted eleven," Hassan said.

"Do you know whose it might be?"

Hassan clucked[75] his tongue and tipped his chin. That was a trademark[76] Hassan gesture, meant he had no idea. The blue kite sliced a purple one and swept twice in big loops. Ten minutes later, he'd cut another two, sending hordes[77] of kite runners racing after them.

After another thirty minutes, only four kites remained. And I was still flying. It seemed I could hardly make a wrong move, as if every gust[78] of wind blew in my favor. I'd never felt so in command, so lucky. It felt intoxicating[79]. I didn't dare look up to the roof. Didn't dare take my eyes off the sky. I had to concentrate, play it smart. Another fifteen minutes and what had seemed like a laughable dream that morning had suddenly become reality: It was just me and the other guy. The blue kite.

The tension in the air was as taut[80] as the glass string I was tugging[81] with my bloody hands. People were stomping their feet, clapping, whistling, chanting, "Boboresh! Boboresh!" Cut him! Cut him! I wondered if Baba's voice was one of them. Music blasted[82]. The smell of steamed mantu[83] and fried pakora[84] drifted from rooftops and open doors.

But all I heard—all I willed myself to hear—was the thudding[85] of blood in my head. All I saw was the blue kite. All I smelled was victory.

*In this part of the story, Amir describes a kite-flying competition that was an important event in his childhood.

Talk about It Does Amir think he's going to win or lose the competition? What words in the excerpt above describe how he is feeling? Discuss your ideas with your classmates.

Think about It Answer these questions about the story on page 20.

1. The story has a past time frame, and most of the verbs are in the simple past. Find an example of the past perfect and the past continuous. Why did the writer choose those forms rather than the simple past?

2. Underline the time adverbials in the story.

WRITING ASSIGNMENT I

Follow steps A–D to write a short narrative about an experience or event you learned from.

A | Planning Follow these steps to plan your narrative.

1. List three important experiences, or events in your life. They can be events that you observed or events that you participated in. Then think about why each event is important. For example, what did you learn from it? Or how did it affect your future actions and decisions? Add this information to your list.

   - *meeting cousins (learned to appreciate my circumstances)*
   - *singing contest (learned that effort was rewarding)*
   - *car breaking down (learned that I still needed help)*

2. Discuss your experiences with a partner. Ask your partner for details about what happened and why it was important. Add details to your list.

B | Writing Choose one of the items from your list. Write a paragraph about your chosen experience. Explain what happened and what you learned. Include at least one full adverb clause or reduced adverb clause of time.

> *When I got my first car, it felt like a ticket to freedom and adulthood. I loved to go for long drives by myself. So when I woke up on an unusually bright and beautiful New Year's Day not long after I got the car, it seemed like a great idea to go for a drive. I took the highway to the coast and drove north, enjoying the sunny day and the empty road. Suddenly I heard a terrible knocking sound, and the engine died. I pulled over to the side of the road and soon discovered there was no phone service. So I locked the car and started walking. Two hours later, I reached a small town and was able to use a phone in a restaurant. I had to wait three hours for my father to pick me up and deal with the tow truck[86] because I had no money and no idea who to call or what to do. That day I discovered that I wasn't quite as adult as I thought I was.*

C | Peer Reviewing Share your writing with a partner. Answer these questions about your partner's story.

1. What time frames does the paragraph have? Do the verb choices fit the chosen time frame(s)?
2. Can you easily follow the order of events? Should your partner add any adverbials to make the order clearer?
3. Do you understand why the experience was important or what your partner learned from it? Should anything be added or removed to make this clearer?

D | Revising Follow these steps to revise your paragraph.

1. Using your partner's feedback, rewrite your paragraph.
2. Check your writing for mistakes and clarity. Underline the verbs and check the verb forms. Did you use at least one full adverb clause or reduced adverb clause of time? Make any final corrections necessary.

1.6 Adjectives and Adjective Complements

A

ADJECTIVES AND DESCRIBING NOUNS

1 The **long-term** savings from the **budget** cuts were substantial.

2 Anabel looked **exhausted** after the long race.

ADJECTIVE + ADJECTIVE COMPLEMENT

3 The doctors were **unaware** of the medicine their patients were taking. (prepositional phrase)

4 The students were **happy** to have an extra day of vacation. (to- infinitive clause)

5 Tom felt **sure** that the project would not succeed. (*that* clause)

One way that writers add descriptive detail is by using **adjectives** and **describing nouns** before a noun, as in **1**, or **adjectives** after a linking verb (*seem, look, be, feel*, etc.), as in **2 – 5**.

Sometimes we add even more detail to adjectives with:

- prepositional phrases, as in **3**
- *to-* infinitive clauses*, as in **4**
- *that* clauses (noun clauses), as in **5**

GRAMMAR TERM: The words that add detail after adjectives are called **adjective complements**.

*These *to-* infinitive structures can be considered clauses because the to- infinitive clause has an understood subject and a verb. For more information, see the Resources, page R-49.

B

6 Dana was no longer **certain** that she was going to find what she needed.

7 Anderson was **pleased** that the book had received such good reviews.

Adjectives commonly followed by *that* clauses usually describe:

- degrees of certainty, as in **6**
- feelings, as in **7**

Notice that the subject and verb form in the *that* clause can be different from those in the main clause.

For more information on *that* clauses as complements, see the Resources, page R-25.

C

8 She had convinced her boss that she was **sure to return** from the trip with some useful material.

9 I'm grateful to all the people who were **willing to come** out so early this morning.

10 Marcus was obviously **happy to be included** in the group.

11 Potatoes were **easy to grow** and very nutritious.

COMPARE

12a At first most of the children were **afraid to get into** the water.

12b Some of the parents were **afraid** that the water was not safe.

Adjectives commonly followed by **to- infinitive clauses** usually describe:

- degrees of certainty, as in **8**
- ability or willingness, as in **9**
- feelings, as in **10**
- ease or difficulty, as in **11**

Many adjectives that describe feelings or degrees of certainty can be followed by either a **to- infinitive clause** or a *that* clause, as in **12a – 12b**.

GO ONLINE For more practice with adjective complements, go to the Online Practice.

19 | Noticing Adjectives and Adjective Complements Circle the adjectives that are followed by a prepositional phrase, a *that* clause, or a *to-* infinitive clause. `1.6 A–C`

DESCRIPTIVE DETAILS

1. The student unrest began with the state of research in France after World War II. A number of eminent[87] French scientists were (concerned) that French research was behind the times, and they knew that scientific research would play an increasingly important role in the economy.

2. Many volunteers came to rescue work after getting hurt or lost in the woods themselves. Rescue unit leader Wally Mann, 32, once hiked out in pain from New Hampshire's Mahoosuc Mountains, and was relieved to find a rescue party ready to go in after him. That vision of hope prompted[88] him to sign on for search and rescue work himself.

3. Welch was careful to note the exact time of the eclipse[89] and to describe in detail the effect it had on the people around him.

4. My husband and I recently met friends for dinner downtown. We were happy to find on-street parking a few blocks from the restaurant, a new place we were eager to try. But when we got back after dinner, we were greeted with a $25 parking ticket.

5. He looked cold, even though he was well covered. He wore a thick, tightly buttoned sweater under his jacket and a wool blanket over his shoulders. The ancient buildings were impossible to heat, even when there was plenty of fuel.

6. A teacher came to class with a set of 30 photographs with the captions removed. The students discussed the pictures and tried to identify the country. Most were convinced that the photographs were scenes from Spain.

7. I arrived early and that turned out to be a good idea. Before long the large auditorium was full of students waiting to see the great man. Most of us, I suspect, were willing to believe just about anything he said.

> **F Y I**
>
> In writing, we do not usually omit the *that* in adjective complements. In conversation, we sometimes leave it out.
>
> **Writing:** He was sure that the policy would improve the circumstances of low-income families.
>
> **Conversation:** "I'm sure (that) I left my keys here."

Think about It Of the adjectives you circled above, write the ones that describe:

degrees of certainty _____

ability or willingness _____

feelings *concerned* _____

ease/difficulty _____

Think about It Underline all of the describing noun + noun combinations in Activity 19.

20 | Using Adjectives with *That* Clauses Read each passage. Then complete the sentences below with the adjectives in parentheses and a *that* clause based on the story. (Different answers are possible.) `1.6 B`

Vasco da Gama's Voyage

Vasco da Gama

A The Portuguese explorer Vasco da Gama was the first European to find a sea route to India. Before da Gama's famous voyage, Portuguese explorers had traveled down the west coast of Africa in search of treasure. However, having received little profit from these journeys, the Portuguese crown[90] did not want to pay for further exploration. This changed in 1481, when John II of Portugal became interested in the spice trade with Asia. He believed that spices could be an important source of income for the crown, but the route over land was long and difficult. He asked his ship captains to find a route to Asia by sailing around the tip of Africa. In 1488, Bartolomeu Dias finally rounded the southern end of Africa and verified[91] that the coast headed northeast after the Cape of Good Hope.

Da Gama set out from Lisbon in July of 1497. After five months of sailing, he reached the Fish River, the point where Dias had turned back. From then on, da Gama was traveling a route unknown to Europeans, hoping that his journey would take him to India.

B Da Gama faced hostility in several of the places that he stopped. In Mozambique, for instance, he did not have an appropriate gift for the ruler. The people became angry and forced him to leave.

C Da Gama's expedition finally arrived in India in May of 1498. However, they did not get the reception they wanted. Local leaders were not impressed with the gifts da Gama brought and told him to pay taxes in gold. Angry, da Gama captured several of the local fishermen and took them away.

D The expedition was expensive. One ship and over half of the men were lost. However, the crown made a huge profit on the spices that da Gama brought back, and the king knew that da Gama's new route would bring great wealth to Portugal.

(A) 1. Early Portuguese explorers ___were hopeful that they would find treasure in Africa___.
(hopeful)

2. After the early explorations, the Portuguese crown _____
(not convinced)
_____.

3. John II _____.
(confident)

4. After Dias' voyage, the Portuguese _____
(sure)
_____.

5. After passing the Fish River, da Gama _____
(not certain)
_____.

(B) 6. The people of Mozambique _____
(angry)
_____.

(C) 7. Da Gama _____.
(probably quite relieved)

8. Da Gama _____.
(annoyed)

24

(D) 9. The king _____.
      (pleased)

   10. The king _____.
      (aware)

   _____.

Think about It Compare the sentences you wrote in Activity 20 with a partner. Identify the subjects in the main clause and the *that* clause. Are they the same or different?

21 | Using Adjectives with *To-* Infinitive Clauses Complete each sentence with one adjective and one verb from the box. (Different answers are possible.) 1.6 C

EXPRESSING FEELINGS AND DEGREES OF DIFFICULTY

ADJECTIVES	VERBS
afraid	be
careful	carry
content	copy
curious	discover
difficult	know
easy	learn
free	leave
grateful	leave
impossible	read
pleased	represent
proud	select
relieved	use

1. He was _____*grateful to be*_____ accepted into the group.

2. Although everyone else had to remain in the area, reporters were

   _____ whenever they wanted to.

3. The teachers were _____ activities that could be

   performed by all of the students.

4. The employees were _____ that their colleagues

   faced similar difficulties.

5. Some of the students preferred using an e-reader because the huge

   textbook was _____ in a backpack.

6. The program received positive evaluations. Students said it was

   enjoyable and _____.

7. The patient suffered from severe anxiety and was _____ the house.

8. Researchers were _____ how children would view the recent events.

9. I was _____ our country at the conference.

10. Many people have suggested that artists in the Middle Ages were _____

    one another and did not make any attempt to draw inspiration from nature.

11. We were _____ that our program had achieved so much success.

12. The print at the bottom of the form was tiny and _____. I have no idea

    what it said.

22 | Using Adjectives with *To-* Infinitive Clauses Rewrite each sentence using an adjective from the box + a *to-* infinitive clause. You may need to change several words in the sentence. (Different answers are possible.) 1.6 C

DEGREES OF CERTAINTY

apt[92]   certain   due   guaranteed   liable[93]   likely   prone[94]   sure

1. It was the kind of community where neighbors often showed up with a cake or a pot of soup.

   It was the kind of community where neighbors were apt to show up with a cake or a pot of soup.

2. Lauren was probably asleep already, so Liz hesitated before slowly turning the doorknob.

   _____

DEGREES OF CERTAINTY							
apt	certain	due	guaranteed	liable	likely	prone	sure

3. The air traffic controllers had day shifts alternating with night shifts. This schedule was definitely going to produce drowsiness[95] in the control room.

_____

_____

4. Matthew said a few things that he would definitely regret later.

_____

ABILITY OR WILLINGNESS				
able	bound	eager	hesitant[97]	welcome
anxious	determined	eligible[96]	inclined[98]	willing

5. She thought that she probably agreed with her doctor.

_____

6. Lana very much believed in keeping the promises that she had made.

_____

7. It took me a while to recover, but eventually I could do my job again.

_____

8. No one really liked talking about the disaster.

_____

23 | Usage Note: Adjectives in Detached Clauses Read the note. Then do Activity 24.

In descriptive writing, we sometimes add an adjective + complement to a **main clause** in a **detached adjective complement clause**. The detached clause describes the subject of the main clause and can be placed at the beginning or end of the main clause. A detached clause is separated from its main clause by a comma.

1 Alexander approached the painting slowly, afraid to touch the canvas.
(Alexander was afraid.)

2 Hopeful that his silence would be viewed as acceptance, **Reynolds decided not to speak up at the meeting.**
(Reynolds was hopeful.)

24 | Using Detached Clauses Combine the sentences, changing the second sentence to a detached clause. You may want to reverse the order of the clauses and/or change some of the words. (Different answers are possible.) 1.6 B–C

SENTENCE COMBINING

1. Charles finished college and applied to law school.
   Charles was determined to become a lawyer like his father.

   Determined to become a lawyer like his father, Charles finished college and applied to law school.   OR
   Charles finished college and applied to law school, determined to become a lawyer like his father.

2. Cameron correctly painted smoke rising from only three smokestacks[99].

   Cameron was aware that the ship had only used three of its four engines.

3. Florence called the local newspaper.

   Florence was certain that she could see bones in the trench[100].

4. Parents petitioned[101] for the construction of a school within walking distance of the community.

   Parents were concerned that children were spending too much time on the bus every day.

5. Community members asked legislators[102] to take action.

   Community members were fearful that the polluted water was making residents sick.

6. The nurses walked quietly through the halls.

   The nurses were anxious not to wake the sleeping children.

7. Residents gathered in protest outside City Hall.

   The residents were angry about the new policy.

8. More and more young people were leaving the country every year.

   The young people were unable to find work at home.

WRITING ASSIGNMENT II

Follow steps A–D to write a detailed description of a place that is or was important to you.

A | Planning Follow these steps to plan your paragraph.

1. Make a list of three places that are or used to be important to you. Next to each place, take some brief notes describing it. Think about what the place looks/looked, smells/smelled, and sounds/sounded like. Make notes about why it is or was important to you.

   - *My room behind the house—small, slanting wooden ceiling with skylights[103], loft bed; a peaceful place; my first experience of privacy*

   - *The beach on Menorca—sun shining, happy people, clear water, relaxing; people seemed freer; important to forget about work for a while*

   - *My college dorm room—small, crowded, too many books, clothes everywhere, the smell of our coffee maker in the middle of the night, music constantly playing from the room next door; the place I met my best friend*

2. Discuss your list with a partner. Ask and answer questions. Why did your partner choose these places? Why are/were they important? What do/did they look like? What feelings, smells, sounds, etc. do/did they bring to mind? Add details to your list.

B | Writing Choose one of the places from your list. Write a paragraph describing that place. Include a brief explanation of why it is or was important to you. Include at least one adjective followed by a *that* clause or *to-* infinitive clause.

> In the backyard of my family's house there was a small building. We called it "the granny unit," but I think it was a converted garage, and when I turned 18, I moved out there. I was eager to have my own private space, and the granny unit was perfect for me. Previous owners had put in a high wood ceiling with two enormous skylights, so the room was bright all day and at night you could look up and see the stars. When it rained, the water came in around the edges of the skylights, loudly dripping into my strategically placed pots and buckets. There was a thin red carpet covering a concrete floor, and the warmth from the tiny electric heater disappeared through the skylight glass, so the room was cold in the winter. But I never cared. It was my refuge[104], a place apart from my younger siblings where I could study and relax in peace, and I loved it.

C | Peer Reviewing Share your writing with a partner. Answer these questions about your partner's paragraph.

1. Can you imagine what the place looks like? Could your partner add details to make the description more vivid?

2. Do you understand why the place was important to your partner? Should anything be added or removed to make it clearer?

D | Revising Follow these steps to revise your paragraph.

1. Using your partner's feedback, rewrite your paragraph.

2. Check your writing for mistakes and clarity. Circle the adjectives in your revised description. Is at least one of them followed by a *that* clause or *to-* infinitive clause? Make any final corrections necessary.

25 | Reading Read this story by author Geoffrey Canada. Then do the tasks on page 29.

CHERRIES FOR MY GRANDMA

by Geoffrey Canada

1 I grew up poor in the Bronx. My mother raised my three brothers and me by herself. When she couldn't find work, we went on welfare[105]. When she could find work, it was in jobs that paid women so little money that we couldn't tell the difference between welfare and work except that our mother wasn't home when she was working. People talk about poverty and the poor like it's so easy to not be poor. But I know a different story.

2 It takes great sacrifice and talent to work your way out of poverty. My mother used to make all of her own clothes. You couldn't raise four boys on her salary and afford to buy dresses to wear to work. When we were young, she used to make our clothes, cut our hair, and make toys for us out of cereal boxes. All her life she sacrificed for us. She put off getting her college degree and her master's degree until we were grown and on our own.

3 And you know what? We hated being poor. We loved our mother but we ruined her Christmas every year with our tears of disappointment at not getting exactly what we wanted. I couldn't help but be angry when my shoes had holes in them and there was no money to buy new ones. And I couldn't help but stare angrily when I needed money to go on a school trip and there wasn't any money to be had.

4 And while there was much love in our family, being poor strained[106] our loving bonds. We had to blame someone, and my mother was the only target. And here she was giving up all she had for us, going without lunch, without movies and nights out, walking ten blocks to the train because she couldn't afford to pay the 15 cents extra to take the bus. And she would come home to four boys with their hands out, angry because we wanted something, needed something she could not give.

5 There are some Americans who think poverty stems from[107] a lack of values and determination. But you can work hard all your life, have impeccable[108] values, and still be poor. My grandfather was the pastor of Mount Pleasant Baptist Church in Harlem. My grandmother was a Christian woman. They were hard-working, moral people. They were poor.

6 I lived with my grandparents during my high school years. My grandmother worked all her life: caring for other people's children, selling baked goods or beauty products, doing whatever she could do to help bring money into the house. She was a beautiful woman, kind and intelligent. She was determined to save my soul.

7 I was a wild and reckless adolescent whose soul was indeed in danger. And I fell in love with my grandmother. A deep love that any of us would develop if an angel came into our lives. The more time I spent with her, the more I loved her. She cooled my hot temper and anger over being poor, and she showed me there was dignity[109] even in poverty.

8   In all the years I knew her, she was never able to afford material things that others took for granted[110]. She worked very hard but never could afford anything of luxury. She taught me how one could enjoy a deep spiritual love of life that was not tied to material things. This is a tough lesson to teach in a country that places so much value on materialism[111].

9   But each summer my grandmother and I would secretly plan to indulge[112] her one vice[113]: cherries. She loved cherries. Two or three times a week when my grandfather was at work, I would walk the mile to the supermarket and buy half a pound of cherries. My grandmother and I would eat them secretly because my grandfather would have had a fit[114] if he'd known we spent an extra dollar a week on them.

10   My summers with my grandmother were measured by how good the cherries were that year. It was our little secret. And I was amazed at how much she loved cherries, and how expensive cherries were. Later when I went off to Bowdoin College in Brunswick, Maine, I would sit in my room and think about how much my mother and grandmother had sacrificed for me to be in college.

11   I would fantasize about how when I graduated and got a good job, the first thing I would buy with my first check in August would be a whole crate[115] of cherries. It would have to be August because our cherry summers taught us that August cherries were the sweetest. I would dream of wrapping the crate up in gift paper, putting a bow on it, and presenting it to Grandma. And many a night I would go to sleep in the cold winter Maine nights warmed by the vision of my grandmother's excitement when I brought her this small treasure.

12   Grandma died during my sophomore year. I never got to give her all the cherries she could eat. And if you want my opinion, the summer of 1971, the last summer she was alive, was really the last great summer for cherries.

13   Poverty is tough on families in many ways. It's not quite as simple to get out of as people make out[116]. We must be careful to make sure we build ladders so children and their families can climb out of poverty. It's not an easy climb. You can climb all your life and never make it out.

14   Grandma, who sacrificed so much for all of us, I just want to say I know that in all I've been acknowledged for, I still haven't reached the level of love and compassion that you tried to teach me. I think you accomplished your goal: you saved my soul. And I hope they let me bring gifts to Heaven. You'll know what's in the box.

Talk about It Discuss these questions about the story in Activity 25 with a partner.

1. What lessons did Canada's grandmother teach him? What do you think about them?
2. What lessons did Canada's mother teach him? What do you think about them?
3. What lessons does society need to learn, according to Canada? What do you think about them?
4. What's in the box that Canada wants to bring to heaven? What are some things that this gift could symbolize?

Think about It Answer these questions about the story.

1. What is the main time frame of paragraph 1? Which verbs are in a different time frame? Why?
2. What forms does the writer use for the habitual past in paragraph 2?
3. What form does the writer use for the habitual past in paragraph 4?
4. What time adverbials does the writer use in paragraph 8?
5. What are the adverb clauses of time in paragraph 11?
6. Underline four of the adjectives followed by *to-* infinitive clauses in the story.
   (See paragraphs 1, 6, 8, and 13.)

FINAL WRITING ASSIGNMENT
Write a Descriptive or Narrative Essay

Your Task

Write a descriptive essay about a childhood relationship with a person who has had a powerful influence over you. Give specific examples and detailed descriptions of things you did together and conversations you had. Show how this relationship helped you to become the person you are today.

Alternative Task

Write a narrative essay about the past experiences of a famous person or a person you know. Tell about his/her experiences in chronological order. Then explain how the experiences influenced him/her.

GO ONLINE Go to the Online Writing Tutor for a writing model and to write your assignment.

A | **Writing Note: Essay Structure** Read the note. Then do Activity B.

An essay can be divided into three parts: the **introduction**, the **body**, and the **conclusion**.

The first paragraph of an essay is the **introduction**. One common pattern in an introduction is to move from the general to the specific. An introduction often begins with a **hook** to capture the reader's attention. The hook can then be followed by some general statements on your topic. The introduction often also includes a main idea, known as a **thesis statement**.

The **body** of an essay may consist of several paragraphs and includes information, examples, or further explanation that supports the thesis statement. This may be in the form of "**SAFER**":

- **s**tatistics (numerical data)
- **a**necdotes (short and interesting stories about real experiences)
- **f**acts (true information)
- **e**xamples (samples or illustrations of an idea)
- **r**easons (explanations of why an idea is true)

The **conclusion** often refers back to the thesis statement. It can sum up important arguments, give advice or an opinion, or leave the reader with something to think about. The conclusion should contain key words and phrases from the introduction and body to unify the essay.

B | **Analyzing a First-Draft Essay** Read this student's first draft and identify the parts of the essay: introduction, body paragraphs, and conclusion. Then answer the questions on page 31 and compare answers with a partner.

Muhammad Yunus

Muhammad Yunus was born on June 28, 1940 in Chittagong, India, which is now in Bangladesh. He is famous for winning the Nobel Peace Prize and for starting Grameen Bank, which gives small loans to very poor people.

Muhammad was the third of nine children. His parents valued education even though they themselves did not go to high school. His father was a successful jeweler. Besides going to school, Yunus was active in the Boy Scouts, especially in the activities that raised money for the poor. After he finished high school, he attended the University of Dhaka, where he earned his BA and MA degrees in economics. He started a printing and packaging business with help from his father, and he began teaching economics courses at the University of Chittagong. Yunus found that he liked teaching, and he knew he would get a better job if he went abroad to study, so he applied for and received a Fulbright scholarship to study in the U.S. He studied economics at Vanderbilt University, and after finishing his course work, he began teaching at Middle Tennessee State University. His college education was important to his later success. There were many problems at that time in Pakistan, and Yunus' experiences there inspired him to help. In 1977, he started the project that would lead to Grameen Bank, which was to give poor people access to the money they needed to establish and develop their own businesses. He maintained contact with the bank as it grew, and eventually became known as "banker to the poor." He won the World Food Prize in 1994 and the first ever Sydney Peace Prize in 1998. He shared the 2006 Nobel Peace Prize with Grameen Bank in recognition of[117] the idea that reducing poverty makes a more peaceful world.

   Forced to retire from Grameen Bank in 2011 because of his age, Yunus is now engaged in promoting "social business," a business model in which investors are repaid their capital but do not receive further profit. Any profit is returned to the business to help support and develop it.

QUESTIONS

1. Is there a thesis statement—one sentence that states the main idea of the essay?

2. Does each body paragraph have a clear main idea?

3. The writer says, "His college education was important to his later success." What kind of details could he or she add to support that idea?

4. What other idea(s) in the essay need(s) support? What details could the writer add to support this idea/these ideas?

5. Is there a conclusion that unifies the essay?

C | Analyzing a Second-Draft Essay Read the student's second draft. Then answer the questions on page 32 and compare answers with a partner.

Muhammad Yunus: A Creative Solution to a Difficult Problem

   "What? Lend money to the poor? It's too risky!" "You can't earn money on small loans. You need big loans to make a profit." "Your proposal will never work." Certainly Muhammad Yunus has heard statements like these throughout his career, but despite his critics, he has demonstrated that some of his proposals, such as making small loans to poor people, can succeed beyond anyone's expectations. Yunus has been able to achieve so much because he has used his formal education and his life experience to find new solutions to old problems.

   Muhammad Yunus is a highly accomplished man. He was born in 1940 in Chittagong, India, which is now in Bangladesh. After high school, Yunus attended the University of Dhaka, where he earned his BA and MA degrees in economics, and in 1964, he received a Fulbright scholarship to study for a PhD in economics at Vanderbilt University in the U.S. In 1969, he began teaching at Middle Tennessee State University. Two years later, Yunus went to Washington, D.C. to educate American politicians about, and raise support for, the independence of East Pakistan, which later became Bangladesh (Counts 34). When Yunus returned to Chittagong in 1972, he got a position at the University of Chittagong. While there, he studied the economics of rural people. In 1977, he established a micro-credit lending project for which he served as project director, and in 1983, this project became the independent Grameen Bank, for which he served as managing director from 1983 to 2011. He shared the 2006 Nobel Peace Prize with Grameen Bank in recognition of the idea that reducing poverty leads to a more peaceful world ("Muhammad Yunus"). He established the Yunus Centre in Bangladesh in 2008 and serves as its chairman, and he has been chancellor of Glasgow Caledonian University, Scotland since 2012 ("CV").

   Yunus was fortunate to have had parents who encouraged him to learn both in school and from the world around him. While his education gave him theories, his observations of the world around him helped him go beyond the theories. Living in Chittagong, Yunus saw many very poor people in the rural areas near his home. After the War of Independence, Bangladesh suffered a severe drought[118], and many of the people around him were slowly starving. Seeing this, Yunus recognized that his academic training could be applied to the problems of poverty and farming practices (Counts 27–28). Among the problems that Yunus addressed was that of poor people borrowing money. Bankers refused to lend them money because the amounts were too low, and the bankers also believed that the poor would not repay the loans. Yunus, perhaps drawing on his experience with American politicians, persuaded bankers to establish a program to give extremely poor people very small amounts of money, micro-loans, with which they could improve their lives. For example, the first loan, the equivalent of $27, served 42 people in a village near Chittagong (Counts 58–59). With capital to control, borrowers began to eat better, send their children to school, and become more self-sufficient. Grameen Bank expanded, eventually extending its model of microfinance[119] around the world, including to programs in the U.S. and Europe. To make the program successful, Yunus learned by working within the system.

Yunus did more than apply his formal education to the problems he saw. He also challenged conventional thinking. Rather than letting his graduate students stay within the grounds of the university, he encouraged them to go into the rural areas to develop new approaches to old problems (Counts 37–38). Instead of accepting common beliefs about the poor, Yunus has long advocated[120] more universal access to loan money as a means of eliminating poverty ("Vision"). Rejecting the idea that businesses must earn a profit for their investors, Yunus promotes social businesses in which, after the investors have regained their start-up money, all profits go back into the businesses ("Social Business").

Professor Muhammad Yunus, Nobel Prize winner and "banker to the poor," learned from the established system and then challenged beliefs in order to make beneficial change. His new ideas in banking and business have led to a better quality of life for many people around the world. Perhaps by imitating him, we too can make the world a better place. Are you willing to give it a try?

Works Cited

Counts, Alex. *Small Loans, Big Dreams: How Nobel Prize Winner Muhammad Yunus and Microfinance Are Changing the World*. Hoboken, New Jersey: John Wiley & Sons, 2008. Print.

"CV of Professor Muhammad Yunus." *Yunus Centre*. 2011. Web. 8 Feb. 2015. <http://www.muhammadyunus.org/index.php/professor-yunus/cv>

"Muhammad Yunus—Nobel Lecture." *Nobelprize.org*. Nobel Media AB 2014. Web. 8 Feb. 2015. <http://www.nobelprize.org/nobel_prizes/peace/laureates/2006/yunus-lecture-en.html>

"Social Business." *Yunus Centre*. 2011. Web. 8 Feb. 2015. <http://www.muhammadyunus.org/index.php/social-business/social-business>

"Vision." *Yunus Centre*. 2011. Web. 8 Feb. 2015. <http://www.muhammadyunus.org/index.php/professor-yunus/vision>

QUESTIONS

1. How has the writer made the introduction more interesting?
2. Underline the thesis statement. Does the rest of the essay support the thesis statement?
3. What is the main idea of the second paragraph? How does the writer support that idea?
4. What is the main idea of the third paragraph? How does the writer support that idea?
5. What is the main idea of the fourth paragraph? How does the writer support that idea?
6. Does the conclusion refer back to the thesis statement and unify the essay?
7. In what ways is the essay format different? Is it better? Why or why not?

D | Writing Note: Hooks Read the note. Then do Activity E.

Just as a fisherman uses a hook to catch a fish, the beginning sentences of an essay often function as a **hook** to capture the reader's attention. There are many ways to do this.

- Begin with a question. The reader will want to respond to the question.

  When someone asks you to think of a hero, whose face do you picture?

- Begin with a famous quote or some dialogue.

  "You can't judge a book by its cover." I learned this the summer I turned 16.

- Use descriptive language related to the topic.

  I was just a little girl. My whole world was made up of my swing hanging above the grass, my best friend next door, and the chocolate I would let melt on the floor behind the living room sofa.

- Begin with clues to arouse interest in the main topic.

  Andrews grew up poor in the Bronx. His mother raised five children by herself.

E | Practicing with Hooks Check (✓) each sentence that would make a good hook for an essay about a person who has influenced your life. Explain your choices and share them with the class.

1. ☐ Many people have been influenced by someone special when they were young.

   "This is not a very interesting hook. It makes a general statement that doesn't make the reader want to read more."

2. ☑ When Arnold Sanders was young, he was not a well-behaved child.

   "This is an interesting hook. I want to know how Sanders misbehaved. I can identify with him because I got in trouble when I was young, too."

3. ☐ "I want to leave home. Now!"
4. ☐ The person who had the most powerful influence over me as a child was my first English teacher.
5. ☐ Have you ever been called "stupid" in class?
6. ☐ Anne Sullivan had many interesting experiences.
7. ☐ He produced about 900 paintings, which are now worth millions of dollars, but in his lifetime he sold only a few.

F | Writing Note: Thesis Statements Read the note. Then do Activity G.

> The **thesis statement** tells the reader what the essay is going to be about—the topic or point of the essay. It also tells the reader how the author thinks or feels about the topic—the **controlling idea**.
>
> In some academic writing, such as a research paper, a thesis statement may state directly what the paper is going to cover.
>
> **1** This paper examines the life of Franklin Roosevelt in order to demonstrate how his experiences influenced the decisions he made during his time in office.
>
> In a descriptive or narrative essay, thesis statements often give this information indirectly, but suggest a little bit of the writer's purpose for the essay. Sometimes a thesis statement will also include information about the organization of the body of an essay.
>
> **2** Franklin Roosevelt's long battle with illness taught him the courage and confidence that allowed him to become a great leader.
>
> NOTE: A thesis statement is similar to the topic sentence of a paragraph. However, the topic sentence presents the main idea of a paragraph, while a thesis statement gives the larger goal of the essay.

G | Practicing with Thesis Statements Check (✓) each sentence that would make a good thesis statement for an essay about a person who has influenced your life. Explain your choices and share them with the class.

1. ☑ It was my mom who taught me not to give up on my dreams.

   "This is a good thesis statement because it tells us who the essay is about and how the author feels about her. It gives us an idea about how his/her mother influenced him/her. It also avoids a broad, generalized statement such as 'The person who influenced me the most is . . .'"

2. ☐ I never understood why so many people enjoyed English class.
3. ☐ Each of these three movies reflects an aspect of his childhood in Calcutta.
4. ☐ George Eliot was influenced by her family and learned many important lessons.
5. ☐ The only person I felt confident with was Eun Jung, who was my playmate, my best friend, and my inspiration.
6. ☐ In my case, my mother highly influenced my character through an incident with a match.
7. ☐ Geoffrey Canada's grandmother taught him spiritual values, self-control, and the meaning of dignity; these are essential lessons for all people.

H | Writing Note: Essay Organization Study the diagram for organizing an essay. Then do Activity I.

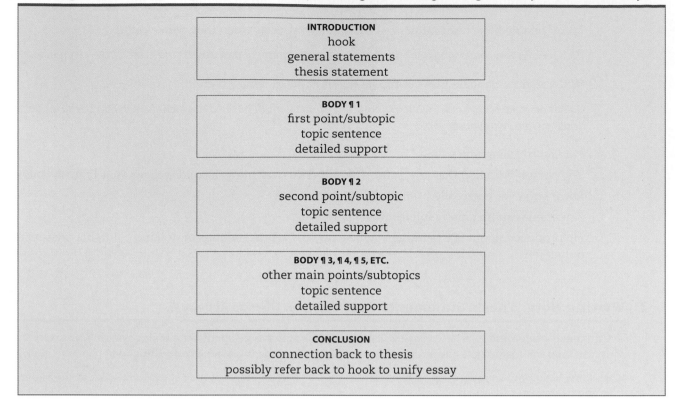

INTRODUCTION
hook
general statements
thesis statement

BODY ¶ 1
first point/subtopic
topic sentence
detailed support

BODY ¶ 2
second point/subtopic
topic sentence
detailed support

BODY ¶ 3, ¶ 4, ¶ 5, ETC.
other main points/subtopics
topic sentence
detailed support

CONCLUSION
connection back to thesis
possibly refer back to hook to unify essay

I | Organizing Your Essay Draw your own diagram like the one above. Write your ideas in each section.

J | Writing a First Draft Using information from your diagram, write a first draft of your essay. Try to use some of the structures that you have practiced in this unit.

K | Peer Reviewing When you have finished writing your first draft, share it with a partner. After discussing your essay, you may want to reorganize your ideas, add more support, and make other changes to strengthen your essay.

Checklist for revising the first draft

When you review your partner's essay and discuss your own, keep these questions in mind.
1. Does the hook capture the reader's attention?
2. Can you find the thesis statement? (Where is it?) Does it make it clear who or what the writer is talking about and how they think or feel about this subject?
3. Are there enough anecdotes, facts, examples, and/or reasons in the body of the essay to support the thesis?
4. Can the reader imagine what the writer is describing?
5. Are there any parts that are unclear or difficult to understand? What are they?
6. Does the first sentence of the conclusion connect back to the thesis in some way?

L | Writing the Second Draft Using your partner's feedback, write a second draft that includes all of your changes.

M|Error Correction Correct the errors in this excerpt from a student essay. Check the verb forms, adjective complements, and adverb clauses. (Different answers are possible.)

When I was a teenager, I thought my aunt was a shallow[121] person, interested only in her appearance, so I was surprised ^to learn that she wanted to go to college and study special education[122]. At the time, I was sure that she would get tired of the hard work of teaching and will soon go back to a life of shopping and long lunches in restaurants. But I was wrong about her. After graduate, she became a special education teacher for children with physical disabilities. She doesn't lose her elegance and sense of style, but she became very focused on her work. Instead of talking about fashion, she would talk about how happy she is being with children. She taught them, but she also learned from them. Many of her students had difficult lives, but they were able overcome their difficulties. When I graduated from high school. I also decided to attend college and study special education. Confident that I could follow in her footsteps, college didn't frighten me. My aunt had succeeded, and I felt certain succeed, too. I took that step and have always been glad that I did.

I didn't respect my aunt when I was young, but now she has become my mentor[123]. She doesn't live near me anymore, but we still talked on the phone regularly, and I am still learning from her.

Think about It Check your essay. Does it contain any errors similar to those in the Error Correction activity above? If so, correct them now.

N|Proofreading Check your essay for the forms in Chart 1.7. Make any final corrections necessary.

1.7 Summary Chart for Proofreading

PROOFREADING QUESTIONS	EXAMPLES
If the paragraph is in a present time frame, do the verb forms primarily fit a **present frame**? Do the **other verbs** show the correct time relationship to the rest of the paragraph?	**PRESENT TIME FRAME** To get to class, Tracy High School students **empty** their pockets and **pass** through metal detectors. Security officers **check** book bags. Most of the windows **have** bars. The fires **have stopped**, but fights between students **are** a regular occurrence. The school's principal, who **started** at Tracy as a teacher some 30 years ago, **is leaving**.
If the paragraph is in a past time frame, do the verb forms primarily fit a **past frame**? Do the **other verbs** show the correct time relationship to the rest of the paragraph?	**PAST TIME FRAME** I **took up** mountain climbing only two years ago, but last year Urs, who **is** also a qualified mountain guide, **told** me I **was** good enough to climb Bear Peak. The feeling of satisfaction when I **got** to the summit **was** amazing, but coming down **was** even more dramatic. There **had been** a rockslide and we **had to** be helicoptered off. And I **don't** mean traveling inside the helicopter—we **were hanging** on a rope beneath it!
Do **adverbs**, **adverbials**, and **adverb clauses** help the reader understand when things happened and follow the events?	Simon had a very favorable opinion of Louisiana, an area that had been very good to him **during the 1820s and 1830s**. Members of his family continued to communicate with each other even **after they left the area**. They **eventually** spread out over an 800-mile area of the lower South.
Did you use **adjectives** to provide descriptive detail? Do the adjectives have the correct **complements** (if necessary)?	In Cortes' early years, he was **anxious to follow the rules of the Spanish crown**. As he gained more power, an **unfavorable** change took place in his relations with Charles V. The change never led to an **absolute** break, but it caused a **gradual** loss of his power.

2

Reporting Ideas

If you have an apple and I have an apple and we exchange these apples, then you and I will still each have one apple. But if you have an idea and I have an idea and we exchange these ideas, then each of us will have two ideas.

—GEORGE BERNARD SHAW,
PLAYWRIGHT AND
LITERARY CRITIC
(1856–1950)

Talk about It What does the quotation above mean? Do you agree or disagree?

WARM-UP

A | Read the survey questions, which researchers asked American scientists and other Americans. Check (✓) *Yes* or *No* to give your opinion. Discuss your answers with a partner.

In your opinion . . .

	YES	NO
1. Are changes in the earth's climate mainly caused by human activity?	☐	☐
2. Is climate change a serious problem?	☐	☐
3. Will increases in the world's population be a problem?	☐	☐
4. To help meet the world's future energy needs, should more nuclear power plants be built?	☐	☐
5. To help meet the world's present and future food needs, should more pesticides (chemicals to kill insects) be used on food crops?	☐	☐

B | Read this summary of some survey results. Then answer the questions below.

In a recent survey, researchers found <u>that scientists and the general public differed in their opinions on various topics</u>. For example, 87 percent of scientists said <u>that human activity was causing changes in the earth's climate</u>, and 77 percent believed <u>that climate change was a serious problem</u>. In contrast, only 50 percent of the public said <u>that human activity was causing climate change</u>, and only 33 percent believed <u>that climate change was a serious problem</u>.

QUESTIONS

1. The underlined clauses give the writer's report of what scientists and the public said in the survey. What word begins these clauses? What verbs come before that word?

2. In the second and third sentences, what verb forms does the writer use in the underlined clauses to talk about present situations? Why do you think the writer uses these verb forms?

2.1 Overview of Reporting Other People's Ideas

In academic writing, we often include other people's ideas. We do this to give readers information and different viewpoints on our topic and to support our own ideas. We can use several techniques for reporting others' ideas, depending on our needs and the specific ideas we are reporting. Whichever technique we use, we must make sure to accurately represent the ideas of our sources—the original authors—and to include **language that appropriately credits our sources** for their ideas. Failure to appropriately credit ideas is called *plagiarism*— copying or other unfair use of others' work. Plagiarism is a serious academic offense.

To see how the techniques for reporting others' ideas work, first read this passage:

ORIGINAL PASSAGE

1 **[a]** At the same time you're taking a test and thinking about your answers, you're sensing many aspects of your environment. **[b]** In addition to things in the external environment, such as the cool breeze from the air conditioner, the distant sounds of traffic, and the movements of the teacher walking back and forth at the front of the room, you sense your internal environment—the slight headache you woke up with, your tensed fingers holding your pen, and a feeling of anxiety about whether you are prepared for the test. **[c]** Even though every one of these environmental stimuli causes activity in your brain and body, you are not really aware of most of them, because of your focus on the test. **[d]** Nevertheless, at any given moment you can shift your focus away from the test and onto any of these things. **[e]** This sort of focus on one stimulus out of many current stimuli—for example, to focus on relaxing by flexing your fingers—is what we call attention. **[f]** Clearly, attention is of fundamental importance in mental life: It determines the contents of our conscious thought at every waking moment. (Adapted from Steven Yantis, *Sensation and Perception*)

A

QUOTATION

2 "Clearly, attention is of fundamental importance in mental life," **Yantis concludes**. "It determines the contents of our conscious thought at every waking moment." (quotes 1f)

3 **According to Yantis**, "[the] focus on one stimulus out of many current stimuli . . . is what we call attention." (quotes 1e)

PARAPHRASE

4 **Yantis explains that** attention is crucially important to our thinking because what we think at any moment depends on our attention. (paraphrases 1f)

SUMMARY

5 Using examples, **Yantis states that** at any time a person is sensing a number of different things in the outside environment and in his or her physical and mental inside environment without being aware of them. **He defines** attention as a focus on one of these things and **explains that** attention is important because it determines what we are thinking about. (summarizes all of 1)

COMBINING TECHNIQUES

6 **Yantis explains that** attention is crucially important to our thinking because it "determines the contents of our conscious thought at every waking moment."

With **quotations**, as in **2** and **3**, we give the author's words exactly, within **quotation marks***. If we need to change or omit any words, as in **3**, we can:

- put any changed or added words in square brackets (**[ ]**)
- indicate omitted words with **ellipses** (**. . .**)

WARNING! Any changes or omissions we make should not change the meaning of the original. Also, be careful not to use too many quotations in a piece of writing. Use a quotation only when you feel that it is important to give the author's exact words.

Paraphrasing, as in **4**, is far more common than quotation. When we paraphrase, we express an author's ideas in our own words. We often use a **reporting verb** + a *that* clause (or another kind of clause) to paraphrase.

We usually use **summaries**, as in **5**, for longer passages or entire articles. With a summary we express the important ideas of a written work but do not include details. A summary is typically much shorter than the original passage.

We can combine paraphrases and quotations, as in **6**. Summaries often include both paraphrases and quotations of ideas that are important and (in the case of quotations) particularly well expressed.

*For more information on the punctuation of quotations, see the Resources, page R-57.

1 | Noticing and Identifying Quotations and Paraphrases Read this passage, the beginning of an article from *National Geographic* about the "Spanish flu" of 1918. Circle the quotations, and underline the paraphrases in *that* clauses. `2.1 A`

1918 Flu Pandemic That Killed 50 Million Originated in China, Historians Say

by Dan Vergano

The global flu outbreak[1] of 1918 killed 50 million people worldwide, ranking as one of the deadliest epidemics[2] in history.

For decades, scientists have debated where in the world the pandemic[3] started, variously pinpointing[4] its origins in France, China, the American Midwest, and beyond. Without a clear location, scientists have lacked a complete picture of the conditions that bred the disease and factors that might lead to similar outbreaks in the future.

The deadly "Spanish flu" claimed more lives than World War I, which ended the same year the pandemic struck. Now, new research is placing the flu's emergence[5] in a forgotten episode of World War I: the shipment of Chinese laborers[6] across Canada in sealed train cars.

Historian Mark Humphries of Canada's Memorial University of Newfoundland says that newly unearthed[7] records confirm that one of the side stories of the war—the mobilization[8] of 96,000 Chinese laborers to work behind the British and French lines on World War I's Western Front—may have been the source of the pandemic.

Writing in the January issue of the journal *War in History*, Humphries acknowledges that his hypothesis[9] awaits confirmation by viral[10] samples from flu victims. Such evidence would tie the disease's origin to one location.

But some other historians already find his argument convincing.

"This is about as close to a smoking gun[11] as a historian is going to get," says historian James Higgins, who lectures at Lehigh University in Bethlehem, Pennsylvania and who has researched the 1918 spread of the pandemic in the United States. "These records answer a lot of questions about the pandemic."

Last of the Great Plagues[12]

The 1918 flu pandemic struck in three waves across the globe, starting in the spring of that year, and is tied to a strain of H1N1 influenza ancestral[13] to ones still virulent[14] today.

The outbreak killed even the young and healthy, turning their strong immune systems[15] against them in a way that's unusual for flu. Adding to the catastrophic[16] loss of lives during World War I, the epidemic may have played a role in ending the war.

"The 1918 flu was the last of the great plagues that struck humanity, and it followed in the tracks[17] of a global conflict," says Humphries.

Talk about It With a partner, discuss reasons why the author of the passage above uses paraphrases and quotations to discuss his topic.

Think about It What information does the author of the passage above give about his sources? Why might this information be useful to readers? After initially introducing a source, how does the author then refer to a writer whose words he quotes or paraphrases?

Write about It Complete the sentences to provide a short summary of the passage above. Compare answers with a partner.

Dan Vergano writes about a new hypothesis proposed by historian Mark Humphries to explain _____ _____. According to Humphries, the flu might have begun with _____ _____. Although more evidence for this hypothesis is needed, other historians such as James Higgins feel that _____.

[1] See page V-3 for the Vocabulary Endnotes for this unit.

In a **paraphrase**, we express the original author's ideas and cite our source but use different words and different sentence structures. Follow these guidelines to paraphrase:

- Make sure that you fully understand the meaning of the sentences. Look up any unfamiliar words before paraphrasing.
- Put the sentences into words that are your own but that keep the meaning of the original. Try to use different sentence structures.
- Include the author's last name or another reference to the original author or work.

Notice how the words in **1** (original passage) are appropriately paraphrased in **2a – 2c**, compared to the inappropriate paraphrases in **2d – 2g**.

ORIGINAL PASSAGE

1 Perhaps more than ever before, video games have become an intensely social activity. Instead of the stereotypical gaming nerd who uses video games to shun social contact, over 70 percent of gamers play with friends, whether as part of a team or in direct competition. (From Romeo Vitelli, "Are There Benefits in Playing Video Games?")

APPROPRIATE PARAPHRASES

2a Vitelli (2014) points out that video games are now very much something that people do together. He notes that more than 70 percent of video game players play with other people, even though many people have an image of video game players as loners.

2b Vitelli writes that video games have turned into a social activity and so today—contrary to our idea of players as people who play to avoid others—almost three-quarters of players play video games with friends.

2c According to Vitelli, more than 70 percent of video gamers play either in teams or in one-on-one competition. Not only does this contradict the stereotype of solitary players who avoid others, he says, but it also suggests that playing video games is now a social activity to a larger extent than ever.

✗ INAPPROPRIATE PARAPHRASES

2d In contrast to the past, video games are now an activity for people to do together. Our image is of gamers as loners, but over 70 percent of gamers play with or against other people. (does not include a citation)

2e Vitelli says that, although in the past, video games were played by nerds who avoided other people, today video game play almost always involves other people. (changes the basic meaning of the original)

2f Vitelli explains that, to a greater extent than in the past, video games are now an activity people do together. He notes that rather than nerds who play to avoid people, most players play with other people. (sentence structure is too similar to the original—uses the same order of information)

2g According to Vitelli, video games today are an intensely social activity. More than 70 percent of players are engaged in team or competition play, in contrast to the stereotypical gaming nerd whose reason for playing is to shun social contact. (too many words are the same as in the original; also, it's not clear that the second sentence is still reporting information from Vitelli)

Notice in **2a – 2c**:

- A good paraphrase includes the source, often just the last name. Citations with the date, as in **2a**, are typical of writing in the sciences and social sciences*.
- Often, the paraphrase is in a *that* noun clause following a reporting verb, as in **2a – 2b**.

(For a list of reporting verbs, see the Resources, page R-50.)

- The same content can be appropriately paraphrased in different ways—with different words and different structures, but keeping the same basic meaning, as in **2a – 2c**.
- If a paraphrase continues beyond one sentence, the writer makes clear that the next sentence or sentences are still part of the paraphrase, as in **2c**.
- An unimportant detail can be omitted, as in **2a** and **2b**. (These writers omitted the detail that social activity can involve a team or direct competition.)

WARNING! When you paraphrase:

- Do not fail to credit the original author, as in **2d**.
- Do not change the basic meaning of the original passage, as in **2e**.
- Do not use structures too similar to those in the original, as in **2f**.
- Do not use the exact words from the original passage, as in **2g**. (Exception: Some words in the paraphrase must be the same as in the original because they are important words for discussing the topic—for instance, *video games* and *play*.)

*For more information on styles for citing sources in academic writing, see the Resources, pages R-58–R-63.

A

2 | Identifying Paraphrases Read the paragraphs. Find each paraphrase introduced by a reporting verb + *that*. In the sentence with the paraphrase, put a box around words referring to the author and/or the author's work, circle the reporting verb, and underline the paraphrase. **2.2 A**

1. In a delightfully provocative[18] section, Devlin compares mathematics with a soap opera[19]. He explains that, just as mathematics is all about understanding connections between patterns, watching a soap opera is all about understanding the outrageous, sometimes ridiculous connections between the characters.

2. "This could be interpreted as a failure by scientists to better communicate with the public," said Alan Leshner, chief executive officer of AAAS. In an editorial[20] in the journal *Science*, Leshner said that scientists should not shy away from addressing controversial topics in public.

3. Films often have a tendency to present historical figures absolutely, in black-and-white[21] terms, in "tidy little boxes with no gray areas," as Joseph Roquemore says, making complicated lives and events into exaggerated[22], overly[23] dramatic history. Yet the historical novelist and screenwriter[24] George MacDonald Fraser has written that Hollywood provides us with more vivid and memorable pictures of past ages than we are ever likely to get from historians and history books.

4. For Aristotle, a genuinely happy life required the fulfillment[25] of a broad[26] range of conditions, including physical as well as mental well-being. In this way Aristotle introduced the idea of a science of happiness in the classical sense, in terms of a new field of knowledge. Essentially, he argues that virtue[27] is achieved by maintaining the Mean, which is the balance between two excesses[28].

5. Another reason that farmers do not use terracing more often is that terraces are very expensive to construct. Djorovic suggests that if the problem of high costs could be solved in a satisfactory way, there would be no further obstacle[29] for the wide use of terraces in hilly or mountainous regions.

6. A Columbia University research team reported that children with higher levels of the chemical BPA at ages 3, 5, and 7 had increased odds[30] of developing respiratory[31] diseases when they were between 5 and 12.

vineyard terraces in Douro Valley, Portugal

Think about It What verbs are used to introduce the paraphrases above? How are these verbs similar, and how do some of the verbs differ in meaning from one another? What are some other verbs you think might be used to introduce paraphrases? Make a list, and compare lists with a partner.

3 | Analyzing Paraphrases Read each original passage and its paraphrase below. Compare the paraphrase to the original and, using the questions in the box as a guide, decide whether the paraphrase is an appropriate paraphrase. Check (✓) the correct column. 2.2 A

- Does it credit the author or source of the original passage?
- Does it include all of the important ideas of the original passage?
- Does it significantly change the words and structure of the original?
- Does it keep the meaning of the original?

FACTORS THAT INFLUENCE OUR HEALTH		
Source, original statement, and paraphrase	Appropriate paraphrase?	
	Yes	No
1. Source: Kevin Hillstrom, *Genetically Modified Foods* Original: *In 1953, scientists James Watson and Francis Crick announced that they had discovered the basic structure of DNA. Their breakthrough opened the door for scientists to learn much more about how genetic information was passed down through generations.* Paraphrase: Hillstrom explains that, with their 1953 discovery of the basic structure of DNA, James Watson and Francis Crick made it possible for scientists to understand the way that genetic information is carried from one generation to another.	✓	
2. Source: Positive Psychology Center, University of Pennsylvania Original: *Positive psychology is the scientific study of the strengths that enable individuals and communities to thrive.* Paraphrase: The Positive Psychology Center at the University of Pennsylvania states that positive psychology scientifically studies people and communities.		✓
3. Source: D. J. Frenk, "Walking and Bicycling Your Way to Health" Original: *Walking is an ideal exercise for many people—it doesn't require any special equipment, can be done anytime, anyplace, and is generally very safe.* Paraphrase: D. J. Frenk writes that, because walking is something that people can safely and easily do at any time and anywhere, many people will find it a perfect kind of exercise.		
4. Source: Mayo Clinic, "Caffeine: How Much Is Too Much?" Original: *Up to 400 milligrams (mg) of caffeine[32] a day appears to be safe for most healthy adults. That's roughly the amount of caffeine in four cups of brewed[33] coffee, ten cans of cola, or two "energy shot" drinks. Although caffeine use may be safe for adults, it's not a good idea for children. And adolescents[30] should limit themselves to no more than 100 mg of caffeine a day.* Paraphrase: The Mayo Clinic states that generally adults who are in good health can safely have as much as 400 mg of caffeine daily (or, for example, four cups of coffee) but that teenagers should not have more than 100 mg and children should not have caffeine.		
5. Source: World Health Organization, "Genes and Human Disease" Original: *Most diseases involve many genes in complex interactions, in addition to environmental influences.* Paraphrase: A majority of diseases are caused by complicated interactions among many genes and also by influences from the person's environment.		

FACTORS THAT INFLUENCE OUR HEALTH		
Source, original statement, and paraphrase	Appropriate paraphrase?	
	Yes	No
6. Source: Cynthia Lightfoot, Michael Cole, and Sheila R. Cole; *The Development of Children* Original: *Indeed, adolescents who engage in higher levels of physical activity experience greater well-being than less physically active adolescents.* Paraphrase: Lightfoot claims that adolescents who engage in more physical activity experience greater well-being than less physically active teenagers.		
7. Source: Christopher J. Gearon, "Treating Hunger as a Health Issue" Original: *Addressing issues like hunger, housing, and education can have more of an impact on people's health than the traditional medical services that hospitals deliver*[31]. Paraphrase: Gearon says that health can be improved more by dealing with problems such as hunger, housing, and education than through hospitals and their services.		
8. Source: Robert Wood Johnson Foundation, "Early Childhood Experiences: Laying the Foundation for Health Across a Lifetime" Original: *The earliest years of our lives are crucial in many ways; these years set us on paths leading toward—or away from—good health.* Paraphrase: A report from the Robert Wood Johnson Foundation argues that our early childhood is important for various reasons; this period gets people started in a direction going to—or away from—a healthy life.		

Think about It Compare your answers in Activity 3 with a partner. Do you agree about which paraphrases are and aren't appropriate? For each item, discuss the paraphrase in terms of the list of questions in the box on page 42, explaining why the paraphrase is or is not appropriate.

"In item 1, the paraphrase writer credits the original source. All the important information from the original is in the paraphrase, and the meaning is the same. The structure of the paraphrase is different, because, for example, the original has two sentences but the paraphrase puts all the information into one sentence."

"In item 2, the paraphrase is not appropriate because the meaning is different from the original. The original says it's the study of the strengths of people and communities that help them to do well, but the paraphrase just mentions people and communities. The structure is a little close to the structure of the original sentence, but this seems OK as it's a simple sentence that can't really be changed around easily."

Think about It With your partner, look again at the appropriate paraphrases and find some unimportant details that have been left out.

Write about It With your partner, rewrite each paraphrase that you think is not appropriate. Then compare paraphrases as a class. Does everyone agree that the paraphrases are now appropriate?

The Positive Psychology Center at the University of Pennsylvania states that positive psychology scientifically studies the kinds of strengths that help people and communities to do well.

2.3 Reporting Verb Forms

A

1 One survey in the late 1980s **found** that two-thirds of high school students had jobs.

2 The poll **finds** that only 20 percent of adolescents get the recommended nine hours of sleep. It also **finds** that sleep declines . . .

3 Pesendorfer et al. (2009) **have argued** that Whiten et al.'s (2005) chimpanzee study was not specifically designed to test conformity.

4 At first, researchers **assumed** that economic growth was not associated with an increase in individual happiness (Easterlin, 1974). Recently, however, researchers **have found** that economic growth is in fact associated with an increase in happiness over time (Stevenson & Wolfers, 2008).

5 Woolf **writes** that she has made a discovery about her characters.

When we paraphrase authors' ideas or report their work in other ways, we usually use one of three forms for the reporting verb:

- **simple past forms**, as in **1**, especially to emphasize that research is from the past or that the content is specific to a particular event or study
- **simple present forms**, as in **2**, especially to make the reported content more vivid and immediate or to suggest that research findings or other ideas are timeless
- **present perfect forms**, as in **3**, especially to emphasize the ongoing nature of research or the relevance of past research to present issues

Notice that in **4** the writer uses the **past** to introduce early research and the **present perfect** to contrast more recent findings.

In general, disciplines in the social sciences (such as psychology, sociology, and economics) and sciences tend to use past and present perfect verb forms, while disciplines in the humanities (philosophy, history, literature, art, etc.) tend to use simple present verb forms. The present is especially common in discussions of literature, as in **5**.

---

4 | Identifying Reporting Verb Forms Circle the reporting verb introducing each paraphrase and underline the paraphrase. `2.3 A`

1. René Descartes, the seventeenth-century French philosopher, (argues) that the mind is indivisible[36] because he cannot perceive himself as having any parts.

2. Other members of the discussion group had similar opinions. For example, Kathleen stated that although she had "really enjoyed" taking part in class discussions about issues or about particular texts, she was not sure what the discussions were meant to achieve. In contrast to the university students, these high school students generally did not use their responses as the basis for discussions.

3. In the 1940s, a linguist[37] named Benjamin Lee Whorf studied Hopi, a Native American language spoken in northeastern Arizona. Based on his studies, Whorf claimed that speakers of Hopi and speakers of English see the world differently because of differences in their language.

4. The "Whorf hypothesis" claims that the way a person views reality is shaped by the language he or she speaks. For example, Whorf claimed that Hopi had no words for time and no grammatical category of tense and that Hopis, as a consequence, did not perceive "time" as a definable[38] phenomenon[39].

5. For over 15 years, Joseph Merlino has been researching what works to increase the breadth and depth of student learning in the areas of science and math. He has concluded that student engagement[40] is a key and too-often-ignored factor in determining readiness to pursue careers in science and technology fields.

6. His approach to psychological therapy is brief but comprehensive[41] and emphasizes flexibility. He has written that an effective therapist is "a chameleon[42]" who adapts his methods to suit the needs of each individual.

Think about It Complete the chart with the reporting verbs you circled in Activity 4. Then, with a partner, look back at the explanations in Chart 2.3 and discuss the questions below.

Verb in base form	Form of verb used
1. *argue*	*argues—simple present form*
2.	
3.	
4.	
5.	
6.	

QUESTIONS

1. How might the discipline of the material in item 1 of Activity 4 help explain the form that the writer chose for the reporting verb? How might the discipline of the material in item 6 help explain the form of the reporting verb there?

2. Item 2 of Activity 4 reports on a conversation that a particular study group held. Why do you think the past form of the verb is more appropriate than the present form there?

3. Items 3 and 4 explain ideas developed by Benjamin Whorf and describe the main claim of his theory, the Whorf hypothesis. Why do you think a present form is used in one place and past forms are used in the other places?

4. In item 5, how does the first sentence help explain why the writer chose a present perfect form for the reporting verb in the second sentence?

2.4 Reporting Verbs with *That* Clauses

A

VERB + *THAT* CLAUSE

1 Keynes **argued that** full employment could not always be reached by lowering wages.

VERB + *TO* + NOUN PHRASE + *THAT* CLAUSE

2 She **points out to** readers **that** these do not represent Micronesian concepts.

(Also possible: She points out that these do not represent . . .)

VERB + NOUN PHRASE + *THAT* CLAUSE

3 He **shows us that** love is sometimes not as beautiful as the books often make it seem.

(Also possible: He shows that love is sometimes . . .)

4 In this new book, he **tells readers that** the largest glacier ever measured is 200 miles long.

(NOT: ~~he tells that the largest glacier~~ . . .)

We often use a **reporting verb** + a ***that* noun clause** to report other writers' ideas. We often place the *that* clause directly after the reporting verb, as in **1**.

Sometimes we want to indicate to whom the material in the *that* clause is directed. We give this information in a **noun phrase** before the *that* clause, as in **2 – 4**.

With some reporting verbs (indicated with * below), we can include **to** + a **noun phrase** before the *that* clause, as in **2**.

With a small number of reporting verbs, like **show** and **warn** (indicated with ** below), we can (but don't have to) use a **noun phrase** right after the verb, as in **3**.

With some other reporting verbs, like **tell** and **remind** (indicated with *** below), we must use a **noun phrase** right after the verb, as in **4**. The sentence is incorrect without the noun phrase.

Common **reporting verbs** that are used with *that* clauses include:

argue	indicate*	show**
claim*	note	state*
conclude	point out*	suggest*
demonstrate*	propose*	tell***
explain*	remind***	think
find	report*	warn**
hypothesize	say*	

For more reporting verbs, see the Resources, page R-50.

*can be followed by to + a noun phrase
**can be followed by a noun phrase
***must be followed by a noun phrase

B

INCLUDING *THAT* IN ACADEMIC WRITING

COMPARE

5a The study **shows** us **that** teachers have the power to change students' attitudes.

5b The study **shows** us teachers have the power to change students' attitudes.

(less common in academic writing)

6a The researchers **said that** despite the slower growth next year, urban employment would likely remain relatively stable.

6b The researchers **said** despite the slower growth next year, urban employment would likely remain relatively stable.

(less common in academic writing)

Although in speech we often omit **that**, in academic writing we usually include it, especially if:

• a noun phrase, prepositional phrase, or other words come between the reporting verb and *that*, as in **5**.

• the subject of the *that* clause does not immediately follow, as in **6**.

Including *that* often makes sentences clearer for readers.

GO ONLINE For more practice with reporting verbs, go to the Online Practice.

5 | Choosing Correct Reporting Verbs
Circle the reporting verb or verbs that can complete the sentences. **2.4 A–B**

1. A writer of poetry and researcher of Latin American history, he ____ that tourism has been an important characteristic of the city for centuries.

   (argues)   (demonstrates)

2. She ____ that teachers should provide adequate guidance for groups and should make their own expectations clear.

   concludes   states

3. Hume ____ that, contrary to what some might think, following the rules of justice does not always produce good results.

4. Anderson ____ to readers that we must all take responsibility for our lives.

5. First, the author ____ us that at the school level teachers do not all agree.

6. She ____ critics that even Einstein's theory of relativity could not be tested completely until space travel made testing possible.

7. Based on this research, he ____ to us that the Mayan rulers were well aware of many of the environmental problems they faced.

8. The writer of this 1839 article ____ to his readers that the best way they can elevate[43] themselves is by living an honest and moral life.

9. She ____ parents that changes in their child's behavior may mean that the child is experiencing online bullying.

notes	reminds
points out	tells
shows	tells
explains	reminds
argues	proposes
says	suggests
suggests	warns

Think about It Look at sentences 4–9 above. Why is it especially important to include (not omit) *that* in these sentences?

6 | Writing Note: Using Specific Reporting Verbs Read the note. Then do Activity 7.

As writers, we give readers information through our choices of reporting verbs, and we make our writing more varied. Through reporting verbs, we can indicate how strong the original author's claim is or how much we agree with the idea we are reporting.

STRENGTH OF CLAIM		EXAMPLES
STRONG	insist, prove, show	In her book, she **proves** that a healthy diet can be flavorful. (The writer's use of *prove* indicates that the original author's claim is strong and that the writer agrees.)
NEUTRAL	believe, think, claim, discuss, explain, note, report, say, state	He **claims** that all behavior has three parts: what we do, what we think, and what we feel. He **believes** that we can't force changes in our behaviors.
WEAK/SOFTENED	hypothesize, suggest	The author **suggests** that negative views about students can affect their performance. He also **hypothesizes** that students' cultural values may not fit those of their schools.

We can also use reporting verbs for particular purposes, such as:

PURPOSE		EXAMPLES
ADDITION OF INFORMATION	add, go on to say	The student indicated that it was hard for her to pay attention in class. She **added** that she did not like her teacher this year.
AGREEMENT; DISAGREEMENT	(not) agree, disagree, (not) doubt, (not) believe, etc.	She **agrees** that mastering English is important, but she **does not think** that English should be the language of instruction.
REACHING A CONCLUSION	conclude, find	Based on his research, he **concludes** that the army's defeat was the result of its generals' lack of ability.

7 | Selecting Specific Reporting Verbs Replace each **bold** form of *say* with a more informative reporting verb from the box. Choose the verb that you think works best. Compare answers with a partner.

`2.4 A`

SOME RESEARCH ON COLLEGE STUDENTS

1. The study explored how university students in various countries spend their time. Based on survey results, the researchers **said** _____*concluded*_____ that many students today are less involved with their universities than were students in previous generations.

> added
> concluded
> suggested

2. Students with mental health issues often do not seek help. The authors of this article looked at blogs to develop some possible explanations. They **said** _____ that one problem might be that students have a negative view of mental health services.

3. The authors of the study said that students generally do not get enough sleep. They **said** _____ that the problem is especially serious at exam time.

4. The author carefully analyzes student errors and finds their causes. She **says** _____ that most of these errors are actually related to reading comprehension problems.

> agrees
> hypothesizes
> shows

5. The author **says** _____ that student writing in the United States and the European Union might have more similarities than differences, despite the differences in the cultures. She proposes to explore this idea through a specially designed study.

6. Previous studies have shown that certain personality characteristics are associated with addiction to the Internet, and the author of this study **says** _____ that personality characteristics can lead to this problem.

7. A study of Internet use **says** _____ that students rely too much on the Internet.

> believes
> finds

8. The author of the Internet study **says** _____ that the problem of excessive reliance might get worse.

Think about It With a partner, try replacing the verbs that you chose above with other verbs from the Writing Note in Activity 6 or from Chart 2.4. For each sentence, what are some other verbs that work? Do you see differences in meaning with the different verbs? If so, discuss these differences with your classmates.

2.5 Backshifting Verb Forms in *That* Clauses

COMPARE

1a Asch **found** that conformity with the opinions of other members of the group **increases** when the size of the majority **increases**. (not backshifted)

1b Asch **found** that conformity with the opinions of other members of the group **increased** when the size of the majority **increased**. (backshifted)

2 Research by Fleming (1992) **suggests** that visual learners **have** a preference for seeing new information. (present reporting verb: backshifting not possible)

3 Studies **have shown** that up to 29 percent of all solid waste **originates** from construction (Horvath, 2004). (present perfect reporting verb: backshifting not possible)

In our summaries and paraphrases, when we use reporting verbs in their **past form**, we often change verb forms in the *that* clause. For example, instead of **simple present forms**, as in **1a**, we may use **simple past forms**, as in **1b**. This is called **backshifting** (we shift verb forms back into the past).

When we use reporting verbs in their **present form**, as in **2**, or **present perfect form**, as in **3**, we do not backshift the verb forms in the *that* clause.

A

ORIGINAL OR QUOTED SPEECH	CHANGE TO VERBS IN THE *THAT* CLAUSE	INDIRECT (REPORTED) SPEECH
4a "Today's world **is** one of crises."	simple present → simple past	**4b** He **said** that today's world **was** one of crises.
5a "The orders **are** now **seen** as an important tool."	simple present passive → simple past passive	**5b** The council member **suggested** that the orders **were** now **seen** as an important tool.
6a "Schools **aren't doing** enough to address the problems."	present progressive → past progressive	**6b** The committee **stated** that schools **were not doing** enough to address the problems.
7a "They **are** now **being treated** at another hospital."	present progressive passive → past progressive passive	**7b** He **said** that they **were being treated** at another hospital.
8a "The temperature there **has risen** at twice the rate of the rest of the world in recent decades."	present perfect → past perfect	**8b** The report **concluded** that the temperature there **had risen** at twice the rate of the rest of the world in recent decades.
9a "The captain **received** several warnings of icebergs."	simple past → past perfect	**9b** The article **mentioned** that the captain **had received** several warnings of icebergs.
10a "The president **was shot** in a theater tonight."	simple past passive → past perfect passive	**10b** A news bulletin 150 years ago **reported** that President Lincoln **had been shot**.
11a "The problems **have been increasing** in recent years."	past progressive → past perfect progressive	**11b** The agency **found** that the problems **had been increasing** in recent years.
12a "Invasive species **will affect** diversity in the region."	will → would can → could may → might must → had to	**12b** The author **claimed** that invasive species **would affect** diversity in the region.
13a "Higher salaries **may solve** the labor problem."		**13b** She **argued** that higher salaries **might solve** the labor problem.

B

CHOOSING NOT TO BACKSHIFT

14 Einstein **concluded** that nothing **can travel** faster than the speed of light.

15 In a new study, the researchers **found** that pizza **is** a large source of calories, fat, and salt in kids' diets.

Although it is possible to backshift after a past form reporting verb, sometimes we choose not to backshift, especially when:

- the clause expresses a general truth, as in **14**.
- the situation in the clause presumably continues into the present, as in **15**.

GO ONLINE For more practice with indirect (reported) speech, go to the Online Practice.

8|Identifying Backshifted Verbs Read the statements. Circle the reporting verb and underline the *that* clause paraphrases. (Remember that *that* is sometimes omitted.) Put a box around the main verbs in the *that* clauses. Have these verbs been backshifted? Check (✓) the correct column. Discuss your answers with a partner. **2.5 A–B**

| | VERBS BACKSHIFTED? | |
| STATEMENTS FROM RESEARCH ON EDUCATION | YES | NO |

1. The school currently offers six study abroad programs. The director of study abroad (said) that students [were] increasingly interested in participating in the programs. ✓ ☐

   "Were is backshifted because the original sentences were about the present ('currently'), not the past: the director must have said, 'The students are interested . . .'"

2. The study found that the teacher's presentation of goals in class is key to reducing cheating. ☐ ☐

3. Parents play a significant role in their children's adjustment to school. A recent study suggested that for children today, a successful start in school depended largely on parents. ☐ ☐

4. West argued that in the nineteenth century there had been a steady improvement in the quantity and quality of education. ☐ ☐

5. In his writings, Aristotle recognized that education is important for personal development. ☐ ☐

6. Interagency[44] work and collaboration need to be part of the vision of the leadership team, according to one school principal. Stressing the moral purpose of schools, she claimed education needed to benefit all schools, not just individual schools. ☐ ☐

7. Commenting on the public versus private school divide in the United States, Ravitch argued that privatization[45] of schools is a dead end[46] for American education. ☐ ☐

8. Seibert, a nursing student, has strong opinions about the value of education today. In an interview, she suggested education was especially important for countries that were now facing health crises. ☐ ☐

9. Studies show that while the achievement gap between white and black students has narrowed significantly over the past few decades, the gap between rich and poor students has grown substantially during the same period. ☐ ☐

10. A recent study claimed that many students are graduating without the sophisticated reasoning skills that they may need for the work world. ☐ ☐

11. The authors concluded that East Asian countries today are reinventing education to maintain their efficiency as student populations change. ☐ ☐

Think about It Look at the items above where verbs are not backshifted. In which one of these items was backshifting not possible? In the other items, why do you think the writer chose not to backshift?

9 | Backshifting Verbs in *That* Clauses Read the sentences. Circle each reporting verb that introduces a paraphrase. Where possible, rewrite the sentences and backshift the verbs in the *that* clause. If backshifting is not possible, write "no backshifting." ‬ **2.5 A–B**

GENETICALLY MODIFIED ORGANISMS[47] (GMOS[48])

GET READY TO READ

You are going to read an article about food crops that are genetically modified organisms (GMOs).

1. The *Oxford Advanced American English Dictionary* (states) that genetically modified organisms are plants or other living things whose genes have been artificially changed to produce some desired result.

   no backshifting

2. Scientific research has generally shown that genetically modified foods do not cause health problems.

   _____

   _____

3. A leading scientist warned that hysteria[49] over genetic modification is confusing the issue and is preventing serious debate.

   _____

   _____

4. Although GMOs are common in foods sold in the United States, a recent study showed that the number one concern for U.S. shoppers is to avoid GMOs.

   _____

   _____

5. In Britain, where GMOs are not allowed, a survey estimated that one in seven loaves of bread may contain traces of genetic modification.

   _____

   _____

6. A report supporting the use of GMOs explained that GM crops generally need less insecticide[50] than other crops.

   _____

   _____

7. In a recent debate, those supporting GMO use pointed out that the world's population has been growing rapidly and argued that GMOs will be needed to feed this growing population.

   _____

   _____

8. In the same debate, opponents of GMOs argued that other methods of agriculture can achieve the same things as GMOs with fewer risks.

   _____

   _____

9. Some GMO opponents have pointed out it will likely be decades before the full range of consequences of GMO use becomes clear.

   _____

   _____

Think about It Look at your backshifted sentences above. For these sentences, both versions (backshifted and not backshifted) are possible. Why might a writer choose *not* to backshift these sentences?

GOLDEN RICE AND THE GMO DEBATE

by Margot Finn

On August 8, 2013, protestors in the Philippines broke down the fences surrounding a field of genetically modified Golden Rice and ripped out all the plants. The fields were part of an experimental trial[51] funded by the International Rice Research Institute and Philippine Rice Research Institute, two nonprofit organizations seeking to demonstrate the potential benefits of the rice, which has been engineered to provide vitamin A to malnourished[52] people. According to the World Health Organization, 124 million people worldwide suffer from vitamin A deficiency, resulting in between 250,000 and 500,000 cases of permanent blindness and between 1 and 2 million deaths every year. However, the protesters argued that Golden Rice could pose unforeseen risks to human health and the environment. One of the farmers leading the protest told the Filipino newspaper *Remate*, "We do not want our people, especially our children, to be used in these experiments." They also claimed Golden Rice was a ploy[53] to further enrich multinational corporations at the expense of poor farmers and consumers in the developing world.

Some of the Filipino protesters' complaints echo[54] points frequently made in the larger debate about genetically modified organisms (or GMOs) around the world. GMOs are living organisms whose DNA has been intentionally altered by inserting new genes into it, often from other organisms. The genes that enable Golden Rice to produce vitamin A come from corn and a common soil bacterium. Activists[55] in North America and Europe are concerned that the process may result in unknown health risks and have asked their governments to ban GMOs or at least require products containing them to carry special labels. They also argue that the foreign DNA might contaminate[56] wild plant species if pollen[57] from GMO crops fertilizes[58] plants in nearby fields, and that even small genetic changes in wild plant populations might have large ecological effects. On the other side of the debate, GMO supporters argue that the crops not only are safe for human consumption[59] but also can make farming more productive. Such an increase in productivity, they say, will be necessary in order to feed a growing world population. GMO supporters often portray[60] their critics as spoiled First-World consumers who completely reject biotechnology[61] without really understanding it and enthusiastically embrace "natural" foods with no evidence the latter are any better for human health or the environment.

Often, the debate over GMOs concerns the extent to which people should trust the corporations that control the GMOs. Most of the GMOs currently used in agriculture were developed and patented[62] by corporations like Monsanto and Dupont, which sell them to farmers with the promise of more efficient farming practices and higher crop yields[63]. For example, Roundup Ready corn and soybeans[64] are genetically engineered to be unaffected by the herbicide[65] Roundup, so farmers can spray enough on their fields to control weeds[66] without tilling[67]. The patents often require farmers to purchase new seed every year, preventing them from saving seed from one year's crop to plant again the next year. GMO critics often claim that it's wrong for corporations to hold patents on seeds, and they accuse the corporations of being overly aggressive in enforcing the patents.

Golden Rice goes against many of the usual arguments about genetically modified organisms on both sides. Unlike Roundup Ready crops, Golden Rice seeks to address a genuine humanitarian[68] concern and seems unlikely to enrich any corporations. Clinical trials have shown that a single serving can provide up to 50 percent of the recommended daily allowance of vitamin A, more than enough to resolve most deficiencies. The developers of Golden Rice have offered to give the seed to subsistence farmers[69] in developing countries for free, and the current patent holders have promised never to charge farmers who earn less than $10,000 a year from it. Additionally, farmers are permitted to save and re-plant the seeds for Golden Rice from year to year. But the Filipino protesters are clearly not spoiled First-World consumers, and some of the concerns that they raise about GMOs are specific to the developing world. Much of the opposition to GMOs in the developing world has more to do with economic and political consequences than with nutrition. For instance, Indian environmentalist Dr. Vandana Shiva has warned that, if approved,

Golden Rice will open the developing world to other GMO crops and exploitation[70] by corporations that are patent owners. Another concern is how anti-GMO movements in the First World could affect the international trade of developing countries. Several African countries have banned GMOs for fear that if they permit them and First-World consumers succeed in getting them labeled or banned, the market for their agricultural exports will collapse.

Even GMO supporters typically agree that the public should have a say about matters that may affect their health and their environment and should be able to limit the sale of products that they object to if the products have no compelling[71] benefit. However, it remains unclear who should get to decide what counts as a compelling benefit. Most consumers don't see any personal benefit from Roundup Ready crops, but by reducing tilling, these crops may help make it possible to significantly reduce greenhouse gas[72] emissions. Golden Rice has an even clearer claim to serving the public good. The problem is that many people don't understand GMOs well enough to make an informed decision about the risks and benefits.

One tendency on both sides that probably doesn't help is lumping all GMOs together[73]. Although there's no evidence that any of the GMOs currently grown have had any negative impact on human health or the environment, that doesn't guarantee that newer crops, like Golden Rice, are necessarily safe. More research by independent, nonprofit groups needs to be done, and the results should be shared with the public, which means experiments like the one sabotaged[74] in the Philippines must be allowed to proceed. The fact that most existing GMOs were primarily designed to increase agricultural productivity and enrich corporations is a poor reason to prevent research on a crop with the potential to significantly reduce suffering and death. However, people in developing countries should be able to grow crops like Golden Rice without having to accept Roundup Ready crops or worry about the collapse of the market for their agricultural exports. Both unquestioning support for GMOs and unquestioning resistance to them ignore the diversity of GMOs today.

Talk about It Discuss these questions with a partner.

1. Why was Golden Rice planted in the Philippines? What did the protestors in the Philippines do, and why did they do this?

2. What are GMOs? What are some reasons why people oppose GMOs? What are some reasons why people support GMOs?

3. What are Monsanto and Dupont? What concern do opponents of GMOs express about Monsanto and Dupont?

4. What are some of the ways in which Golden Rice differs from more "typical" GMOs like Roundup Ready corn?

5. How are developing countries' concerns about GMOs somewhat different from the concerns in First-World countries?

Think about It What information and ideas from other people and organizations are in the first paragraph of the article? What different structures does the author use to introduce and report these views?

11 | Paraphrasing Content Use information from the reading to write answers to the questions. Use reporting verbs followed by *that* clauses, and use backshifting in *that* clauses as appropriate. `2.5 A-B`

1. In her article, Finn makes the point that Golden Rice and the protest against Golden Rice in various ways contradict arguments made by opponents and supporters of GMOs. According to Finn, how does Golden Rice contradict the arguments of GMO opponents and how does it contradict the arguments of GMO supporters?

Finn claims that Golden Rice contradicts GMO opponents' arguments because growing Golden Rice would not benefit large corporations very much. . . .

2. Finn points out that there is general agreement that the public should have a say on GMOs, but she also feels this might be difficult. What does she believe the difficulty might be?

3. In the final paragraph, what does Finn conclude about the GMO debate? What does she argue should be done about GMOs?

Talk about It What is your current opinion of GMOs? What kind of information do you think you would need in order to make more informed decisions about GMOs and their risks and benefits? After discussing these questions with a partner, make a list of questions about GMOs that you would like to ask.

12 | Writing Note: Writing a Paragraph Summary of a Short Passage Read the note. Then do Writing Assignment I.

To summarize a short passage, use a process such as the following:

1 Read the passage carefully. Look up any words that you are unsure about. Make sure you understand the passage.

2 Reread the passage. Underline the main idea and the main supporting points.

3 In the first sentence of your paragraph, give the source and, following an appropriate reporting verb, state the main point in your own words.

4 Write the rest of the paragraph, putting the main supporting points of the original into your own words. As this is a summary of the original passage, be careful not to include your own ideas. Remember also not to include minor points or details. Use the source's last name or pronouns for subsequent references to the source; choose appropriate reporting verbs. (For a sample summary of a short passage, see Chart 2.1, example 5.)

5 Finally, check your summary for the following:

- Does the summary use your own words and structures, different from those in the original passage?
- Does the summary include all main supporting points but **not** anything that is less important?
- Is the summary much shorter than the original passage?
- Do you make it clear that all the ideas are the original author's, and do you avoid including your own ideas?

WRITING ASSIGNMENT I

Follow steps A–D to write a one-paragraph summary of the first and second paragraphs of the reading in Activity 10.

A | Planning Follow these steps to plan your summary.

1. Read the two paragraphs again carefully. For each paragraph, write down the main idea followed by the main points supporting this idea. If possible, write the points in your own words.

2. Compare notes with a partner. Did you include all the same points? Discuss any differences in what you wrote. Based on this discussion, do you want to add any main points that you missed and/or omit any minor points or details that you included? If so, revise your notes.

B | Writing Based on your notes, write a one-paragraph summary of the first two paragraphs of the reading. Your summary should address the following questions: what was the Golden Rice protest and how did protestors' complaints echo points in the larger debate on GMOs? Include a paraphrase of content that you think is particularly important. Follow steps 3–5 of the Writing Note on page 54.

C | Peer Reviewing Share your writing with a partner. Answer these questions about your partner's summary.

1. Does it include the main idea of the original paragraphs and all the main supporting points? Are there any main supporting points you think your partner has not included? Are any of the points included just minor points or details? Has your partner avoided including his or her own ideas?

2. Has your partner appropriately credited the source? Does your partner use his or her own words and structures? Has he or she connected the ideas effectively, for example, through linking adverbials?

D | Revising Follow these steps to revise your paragraph.

1. Using your partner's feedback, rewrite your paragraph.

2. Check your writing for mistakes and clarity. Did you include a paraphrase of content that you think is especially important? Make any final corrections necessary.

2.6 That Clauses with Subjunctive Verb Forms

With certain **reporting verbs** that express urgency, requirement, or an intention to bring about action by others, we often use the **base form** of the verb in the *that* clause, as in **1 – 6a**. We call this a **subjunctive form** of the verb.

A

1 We **demand** that he **appoint** separate officials to deal with these complaints.
(NOT: We demand that he appoints separate officials . . .)

2 The committee **requested** that there **be** more feedback about the work.

3 He **insisted** that tobacco **be regulated** as an addictive drug.

4 The government agency's report **recommends** that scans **not be done** unless medically necessary.

5 The author **urged** that we **not think** of our community as just a college town revolving around students.
(NOT: The author urged that we do not think of our community . . .)

COMPARE

6a Harding **proposes** that scientists **take up** research projects that start from women's lives. (subjunctive; Harding wants scientists to do something—an intention to bring about action by others)

6b Simonton **proposes** that genius **has become** irrelevant in understanding creativity in modern science.
(not subjunctive; Simonton thinks this change has happened)

Use of the base form means that in these clauses:

- We do not use an -s even with third-person singular subjects, such as *he* in **1**.

- We use the base form **be** (instead of *am / is / are, was / were*), as in **2**, including in passive clauses, as in **3** and **4**.

- We use **not** + the **base form** in negatives, as in **4** and **5**. (Notice that we do not use the helping verb *do*.)

Verbs that can be followed by subjunctive forms in *that* clauses include:

advise	insist	propose	require
ask	intend	recommend	suggest
demand	prefer	request	urge

Notice that we can use these verbs with subjunctive and non-subjunctive forms, as in **6a – 6b**. (In **6b**, *propose* is not used to express urgency, requirement, or an intention to bring about action, so a non-subjunctive form is used.)

GO ONLINE For more practice with the subjunctive form of verbs, go to the Online Practice.

13 | Identifying *That* Clauses with Subjunctive Forms Read the passage. Circle each reporting verb followed by *that* and put a box around the main verb in the *that* clause. Then write each reporting verb in the chart below. **2.6 A**

The 1916 Report of the Commission[75] on Industrial Relations[76]

The early years of the twentieth century were a time of labor unrest[77] in the United States. Workers had few rights, and violence between workers and employers was common. Because of this conflict, in 1912 President William Howard Taft (proposed) that a committee [be established] to investigate conditions. In response, Congress set up the Commission on Industrial Relations and requested that its members investigate "the general condition of labor in the principal industries of the United States."

Over a period of several years, the commission traveled around the United States, holding hearings[78] and taking testimony[79] from many people, ranging from poor workers to the wealthiest employers such as John D. Rockefeller. Workers testified about the difficult conditions. For example, some testified that they paid fines for laughing or talking at work, and others said that they had been forced to work days of 12 or more hours.

In 1916, the commission published its final report—a 1,200-page document with recommendations that some or all commission members supported. The report urged[80] that workers be allowed to organize, and it argued that government should protect worker rights. The report also addressed conditions for particular types of workers, including farmers, migrant workers, and domestic workers. For example, it recommended that Congress make borrowing easier for farmers and that it set a minimum wage for domestic workers. It even suggested that it be a crime to have people work more than six days a week. The report also looked beyond the workplace for explanations of problems in the workplace. It proposed, for example, that female workers were handicapped[81] by not being able to vote.

Did the commission's report make a difference for workers in the United States? Historians do not agree on the answer to this question. Some feel that Congress largely ignored the report. Others believe that the report's findings[82] and recommendations set[83] important changes in motion. For example, Dan Jacoby suggests that labor unions today owe much to the recommendations of the commission.

Verbs followed by subjunctive verb forms	Verbs followed by regular verb forms
propose	

Think about It Which two verbs occur in both columns of the chart in Activity 13? For each of these verbs, compare the sentence where it is followed by a subjunctive verb form with the sentence where it is followed by a regular (non-subjunctive) verb form. What is the difference between these two sentences?

Write about It For each of the two verbs you identified in the Think about It activity above, write a pair of sentences of your own—one with the following verb in its subjunctive form, and one with the following verb in its regular form.

Write about It Write a brief summary of the essay by completing these sentences in your own words.

The paper explains that the Commission on Industrial Relations was established _____ _____ and that the commissioners worked by _____.

It states that the commission's final report _____ _____. The author points out that historians _____ _____.

14 | Choosing Subjunctive or Other Verb Forms for *That* Clauses Complete these sentences with a correct form of the verb in parentheses. Where possible, use subjunctive forms. **2.6 A**

1. The author suggests that the student-reader _____ some time with each example.
   (take)

2. He suggests that the typical student _____ frustration when material is
   (experience)
   too difficult.

3. Sidney proposes that proper imitation _____ the successful learning of
   (result in)
   what is imitated.

4. The article recommends that women who are pregnant _____ a strictly
   (not / eat)
   vegetarian diet.

5. The Department of Agriculture suggests that the beekeeper

   _____ beehives when spraying with insecticides.
   (cover)

6. Despite the offer, many fishermen said that they would still prefer

   that the project _____.
   (not / passive be / build)

7. Far from[84] blaming unequal development for poverty, he suggests

   that development actually _____ to lessening poverty
   (contribute)
   in his country.

8. They requested that the committee _____ on the most
   (focus)
   important issues affecting athletes.

a beekeeper working with a beehive

9. The report insisted that, contrary to what some had claimed, diet and nutrition in the

   community today in fact _____ any different from what they had been in the
   (not / be)
   past, as surveys made clear.

10. In *Death of a Salesman*, the aging Willy Loman insists that his reputation still _____ (be) as great as ever.

11. The rules require that any applicant for teacher certification _____ (pass) both an exam of subject matter knowledge and an exam of professional knowledge.

2.7 Reporting Verbs with *To-* Infinitive Clauses

With certain **reporting verbs**, we can use **to- infinitive clauses***. These clauses often give us a shorter way to express the meaning of a *that* clause, as in **1a – 1b**.

1a The author **claims to measure diversity of plants in the wetlands in three different ways.**
(reporting verb + *to-* infinitive clause)
1b The author **claims** that he measures diversity of plants in the wetlands in three different ways.
(reporting verb + *that* clause)

A

VERB + *TO-* INFINITIVE

2 The researchers **expect to expand their work to other problems and to child behavior in general.**

3 In the article, he **claims to have sold the painting for fear that it would be damaged or stolen.**

VERB + NOUN PHRASE + *TO-* INFINITIVE

4 Salisbury and his colleagues found evidence of six major eruptions and **estimated these eruptions to be at least from 3.0 to 5.0 on the Volcanic Explosivity Index.**

5 Investigators **believe the fire to have been caused by sparks from the engine.**

6 Their analysis **showed the 33,000-year-old skeleton to have been of a young male.**

COMPARE

7a They **expect interest rates to increase gradually over the year.** (*expect* + *to-* infinitive clause)
7b They **expect** that interest rates will increase gradually over the year. (*expect* + *that* clause)

VERB + NOUN PHRASE + *TO-* INFINITIVE WITH SUBJUNCTIVE MEANING

8 The chapter **challenges readers to view soil not as dirt, but as living material.** (intention to bring about action by others: *the chapter* is encouraging *readers* to do something)

9 In her lecture, she **urged students to get involved and help others who are less fortunate.** (*She* is urging *students* to do something.)

COMPARE

10a The report **advised parents not to let their children have too much caffeine.** (*advised* + *to-* infinitive clause)

10b The report **advised** that parents not let . . . (*advised* + *that* clause with subjunctive form)

With some verbs, the *to-* infinitive is used directly after the **reporting verb**, as in **2 – 3**. Verbs that can be followed directly by a *to-* infinitive include:

claim	expect	propose

With other reporting verbs, such as *estimate* and *show*, a **noun phrase** is used between the **reporting verb** and the *to-* infinitive, as in **4 – 10a**. In these sentences, the noun phrase is the subject of the *to-* infinitive (*these eruptions* in **4**, *the fire* in **5**, etc.).

Reporting verbs that must be followed by a noun phrase include:

advise*	believe	estimate	prove	tell*
ask*	challenge*	expect	show	urge*
assume	consider	find	suppose	

*used to express an intention to bring about action by others

Many sentences with the verbs above are similar to sentences with *that* clauses with regular (non-subjunctive) verb forms, as in **7a – 7b**.

A few verbs, such as *challenge* and *urge* (indicated with * above), are used to express an intention to bring about action by others, as in **8 – 10a**. These types of sentences are therefore similar in sense to sentences with *that* clauses with subjunctive forms, as in **10a – 10b**. (See Chart 2.6 for more information about subjunctive forms.)

*For more information on *to-* infinitive clauses, see the Resources, page R-49.

GO ONLINE For more practice with *to-* infinitive forms, go to the Online Practice.

15 | Writing Sentences with _To-_ Infinitive Clauses Change each sentence with a _that_ clause into an equivalent sentence with a _to-_ infinitive clause. Use the appropriate form of the _to-_ infinitive. **2.7 A**

1. The speaker expects that worsening economic conditions will play a crucial role.

   The speaker expects worsening economic conditions to play a crucial role.

2. In the movie, eventually Jerome advises that Antwone search for his blood relatives[85].

   _____

   _____

3. A new study has found that friendships increase longevity[86].

   _____

4. The final report urges that the health system address mental health with the same urgency as physical health.

   _____

   _____

5. The researchers proposed that they would simplify the test so they could use it more easily in their research.

   _____

   _____

6. Wu claimed that his daughter's health problem was directly related to secondhand smoke[87].

   _____

   _____

7. The proposal would require that all subjects be taught only in English.

   _____

8. The agency estimated that the compensation[88] from fishing agreements amounted to[89] about $330 million in 2013.

   _____

   _____

9. The researchers expected that they would be able to work on other types of research while they conducted this study.

   _____

   _____

10. The study found that the level of air pollution had been declining since at least 2000.

    _____

    _____

16 | Paraphrasing with *To*- Infinitive Clauses
Complete each sentence with the past form of a reporting verb from the box followed by a *to*- infinitive clause with content from the quotation. If appropriate, include a noun phrase before the infinitive clause. Paraphrase the content, putting it in your own words. (Different answers are possible.) **2.7 A**

A speech given to graduating university students

1. "Please be sure to say two simple words to your parents after today's ceremonies: thank you."

   The speaker _____

   _____ .

2. "Have the courage to seek the truth, and speak the truth, to stand up for the underdog[90], and to stand up against intolerance[91]—even if yours is the lone[92] voice doing so."

   She _____

   _____ .

| tell |
| urge |

> **F Y I**
>
> As part of reporting another person's words, we often need to change pronouns and time and place words.
>
> John F. Kennedy: "Ask not what your country can do for you—ask what you can do for your country."
>
> In his speech, Kennedy told Americans to ask what **they** could do for **their** country.

A request for people to participate in a study

3. "In our study, we will try to understand how soccer injuries affect the brain."

   The researchers _____

   _____ .

4. "If you are a soccer player, help us make soccer safer by joining our study."

   They_____

   _____ .

| ask |
| propose |

A discussion of the results of several studies

5. "The effectiveness of the flu vaccine[93] differs greatly from season to season."

   The studies _____

   _____ .

6. "These differences are probably explained by differences in how well the vaccine matches the viruses."

   The writer _____

   _____ .

7. "In one study, the flu vaccination was associated with about 70 percent fewer hospital stays by adults."

   One study _____

   _____ .

| believe |
| estimate |
| show |

Talk about It Compare your answers in Activity 16 with a partner. Did you use the same reporting verbs and include noun phrases in the same sentences? Discuss the choices that you made in paraphrasing. If you made different choices, do both versions seem effective? Why or why not?

2.8 Wh- and *If / Whether* Noun Clauses

We use certain **reporting verbs** with **noun clauses** that begin with **wh- words** or with *if / whether*. The clauses use statement word order, as in **1a**, not question word order, as in **1b**.

COMPARE

1a He **asks why the assumption is** widely held. (subject before verb)
1b Why **is the assumption** widely held? (verb before subject)

A

WH- NOUN CLAUSES

2 He **does not indicate why young people in rural areas do not experience similar problems.**
(wh- question: Why don't young people in rural areas experience . . . ?)

3 They **inquire about how cultural factors might affect families' views of therapy.**
(wh- question: How might cultural factors affect . . . ?)

NOUN CLAUSES WITH *IF / WHETHER*

4 The author **wonders whether these results can be repeated in a larger study.**
(yes/no question: Can these results be repeated . . . ?)

5 Hosking **does not explain whether the power of trust works consistently across different parts of the world economy.**
(yes/no question: Does the power of trust work . . . ?)

We use **why, how, who, what, when,** and **where** to begin clauses that correspond to a wh- question, as in **2 – 3**.

We use **whether** or **if** to begin clauses that correspond to a **yes/no** question, as in **4 – 5**. In academic writing, *whether* is more common than *if*.

Some verbs are usually used in negative sentences when they are used with *whether* or *if*, as in **5**.

Verbs that can be followed by wh- or if / whether noun clauses include:

ask	explain*	say*
consider	indicate*	talk about
discuss	inquire (about)	tell*
establish*	question	wonder

*usually negative when followed by *if* / *whether*

For more information on wh- clauses and if / whether clauses, see the Resources, pages R-23–R-24.

B

OTHER USES OF *WH-* CLAUSES

6 Scientists **do not know whether insect sounds are a method of communication.**

7 The number of residents is not yet at an optimum level. **When that level will be reached** is not certain.

8 According to Picasso, every child is an artist, and the problem is **how we can remain artists when we grow up.**

9 We need to look at **why urbanization promotes both conflict and cooperation.**

10 Scientists seem to keep changing their minds about **whether coffee is bad for you.**

11 Many of the students were not certain **what they wanted to study.**

Like other noun clauses, **wh- noun clauses** can serve various functions in a sentence. We can use them as:

- objects of (certain) other verbs, as in **6**
- subjects, as in **7**
- subject complements, as in **8**
- objects of a preposition, as in **9 – 10**
- adjective complements (with certain adjectives), as in **11**

GO ONLINE For more practice with wh- and if/whether noun clauses, go to the Online Practice.

17 | Using *Wh-* Noun Clauses to Report Information
Complete each sentence with a *wh-* clause beginning with an appropriate question word and using the content of the question. **2.8 A**

ARTICLE TITLES PHRASED AS QUESTIONS

1. Are altruism[94] and cooperation natural?

   The author asks *whether altruism and cooperation are natural* .

2. Is computer hacking[95] a crime?

   The author inquires about _____.

3. Why do people use drugs?

   The author examines _____.

4. Where do we go for help and guidance?

   The author talks about _____.

5. Should we measure our success by what others have accomplished?

   The author wonders _____

   _____.

6. Will our jobs be exported?

   The author wonders _____

7. What are schools for?

   The author discusses _____.

8. Can the world's small languages be saved?

   The author looks at _____.

9. How are our schools doing?

   The author asks _____.

10. Do children have rights?

    The author explores _____.

11. Have women changed the way business is done?

    The author inquires about _____.

12. What is advertising good for?

    The author asks _____.

---

18 | Identifying *Wh-* Noun Clauses Read the passage. Underline each *wh-* noun clause. Then label
each noun clause as *S* (subject), *SC* (subject complement), *O* (object), *OP* (object of preposition), or
AC (adjective complement). Be careful: Some *wh-* words introduce adjective clauses or adverb clauses;
label only *wh-* noun clauses. **2.8 B**

How Young Children Think

$\overset{S}{\underline{\text{Whether children's ability to think like adults develops in}}}$
<u>definite stages or at different rates in different areas of thinking</u>
is not clear. Nevertheless, when a young child claims that the
weather is cold because snow is falling, it is clear that children's
thinking is quite different from adults' thinking. The Swiss
psychologist Jean Piaget originated[96] the stages theory of
children's cognitive[97] development. According to his theory, for
example, children who are younger than about six years old
cannot really understand cause and effect. That is, they cannot
understand why cold weather is a cause of snow, and not the
other way around. Children in that stage also cannot imagine

WARNING!
Do not confuse noun clauses
with adverb or adjective clauses.

A **noun clause** is generally
used where a noun phrase
could be used; it answers
the question *what*.

In an astronomy database, you can
learn **when the next solar eclipse
will occur**.

An **adverb clause** is used before
or after a main clause.

When a solar eclipse occurs, the
moon appears to cover the sun.

An **adjective clause** follows
a noun and gives more
information about it.

The perigee of the moon's orbit
is the point **where it is closest
to Earth**.

what other people are thinking or perceiving. This is what Piaget calls "egocentrism"—that is, young children are self-centered and can see only their own point of view[98].

However, other psychologists question that the stages theory can really tell us why young children seem able to think more accurately about some things than about others. For example, in the area of physics, infants just a few months old know when two objects seem to violate[99] a basic principle like not being in the same place at the same time. In the area of psychology, in contrast to what Piaget says about children's self-centeredness, it seems that children as young as three can predict how other people will perceive certain situations. Studies with such results make us unsure whether a strict stages theory can fully explain children's thinking.

Piaget's Liquid Conservation experiment examines logical thinking ability in children aged 7–12.

19 | Error Correction Correct any errors in these sentences. The errors relate to *that* clauses, *to-* infinitive clauses, and *wh-* clauses. (Some sentences may not have any errors.)

1. The researcher recommends that elementary school students ~~are~~ *be* forbidden to play violent video games for more than one or two hours per week.

2. Based on recent observations, Wilton suggests that solar systems with two or more planets in the habitable[100] zone are rare.

3. In *Animal Farm*, George Orwell shows to readers that a society of equals would be very difficult to achieve, if not impossible.

4. He tells that the media's images of marriage are deliberately distorted to promote consumerism[101].

5. She is correct to remind that Losey's film is about the servant as intruder[102] and ultimately as conqueror.

6. The law requires that business enterprises and governmental organizations do not attempt to influence employees' political activities.

7. To make planning easier, the department requested that regular maintenance operations be scheduled at least six months in advance.

8. The group discussed why was it dangerous to expose youngsters to violent contact sports.

9. In their important work, Davidoff and Wardwell demonstrated that the virus will always develop resistance to this type of therapy.

10. Several studies near the end of the twentieth century reported that this family form is likely to become the most common in America.

11. The author explains what action should have been performed and points out it wasn't performed.

12. Blodgett urged medical students to do not treat patients as children who need to be shielded from disturbing information.

13. Daskel advises the translator find a neutral term that is similar to the source term and is common in the target culture.

14. This study claims the results to show that current feminist ideas stand in opposition to the basic concepts of feminism[103].

15. At the conference, users explained whether the medication had unexpected side effects.

16. This study tried to establish whether would it be more beneficial to teach British English or American English as a model accent to Hungarian learners of English.

2.9 Other Ways of Introducing and Reporting the Ideas of Others

In addition to the structures covered in Charts 2.3 – 2.8, there are other sentence structures we can use to introduce and report other people's ideas. By using a variety of reporting techniques in our writing, we can make it more interesting and can emphasize different elements in our sentences.

USING A REPORTING VERB IN AN ADJECTIVE CLAUSE OR ADVERB CLAUSE

1 This perspective is supported by Sato (2006), **who argues that other organizations took a similar approach to environmental education.** (reporting verb in an adjective clause)

2 **Although the study found that** companies run by women had stronger event planning and a greater online presence, it appears that men are more aggressive when asking for what they want. (reporting verb in an adverb clause)

We can introduce the reported idea with a reporting verb + *that* clause within an **adjective clause**, as in **1**, or within an **adverb clause**, as in **2**.

For more information on adjective clauses and adverb clauses, see the Resources, pages R-27 and R-43.

REFERENCING A SOURCE IN A PREPOSITIONAL PHRASE OR ADVERB CLAUSE

3 Many of the nation's adolescents are falling asleep in class, arriving late to school, feeling down, and driving drowsy because of a lack of sleep, **according to a survey by the National Sleep Foundation.**

4 **According to the American Chemistry Council,** about 1,800 U.S. businesses are involved in the recycling of plastics.

5 **In Thompson's opinion,** the present is preferable to the past, whose glories are more imagined than real.

6 In conclusion, **in the authors' view,** leaving an uninformed learner in control of his learning journey leads to three problems.

7 What got the city where it is now was a combination of market forces and efforts by city government. **As Jones argues,** good urban development needs both of those pieces.

We can put the reported idea in the main clause of a sentence and use a **prepositional phrase** or **adverb clause** to reference the author or work. We may use:

- a **prepositional phrase** with *according to* + the author's name, as in **3 – 4**
- a **prepositional phrase** with *in* + a reference to the work, as in **5 – 6**
- an **adverb clause with** *as*, as in **7**

Notice: When we use **as . . . argues** (or *states, explains, points out,* etc.), we express agreement with the author's idea.

USING A REPORTING NOUN + A NOUN CLAUSE

8 It is the author's **argument that all fan fiction essentially comments on the original work by transforming a piece of the original, no matter how small.**

9 I agree with Bennett's **statement that** "great things happen in gardens."

Sometimes we introduce the reported idea with a **reporting noun**—the noun form of a reporting verb (*statement, argument, claim,* etc.). The reported idea then follows in a **noun clause,** as in **8** and **9**.

20 | Identifying Structures That Introduce and Report Other Writers' Ideas Read the passages. Underline the reported ideas (the paraphrases and quotations of others' ideas). Put a box around the source (the author or work). Circle the words that introduce the reported ideas (the reporting verb, prepositional phrase, or reporting noun). Then write each sentence number in the chart on page 66. (Different answers are possible.) `2.9 A`

GET READY TO READ

You are going to read some further views on GMOs.

GMOS

1. As scientists, physicians, academics, and experts from disciplines relevant to the scientific, legal, social, and safety assessment aspects of genetically modified organisms (GMOs), we strongly reject claims by GM seed developers and some scientists, commentators[104], and journalists that there is a "scientific consensus[105]" on GMO safety and that the debate on this topic is "over."—European Network of Scientists for Social and Environmental Responsibility

2. GMOs alone probably won't solve the planet's food problems. But with climate change and population growth threatening food supplies, genetically modified crops could significantly boost crop output[106]. "GMOs are just one tool to make sure the world is food-secure when we add two billion more people by 2050," says Pedro Sanchez, director of the Agriculture and Food Security Center at Columbia University's Earth Institute. "It's not the only answer, and it is not essential, but it is certainly one good thing in our arsenal[107]."—Brooke Borel, "Core Truths," *Popular Science*

3. The Organic Consumers Association . . . says genetic engineering will never deliver on promises to feed a growing population and isn't a trustworthy technology. "The dirty secret of the biotech industry is, after thirty years, they haven't done anything for consumers," said Andrew Kimbell, the founder[108] and executive director of the Center for Food Safety.

   According to Robert Fraley, Monsanto's chief technology officer and executive vice president, his company has been studying the impacts of climate change since 2006. But it has created only one line of GM plants designed to deal with environmental stress. . . .

   The high cost of GMO field-testing[109] may explain why the only genetically modified crops that have made it to market are, in the words of environmental scientist Jonathan Foley, "very disappointing" and "come with some big problems."—Madeline Ostrander, "Can GMOs Help Feed a Hot and Hungry World?" the *Nation*

4. The claim made by the British government that we need 40 percent more food by 2050 just to keep up with the rising population and increased demand is not true. As Hans Herren, president of the Millennium Institute, points out, the world already produces enough food and energy to sustain[110] 14 billion people, a number which is twice the present world population and 50 percent more than the population that we will have in 2050. But what happens is that most of that food is wasted, and this is obviously a huge problem.—Colin Tudge, in "A Debate between Mark Lynas and Colin Tudge," *Journal of International Affairs*

5. Two agricultural economists from the University of Göttingen in Germany who analyzed 147 papers from the peer-reviewed literature found that on average, genetically engineered crops reduced chemical pesticide use by 37 percent, increased crop yields by 22 percent, and increased farmer profits by 68 percent.—Peter J. Davies, "Conflicting Views on GMOs: How Do We Know What to Believe?" Genetic Literacy Project

6. According to a survey conducted by the Pew Research Center in association with the American Association for the Advancement of Science, 88 percent of scientists believe GM foods are safe to eat, compared with only 37 percent of the public—a gap of 51 percentage points.

   Unfortunately, this [denial of science] has victims. . . . As [a paper from the World Resources Institute] points out, farmers need to close a 69 percent gap between the crops they produced in 2006 and the food the world will need, given population growth, by 2050.—Fred Hiatt, "Science That Is Hard to Swallow[111]," the *Washington Post*

Form in which others' ideas are given	Way in which paraphrase or quote is introduced
In a sentence that is a quotation:	With a reporting verb + *that* (including where *that* is omitted):
In a sentence that gives a paraphrase:	With *according to*:
In a sentence that includes both a quotation and a paraphrase: *1*	With a prepositional phrase with *in*:
	With an adverb clause with *as*:
	With a reporting noun: *1*

Talk about It With a partner, discuss which issue(s) the writer in each passage in Activity 20 addresses. In your own words, summarize the points they make and the position on GMOs they seem to take.

Who discusses
- whether GMOs are needed to feed the world now and in the future?
- whether GMOs are increasing or reducing the use of pesticides?
- how wide-ranging the benefits of GMOs are and who benefits from GMOs?
- whether there is scientific consensus about GMOs?
- how the public feels about GMOs and why the public feels this way?

Talk about It On controversial topics such as GMOs, there are often differences of opinion. What are some of the differences of opinion between the writers of the excerpts in Activity 20?

EXCERPTS ABOUT GMOS

Whether you're looking at modern-day corn or tomatoes, or you're looking at peaches or soybeans, we've been moving genes around from the beginning of time. But through biotechnology, we're able to do it even more precisely, literally one gene at a time.

—Robert Fraley, Monsanto, Intelligence Squared U.S. debate: Genetically modify food

eggplant

There is no reliable evidence that ingredients made from current GE crops pose any health risk whatsoever. Numerous governmental and scientific agencies . . . have conducted reviews that did not identify any health concerns. Indeed, even the fiercest opponents have not shown any health risks.

—Greg Jaffe, "What You Need to Know about Genetically Engineered Food," the *Atlantic*

University researchers are working to develop GM oranges that are resistant[112] to citrus greening disease, something that is devastating[113] the Florida orange industry. . . .

cassava

There are many publicly funded groups around the world, working to develop GM-disease resistant varieties of crops, including apples, bananas, cassava, cowpea, eggplant, grapes, potatoes, rice, sweet potatoes, and wheat. Some of these staple[114] crops are an essential source of nutrient[115] in the diets of the poor. And it doesn't stop at plants. Researchers . . . are working . . . to develop genetically engineered cattle that are resistant to African Sleeping Sickness, a disease that kills several thousand people and three million cattle annually. . . . All of these GM applications[116] focus on controlling disease with genetics rather than chemicals, an objective that I would argue is compatible with agroecology[117], sustainability[118], and feeding more people better with less environmental impact. There are literally dozens of other applications and field trials globally.

cowpea

—Alison Van Eenennaam, University of California Davis, Intelligence Squared U.S. debate: Genetically modify food

Ecosystems[119] are complex. Plants interact with everything. . . .

Ecologists understand that 10, 15, or even 20 years . . . may be insufficient to really know how [an ecosystem] functions (Luo et al. 2011, Reich et al. 2012). Twenty years . . . may only be a fraction of the time necessary for an ecosystem to stabilize[120] in response to a changing environment—if stability is even realistic. To add even more complexity, it may take several generations to detect how GE crops affect individual species and species interactions at the genetic level.

—Sasha Wright, "Why the GMO Debate Misses the Point," *Popular Science*

[T]here's no shortage of land devoted to GMOs. Since the . . . seeds hit the market in 1996, global GM crop acreage[121] has expanded dramatically, reaching 420 million acres by 2012, reports the International Service for the Acquisition of Agri-biotech Applications. That's a combined landmass more than four times larger than California. The pro-GMO ISAAA hails this expansion as [the] "fastest adopted crop technology in the history of modern agriculture."

Yet, for all of that land devoted to GMOs, there are just two traits[122] in wide use: herbicide resistance and pest resistance. . . . [T]he percentage of all global GMO acres planted in crops that aren't either herbicide- or pesticide-tolerant [is] less than 1 percent.

Now, one might ask: But isn't the industry on the brink of[123] rolling out wonder crops—new varieties that are more nutritious, or use water more efficiently, or need less fertilizer[124]? One way to tell is to peek into[125] the U.S. Department of Agriculture pipeline[126] of new GMO products being considered. . . . Here we can expect to find the stuff the industry has tested and found . . . ready for field conditions. What's in there? Thirteen products—nine of which involve herbicide tolerance or insect resistance. Of those nine, five are engineered to resist two herbicides—a dispiriting[127] trend. . . .

[W]here's the progress? For that, I think, we have to look to the fact that genes and traits (the cool things we want plants to do in the field) don't always track on a one-to-one basis. There are single genes that confer[128] resistance to particular herbicides. . . . But there's no one gene that regulates the way a plant uses water—which probably explains why Monsanto's "drought-tolerant" corn . . . has fallen with such a thud.

—Tom Philpott, "Crop Flops: GMOs Lead Ag Down the Wrong Path," *Grist*

Talk about It With a partner, look over the excerpts in Activity 21. Supporters of GMOs often try to show that GMOs are really very similar to other crops—and therefore not risky in any way—and offer important benefits. Opponents often try to show that GMOs *are* different, and therefore risky, and that they do not offer important benefits. Which authors make points supporting the use of GMOs, and which authors make points opposing their use? State the main point of each excerpt in your own words.

22 | Referring to Other Writers' Ideas Answer the questions with ideas from the excerpts in Activity 21. The speaker or writer is indicated in parentheses. Because you are giving the ideas of other writers, make sure to include an appropriate structure from the box below. `2.9 A`

1. How might biotechnology (the process through which GMOs are developed) compare to what farmers have always done? (Fraley)

   Fraley argues that biotechnology is . . .

2. Is there evidence of health risks from GMOs? (Jaffe)

3. Are GMOs that are now being developed likely to serve a wide range of helpful purposes? What are two different opinions on this point? (Van Eenennaam, Philpott)

4. Why might GMOs pose environmental risks? (Wright)

5. Philpott raises a question about GMOs being developed. What question does he raise?

6. Why might it be easier to develop GMOs that are herbicide-resistant than to develop GMOs that might be more generally useful? (Philpott)

according to
in the opinion / view of   OR   in ____'s opinion / view
writes / argues / other verb + that
wonders / asks / inquires / other verb + whether / what / other *wh-* word

Write about It Think about your answers above. First, find a statement that you agree with. Express it in a sentence using the following structure:

as . . . claims/states/points out/other verb

Then find a statement that you do not agree with or are not sure about. Give your thoughts about it in a sentence using the following structure:

's statement/argument/claim that

Share your sentences with a partner.

Follow steps A–D to write a paragraph summarizing the Philpott excerpt in Activity 21.

A | Planning **Follow these steps to plan your summary.**

1. Read the excerpt again carefully. Look up any important words that are unfamiliar. Make sure that you understand all of the ideas in each paragraph. Then write a single sentence stating what you see as the author's main point in each paragraph. Next, for each paragraph, write an informal outline, with the main idea of the paragraph followed by a list of main points that support it (some paragraphs will have more points than others).

   Main point:

   Paragraph 1: main idea: ____

   1st supporting point: ____

   . . .

   Paragraph 2: main idea: ____

   . . .

2. Compare outlines with a partner. Discuss any differences between your outlines. Then make any revisions that you want to make based on your discussion.

B | Writing **Based on the main points and supporting points that you listed in Activity A, write a one-paragraph summary of what Philpott is saying. Before summarizing, review the Writing Note on page 54. Begin your summary with a sentence that introduces the source and his topic and/or his main idea. Use the ideas in your list so that you summarize the excerpt paragraph by paragraph, including the main idea and important supporting points from each paragraph. Use different ways of introducing your paraphrases.**

C | Peer Reviewing **Share your writing with a partner. Answer these questions about your partner's summary.**

1. Did your partner include the main idea of the original paragraphs and all the important supporting points? Are there any important supporting points that are not included? Do any of the points seem to be just minor points or details? Did your partner avoid including his or her own ideas?

2. Did he or she appropriately credit the source? Did your partner use his or her own words and structures? Have the ideas been connected effectively, for example, through linking adverbials?

D | Revising **Follow these steps to revise your paragraph.**

1. Using your partner's feedback, rewrite your paragraph.

2. Check your writing for mistakes and clarity. Did you use different ways of introducing your paraphrases? Make any final corrections necessary.

In academic writing, we often combine several clauses in a sentence, as in **1** and **2**. We can do this by:

- combining main clauses together with a conjunction such as *and* or *but*
- adding various other kinds of clauses to or within main clauses. These may include:
  - adjective clauses beginning with a relative pronoun such as *that*, *who*, or *which*
  - *that* clauses, *wh-* noun clauses, and *to-* infinitive clauses (See Charts 2.4–2.8 for more information on these types of clauses.)
  - adverb clauses beginning with a subordinator such as *because*, *when*, or *although*

A

1 Even though we have overwhelming evidence that GMO crops are safe to eat, the debate over their use continues, and in some parts of the world, it is growing ever louder.

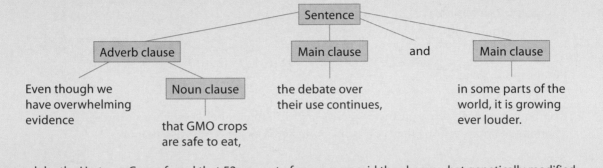

2 Research by the Hartman Group found that 52 percent of consumers said they knew what genetically modified organisms were, but that less than a third could identify the crops that now are grown with genetically modified seeds.

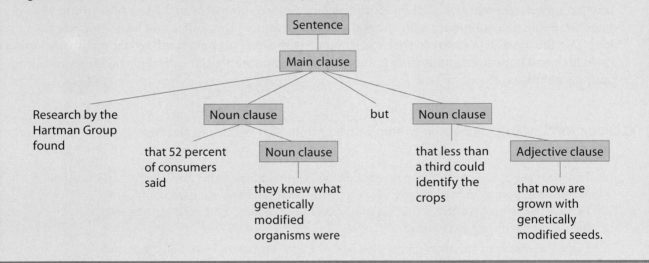

B

COMBINING CLAUSES FOR COHESION

COMPARE

3a A majority of divorced persons eventually remarry. However, the growth of divorce has led to a steep increase in the percentage of all adults who are currently divorced. This percentage was only 1.8 for males and 2.6 for females in 1960. It quadrupled by the year 2000.

3b Although a majority of divorced persons eventually remarry, the growth of divorce has led to a steep increase in the percentage of all adults who are currently divorced. This percentage, which was only 1.8 for males and 2.6 for females in 1960, quadrupled by the year 2000.

By combining clauses, we can avoid having numerous short sentences. Readers will find our sentences smoother, clearer, and more cohesive. Combining clauses allows us to signal relationships between ideas and organize information within sentences. Compare **3a** with **3b**. The four sentences of **3a** are two sentences in **3b**.

In each sentence in **3b**, the writers combine related ideas. Notice that they:

- express their main idea in the main clause of the two sentences.
- express the less important ideas (background or additional information) in other types of clauses.

23 | Identifying Clauses within a Sentence In each sentence, circle the words that introduce clauses that are not main clauses. Then read the list of clauses below the sentence, and label each clause as *MC* (main clause), *NC* (noun clause), *AdjC* (adjective clause), or *AdvC* (adverb clause). **2.10 A**

SCIENCE NEWS AND COMMENTARY

1. (When) voters were asked (whether) they would support a plan (that) would develop a green[129] economy and create new manufacturing jobs, 72 percent said (that) they would strongly support it.
   a. When voters were asked . . . ___*AdvC*___
   b. whether they would support a plan . . . ___*NC*___
   c. that would develop a green economy and create new manufacturing jobs ___*AdjC*___
   d. 72 percent said . . . ___*MC*___
   e. that they would strongly support it ___*NC*___

2. The study team reports that the genetically engineered plant attracted insects that preyed on[130] other, plant-eating insects.
   a. The study team reports . . . _____
   b. that the genetically engineered plant attracted insects . . . _____
   c. that preyed on other, plant-eating insects _____

3. Scientists who are developing genetically engineered poplar[131] trees argue that this can save native forests and the environment.
   a. Scientists . . . argue . . . _____
   b. who are developing genetically engineered poplar trees _____
   c. that this can save native forests and the environment _____

genetically engineered poplar trees

4. While the government produces lengthy reports on Britain's unhealthy diet of starchy[132], salty, and sugary processed foods and recommends that this diet be modified, it puts obstacles in the way of producers who could bring about the changes required.
   a. While the government produces lengthy reports on Britain's unhealthy diet of starchy, salty, and sugary processed foods and recommends . . . _____
   b. that this diet be modified _____
   c. it puts obstacles in the way of producers . . . _____
   d. who could bring about the changes required _____

5. Four out of five firefighters in the U.S. are overweight or obese, and roughly half of all firefighters who die in the line of duty each year are killed by heart attacks.
   a. Four out of five firefighters in the U.S. are overweight or obese _____
   b. and roughly half of all firefighters . . . are killed by heart attacks _____
   c. who die in the line of duty each year _____

6. Scientists at Scripps Research Institute said that they had developed an artificial antibody[133] that grabbed hold of the virus and inactivated[134] it.
   a. Scientists at Scripps Research Institute said . . . _____
   b. that they had developed an artificial antibody . . . _____
   c. that grabbed hold of the virus and inactivated it _____

7. Data in a 2013 study indicates that one in five restaurant workers went to work despite virus symptoms.

   a. Data in a 2013 study indicates . . . _____

   b. that one in five restaurant workers went to work despite virus symptoms _____

Think about It In sentence 6 of Activity 23, why is "inactivated it" not a clause by itself? In sentence 7, why is "despite virus symptoms" not a clause?

24 | Breaking a Sentence into Clauses
Each sentence contains two or more clauses. Put square brackets ([ ]) around each clause that is not a main clause, and label it as *NC* (noun clause), *AdjC* (adjective clause), or *AdvC* (adverb clause). If a sentence has only main clauses, write *MC* after the sentence. `2.10 A`

NEWS ABOUT THE WORLD'S FOOD

1. [Although vegetable staples are nutritious], they generally do not provide a full range of nutrients, so other kinds of foods are needed as well.
   AdvC

2. While insects can be slimy[135] creatures, a new book says that beetles, wasps, and caterpillars are also a relatively unexplored[136] nutrition source that can help address the world's food shortage.

beetle

3. The world's population will hit 9 billion by 2050, so having enough land for farming will be an increasing concern, and insect farms offer nutrition at less cost to the environment.

4. New research revealed a worldwide rise in the consumption of healthy food, but this was overtaken by a worrying increase in consumption of junk food.

wasps

5. Fast food has long been linked to childhood obesity, but a new study suggests that it may also affect educational achievement.

6. When you were a child, if you were like many people, you may have developed phobias[137] toward some vegetables, but as adults we can overcome these phobias.

caterpillar

7. Researchers found that people can make healthier food choices overall if they occasionally indulge[138] in less healthy food that they truly enjoy.

8. The beginning of the twenty-first century, which witnessed a massive growth in globalization, was good for the fast-food industry as well.

9. A new study confirms that worldwide we're increasingly eating foods from the same small number of staple crops, and this trend makes the global food supply vulnerable[139] to new diseases and pests.

10. In the survey, although financial concerns were a major obstacle to healthy eating around the world, a perceived time crunch[140] was the biggest barrier.

11. If a recent report is correct, unless the world's population adopts a vegetarian diet over the next 40 years, we may face a global food shortage that could end in catastrophe.

12. According to a new study, over the past two decades the levels of healthy fats in people's diets worldwide increased while their intake[141] of harmful fats stayed about the same.

25 | Writing Note: Prepositional Phrases Read the note. Then do the task below.

Many sentences contain one or more **prepositional phrases**, as in **1a – 1c.**. Writers often use prepositional phrases to combine ideas, as in **1c**. Some kinds of clauses can be rephrased as prepositional phrases.

TWO SENTENCES	**1a** The predictions are **for a relatively inactive storm season**. However, forecasters stress that a single storm can cause great damage. (The first sentence contains a prepositional phrase.)
SENTENCE WITH AN ADVERB CLAUSE	**1b** Although the predictions are **for a relatively inactive storm season**, forecasters stress that a single storm can cause great damage. (The adverb clause contains a prepositional phrase.)
SENTENCE WITH A PREPOSITIONAL PHRASE	**1c** Despite the predictions **for a relatively inactive storm season**, forecasters stress that a single storm can cause great damage. (The prepositional phrase with *despite* contains another prepositional phrase.)

Remember: A phrase is different from a clause because it is missing a subject, a complete verb, or both.

For a list of common prepositions, see the Resources, page R-56.

Think about It Look again at the sentences in Activity 24. Identify the prepositional phrases in the sentences and write them in a chart like the one below. (Note: some prepositions may be more than one word.) In your chart, underline the preposition in each phrase. Compare charts with a partner.

Sentence	Prepositional phrases
1	of nutrients; <u>of</u> foods
2	none

26 | Combining Simple Sentences In each item, combine the simple sentences into a single sentence with two or more clauses. Add and omit words as needed, and make any other changes that are necessary. (Different answers are possible.) 2.10 B

THE COMMON COLD

1. The common cold is a viral infection of the nose and throat. A common cold is usually harmless.

   The common cold, which is a viral infection of the nose and throat, is usually harmless.

2. More than 200 viruses can cause a cold. A recent study confirmed this. Cold symptoms vary greatly for this reason.

3. Many viruses can cause colds. The rhinovirus is most often to blame, though. It causes up to 50 percent of colds.

4. Most people get colds in winter and spring. It is possible to get a cold at any time of year.

5. Parents often catch colds from their children. Their children catch them from other children at schools or daycare centers. Colds spread quickly at schools and daycare centers.

6. People are infected first. Then people develop symptoms. For this reason, people spread colds without realizing it.

7. Rhinoviruses usually live for about 3 hours on the skin or on another surface. Sometimes they live for up to 48 hours. Hand washing is important.

8. A sick person coughs or sneezes. He or she expels[142] virus-containing droplets[143]. These droplets can travel up to 6 feet.

9. People should stay home from work at the beginning of a cold. A cold is most contagious[144] at the beginning. People usually stay home later. At this point their cold feels worse but is actually less contagious.

10. Most people recover in about a week from a cold and its symptoms. The symptoms include sore throat, runny nose, and headaches. But people with weakened immune systems may develop a more serious illness.

11. Traditional remedies like chicken soup can actually promote recovery from colds. A new study suggested this. The person must believe in these remedies.

Think about It Compare your answers in Activity 26 with a partner. For answers that are different, do you prefer one version over the other? Why?

Write about It Use some of the sentences in Activity 26 to write a short paragraph about the common cold. Revise sentences as needed to make the paragraph flow smoothly and cohere.

FINAL WRITING ASSIGNMENT
Write a Summary/Response Essay

Your Task
Write an essay summarizing and responding to "Golden Rice and the GMO Debate" on pages 52–53.

Alternative Task
Choose another article from a newspaper, a magazine, or the Internet on another recent technology about which there are conflicting opinions. Write an essay that summarizes and responds to the article.

GO ONLINE Go to the Online Writing Tutor for a writing model and to write your assignment.

A | Reading a Model Read the model summary/response essay. Then do Activity B.

The Debate Over Fracking

Water is not just for drinking and agriculture anymore. Today, it has also become a key player in the energy industry. Fracking is the latest method used to extract oil and gas from underground. It works by forcing many gallons of water deep into the ground at very high pressures. According to Mark Koba's article from NBC News, "Fracking or Drinking Water? That May Become the Choice," there is now a debate about whether fracking will threaten global water supplies. Koba offers a clear and objective review of this debate, but readers can also infer that the dispute ultimately stems from conflicting agendas among environmentalists and the oil and gas industry.

In the article, Koba reports that experts do not agree on whether fracking is beneficial or not. He cites a recent study from the World Resources Institute (WRI), which suggests that fracking could compromise the earth's natural water reserves. According to the report, many countries are using fracking, including the United States, Germany, and New Zealand. The report notes that fracking requires millions of gallons of water for drilling, which could potentially cause these countries to contend with water scarcity in the future. Another concern relates to countries planning to employ fracking to search for new sources of oil and gas below ground, such as China, India, and Mexico. "If they are developed," says the report, "the need of water for oil exploration could conflict with farming and daily use." Finally, experts caution that fracking produces significant amounts of toxic wastewater, which is not reusable for drinking or agriculture, and is thus lost forever.

However, Koba also points out that some energy experts disagree with the suggestions of the report. They argue that fracking demands much lower quantities of water than agriculture and is therefore not a serious threat to future water supplies. They also say that the oil industry is aware of the potential risks of wasted water, and is working diligently to develop ways to recycle it. Finally, even though the report claims that there is a connection between fracking and potential earthquakes, they contest this finding. However, they do admit that drilling for oil and natural gas is never "without risk," no matter how it is done.

It is clear that experts are divided on this matter, but Koba succeeds at presenting both sides in a clear and balanced way. He not only presents the negative findings of the report, but notes that the study highlights favorable aspects of fracking as well, such as the fact that it could "boost gas resources by 47 percent." To discuss the situation, Koba relies predominantly on the opinions of others rather than his own, which gives the article a more objective tone. Instead of ending with his own assessment of the situation, he concludes with a quote from a professor, who suggests that it might be too early to determine whether fracking is the most practical way to drill for new oil and gas. Therefore, readers are left to make their own decision about what the various facts and conflicting opinions suggest.

Still, a careful reading of Koba's article reveals a very important but understated point. The experts who wrote the report are scientists from the World Resources Institute, a nonprofit, global organization dedicated to preserving the earth's natural resources ("About WRI"). In contrast, the energy experts who question the report's findings represent a research firm of the Independent Petroleum Association of America (Koba). This firm exists to serve the best interests of oil and gas companies, not the environment ("About IPAA"). In my opinion, it is therefore not surprising that they downplay the negative effects of fracking. I am not convinced that they truly believe fracking is safe and good for the future. In other words, it is possible that they are denying the dangers of fracking because they want to protect the oil industry and its financial prosperity, and are less concerned about fracking's potentially negative impact on future water supplies.

Overall, Koba's article helps readers understand the nature of the fracking debate. He effectively presents what the WRI's report suggests about the present and future dangers of fracking, but also considers the opinions of those in the oil and gas industry who question whether these dangers are legitimate. I think it is important to look at both sides in order to make an informed decision. In my opinion, it is too early to tell whether or not fracking will jeopardize global water supplies, but if scientists are already sending a strong warning, I believe we should listen to them.

Works Cited

"About IPAA." *Independent Petroleum Association of America*. Web. 13 May 2015. < http://www.ipaa.org/about/>
"About WRI." *World Resources Institute*. Web. 13 May 2015. < http://www.wri.org/about>
Koba, Mark. "Fracking or Drinking Water? That May Become the Choice." *NBC News*. 12 Sept. 2014. Web. 12 May 2015.
       < http://www.nbcnews.com/business/business-news/fracking-or-drinking-water-may-become-choice-n202231>

B | Analyzing Essay Structure Look again at the model summary/response essay in Activity A, and identify the introduction, body paragraphs, and conclusion. Then answer the questions.

Introduction

1. Does the introduction include a hook? If so, what is it?

2. What issue will the essay address? What background information, if any, does the writer include on the issue, and why do you think he or she has given readers this information?

3. What is the thesis statement? What does it tell readers about the writer's response to the article?

Summary

4. In which body paragraph(s) does the writer give a summary of the article?

5. What words does the writer use to introduce the ideas from the article? Is it clear that all of the ideas are from the original article, and not the writer's ideas? Does the writer use a variety of structures to introduce these ideas?

6. Does the writer include any quotations from the original article? Were the quotations well chosen—that is, can you see why the writer used them rather than paraphrasing?

Response

7. In which body paragraph(s) does the writer give his or her response to the article?

8. Does the writer clearly express his or her thoughts and opinions about the article? What are those thoughts and opinions?

9. Does the writer give clear reasons for his or her thoughts and opinions? Does he or she support them with evidence? Does the writer include other writers' ideas as part of this support? If so, does he or she correctly introduce them as other writers' ideas? What words does the writer use to introduce them?

10. Are the points in the response set up by the summary? That is, does the summary give readers the information needed to understand the response?

Conclusion

11. Does the conclusion include a restatement of the thesis? If so, what is this restatement?

12. What are the writer's concluding thoughts? Do these concluding thoughts seem like an effective way of ending the essay? Why or why not?

Think about It Compare the summary in Activity A to the original article in the Online Resources. Does the summary include the main idea of the article and the main ideas of each of the article's paragraphs? Does it include only the important ideas? Does the essay writer basically use his or her own words, rather than words from the original article?

C | Writing Note: Tips for Writing a Summary/Response Essay Read the note. Then do Activity D.

THE SUMMARY PART

Remember: A summary of a piece of writing gives all of its main ideas in your own words. A summary does not include minor points or details or your own ideas. In your summary:

- Include references to the author with appropriate reporting verbs.
- Use quotations if you feel it is important to use some of the author's exact words.
- Connect the main ideas that you are paraphrasing so that your summary will read smoothly.
- If there are ideas that you will respond to, make sure that these are clear from the summary.

THE RESPONSE PART

Your response gives your thoughts and opinions about the piece of writing that you have summarized. In your response, you say what you thought about the main idea of the essay and some of the main points that support it. Your response might include your thoughts on some of the following:

- Is the article well written? Is it clear and easy to understand? Why or why not?
- Does the author support the ideas well? Why or why not?
- Do you agree with the author? Why or why not? Are there specific points that you do not agree with? What are these?
- Is there anything that the author should discuss but does not? If so, what?

In your response, you can:

- Include paraphrases and/or quotations from the article to support your points, making sure to clearly indicate them as the author's ideas.
- Support your ideas with paraphrases and/or quotations from other authors, making sure to clearly indicate whose ideas they are.

D | Planning the Summary and the Response Follow these steps to plan the content for your summary/response essay.

1. Reread the article "Golden Rice and the GMO Debate" on pages 52–53. Then answer these questions.

   - In your opinion, what is the main idea of this article?
   - What conclusions does the author reach about the GMO debate? How does she support these conclusions?
   - In your opinion, is the author's decision to use Golden Rice as a way to approach the GMO debate a good decision? Why or why not?
   - Do you believe the author is fair to both sides of the debate? Why or why not?
   - Do you agree or disagree with the author's opinions?
   - What other factors should be considered when discussing this subject? Is there anything important that the author should have included but did not include?

2. Carefully reread the article, paragraph by paragraph. As you read each paragraph, complete this chart.

Paragraph	Main idea of the paragraph	Main points in the paragraph related to/supporting this main idea	Any questions/thoughts I have about this content
1	*Protestors in the Philippines destroyed a field of GMO Golden Rice, arguing that it could affect their health and the environment.*		
2			
3			
4			
5			
6			

3. Look over your completed chart, especially the column with your questions and thoughts. What points do you agree with? What points do you disagree with or feel uncertain about? Return to Activity 20 on pages 65–66 and to the reading "Excerpts about GMOs" in Activity 21 on pages 67–68. Do any of these excerpts make points related to your questions and thoughts? Take notes on points that might be relevant to your response.

E | Writing Note: Essay Organization Study the diagram for organizing a summary/response essay. Then do Activity F.

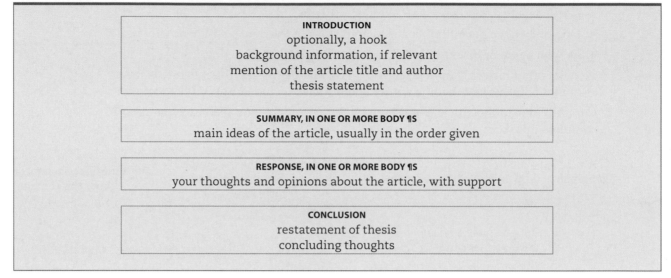

INTRODUCTION
optionally, a hook
background information, if relevant
mention of the article title and author
thesis statement

SUMMARY, IN ONE OR MORE BODY ¶S
main ideas of the article, usually in the order given

RESPONSE, IN ONE OR MORE BODY ¶S
your thoughts and opinions about the article, with support

CONCLUSION
restatement of thesis
concluding thoughts

F | Organizing Your Essay Draw your own diagram like the one above. Write your ideas in each section.

G | Writing a First Draft Using information from your diagram, write a first draft of your essay. Try to use some of the structures that you have practiced in this unit.

H | Peer Reviewing When you have finished writing your first draft, share it with a partner. After discussing your essay, you may want to reorganize your ideas, add more support, and make other changes to strengthen your essay.

Checklist for revising the first draft

When you review your partner's essay and discuss your own, keep these questions in mind.
1. Does the thesis statement clearly express the argument that the writer will make?
2. Does the introduction capture the reader's interest and give any basic background information needed?
3. In the body paragraph(s) presenting the summary, does the writer clearly present the main ideas of the article and introduce them clearly as the ideas of the author of the article?
4. In the body paragraph(s) presenting the response, does the writer clearly express his or her thoughts about the article and its main ideas?
5. Does the writer provide support for the points in his or her response and, if including support from other writers, clearly indicate the ideas as belonging to the other writers?
6. If the writer uses quotations, are the quotations effective and are the authors clearly indicated?

I | Writing the Second Draft Using your partner's feedback, write a second draft that includes all of your changes.

J | Proofreading Check your essay for the forms in Chart 2.11. Make any final corrections necessary.

2.11 Summary Chart for Proofreading

PROOFREADING QUESTIONS	EXAMPLES
Did you correctly use quotations where you felt it was important to use the author's exact words?	From a battlefield in England, Canadian soldier Thomas Marion wrote his mother, "Many a mother's heart is breaking for her boy who will never return."
Do paraphrases give the author's ideas in your own words and sentence structures?	Technology allows the rural people to get more access to knowledge and resources, and that will help them to gain economic benefits. (original) In his article, Shaijumon writes that villagers' economic situation will improve because through technological developments they will get the information and goods that they need.
Are **reporting verb forms** consistent, and are **verbs backshifted** following past-form reporting verbs? Did you use specific reporting verbs that are appropriate in meaning? Are reporting verbs followed by the right kinds of clauses—*that* clauses, *to-* infinitive clauses, and *wh-* clauses?	In his article, Pillalamarri **pointed out** that the Indus Valley Civilization (IVC) in South Asia **had existed** at about the same time as the civilizations of ancient Egypt and Sumer. He **described** new discoveries of IVC sites in India that **dated** back to 7500 BCE, and he **expected** future discoveries to push the beginnings of South Asian civilization as far back as 10,000 BCE. Finally, he **wondered** what the inscriptions in the still-undeciphered writings of IVC peoples **would reveal** about this ancient culture.
Are sentences varied in structure? Did you combine clauses in different ways to make your writing smoother and more cohesive and to signal relationships?	According to Tracey, despite widespread belief in the story that Marco Polo introduced pasta into Italy in 1295 when he returned from China, evidence shows that this story cannot be true. However, as Tracey points out, Marco Polo encountered pasta in China, and pasta in China predated pasta in Italy. Of course, this is not surprising, because Chinese civilization originated over 5,000 years ago.

3

Expanding and Condensing Information

> Every truth has two sides; it is as well to look at both before we commit ourselves to either.
>
> —AESOP, GREEK STORYTELLER
> (c. 620–c. 564 BCE)

Talk about It What does the quotation above mean? Do you agree or disagree?

WARM-UP

A | Read these paragraphs. Which sounds more formal and academic? What do you think makes it sound that way?

A	B
Do employees have a right to privacy? This is a controversial legal topic. And it's getting more controversial. These days, companies are relying more and more on computers and email. They use these technologies to do business. In addition, employers can use new technology to monitor their employees. They can see almost all workplace communication on the computer. **Many employers now have new email systems. They copy all email messages as they pass through the system. They check to see if employees are being productive or if they're doing illegal things. They also check for other problems.** Employers frequently use emails as evidence during trials. The emails prove that employees have behaved improperly at work.	An employee's right to privacy in the workplace is an increasingly controversial legal topic in an age of increased reliance[1] on computers and email to do business. Technology has enabled employers to monitor virtually all workplace communication by employees using computers. Many employers now have email systems that copy all email messages as they pass through the system to check for productivity[2], illegal use, and other issues. Emails are frequently being used as evidence during trials to prove employee misconduct[3].

B | Discuss these questions with a partner.

1. How many sentences are there in paragraph A? In paragraph B?

2. Look at the first sentence in paragraph B. How many sentences does paragraph A use to express the same ideas?

3. Underline the complete subject of the first sentence in paragraphs A and B. How are the two subjects different?

4. Look at the four **bold** sentences in paragraph A. How many sentences does paragraph B use to express the same ideas? How did the writer condense the ideas?

5. Besides the number of sentences, what else is different about the language, including the vocabulary, in these two paragraphs? (For example, paragraph A says "more controversial," while paragraph B says "increasingly controversial.")

[1] See page V–5 for the Vocabulary Endnotes for this unit.

3.1 Overview of Expanding Structures by Adding Information

A

NOUN PHRASES: ADDING INFORMATION BEFORE AND AFTER A MAIN NOUN

One common way to expand the information in a sentence is to add words and phrases to a **main noun** to form a noun phrase, as in **1**.

noun phrase

1 We will discuss | the surprising **results** of a study that was conducted by some of our colleagues last year | .

Notice the grammatical elements that can be added before and after a main noun:

NOUN PHRASE							
DETERMINER / NUMBER	ADJECTIVE(S)	DESCRIBING NOUN	MAIN NOUN	APPOSITIVE	PREPOSITIONAL PHRASE	(REDUCED) ADJECTIVE CLAUSE	COMPLEMENT CLAUSES
The (one)	unexpected		**result**		of a study	(that was) published in August	
		government	**officials**			who make policy	
			Charles,	the owner,			
an			**agreement**				to change the rules

For more information on noun phrases, see the Resources, pages R-17–R-20.

B

VERB COMPLEMENTS

verb + *that* clause

2 Patients **understand** that they need to consult a health-care professional.

verb + *wh-* clause

3 Many of the doctors **wondered** what benefits the new drugs were bringing to their patients.

verb + *-ing* clause

4 The procedure **involved** using surveys to gather information.

verb + *to-* infinitive clause

5 Researchers **hope** to continue the work that began a decade ago.

NOUN COMPLEMENTS

noun + *that* clause

6 One investigation concerned the common **belief** that certain birds were not strong enough to fly during winter.

noun + *wh-* clause

7 The new laws were written at a **time** when unemployment was high.

noun + *to-* infinitive clause

8 Increasing humidity is a practical **way** to reduce dust.

ADJECTIVE COMPLEMENTS

adjective + *to-* infinitive clause

9 Some of the people were **happy** to help neighbors who had been affected by the disaster.

We can also expand sentences by adding different types of clauses to verbs, as in **2 – 5**; to nouns, as in **6 – 8**; and to adjectives, as in **9***. These are called **complement clauses**.

Most complement clauses are:

- *that* clauses
- *wh-* clauses
- *-ing* clauses
- *to-* infinitive clauses

*For information on adjective complements, see Unit 1, page 22.

GO ONLINE For more practice with parts of a noun phrase, go to the Online Practice.

1 | Noticing Noun Phrases Read the excerpt and notice the structures of the **bold** noun phrases. Copy each noun phrase into a chart below that describes its structure. `3.1 A`

Social Media Monitoring of Job Candidates: Some Concerns

Looking at social media for hiring purposes can obviously have **some benefits for employers**ᵃ, but there are also **possible negative consequences that need to be considered**ᵇ.

When employers look at **private social media accounts**ᶜ, they may find **information that is irrelevant⁴ to an employee's job performance**ᵈ, but that may unfairly influence the hiring decision. For example, employers may learn **the age, marital status, or religion of the prospective⁵ employee**ᵉ.

There are several problems with this. For one thing, managers are **people with prejudices and biases⁶**ᶠ like anyone else, and this information may cause them to reject **talented candidates, individuals likely to benefit the company as employees**ᵍ. In addition, if an employee is rejected, an employer who had **access to this private information**ʰ might be accused of discrimination⁷.

For all of these reasons, some people recommend that **these types of searches**ⁱ be performed by a third party⁸. Employers can request to be informed only of relevant information, such as illegal behavior, and this protects them from lawsuits⁹.

> **FYI**
> The forms we can put before the main noun must usually be in a specific order. The forms we can put after the main noun can be longer, and their order is more flexible.

1.

main noun	prepositional phrase
access	*to this private information*

2.

main noun	prepositional phrase

3.

determiner	main noun	prepositional phrase

4.

determiner	main noun	prepositional phrase

5.

determiner	main nouns/noun phrases (three)	prepositional phrase

adjective	describing noun (two words)	main noun
6.		

main noun	adjective clause	prepositional phrase
7.		

adjective	adjective	main noun	adjective clause
8.			

adjective	main noun	appositive
9.		

Talk about It What concerns does the writer in Activity 1 have about monitoring social media for hiring purposes? Discuss as a class.

2 | **Noticing *That* and *Wh-* Clauses** Read this passage. Underline the complement clauses beginning with *that* and *wh-* words. **3.1 B**

Checking Up on Job Applicants[10]

Everyone knows <u>that nowadays many employers check the social media presence of job seekers[11] before they make a hiring decision</u>. Some people regard this as an invasion of privacy[12], but two recent studies have added support to the argument that employers can gather valuable information from social media. These studies have demonstrated that social media often reveal what a person will be like as an employee.

For the first study, researchers asked employers to look at the publicly[13] available information on a group of college students. The employers gave each student a score on personality and other qualities, such as emotional stability[14] and friendliness. The researchers predicted that the students with the highest scores would make the best employees. Later, the researchers contacted the actual employers of the students. They found that the employers' evaluations were very similar to the results from the social media evaluations.

In another study, researchers evaluated social media profiles in a similar way, this time to predict how successful students would be in school. In this study, the students were also given traditional personality and intelligence tests. The researchers made separate predictions based on the tests. When they compared their predictions to the students' college transcripts[15], they discovered that the social media profiles were a better predictor[16] of student success than the personality and intelligence tests.

Based on these two studies, it is clear that employers have excellent reasons for looking at the social media profiles of potential employees.

Talk about It What did the two studies in the article in Activity 2 show?

Think about It Do the clauses you underlined in Activity 2 add information to verbs, nouns, or adjectives? Label the word or words before each clause as *noun*, *verb*, or *adjective*.

3 | Noticing *-ing* and *To-* Infinitive Clauses Underline the *-ing* and *to-* infinitive clauses in this passage. `3.1 B`

In Favor of Social Media Monitoring

Most people can understand why employers check the social media profiles of job applicants. They want to avoid hiring the wrong people, and social media accounts often provide valuable information. Many employers have learned that applicants were dishonest about their experience and skills, that they enjoy making aggressive or rude remarks, or that they have engaged in an illegal activity. Employers have the right to know all of these things before they decide to hire someone.

However, some employees are not happy when the boss continues checking up on them after they are hired, and many refuse to give their social media passwords to employers who ask for them. Despite this resistance[17], employers have good reasons to monitor employees' online behavior. The things that employees say on their private accounts can damage an employer's reputation or even get an employer into legal trouble. Employees have been caught discussing private customer information and even revealing company secrets online. They may also criticize customers or co-workers, or make other statements that reflect poorly on the company. Nothing on the Internet is really private, and wise employers will insist on access to all of their employees' social media accounts.

Talk about It What reasons does the writer give above in support of social media monitoring? Discuss as a class.

Think about It Do the clauses you underlined above add information to verbs or nouns? Label the word before each clause as *noun* or *verb*.

4 | Usage Note: Expanding Subjects with Phrases with *Of* Read the note. Then do Activity 5.

We can use a **quantifying determiner** + *of*, as in **1**, or a **category noun phrase** + *of*, as in **2**, to add information to a noun phrase.

	QUANTIFYING DETERMINER + *OF*	NOUN PHRASE			CATEGORY NOUN PHRASE + *OF*	NOUN PHRASE
	all of	their ideas			a group of	23 economists
	most of	the information			a mass of	supporters
1	many of	the benefits		**2**	several pieces of	analysis
	a number of	the employees			a set of	research studies
	several of	the problems			a few types of	evidence

SUBJECT-VERB AGREEMENT

When there is a quantifying determiner, the **verb** usually agrees with the **noun phrase after *of***, as in **3 – 4**.

3 | Most of **the reports** | **provide** a broad picture.   **4** | Most of **the research** | **has been done** in the last five years.

When there is a category noun phrase, the verb often agrees with the **category noun phrase**, as in **5 – 6**.

5 | **A set** of experiments | **was conducted** to address these issues.

6 | **Several pieces** of information | **were considered** helpful in resolving this issue.

---

5 | Using Category Noun Phrases and Quantifying Determiners Circle the correct verb form. Underline the complete subject noun phrase for each circled verb.

SCIENCE AND TECHNOLOGY

1. Data sets were obtained from published sources as well as from some unpublished sources provided by specialists. <u>All of the data sets</u> (was / were) then fed into the system.

2. Rocks as old as 3.2 billion years have been found. Many pieces of evidence from these rocks (indicates / indicate) that early Earth must have had an abundant[18] supply of liquid water.

3. A set of standards (was / were) developed for evaluating the research.

4. After every oil spill, a number of marine animals (is / are) saved by volunteers who clean them and later return them to their native waters.

5. A key piece of equipment known as a heat exchange (is / are) used by oil refiners to control temperatures and make processes run more efficiently.

6. Previously, a mass of different technical documents (was / were) generated every time engineers designed a new product. This system has now been greatly simplified.

7. A group of more than 20 programmers and biologists (is / are) working to finish the project.

8. Several types of new technology (has / have) changed the practice of modern agriculture.

9. Field researchers may spend hours waiting quietly by a trail because they know a certain type of animal often (passes / pass) that way.

10. Most of the world's remaining wild oysters (come from / comes from) just five areas on the East and Gulf coasts of North America.

wild oysters

Think about It Which of the underlined noun phrases above include quantifying determiners? Which include category noun phrases?

3.2 Expanding Verbs with Verb Complements

Many verbs have **direct objects**. Direct objects usually answer the question *what*. They help complete the meaning of the verb, so they are called **verb complements**. Some verb complements are single words or phrases, as in **1**. Verb complements can also be clauses, as in **2**.

1 The researchers found **a solution**. (noun phrase as direct object/verb complement)

2 The researchers found **that the number of smokers had decreased from 1980 to 2009**.
(*that* clause as direct object/verb complement)

A

3 Less attention has been devoted to older children with reading. This **means that they encounter new problems in reading when they enter the upper elementary grades.**

4 The policymakers **assumed that improved economic numbers would bring higher employment rates**, but it didn't work out that way.

Sometimes we complete **verbs** using *that* **noun clauses**, as in **3 – 4**. Some common verbs used with *that* clauses in academic writing include:

> **Thought verbs:** assume, believe, conclude, decide, doubt, expect, feel, find, hear, hope, imagine, know, mean, notice, read, realize, recognize, remember, see, suppose, think, understand, wish

> **Reporting verbs:** argue, ask, explain, prove, recommend, say, show*, suggest, tell**

*can be followed by a noun phrase (indirect object)
**must usually be followed by a noun phrase (indirect object)

For more information on reporting verbs, see Unit 2, page 46.

For more information on *that* clause verb complements, see the Resources, page R-24.

B

5 People do not necessarily **know where the information came from.** (= the place that the information came from)

6 This paper **explains why certain animals need to be protected by law.** (= the reason that certain animals are protected by law)

7 The public did not want to **accept what could be long-term consequences.** (= the things that could be long-term consequences)

Sometimes we complete **verbs** using *wh-* **noun clauses**.

The verbs most often used with *wh-* clauses are thought or reporting verbs, as in **5 – 6**. These verbs, which can also be used with *that* clauses, include:

> explain   know   realize   show*   understand

*can be followed by a noun phrase (indirect object)

However, most transitive verbs (verbs that take objects) can be used with a *wh-* clause. These clauses can often be restated as adjective clauses with *that* or *who*, as in **5 – 7**.

GRAMMAR TERM: We sometimes call verb complement *wh-* clauses **indirect questions**.

For more information on *wh-* noun clauses, see Unit 2, page 61, and the Resources, page R-23.

C

8 Genetic data **seems to indicate that the population has moved.**

9 The two countries have **agreed to work together for their mutual benefit.**

10 Teachers **expect** students **to identify strategies that will help them succeed.**

Sometimes we complete **verbs** using *to-* **infinitive clauses**, as in **8 – 10**. Common examples from academic writing include:

> agree, allow**, appear, attempt, begin, continue, enable**, expect*, fail, intend, require*, seem, tend, try, want*

*can be followed by a noun phrase (indirect object)
**must usually be followed by a noun phrase (indirect object)

For more information on *to-* infinitive verb complements, see the Resources, page R-48.

D

11 The team **began working on the project in the 1990s.**

12 Doctors **started achieving better results when they gave patients a combination of treatments.**

Sometimes we complete **verbs** using *-ing* **(gerund) clauses**. These verbs often refer to an ongoing activity, as in **11 – 12**. Some examples from academic writing include:

> begin   involve   keep   see**   start   stop

**must usually be followed by a noun phrase (indirect object)

For more information on *-ing* (gerund) verb complements, see the Resources, page R-46.

6 | Noticing Verb Complements Choose one or two verb complements from the box to add to each passage below. 3.2 A–D

> **VERB COMPLEMENTS**
> a. that distrust of the legal system has had a negative effect on the quality of medical care
> b. why they did not enjoy activities
> c. using email to communicate with colleagues
> d. how any sunlight at all gets to the moon
> e. what's going on in the natural world
> f. that it was not only safe but also important
> g. to gain access to information in their special field
> h. using the network's radiometric[19] system and the spacecraft's cameras
> i. that the normally bluish-white moon appears reddish-brown during an eclipse[20]

SENTENCES FROM ACADEMIC JOURNALS

1. NASA's Deep Space Network (DSN) is the largest and most sensitive scientific telecommunications system in the world. The DSN was able to track[21] *Voyager*'s position at Saturn with an accuracy of nearly 150 kilometers (about 90 miles) during its closest approach. Achieving this accuracy involved __h__.

2. One needs no sophisticated equipment to recognize ____, and many describe the moon as taking the color of blood. Many have wondered ____ to provide it with that red light.

3. The Institute of Medicine has conducted studies showing ____ because doctors are hesitant[22] to be honest with each other. They avoid ____ because it leaves a written record. They don't want to admit fault even in cases when no harm is done to the patient.

4. Krause suggests the creation of a virtual library that will enable scientists ____ from many sources around the world.

5. As a young researcher, Paul Cohen decided ____ to dive freely among hammerhead sharks to acquire a better understanding of these magnificent animals. "I believe that you can only really learn ____ by observation," he said in a recent interview.

6. Because there was not a place on the student attitude surveys for students to explain ____, it is difficult to know why the students were not as positive about certain activities.

hammerhead shark

Talk about It Use these sentence beginnings to make statements about science. Use a verb complement. Discuss your ideas with a partner.

1. Success in a scientific field involves ____.
2. Many scientists have wondered ____.
3. There have been studies showing ____.
4. Scientists should avoid ____.
5. Technology enables scientists to ____.

7 | Using *That* Clauses as Verb Complements
These passages contain verb complements without *that*. Insert the missing word *that* where it belongs. `3.2 A`

Our Moon and Our Solar System

1. Recent research by Rick Carlson suggests ^*that* Earth's moon is somewhat younger than previously thought.

2. Computer models have shown the moon was created when another body collided[23] with Earth in the early days of the solar system.

3. The moon's surface is covered with approximately 300,000 large craters[24]. The lack of weather, water, and other changing conditions means many of these craters are well preserved.

4. By the start of the twentieth century, most astronomers recognized Mars was far colder and drier than Earth.

5. People have suspected the existence of water on Mars since the invention of the telescope. Early observers[25] correctly assumed the white polar caps and clouds were indications of water's presence.

6. The Mars ocean hypothesis[26] proposes nearly a third of the surface of Mars was once covered by ocean. One study concluded such an ocean would have covered 36 percent of Mars, while other evidence points to a much larger ocean.

7. In 1966, the tenth satellite of Saturn was discovered by Audouin Dollfus. It was named Janus. A few years later astronomers realized there had to be another satellite near Janus with a similar orbit.

8. William Herschel discovered infrared radiation[27] when he placed a thermometer in sunlight of different colors and noticed the temperature increase was highest just beyond the red color.

Earth's moon

8 | Using *Wh-* Clauses as Verb Complements
Replace each *that* clause with a *wh-* clause complement. `3.2 B`

Exploring Planets

1. Unlike its predecessors[28], the Mars rover[29] was able to move slowly over the surface of Mars and discover ~~the things that~~ *what* lay beyond the next hill or across a dry riverbed.

2. In 1968, one of NASA's highest-priority projects was to explain the reasons that the spacecraft[30] being used in navigation[31] tests were experiencing large numbers of errors.

3. Jupiter has over 300 times the mass of Earth, and we want to understand the way that such a large planet could have formed.

4. It is possible to find very faint objects without the help of a telescope if you know the place that they are located.

5. A special environment was set up in the desert to test the spacecraft and demonstrate the things that it could do if it were sent to the moon.

6. It requires at least a 15-mm-diameter[32] telescope to see Saturn's rings, so they were not known to exist until Galileo saw them in 1610. He wasn't able to interpret the things that he was seeing, and thought the rings were two moons on Saturn's sides.

7. Édouard Roche described the way that a satellite that came within a certain distance of Saturn could break up and form rings.

8. In 1609, Galileo was one of the first to turn his telescope toward the sky and record the things that he saw.

Saturn

9 | Using *That* and *Wh-* Clauses as Verb Complements Read the passages. Then complete the verbs in the sentences on page 91 with *that* or *what* complement clauses. (Different answers are possible.)
3.2 A–B

Opinions about Workplace Surveillance

Jerry, a waiter

I'm ready to quit. I'm being videotaped in the bathroom!! My boss installed some video surveillance[33] equipment in the restroom because he wants to be sure that the employees wash their hands before leaving. He's worried that some customer might sue[34] him if they don't. This certainly feels like an invasion of privacy. If the restroom isn't private, what is?

Jane, an office supervisor

My employees used to spend hours playing video games and downloading music. I sent everyone a memo making it clear that playing games wastes company time and money, but they just closed their office doors. I couldn't see them, but I knew they were still playing games. So I bought equipment that enables me to monitor what they are doing whenever they are online. I had mixed emotions about spying on them, but how else was I supposed to dissuade[35] them from wasting company time when they refused to listen to me? It was my only choice.

Anna, a systems manager

I need advice!!! I work with my company's computer system. My boss asked me to look at the social media profiles of other employees. I agreed, but I wasn't really thinking about what it meant. My office manager has mentioned online that she is thinking about leaving the company. She's not doing anything illegal, and she hasn't decided yet, so I don't feel right about telling my boss. But if she leaves and my boss looks at these emails, I might get in trouble. What should I do?

JERRY

1. Jerry doesn't agree with _what his boss is doing_____.

2. Jerry believes _____.

JANE

3. Jane noticed _____.

4. She tried to explain _____.

5. Employees closed their office doors so that Jane wouldn't see _____.

6. She finally decided _____.

ANNA

7. When her boss asked her to read people's social media profiles, Anna didn't realize

_____.

8. She discovered _____.

9. She doesn't know _____.

10 | Using *To-* Infinitive and *-ing* Clauses as Verb Complements Choose a verb from the box to complete each sentence. Use a *to-* infinitive or *-ing* form. (Different answers are possible.) **3.2 C–D**

SENTENCES FROM ACADEMIC JOURNALS

complete
express
find
grow
make
measure
participate
think
use
vary

1. The results of the study must be interpreted with caution[36] because all of the participants[37] were from a similar background. We do not know how much they differ from people who did not agree _____ in the study.

2. After World War II, farmers began _____ new technology to increase food production.

3. For this study, we intend _____ children's monthly growth over time.

4. Small details can have a big impact on local climate, which is one reason that we expect the effects of climate change _____ depending on geographic location.

5. Researchers in Sydney are attempting _____ the cause of certain speech problems by scanning the brains of newborn babies.

6. Research shows that most girls have stopped _____ by the time they are 17 years old.

7. Barnes hopes _____ the study of the recycling program by the end of next year.

8. An open-ended survey allows participants _____ their ideas freely within the categories created by the examiner.

9. It is not reasonable to insist that environmental objectives take precedence over all other goals. Public policy involves _____ choices.

10. Feldenkrais exercise activities require concentration. Individuals are expected _____ about what they are doing as they move their muscles.

11 | Using -*ing* and *To*- Infinitive Clauses as Verb Complements Read the passage. Then complete the sentences below with an -*ing* or *to*- infinitive clause. (Different answers are possible.) **3.2 C–D**

Against Social Media Monitoring of Employees

Checking the social media profiles of job candidates is one issue, but monitoring current employees is a different practice, and it usually does more harm than good. Most of what people do online is done during their own time on their own equipment and has no relationship to work. Employers should not be firing good employees because of private behavior that does not affect their ability to do a good job. Employers should also not be spying on employees' online presence any more than they should be peeking[38] in the windows of their homes or following them to restaurants to see how they behave when they're off-duty. If an employer asked for access to my private accounts, I would look for work elsewhere. Monitoring is only appropriate when employers have a reason to suspect illegal behavior. Routinely investigating employees' private lives uses a lot of company time and resources. It can also result in employees' being fired unfairly. If an employer has a personal dislike of things that employees do during their free time, he or she may be more likely to fire them, even if the behavior has no influence on their jobs.

1. According to this writer, employers should not attempt _to monitor current employees_____.

2. Monitoring current employees tends _____.

3. Information about private behavior should not be used _____.

4. The writer thinks that employers should stop _____.

5. The writer would not agree _____.

6. If an employer asked for access to the writer's private accounts, the writer would start

   _____.

7. Monitoring enables employers _____

   _____.

WRITING ASSIGNMENT I

Follow steps A–D to write a paragraph about the advantages and disadvantages of social media monitoring in the workplace.

A | Planning Follow these steps to plan your paragraph.

1. Review the reading passages in Activities 1, 2, 3, 9, and 11. In this chart, list some of the advantages and disadvantages of monitoring job candidates and current employees.

A. Investigating the social media profiles of *job candidates*
Advantages
Disadvantages *The information might unfairly influence the hiring process.*

B. Monitoring the social media profiles of *current employees*
Advantages
Disadvantages

2. Discuss your chart with a partner. Did you include all of the arguments from the readings? Can you think of any other arguments to add to the chart?

B | Writing Write a paragraph explaining some of the arguments for and against social media monitoring in the workplace. Use the information from the chart in Activity A to help you organize your paragraph. Focus on Part A (job candidates) OR Part B (current employees) of the chart, not on both parts. Conclude your paragraph with a brief explanation of your own opinion on the topic. Include some verbs with complement clauses to explain your own and others' opinions.

> *Social media monitoring in the workplace has become very common. Some people believe . . .*
> *Others, however, think . . .*

C | Peer Reviewing Share your writing with a partner. Answer these questions about your partner's paragraph.

1. Did your partner explain the opinions of others on the topic? Should anything be added or removed to make the opinions clearer?
2. Did your partner explain his or her own opinion? Should anything be added or removed to make it clearer?
3. Did your partner include any verb + complement clauses? Were the correct complements used in each case?

D | Revising Follow these steps to revise your paragraph.

1. Using your partner's feedback, rewrite your paragraph.
2. Check your writing for mistakes and clarity. Did you use any verb + complement clauses? Make sure that the complement fits the verb. Make any final corrections necessary.

3.3 Expanding Noun Phrases with Adjective Clauses

One way we can expand **noun phrases** is with an **adjective clause** after the main noun. Writers use adjective clauses to add information to sentences. Compare:

1a The accountant could not explain the mistakes. These mistakes had recently appeared in the documents.
1b The accountant could not explain the mistakes that had recently appeared in the documents.

A

DEFINING ADJECTIVE CLAUSES

2 The tools provide valuable information about the **people** who lived in the area. (Which people? The ones who lived in the area.)

NON-DEFINING ADJECTIVE CLAUSES

3 Vonnegut, who was a prisoner of war in Dresden at the time of the bombing, had been captured.

4 This group of anthropologists focused on **culture**, which they studied by living among their subjects.

5 Prices have risen dramatically in the last few years, which has made it difficult for many families to pay their bills.

Defining adjective clauses help identify the **main noun**, as in **2**. They usually answer the question *which*, *which one(s)*, or *what kind*.

Non-defining adjective clauses give extra information about the main noun, as in **3 – 4**.

Sometimes non-defining adjective clauses give extra information about an entire clause, as in **5**.

Non-defining adjective clauses are usually separated from the rest of the sentence with a comma, as in **3 – 5**.

For more information on defining and non-defining adjective clauses, see the Resources, page R-29.

B

6 There are many factors which need to be considered. (The factors need to be considered.)

7a The patients refused to eat even the food that they liked. (They liked the food.)

7b The patients refused to eat even the food they liked. (less common in academic writing)

Most adjective clauses begin with the **relative pronoun** *who*, *which*, *that*, or *whose*.

- Sometimes the relative pronoun is the subject of the adjective clause, as in **6**.
- Sometimes the relative pronoun is the object of a verb in the adjective clause, as in **7a**.

We can delete object relative pronouns, as in **7b**, but this is not common in academic writing.

For more information on subject and object relative pronouns, see the Resources, page R-28.

C

8 They wanted to create a society in which the health of the people was a high priority.

9 The nurses described the difficulties faced by the people for whom they were caring.

10 Contamination often occurs in areas where the water is shallow.

11 There were serious problems in the community at a time when residents needed to work together to succeed.

12 He saw no reason why others could not achieve success through hard work.

We sometimes use adjective clauses with a **preposition** + *which* or *whom**, as in **8 – 9**.

We can also use clauses with *where*, *when*, or *why* to add information after a noun, as in **10 – 12**.

We usually use clauses with *when* after the noun *time* and clauses with *why* after the noun *reason*, as in **11** and **12**.

GRAMMAR TERM: *Where, when,* and *why* in clauses that add information to nouns are called **relative adverbs**.

*For more information on relative pronouns after prepositions, see the Resources, page R-29.

GO ONLINE For more practice with adjective clauses, go to the Online Practice.

12 | Noticing Adjective Clauses Underline the adjective clauses in these passages. Add commas to signal non-defining clauses. `3.3 A–C`

EXCERPTS FROM CRITICAL REVIEWS OF BOOKS, JOURNALS, AND PLAYS

1. According to the authors, motherhood promises a human connection in a world <u>where trusting relationships are rare</u>, and it gives poor women a social role whose value is only increased by their difficult circumstances.

2. This essay collection appears at a time when the relationship between working environment and productivity is attracting much interest, especially in offices where most of the workforce[39] is employed. The decisions that are made about these issues could have huge economic consequences.

3. All of Havel's plays that are performed in Prague have a very different quality than they have when they are translated or performed in other areas. His plays were written out of a real situation in which people were surrounded by lies, so his satire[40] is much more effective if everyone in the audience has had a similar experience.

Prague

4. In 1916, Robert Bridges published a highly successful book, *The Spirit of Man* which included six poems by Hopkins. In 1920, he published "The Testament of Beauty" which is regarded as his greatest achievement as a poet.

5. The journal[41] *Applied Computing Review* is available in electronic format[42] only. This publication which focuses on current trends in the field contains invited papers from well-known researchers.

6. The novel *1Q84* is a work that is largely an investigation of very strange ideas. The book is best in its first third which is where the author discusses the nature of writing. At one point, one character notes, "When you introduce things that most readers have never seen before into a piece of fiction, you have to describe them with as much precision[43] and in as much detail as possible. What you can eliminate[44] from fiction is the description of things that most readers have seen."

7. Elizabeth Wane, a romantic novelist whose works include *The Trials of Rebecca* and *The Making of Mandy Mason*, has confessed that she's given "generous" praise to terrible books at least four or five times. The purpose, she says, was to increase her own fame by having her name on the cover of books that might just turn out to be best sellers.

FYI

Without punctuation, it may not be clear whether an adjective clause is defining or non-defining. Writers signal that a clause is non-defining by setting it apart from the rest of the sentence with a comma/commas.

Refunds were given to the passengers whose flight was postponed.
(Some passengers received refunds.)

Refunds were given to the passengers, whose flight was postponed.
(All passengers received refunds.)

Think about It Discuss these questions with a partner.

1. Could any of the adjective clauses above possibly be either defining or non-defining? Which ones?

2. Which relative pronouns above are objects of the verbs in adjective clauses?

13 | Using Relative Adverbs Complete these sentences with *when, where,* or *why*. `3.3 C`

1. Participants were asked to write only their first name and the town _____ they lived.

2. I haven't entirely lost hope for the future of newspapers and print journalism, despite there being a growing list of reasons _____ I should.

3. Conflicts over taxation[45] emerged at a time _____ economic anxiety was high.

4. You can choose to download from the app store, _____ you know they are not going to give you a virus, or you can download from the Internet.

5. He had a dream of a country _____ the color of skin did not influence the assessment of character.

6. It seems to me that public policy is an area _____ some scientific knowledge is now extremely important.

7. There have been rare occasions _____ an entire mammoth[46] has been discovered in places such as Alaska or Siberia, frozen solid for millions of years.

8. The leaders are often held responsible for the actions of the group, but there are many reasons _____ leaders do not have the authority to enforce[47] their will.

9. Many of the study participants said that they had reached a point _____ they wanted to quit.

10. On the rare occasions _____ inspectors have visited the site, they have not reported any problems.

> **RESEARCH SAYS...**
>
> In academic writing, clauses with *where* do not always refer to places. They are most common after the nouns *place, area, point, case, world,* and *situation.* In some cases, they have a meaning closer to *when.*
>
> The environmental health officer is trained to prepare for a **situation where** drinking water is contaminated or in short supply.
>
> **C**ORPUS

woolly mammoth

14 | Usage Note: Relative Pronouns in Academic Writing Read the note. Then do Activity 15.

Academic writers often choose the more formal relative pronoun *which* or a preposition + *which / whom* instead of the less formal relative pronoun *that,* as in **1a – 1b** and **2a – 2b**.

1a The study analyzed the amount of time **that** was devoted to physical activity each week. (less formal)
1b The study analyzed the amount of time **which** was devoted to physical activity each week. (more formal)
2a The health professionals **that** these patients are referred **to** should be qualified in several specific areas.
   (less formal)
2b The health professionals **to whom** these patients are referred should be qualified in several specific areas.
   (more formal)

Preposition + *which* is also more formal than *where, when,* or *why,* as in **3a – 3b**.

3a This was the first study **where** the authors investigated this particular effect. (less formal)
3b This was the first study **in which** the authors investigated this particular effect. (more formal)

15 | Using Relative Pronouns in Academic Writing Edit the underlined clauses in these sentences to make them more formal and academic. **3.3 C**

1. Bayles presented her 2007 study, *in which* ~~where~~ nearly all individuals were able to answer the first three questions.

2. We found that many doctors were prescribing[49] treatments <u>that there was no solid evidence of effectiveness[50] for.</u>

3. Our results refer only to the participants <u>that complete data is available for.</u>

4. This is the first study of its kind <u>where authors investigated this particular effect.</u>

5. Our model included the year <u>when the participants' housing was built.</u>

6. Because of the way <u>that stroke[51] affects the body</u>, the condition carries a risk of long-term effects.

7. Maori oral history refers to people who lived in New Zealand before the canoes[52] arrived, <u>whom archeologists can find no direct evidence for.</u>

8. This study found different patterns among the 11 Canadian cities <u>where observations were available.</u>

Think about It Which of the clauses above are non-defining? How did you figure out which preposition to add in the sentences above?

16 | Writing Sentences with Adjective Clauses Read the information about restaurant software. Then complete each sentence below with an adjective clause using *who*, *which*, or *that*. (Different answers are possible.) **3.3 A–C**

RESTAURANT TECHNOLOGY

One doesn't usually think of a restaurant as a high-tech workplace, but even in this simple setting, technology is making major changes in the way work is done. Customers use the Internet to make reservations, hosts use software to plan and arrange seating, and servers send orders to the kitchen using hand-held tablets. Because so much technology is used, restaurant activity is easier to monitor than it has ever been before. In some restaurants, employers use intelligent software to track servers and orders. The software looks for patterns. Employers can use the patterns to detect[53] employee theft and to check productivity. Now the restaurant owner knows who is selling the most food, who is collecting the most tips, and who makes the fewest mistakes with orders. Employers argue that the program motivates[54] servers: when they know their sales are being tracked, they are more likely to suggest that guests order appetizers[55] or desserts. This information is also valuable for evaluating managers. If the software shows that a manager runs particularly efficient work shifts, that manager can be targeted for promotion.

1. These days many restaurants use technology _that is changing the way work is done_____.

2. Nowadays, there are many customers _____.

3. In many restaurants, you'll see servers _____.

4. Some restaurants are using intelligent software _____.

5. Intelligent software can reveal patterns _____.

6. Managers can identify servers _____.

7. The software provides owners with information _____.

8. Owners may promote managers _____.

3.4 Condensing Information with Reduced Adjective Clauses and Appositives

Instead of using full adjective clauses, writers often condense information into complex noun phrases with **reduced adjective clauses** and related structures.

A

REDUCED ADJECTIVE CLAUSES

1 Treatments (that were) **suggested for weight loss** include a five-hour, high-risk surgery to remove a portion of the stomach.

2 As an executive (who is) **currently working in three different locations**, Kellen spends much of her time traveling.

3 The people (who were) **in the auditorium** were listening to a man (who was) **in his 30s**.

COMPARE

4a The area contains diverse vegetation, **which consists of** species that are found throughout the Southeast.

4b The area contains diverse vegetation, **consisting of species that are found throughout the Southeast**.

COMPARE

5a The new procedure has worked well for patients **who have** heart failure.

5b The new procedure has worked well for patients **with** heart failure.

We can reduce adjective clauses that have a subject relative pronoun and the verb *be* by removing the relative pronoun and *be* verb, as in **1 – 3**.

These reduced clauses may contain:

- an *-ed / -en* verb form (usually from a passive verb), as in **1**
- an *-ing* verb form (usually from a progressive verb), as in **2**
- a prepositional phrase, as in **3**

We can also reduce adjective clauses with other simple present or past verb forms by omitting the relative pronoun and replacing the verb with:

- an *-ing* form, as in **4b**
- a prepositional phrase (often when the verb is *have*), as in **5b**

We form many *-ing* phrases from certain verbs. These *-ing* forms include:

arising from	containing	relating
concerning	corresponding to	requiring
consisting of	involving	resulting from

For more information on reduced adjective clauses, see the Resources, page R-31.

B

APPOSITIVES

6a *The Trumpet Major*, **which is a novel by T. Hardy,** was published in 1880.

6b *The Trumpet Major*, **a novel by T. Hardy,** was published in 1880.

7 The items were discovered at the Maya site of Rio Azul—**a city that at its height was home to 400,000**.

We can also add information to nouns using **appositives**. An appositive is usually a noun phrase. It can be seen as a kind of reduced adjective clause, as in **6a – 6b**.

An appositive can be very short, as **6b**.

Sometimes appositives are quite long and include other structures like prepositional phrases or adjective clauses, as in **7**.

We usually separate appositives from the rest of the sentence with commas, dashes, or parentheses.

For more information on appositives, see the Resources, page R-32.

GO ONLINE For more practice with reduced adjective clauses and appositives, go to the Online Practice.

17 | Noticing Reduced Adjective Clauses Underline the reduced adjective clauses in these sentences. Circle the main nouns they describe. `3.4 A`

SENTENCES FROM MAGAZINES

1. The writer refers to a recent (article) concerning the destruction of historic houses and homes.
2. The group's primary mission is to provide humanitarian[56] support to the local population, consisting mainly of Kosovo Albanians.
3. We participated in a ten-year software project involving many people.
4. According to a study done in Europe, many workers are asking their bosses to cut their hours and salary just to gain back some control over their lives.
5. The community health program is designed for families with young children.
6. Occupancy of the building, designed by Tokyo architect Fumihiko Maki, was set for late summer 2009.
7. Clients were asked to report any defects[57] discovered in the software.
8. The patient had difficulty with skills requiring long-term memory.
9. There are a number of potential problems arising from the new strategy.
10. The apartments, constructed in the 1970s with government funding, are not in good condition.
11. The number of factories with safety violations[58] far exceeded[59] the expectations of the inspectors.

Think about It Work with a partner to answer the questions and complete the chart below.

1. Which of the underlined adjective clauses above are non-defining? How do you know?
2. Rewrite the reduced adjective clauses from sentences 1–5 above as full adjective clauses in this chart.

Main noun	Relative pronoun	Verb	Rest of clause
1. *article*	*which/that*	*concerns*	*the destruction of historic houses and homes*
2.			
3.			
4.			
5.			

3. Look at Chart 1.4 B on page 15 on reduced adverb clauses. What is similar about the ways in which we form these two types of reduced clauses?

18 | Using Reduced Adjective Clauses Combine the sentences using reduced adjective clauses that describe the underlined main nouns. `3.4 A`

COMBINING IDEAS

1. The <u>results</u> are expected to be the best in the exam's 56-year history. Results are being collected from schools and colleges today.

   The <u>results</u> being collected from schools and colleges today are expected to be the best in the exam's 56-year history.

2. The newspaper article did not identify the <u>man</u>. The man was being questioned by police.
3. There have been several recent <u>studies</u>. They reveal variability[60] in the ingredients of vitamins and other dietary <u>supplements</u>[61]. These supplements are being sold in markets today.
4. The <u>customers</u> are not just there to send packages. The customers are waiting in line at German post offices.

5. The <u>garden</u> has been well cared for and is filled with flowers and vegetables. The garden is behind the house.

6. The study included 30 men who had been referred to a program for <u>patients</u>. The patients had heart failure.

7. The medical professionals reported no positive <u>changes</u>. No positive changes resulted from the programs they assessed.

8. A search of <u>articles</u> revealed that little attention has been paid to the topic. The articles were written in recent years.

9. Hublin is referring to the <u>period</u> when people started making a wider variety of tools. The period was beginning roughly 40,000 years ago in Europe.

10. We are studying behavior in <u>animals</u>. These animals have complex nervous systems.

19 | Usage Note: Phrases with Noun Phrase + *Of* + Noun Phrase Read the note. Then do Activity 20.

In academic writing, many common phrases follow the pattern **noun phrase + *of* + noun phrase**. Some common phrases include:

PHYSICAL DESCRIPTIONS		ABSTRACT QUALITIES		PROCESSES OR EVENTS (LASTING A LONG TIME)	
the surface of the size of the position of other parts of	+ noun phrase	the nature of the value of the use of the presence of	+ noun phrase	the development of the course of	+ noun phrase

1 Beneath **the surface of Mexico's Yucatan peninsula**[62] is a massive network of caves. (physical description)

2 There was no evidence that the results were affected by **the presence of medical conditions in the participants**. (abstract quality)

3 Political concerns deeply influenced **the course of public health policy**. (process lasting a long time)

20 | Noticing Prepositional Phrases Underline the prepositional phrases that describe nouns in these sentences. Draw an arrow to the nouns they describe. `3.4 A`

1. The national labor union[63] began a series <u>of marches</u> <u>in opposition</u>[64] <u>to the gas deal</u>.

2. In her research, she has surveyed farmers across the United States.

3. The health insurance program means that employees with fewer financial obligations don't have to earn as much as they once did.

4. There are several reasons that the development of technology has influenced the law.

5. The satellite images show how the shape of the coastline has changed over time.

6. The project took place over the course of five weeks.

7. The three service programs have complementary[65] methods, including the use of local teams of experts.

8. As people began to develop societal organizations, we can see an increase in the sophistication of the design of their structures.

> **F Y I**
>
> Some of the **prepositional phrases** that we use to describe nouns cannot easily be rephrased as adjective clauses. These prepositional phrases usually answer the question *what kind* or *which one*.
>
> State officials are reviewing the recent changes **in local government**. (What kind of changes?)
> (NOT: ~~State officials are reviewing the recent changes that are in local government.~~)

9. According to Jeff D. Smith, the value of the new technology lies in its ability to uncover potentially troublesome[66] engineering issues early in the process.

10. Recent research in Nebraska has shown that a combination of control measures can combine the strengths of each method while overcoming most disadvantages.

Think about It Which prepositional phrases in Activity 20 could be rewritten as full adjective clauses using *have* or *be*?

Write about It Choose four of the prepositional phrases in Activity 20 and write a sentence using each one.

The governor gave a speech <u>in opposition</u> to the new law.
People <u>with fewer financial obligations</u> are able to save more money.

21 | Using Appositives Rewrite each passage. Combine the sentences by rewriting the **bold** sentences as appositives. `3.4 B`

Famous People

1. For hundreds of years the main authority in Western medicine was Galen of Pergamon, who had been physician[68] to the Roman emperor. **Galen was a philosopher of the second century CE. The Roman emperor was Marcus Aurelius.**

   For hundreds of years the main authority in Western medicine was Galen of Pergamon, a philosopher of the second century CE who had been physician to the Roman emperor, Marcus Aurelius.

2. Lewis Carroll was a gifted photographer. **He was the author of *Alice's Adventures in Wonderland*. He was one of the best photographers of his time**.

3. Mark Saunders developed the computer forecasting model with his colleague. **Saunders is a climate physicist at University College in London. His colleague's name was Adam Lea.**

4. Mary Shelley wrote *Frankenstein*. **Shelley was a 21-year-old English writer. *Frankenstein* is a novel that people still read today**.

5. Alexander Hamilton lost both of his parents at a young age. **He was one of the founding fathers of the U.S.** His older brother went to work for a carpenter[69], while Alexander was taken into the home of Thomas Stevens. **The older brother was named James. Thomas Stevens was a family friend**.

6. Nicholas Humphrey is a distinguished scientist. **He is a psychologist and neuroscientist whose early work helped to pioneer[70] modern theories of intelligence**. But he is also a rebel. **He is an intellectual who is always willing to ask the difficult questions**.

7. Ozolua ruled the Kingdom of Benin in the late fifteenth and early sixteenth centuries. **It was an era of intensive Portuguese interaction with Benin**.

8. Admission to the World Trade Organization could be offered in return for major economic reforms[71]. **The World Trade Organization is known as the WTO**.

Mary Shelley

Think about It Work with a partner to answer these questions.

1. Which of the appositives in Activity 21 contain one or more prepositional phrases describing a noun?
2. Which contain an adjective clause?
3. Which sentences have two or more appositives?
4. Which appositive would most likely be in parentheses?

22 | Using Adjective Clauses Read the passage. Then write sentences with adjective clauses that describe the nouns in parentheses. Use information from the passage or your own ideas. Try to use a variety of adjective clause types (full, reduced, defining, and non-defining) and appositives. `3.4 A-B`

Employee Monitoring

Employers are increasingly using high-tech monitoring systems to influence decision making, and there are growing numbers of companies specializing in workplace monitoring. One such company, XPin Corp, helps employers analyze the efficiency of their workers by supplying them with high-tech ID badges. The badges contain sensors[72] and microphones that track the employees' movements and interactions with others throughout the day. XPin Corp can use the information to determine[73] how long employees spend on break and who they speak to the most. The devices even analyze posture[74] and body language. It should be noted that not all workers wear these ID badges. Employees are asked for permission before they are given the badges, and XPin Corp doesn't provide information to the employers about individual workers. Instead, the information is used to analyze the workplace as a whole. It helps employers arrange the workplace in a way that is more productive. For example, some businesses have discovered that employees are more productive when they can easily work together, so the furniture has been rearranged in a way to make collaboration[75] easier.

---

1. (employers) _Nowadays, there are many employers using high-tech monitoring systems._

2. (companies) _____

3. (XPin Corp) _____

4. (ID badges) _____

5. (information) _____

6. (devices) _____

7. (workers) _____

8. (businesses) _____

23 | Usage Note: Complex Noun Phrases Read the note. Then do Activity 24.

In academic writing, noun phrases often contain more than one (reduced) adjective clause (or other kind of clause), appositive, or prepositional phrase. These **complex noun phrases** can be arranged in a variety of ways. For example:

ONE ADJECTIVE CLAUSE INSIDE ANOTHER

1 Bank employees can learn how to process **a customer payment** | involving 10 to 20 steps | that have to be learned and practiced until the employee is competent.

Notice that the adjective clause in **1** also contains an adverb clause: *until the employee is competent.*

PREPOSITIONAL PHRASE + ADJECTIVE CLAUSE

2 They established **a program** | of exhibitions and lectures | that was designed for the community.

PREPOSITIONAL PHRASE + PREPOSITIONAL PHRASE (+ PREPOSITIONAL PHRASE)

3 Researchers are attempting to measure **the human health impacts** | of changes | in a variety | of natural systems.

24 | Noticing Complex Noun Phrases Underline the (reduced) adjective clauses in the **bold** noun phrases. Double-underline adjective clauses that are inside other adjective clauses. `3.4 A`

History of Technology

1. Many scientific endeavors are made possible by **technologies which <u>allow humans to travel to places we could not otherwise go</u>**, and by **scientific instruments with which we study nature in more detail than our natural senses allow**.

2. It was **the growth of the ancient civilizations which produced the greatest advances in technology and engineering, which in turn stimulated other societies to adopt new ways of living**.

3. Ancient Greek innovations[76] included **the groundbreaking invention of the watermill[77], which was the first human-made force that did not rely on muscle labor[78]**. Greek inventors also created **the earliest steam engine, which opened up entirely new possibilities for using natural forces whose full potential would not be exploited until the Industrial Revolution**.

4. **Naturally occurring glass, which was used by people across the globe for the production of sharp cutting tools,** was extensively traded during the Stone Age. But archeological evidence suggests that the first true glass was made in coastal north Syria, Mesopotamia, or ancient Egypt. The earliest known glass objects were **beads[79] from the mid-third millennium[80] BCE that were perhaps initially created as accidental byproducts of metalworking**.

5. A match is a tool for starting a fire. Typically, modern matches are made of small wooden sticks or stiff paper. One end is coated with **a material that can be ignited[81] by heat generated by striking the match against a surface. A note in the text *Cho Keng Lu*, written in 1366,** describes **a match used in China by "court ladies" in 577 CE during the conquest[82] of Northern Qi**.

6. A horseshoe is **a metal item designed to protect a horse's hoof from the wear that results from walking on hard surfaces**. Shoes are attached on the surface of **the hoof, which is similar to the human toenail, though much larger and thicker**. Historians have expressed differing opinions on the origin of the horseshoe. **The assertion[83] by some historians that the Romans invented "mule[84] shoes" sometime after 100 BCE** is supported by a reference by **Catullus, who died in 54 BCE**. However, this reference may have been to a kind of leather boot rather than to nailed horseshoes. There is **very little evidence of any sort that suggests the existence of nailed-on shoes prior to[85] 500 or 600 CE**.

horseshoe

Think about It Answer these questions with a partner.

1. Draw an arrow from each adjective clause in Activity 24 to the main noun it describes. Which adjective clause describes another entire clause, not just a noun phrase?

2. Three of the noun phrases in Activity 24 include prepositional phrases between the main noun and the adjective clause. Draw a box around those three prepositional phrases.

3. Look at the first noun phrase in passage 4 of Activity 24. It contains four prepositional phrases. Which ones are used to describe nouns? What is the function of the others?

4. Can you identify the overall sentence structure of passage 1 and of the first sentence in passage 6 in Activity 24? If you take out the complex noun phrases, are the sentences simple or complex?

Write about It Write sentences about technology. Use prepositional phrases and adjective clauses as indicated.

TECHNOLOGY

1. Nowadays, there are many _____*fuel-efficient cars*_____ _____*being manufactured by car companies*_____
                       main noun (phrase)   adjective clause
   _____*hoping to appeal to consumers*_____ _____*who want to save money on gas*_____.
                adjective clause   adjective clause

2. Today there are cameras _____ that take better pictures than the
                               prepositional phrase
   digital cameras _____.
                                  adjective clause

3. The best _____ are made _____
             main noun (phrase)   prepositional phrase
   _____ _____.
          prepositional phrase   prepositional phrase

4. _____ was invented _____
       main noun (phrase)   prepositional phrase
   _____.
                          adjective clause

5. The invention _____ _____
            prepositional phrase   adjective clause
   is _____.
                    rest of sentence

3.5 Expanding Noun Phrases with Noun Complements

Another way we can expand noun phrases is by adding *that* clauses and *to-* infinitive clauses after the **main noun**. We call these clauses **noun complements**. A noun complement completes the meaning of the noun.

A

THAT CLAUSES AS ADJECTIVE CLAUSES

1 The researchers investigated several **topics that would be interesting to eighth-grade students.**
(NOT a complete sentence: ~~Would be interesting to eighth-grade students.~~)

2 They asked for help with a **problem** (that) **they had created themselves.**
(NOT a complete sentence: ~~They had created themselves.~~)

THAT CLAUSES AS NOUN COMPLEMENTS

3a The researchers investigated the idea **that eighth-grade students would be interested in these topics.** (*That* is a connecting word only. The rest of the clause is complete without it.)

3b Eighth-grade students would be interested in these topics.

In Chart 3.3, we discussed **adjective clauses** with the relative pronoun *that*.

Notice that an adjective clause without *that* cannot stand on its own as a complete sentence, as in **1 – 2**.

That **clause noun complements** look similar to adjective clauses, but they are different. Like many adjective clauses, noun complement clauses contain the word *that*, as in **3a**. However, unlike an adjective clause, a noun complement clause without the word *that* can stand alone as a complete sentence, as in **3b**. It is not missing any necessary parts. The word *that* is a connecting word only.

Because the word *that* in a noun complement clause is a connecting word, it cannot be deleted.

B

COMPARE

4a He offered the **suggestion** that a good job is one that a worker can come back to when the economy has improved.

4b He **suggested** that a good job is one that a worker can come back to when the economy has improved.

5 This article highlights the **fact that more work needs to be done in the area of consumer education.** (A fact is something certain.)

6 Today's society operates around the **belief that people face the challenges of life.** (The information in the noun clause comes from a belief.)

That **clause noun complements** occur most commonly after certain nouns. These nouns include:

assumption	fact	notion	sense
belief	hypothesis	observation	suggestion
claim	idea	possibility	view
conclusion			

Notice that these nouns:

- are often singular abstract nouns related to verb or adjective forms of the same word (e.g., *believe–belief; possible–possibility; suggest–suggestion*), as in **4a – 4b**.
- often express a degree of certainty about the information in the *that* clause, as in **5**, or tell us about where the information came from, as in **6**.

C

TO- INFINITIVE CLAUSES AS NOUN COMPLEMENTS

7a The two groups have met several times in an **attempt to make a deal.**

7b The two groups **attempted** to make a deal.

8 We have lowered the levels of unemployment. We have given young people the **opportunity to get jobs.**

We can also add *to-* infinitive noun clause complements after some nouns. Nouns commonly followed by *to-* infinitive clauses include:

ability	decision	failure	right
attempt	desire	opportunity	tendency
capacity	effort	power	willingness

Notice that these nouns:

- are usually singular abstract nouns related to verb or adjective forms of the same word (e.g., *able–ability; fail–failure*), as in **7a – 7b**.
- often refer to actions, goals, or opportunities, as in **8**.

25 | Noticing *That* Clauses Underline the *that* clauses after nouns. Label them as adjective clauses (*AC*) or noun complements (*NC*). `3.5 A–B`

1. One can accept the necessity for a strong state and still believe that there should be institutions of local self-government. Most people accept the idea <u>*NC* that we ought to have institutions of local self-government as well as state government</u>.

Mount Kilimanjaro

2. The article came to the conclusion that globalization[86] has both a dark and a bright side. The authors made the argument that the advantages of globalization outweigh[87] the disadvantages.

3. The aspect of the paper that has attracted the most attention is the claim that the retreat[88] of the Mount Kilimanjaro glaciers[89] can be explained by a reduction in rainfall rather than higher temperatures.

4. Although the two newly constructed surveys have demonstrated reasonably good results, they need to be tested further in future studies that involve more participants.

5. Only brief summaries have been reported for this major national study, and the reports exclude[90] information that would be helpful for evaluating the effectiveness of various programs.

6. It is a widely held assumption[91] that parents play an important role in the development of their children.

7. These small aircraft can be launched[92] in a matter of minutes. The key ingredient is an intelligent control system that makes operating one aircraft as easy as operating ten.

8. Einstein's equations[93] supported the observation that galaxies appear to be flying apart.

9. Eighty-one percent of the population shares the opinion that the government could deliver more services for less money.

10. Thomas Charles Hope determined why icebergs[94] could float in an experiment that now bears his name (Hope's experiment).

Think about It Copy the noun described by each noun clause in the activity above. Then, if possible, write a corresponding verb form of the noun.

1. idea (no corresponding verb)   *2. conclusion— conclude*

26 | Noticing *To-* Infinitive Clauses Choose a *to-* infinitive clause from the box to add to each sentence. `3.5 C`

1. The ability _d_ may ultimately[96] determine whether patients can obtain hospital care and how long the care will last.

2. The new banking program offers people the chance ____, and also to borrow at low interest rates[97].

3. The weather forecast this morning confirmed their decision ____.

4. Three reliable witnesses can confirm the event and I have no reason ____.

a. to get the support of the public
b. to wait for more consistent[95] wind
c. to doubt them
d. to pay for hospitalization
e. to study inland areas
f. to enter the building after the offices were closed
g. to understand outer space
h. to save as much or as little as they can afford
i. to explain various issues regarding the Internet and its contents

5. The reporters had to obtain the building manager's permission ____.

6. Some officials have expressed unhappiness with the governor's plan and what they view as his failure ____.

7. The technology writer has made a significant attempt ____, and for the most part has done so quite clearly.

8. From ancient Native American observatories[98] at Chaco Canyon to current facilities such as the Very Large Array observatory in Socorro, this permanent exhibition explores the human effort ____.

9. Researchers are interested in focusing on coastal sites. Until now there has been a tendency[99] ____.

Think about It Copy the noun described by each *to-* infinitive clause in Activity 26. Then, if possible, write a corresponding verb or adjective form of the noun.

1. ability—able (adj)

27 | Using *To-* Infinitive and *That* Clauses as Noun Complements Think about the issue of privacy in the workplace and complete each sentence with your own ideas. Use a *to-* infinitive or *that* clause. (Different answers are possible). **3.5 A–C**

1. Many employers are concerned about the possibility
   that employees are wasting time at work _____.

2. Some employers have made the decision
   _____.

3. Some employers have made the claim that
   _____.

4. Some workers feel that their employers don't have the right _____.

5. Some employees have a tendency _____.

6. Employees should make an effort _____.

7. Employees may not like the fact _____.

8. Companies have the power _____.

> **GET READY TO READ**
> You are going to read an article about workplace email monitoring.

28 | Reading Read the *New York Times* article. Then do the tasks on page 109.

YOU'VE GOT INAPPROPRIATE MAIL

by Lisa Guernsey

1 Andrew Quinn, a systems manager at a toy company near Montreal, has learned more about his fellow employees than he ever wanted to know. He has found that one co-worker has a weakness for herbal remedies, another likes jokes about women drivers, and another checks the lottery numbers each morning.

2 He knows these things because software on the company's computer network enables him to monitor not only every website that his employees browse[100], but every email message that they send or receive. With a few clicks, he can open a window on a computer screen and see the senders, recipients[101], and subject headings of each message.

3   Ritvik Toys is just one of many companies that look at workers' correspondence[102] on a routine basis. And the number of companies regularly doing so is soaring[103]. Managers give a variety of reasons for installing such software. Some, like Mr. Quinn, are on the lookout for[104] oversize email attachments that clog[105] networks. Others seek to discourage employees from using their systems for personal activities. And others want to make sure employees are not sending messages that disturb or hurt others.

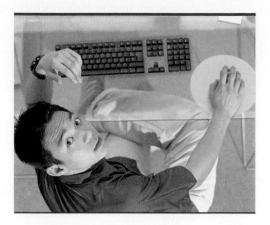

4   Whatever the reason, the monitoring raises ethical[106] questions. Should managers really be peeking into people's private lives like this? And what should they do with sensitive information that, if made public, could jeopardize[107] an employee's career?

5   Like most manufacturers, Ritvik relies on the Internet to get the job done. Its 200 salaried employees file purchase orders, do product research, and make sales calls by email and on the Web. This week, a month after installing the software, Ritvik planned to put into practice a new policy requiring employees to use good judgment in their use of the network. It will also warn them that their email messages may be monitored.

6   Revealing that employees are being monitored is a good business practice, according to the American Management Association. Mr. Quinn is hoping that monitoring will be a powerful deterrent[108] and convince employees not to waste company time and bandwidth[109]. From what he has seen, at least 50 percent of the company's email is not related to work. And, he says, certain names keep appearing on lists of heavy email users, including an employee he has nicknamed the herbal-remedy guy, who has spent hours looking at the website of Deepak Chopra.

7   Others send jokes. "Look at this guy," he said, as he pointed to a subject heading titled "Joke of the Day" and another titled "Women Drivers." He scrolled[110] further, displaying even more jokes all sent by the same employee. "That's all he's been doing for the last hour," Mr. Quinn said, throwing up his hands in irritation. It is not his responsibility to monitor employee productivity, he said, but he cannot help but wonder how such people get their work done.

8   Ritvik employees had mixed emotions about the policy. "It is an invasion of your privacy, I guess," said Karen Trainor, the company's North American distribution supervisor. "If someone knows everything you are writing, that's not really fair." But, she added, she had heard that the company was trying to strengthen its networks and might need to check email traffic to do so. Besides, she has known Mr. Quinn for years and trusts him. "If that's what they are doing, I guess they have a reason to do it," she said.

9   A few lawyers have argued that a casual email exchange is more like a telephone conversation than a printed memo and should be protected in the same way that wiretap[111] laws generally prohibit government agencies and some businesses from secretly listening to personal conversations.

10   "Would you entrust[112] the government with this kind of information?" asked Jeremy E. Gruber, legal director for the National Workrights Institute at a recent New York Bar Association discussion on electronic privacy. "Why do we think that employers will use it in a wonderful way?"

11   Mr. Quinn acknowledges that monitoring systems can be abused. For example, he has no trouble imagining a network manager who takes offense[113] at an email message most people would consider harmless—and who makes life difficult for the sender as a result. "You have to ask: whose opinion draws the line?" Mr. Quinn said.

Talk about It Work with a partner. Discuss how each of these people from the article in Activity 28 feels about email monitoring. Write notes about each person in the chart.

Andrew Quinn	
Karen Trainor	
Jeremy Gruber	

Think about It Underline these structures in the reading in Activity 28.

prepositional phrase describing a noun phrase (paragraph 1)

verb complement *that* clause (paragraph 1)

full defining adjective clause (paragraph 2)

verb complement *to-* infinitive clause (paragraph 3)

reduced defining adjective clause with *-ing* (paragraph 5)

appositive (paragraph 5)

reduced non-defining adjective clause with *-ing* verb form (paragraph 6)

full non-defining adjective clause (paragraph 6)

reduced adjective clause with *-ed/-en* verb form (paragraph 7)

noun complement *to-* infinitive clause (paragraph 7)

noun complement *that* clause (paragraph 9)

WRITING ASSIGNMENT II

Follow steps A–D to write a summary of and response to the article in Activity 28.

A | Planning Write answers to these questions.

1. What is the topic of the article?
2. What are the main questions raised by the article?
3. What opinions are presented in the article? How are they supported?

B | Writing Write a summary of the article "You've Got Inappropriate Mail." Conclude your summary with a brief response that explains your opinion about the topic. Use some noun phrases that include (reduced) adjective clauses, appositives, and/or noun complements. Review the information on writing a summary and response in Unit 2, page 76.

In the article "You've Got Inappropriate Mail," Lisa Guernsey . . .

C | Peer Reviewing Share your writing with a partner. Answer these questions about your partner's summary and response.

1. Did your partner include all of the important ideas from the article? Were these ideas correctly reported? Are there any ideas that should be added?

2. Did your partner include the right amount of detail? Should any details be removed or added?

3. Is your partner's opinion on the topic clearly explained? If not, what was unclear?

4. Did your partner expand noun phrases with (reduced) adjective clauses, appositives, and/or noun complements? Underline any examples of these. Were all of them used correctly?

D | Revising Follow these steps to revise your summary and response.

1. Using your partner's feedback, rewrite your summary and response.

2. Check your writing for mistakes and clarity. Underline any long noun phrases. Did you use some (reduced) adjective clauses, appositives, and/or noun complements? Make sure that there are no mistakes with them. Make any final corrections necessary.

3.6 Condensing Information: Referring Back to Previous Ideas

One way to condense information in academic writing is by using **pronouns and other noun phrases to refer back** to previous ideas. This avoids repetition, improves the flow of ideas, and helps make writing cohesive.

A

1 The main concern for computerized flight systems is reliability. **This** is because if the computer has problems, the pilot may be unable to control the airplane.

2 Over the years, the program trained hundreds of volunteers in basic medical procedures. **These volunteers** used their skills to help local communities. (*volunteers* = repeated noun)

3 Over 500 women attended the conference in India in December 2010. **This event** was held in Bangalore and featured leaders from industrial, academic, and government communities. (*Event* is a synonym for *conference*.)

4a Three hundred subjects in Detroit and Chicago were sent a letter and a survey. **Those in Chicago** also received a phone call. (*those* + prepositional phrase)

4b . . . **Those who chose to participate** were asked to sign a consent form. (*those* + adjective clause)

4c . . . **Those choosing to participate** were asked to sign a consent form. (*those* + reduced adjective clause)

Writers often use **this**, **these**, and **those** in academic writing to refer back to previous ideas. We use them:

- as pronouns, as in **1**
- as determiners with a repeated noun, as in **2**
- as determiners with a synonym, as in **3**
- as pronouns before a prepositional phrase or (reduced) adjective clause, as in **4a – 4c**

That is also used to refer back to previous ideas, but it is more common in speaking than in writing.

B

5 Each person received a five-page survey with a cover letter. **The latter** contained details about the aims and method of the study. (*the latter* = cover letter)

6 We examined test scores of students in the morning program and students in the evening program. **The former group** had slightly better scores on average. (*the former group* = students in the morning program)

Sometimes writers use *the latter* and *the former* to refer back to previous ideas. *The latter* refers to the second of two ideas mentioned, as in **5**.

The former refers to the first of two ideas mentioned, as in **6**.

We usually use these words as pronouns to refer back to a noun, as in **5**.

It is also possible to use them with a repeated noun or a synonym, as in **6**.

GO ONLINE For more practice with referring back, go to the Online Practice.

29 | Noticing Pronouns and Other Noun Phrases That Refer Back Read the passages. Underline each pronoun or other noun phrase that refers back to a previous idea. `3.6 A–B`

RESEARCH RESULTS

1. Cell differentiation[114] determines the properties and characteristics of cells as they develop into eyes, skin, bone, etc. <u>This process</u> is an important area of research for cell biologists.

2. Research studies must involve (a) the introduction of a treatment that is under control of the researchers and (b) a meaningful comparison situation. To address the latter issue, true experiments use a control group that does not receive the intervention[115].

3. People of different ages were surveyed about their multicultural[116] experiences. Those respondents[117] in the 31–40 year age category had significantly more multicultural experiences than those in the 20–30 year age group.

4. Defensive measures[118] are an inefficient way to reduce the environmental impact of wood pests[119], but nations have not been able to agree on a strategy to fight the invaders[120]. Two promising exceptions to this lack of international agreement are the ISPM and IMO standards. The former were developed in response to the large number of forest pests that have been spread in untreated[121] wood.

5. Participants reported on any pain they had experienced within the past year. Those who reported work-related pain or discomfort in a particular body part were asked to rate the severity[122].

6. The data was analyzed using scores that have been developed recently. The low-anxiety group included adolescents[123] who scored below 39 and the high-anxiety group included those who scored above 49. Those scoring between 39 and 49 were excluded from the analysis.

7. While using the Internet to search for information is positively linked with later academic performance, Internet use for recreational[124] and social purposes has a negative impact on academic achievement. These results are generally consistent with[125] earlier studies.

8. It is expected that most states will revise their permitting processes to comply[126] with federal law. Those which fail to do so risk losing federal highway funds[127].

Think about It Answer these questions with a partner.

1. Circle the noun phrase, clause, or sentence above that each underlined phrase refers to. Which of the underlined phrases refer back to a noun phrase? Which refers back to a clause? Which refers back to a whole sentence?

2. Can you find any other words or phrases above that the writers used to refer back to a previous idea? What are they?

   In number 1, "area of research" refers back to "cell differentiation."

30 | Using Pronouns and Other Noun Phrases That Refer Back Write a sentence to follow up on each idea. Use a pronoun or other noun phrase from the box or your own idea to refer back to a previous idea or concept. (Different answers are possible.) 3.6 A–B

ADVANTAGES OF MODERN TECHNOLOGY

1. There have been major advancements[128] in medical technology in recent years. *These technological improvements have saved many lives.* _____

   _____

2. Students are able to complete courses and sometimes entire degree programs online. _____

   _____

the former
the latter
these improvements
this convenient method
   of communication
this method of learning

3. Patients can now easily contact their doctors by email. _____

   _____

4. It is easier to maintain patient records, and the cost of many medical procedures has fallen.

   _____

   _____

5. Mobile technology allows employees to work away from the office, and improved software allows them to collaborate easily with co-workers in different locations. _____

   _____

DISADVANTAGES OF MODERN TECHNOLOGY

6. Many employees are expected to check work email and messages long after they have left the office. *This constant access to work communication interferes with people's personal lives.* OR *This expectation by employers is unreasonable.*

access
advancements
behavior
dependence
desire
distraction
expectation
impatience
need
theft

7. As technology advances, people become more and more dependent on their computers and phones. _____

   _____

8. Customers have grown used to instant communication, so they expect all of their concerns and complaints to be dealt with immediately.

   _____

   _____

9. The number of successful hacking[129] attempts has been growing in recent years, and large amounts of private data have been stolen. _____

   _____

10. People feel pressured to constantly respond to emails, messages, and phone calls, even when they are in the middle of a project. _____

   _____

11. Because the Internet is anonymous[130], many people are rude and unpleasant online.

_____

_____

12. Students have trouble focusing on their studies because of their computers, phones, and gaming devices.

_____

_____

Think about It Underline the idea that each pronoun or other noun phrase you chose in Activity 30 refers back to.

31 | Expanding Sentences and Condensing Ideas Use ideas from this box to write a short paragraph about the advantages of online courses. Include adjective clauses, pronouns, and other noun phrases to refer back to ideas. Try to include a complex noun phrase. Look back at Charts 3.1–3.6 if necessary.

> Online courses are flexible.
>
> A student can study at any time.
>
> Some students work. They can arrange the class around their schedule.
>
> Some students have families. They can complete degree programs. In the past, they might not have been able to complete a degree program.
>
> Students have direct access to a professor.
>
> Some students are shy. They can ask questions. They don't have to speak in front of others. They can get answers back almost immediately.

One major advantage of online courses is their flexibility, which allows busy working students to arrange classes around their schedules. . . .

FINAL WRITING ASSIGNMENT
Write an Advantages/Disadvantages Essay

Your Task

Write an essay about the advantages and disadvantages of workplace monitoring of employees by employers. Consider various types of monitoring, such as social media profiles, email, cameras in the workplace, and tracking software. Support your opinions with summary information from the reading on pages 107–108 as well as information from other sources and from your own experience. Include your own opinions on the topic.

Alternative Task

Write an essay about the advantages and disadvantages of another topic of your choice (for example, studying abroad, providing government support for the poor, or outlawing cars in city centers). Research the topic, and use summary information from multiple sources as well as information from your own experience as support for your opinions.

GO ONLINE Go to the Online Writing Tutor for a writing model and to write your assignment.

A | Writing Note: Brainstorming Read the note. Then do Activity B.

Charts and outlines help you brainstorm ideas before you begin writing an essay. It is important to write down anything you can think of, even though you might not use it in your essay. It is also important to put the ideas in your own words.

B | Brainstorming with a Chart Use this chart to help you start organizing your thoughts. In each box, include facts, statistics, or quotes that support your ideas.

Advantages	
Disadvantages	
My opinion	

C | Writing Note: Introductions and Conclusions Read the note. Then do Activity D.

USING A SUMMARY AS AN INTRODUCTION

Many essays are based on readings. One way to use a reading is to include a summary of it in the introduction to your essay. Then you can respond to the reading in the body paragraphs of your essay and/or add more support from other sources, such as articles, graphs, or charts.

(For more information on summary writing, see Unit 2, page 54.)

USING THE CONCLUSION TO UNIFY YOUR ESSAY

The conclusion for an essay often includes a restatement of the thesis. This restatement can rephrase, but should not simply repeat, the thesis. Other features of a good conclusion may include:

- key words and phrases from the thesis to unify the essay
- a summary of the main points from the body of the essay (but restated a little differently)
- suggestions, advice, or a warning to readers about the consequences of not following any advice given
- something to think about after the reader has finished the essay

D | Analyzing Introductions and Conclusions Read this student's essay about the advantages and disadvantages of using instant replay video in soccer games. Identify the introduction, body paragraphs, and conclusion. Then answer the questions on page 115 and compare answers with a partner.

Why FIFA Needs Instant Replay

"The answer as to whether FIFA (Fédération Internationale de Football Association) and the game of soccer can benefit from the use of instant replay at the World Cup is undoubtedly . . . of course they can," says sportswriter Jason Barmasse in his article "Implementing video replay at the World Cup." Barmasse cites examples from the 2014 FIFA World Cup, in which videos demonstrated that referees had made incorrect calls, and he examines the difficulties of using instant replays to assist referees in making decisions at important soccer matches. He then goes on to outline a proposal for how the use of replays could be implemented, including limiting the number of replays allowed in a match as well as the types of situations that could lead to using video technology. Opponents of instant replay assert[131] that it would change the game of soccer forever; however, as this essay will argue, the resulting changes would make the game fairer to both teams and improve its public image.

Soccer players pride themselves on a fast-action game, in which the momentum[132] of play can shift in an instant. A possible disadvantage of using instant replays is that the time it takes to review a play could slow down the game. In reality, however, time is also often wasted when players argue against a call by the officials. Since replay is very fast these days, a decision could be made by a special video official in the same amount of time that the players use to argue their cases with the field referee. Any time taken can be added to the stoppage time at the end of the half, as is current practice. Furthermore, as Barmasse proposes, the use of replays can be limited to "game-changing" incidents, such as controversial goals and penalties. These events often stop play anyway, and even if they do not, the accuracy of the call is worth the investment of a small amount of time.

The main way that instant replay would change the game is by decreasing human error and the opportunities that arise[133] from these errors. Diego Maradona's famous goal in the 1986 World Cup match of Argentina against England was the first goal of the game. Later replays clearly showed that Maradona had used his hand, so the goal should not have counted. Opponents of replay say that capitalizing on[134] such mistakes by the officials is all part of the game. However, the English team, who lost the game by one goal, would likely support the idea that the referee's decisions should be based on the most and best information available. The teams are more likely to be treated justly when the referee or a special video official can review and act on a controversial play. Barmasse asserts that the "purpose of officials has forever been to make the correct call, and . . . replay technology only serves as [a] method of ensuring a proper match result." There will always be miscalls, even with instant replay, and players will always capitalize on them. Using technology to reduce the number and severity of miscalls will result in a fairer game.

Opponents of the use of video replay do not want the technology to change the game, but it already has. Replays are shown in the stadiums and on television, repeatedly and from a variety of perspectives, but the officials cannot act on them, even when they know that they were not in a good position to make an objective call. The immediate protests against controversial decisions following the individual 2014 World Cup matches, as discussed by Barmasse, demonstrate that much of the public sees the way the games are officiated as unfair, especially to teams that are not favored to do well. To counter that view and to help ensure a more honest outcome for all involved, World Cup officials should have access to video replay. From that, as Barmasse says, "FIFA and the game of soccer can benefit."

Works Cited

Barmasse, Jason. "Implementing video replay at the World Cup." *The Fields of Green*. 20 June 2014. Web. 30 June 2015. <http://thefieldsofgreen.com/2014/06/20/implementing-video-replay-at-the-world-cup/>

Kiernan, Paul. "FIFA Head Proposes Rough Guidelines for Instant Replay." *Wall Street Journal*. 27 June 2014. Web. 30 June 2015. <www.wsj.com/articles/fifa-head-sepp-blatter-proposes-rough-guidelines-for-instant-replay-1403916530>

Nipper, Nathan. "Bosnia Elimination Should Renew Calls to FIFA For Instant Replay." *World Soccer Talk*. 21 June 2014. Web. 30 June 2015. <http://worldsoccertalk.com/2014/06/21/bosnian-elimination-should-renew-calls-to-fifa-for-instant-replay/>

QUESTIONS

Introduction

1. Underline and label the hook. What makes this hook interesting?
2. Does the summary include information that relates to the rest of the essay?
3. Underline and label the thesis statement.

Body

4. What is the main idea of the second paragraph? How does the writer support that idea?
5. What is the main idea of the third paragraph? How does the writer support that idea?

Conclusion

6. Underline and label the restatement of the thesis. Which key words are used?
7. Does the writer offer any recommendations?
8. How does this conclusion help unify this essay?

E | Writing Note: Essay Organization Study the diagrams of possible ways to organize an advantages/disadvantages essay. Then do Activity F.

BLOCK	POINT BY POINT
INTRODUCTION hook summary or general statements thesis statement	**INTRODUCTION** hook summary or general statements thesis statement
BODY ¶ 1 advantages only (or disadvantages only) topic sentence detailed support	**BODY ¶ 1** an advantage and disadvantage of one aspect of the topic topic sentence detailed support
BODY ¶ 2 disadvantages only (or advantages only) topic sentence detailed support	**BODY ¶ 2** an advantage and disadvantage of another aspect of the topic topic sentence detailed support
BODY ¶ 3, ¶ 4, ¶ 5, ETC. your opinion on workplace monitoring topic sentence summary of research as support concluding sentence	**BODY ¶ 3, ¶ 4, ¶ 5, ETC.** another advantage and disadvantage, or a focus on your opinion topic sentence detailed support
CONCLUSION connection back to thesis possibly: summary of main points advice and/or warning refer back to hook to unify essay	**CONCLUSION** connection back to thesis possibly: summary of main points advice and/or warning refer back to hook to unify essay

F | Organizing Your Essay Decide how you would like to organize your essay. Then draw your own diagram and write your ideas in each section.

G | Writing a First Draft Using information from your diagram, write a first draft of your essay. Try to use some of the structures that you have practiced in this unit.

H | Peer Reviewing When you have finished writing your first draft, share it with a partner.

Checklist for revising the first draft

When you review your partner's essay and discuss your own, keep these questions in mind.
1. Does the introduction grab your interest with a hook? If not, how could it be improved?
2. Is information from the reading(s) summarized well? Is it used to support opinions?
3. Are any quotes from the reading(s) used? If so, are they properly presented (see page R-57)?
4. Are the advantages and disadvantages clearly presented? Are there any that you think could or should be added or removed?
5. Is the writer's opinion on the subject clear?
6. Does the conclusion have a clear connection back to the thesis?
7. Does the author leave the reader with something to think about?

I | Writing the Second Draft Using your partner's feedback, write a second draft that includes all of your changes.

J | Proofreading Check your essay for the forms in Chart 3.7. Make any final corrections necessary.

3.7 Summary Chart for Proofreading

PROOFREADING QUESTIONS	EXAMPLES
Have you expanded or condensed information where appropriate by writing complex noun phrases? You can do this with: • **adjective clauses** with relative pronouns (*who, which, that, whose*, or preposition + *which* or *whom*), as in **1 – 6**	**1** An architect is a person **who plans, designs, and oversees the construction of buildings.** **2** The ancient village has been reconstructed, and inside the houses are tools and other items **which the people used for their everyday needs.** **3** The new building should be located in an area **that is convenient for all of the residents.** **4** Edwin Booth did not know the identity of the man **whose life he had saved.** **5** Alabama has an average of 35 days each year **in which the temperature falls below the freezing point.** **6** Napoleon held a dinner for the local farmers, **with whom he was celebrating a new agreement.**
• **reduced adjective clauses** with *-ing* or *-ed / -en* forms or prepositional phrases, as in **7 – 9**	**7** By 1878 there were 25 families **living in the valley at Knox Corner.** **8** *A Brief History of Time* is a popular-science book **written by British physicist Stephen Hawking.** **9** Our study found that the largest educational gains were among people **with some college education but without degrees.**
• **appositives**, as in **10**	**10** Pierre Bouguer, **a man would become known as the father of naval architecture**, won the competition.
• other **prepositional phrases that describe nouns**, as in **11**	**11** The fact that someone remains silent is no proof of their lack of knowledge of a specific piece of information.
Have you condensed information where appropriate by referring back with pronouns, as in **12,** or other noun phrases, as in **13**?	**12** Throughout the eighteenth century, Amsterdam was heavily influenced by French culture. **This** is reflected in the architecture of that period. **13** The new program allows scientists to easily share knowledge with others around the world. **The access to information this has provided** has been an important benefit to researchers.
Have you expanded any noun or verb phrases with **complements**? These include: • *that* clause complements, as in **14 – 15**	**14** Employers know **that when wages decrease, workers will put less effort into their jobs.** **15** Liszt left his job as president of the Royal Academy because he was of the opinion **that his colleagues could do the job without him.**
• *to-* infinitive clause complements, as in **16 – 17**	**16** Tasman had intended **to go north**, but the winds were against him, so he headed east. **17** The more complex games have a tendency **to be more popular because children find them interesting.**
• *-ing* clause complements, as in **18** • *wh-* clause complements, as in **19**	**18** David Ricardo began **working with his father at the age of 14.** **19** Galileo explained **why rocks dropped from a tower fall straight down even if the earth rotates.**

4

Making Comparisons

Do not compare yourself with anybody. Compare yourself with yourself, for yourself and by yourself.

—IFEANYI ENOCH ONUOHA,
EDUCATOR AND AUTHOR
(1984–)

Talk about It What does the quotation above mean? Do you agree or disagree?

WARM-UP

A | Read these statements and check (✓) *Agree* or *Disagree*. Then discuss your answers with a partner.

Personality

	AGREE	DISAGREE
1. People who have the same interests tend to have similar personalities. For example, those who like sports are more extroverted[1], **whereas** those who like to read are more introverted[2].	☐	☐
2. Everyone knows that first impressions are important. **While** you cannot learn everything about people in the first moments of meeting them, you can learn the most important aspects of their personalities.	☐	☐
3. Personality tests can provide valuable information about our potential strengths and weaknesses. **However**, personality is not fate. We can always change.	☐	☐
4. It is possible to gain an accurate impression of someone's personality just by looking at a picture of them. **In the same way**, you can learn a lot about someone just by speaking to them on the phone for a couple of minutes.	☐	☐
5. There are certain traits[3] we are born with that do not change over time. If you are shy as a young adult, you will stay that way for the rest of your life. **Unlike** our exterior appearance, our interior selves change little throughout adulthood.	☐	☐
6. Certain personality types are **more likely** to succeed in certain careers. You shouldn't pursue[4] a career that doesn't suit your personality.	☐	☐
7. The personalities of good friends are usually very **similar**.	☐	☐

B | The words and phrases in blue above signal relationships between ideas. Write them according to the kind of relationship they show.

Contrast (differences) _____

Similarity _____

[1] See page V–7 for the Vocabulary Endnotes for this unit.

4.1 Overview of Making Comparisons

When writers **compare**, they look at similarities and differences.

A

MAKING COMPARISONS WITHIN SENTENCES

1 On average, Neanderthals had brains that were **larger** than those of people living today. But this difference is likely due to their **greater** overall body size.

2 Scientists work together in many different ways, some of which are **more easily** understood than others.

3 São Paulo, Brazil is the city with **the greatest** number of Portuguese language speakers in the world.

4 In many ways, a giant tiger and a house cat are surprisingly **similar**.

5 Many words are spelled **differently** in American and British English.

6 Some animals are difficult to see because they have colors and patterns that **resemble** the things around them.

7 Our study examined **similarities** and **differences** among teachers around the world.

8 A study of people living in the city found that 15 percent lived in government housing, **whereas** 60 percent lived in homes they owned.

Comparisons can be made within sentences in a number of ways. For example, we can use:

- **comparative adjectives** (+ *than*), as in **1**

- **comparative adverbs** (+ *than*), as in **2**

- **superlative adjectives**, as in **3**

- other **adjectives**, as in **4**

- other **adverbs**, as **5**

- **verbs**, as in **6**

- **noun phrases**, as in **7**

- adverb clauses with **subordinators** like *whereas* or *while*, as in **8**

MAKING COMPARISONS ACROSS SENTENCES

9 In the U.S., the purpose of master's programs is to prepare for doctoral programs, to provide the knowledge necessary for teaching in middle and high schools, and to train highly qualified workers and researchers. **In comparison**, the purpose of doctoral programs is to train scientists, faculty members, and researchers.

Often, however, writers need to compare ideas across sentences. This is sometimes done with **linking adverbials**, as in **9**.

---

1 | Noticing Comparisons Underline the forms used for comparison. **4.1 A**

Generational <u>Differences</u> in the United States

The people born between 1946 and 1964 in the U.S. are called baby boomers, and their children born between 1981 and 1995 are called millennials. The two generations <u>are</u> often <u>compared</u>, with one of <u>the most obvious</u> <u>differences</u> being that millennials grew up in the age of the Internet, whereas most baby boomers never saw a computer until they reached adulthood. Another important difference that may not be quite so obvious is that millennials are less affluent[5] than their parents. They have higher unemployment rates and higher student debt rates. In fact, they are the first generation in a long time to be less well-off than the one before. Perhaps unsurprisingly, adult millennials **live with their parents in numbers that haven't been seen** since World War II. This may not be such bad news, however, because they also get along very well with their parents and **don't suffer from the troubled relationships that characterized[6] many late baby boomer families**. Despite the negative economic news, there are some positive aspects of life as a millennial. Driven by high unemployment rates and technological demand, millennials are enrolling in college in record numbers. In 1970, around 50 percent of high school graduates enrolled in college; **in 2012, about 66 percent did**. Combine that with increased rates of people in their 20s returning to college and graduate school, and millennials are fast becoming the most educated generation the U.S. has ever seen.

Think about It Write the words and phrases you underlined in Activity 1 in this chart.

WORDS AND PHRASES USED FOR COMPARING					
Verb	Comparative adjective	Superlative adjective	Noun or noun phrase	Subordinator	Linking adverbial

Share your chart with a partner. Work together to add another example (not from Activity 1) to each column.

Think about It Writers often compare things without using special comparative language. Look at the **bold** phrases in the reading passage on page 120. What is being compared?

2 | Usage Note: Softening and Strengthening Comparisons Read the note. Then do Activity 3.

	STRENGTHENING	SOFTENING
Writers often use **adverbials** like those in **1 – 5** to make **comparative adjectives and adverbs** stronger or softer.	**1** considerably longer **2** a great deal more difficult **3** significantly more slowly	**4** somewhat higher rates **5** slightly less often
Writers use **adverbials** like those in **6 – 11** to make *the same* stronger or softer.	**6** exactly the same amount as **7** precisely the same result	**8** in virtually the same way **9** practically the same response **10** nearly the same level **11** at approximately the same time
Writers use **adverbials** like those in **12 – 15** to make *different* stronger or softer.	**12** a completely different level **13** an entirely different industry	**14** in a somewhat different manner **15** a slightly different focus

For more information on softening and strengthening language, see Unit 5.

3 | Softening and Strengthening Comparisons Circle the adverbial in parentheses that best completes each passage. Then compare choices with a partner. (Different answers are possible.) [4.1 A]

RESEARCH RESULTS

1. In our employee satisfaction survey, nearly three of every four employees (73 percent) said that the direction of the company was significant in evaluating their employer. (Considerably / Completely) less crucial, according to results, were managers (48 percent), followed by pay and benefits (39 percent).

2. Several community colleges have tried to offer four-year degrees. In almost all of these cases, local universities have opposed the move. The universities' concern is that if a community college offers (completely / exactly) the same kinds of programs, there will be competition for students.

3. In a recent survey of health-care specialists, job satisfaction scores for security, pay, co-workers, and supervisors are all (slightly / approximately) lower than previous scores, but the decreases are not significant.

4. In New Guinea, a country with extreme language diversity[7], people who live on one side of a mountain may not be able to communicate with people who live less than a kilometer away on the other side. Although the two communities are close together, they may speak (entirely / a great deal) different languages.

5. We asked students whether they thought reference letters were an important part of a job search. Most students viewed the letters as useful tools for employers. For example, one student said, "They are a good way for employers to see how others in society view your character." Making (virtually / significantly) the same comment, another student said, "They are good to use as a character witness of the job applicant[8]."

6. In a review of beverages sold on elementary school campuses, researchers found that only 18 percent had any nutritional[9] value. (Significantly / Entirely) more items in public schools were nutritious as compared to private schools.

7. With a land area of about 7.7 million square kilometers[10]—(somewhat / completely) smaller than the U.S. at 9.2 million square kilometers—Australia is the world's smallest continent.

8. We must be careful when we base our conclusions on statements that have been translated. It is impossible to know if the item means (precisely / significantly) the same thing in another language.

9. Very few musicians, including successful performers, are equally good at playing more than one instrument. Someone whose primary instrument is flute[11] may not have an equal ability on trombone[12]. Different instruments require (an approximately / a completely) different set of skills.

Think about It Which adverbials from Activity 2 could replace the adverbial in each sentence in Activity 3 without significantly changing the meaning? Discuss as a class.

4.2 Making Comparisons with Linking Adverbials

Writers use **linking adverbials** to connect ideas between sentences. Certain linking adverbials are often used in comparisons to express contrast (differences) or similarity.

A

SHOWING CONTRAST

1 The school lunch program had a positive effect on all of the children; **however**, the nature of the effect was different for different age groups.

2 The majority of students in our study said they increased the volume on their music players when listening to favorite songs and while exercising. **Nevertheless**, most of these students will probably not have trouble with their hearing.

3 Misty Copeland began studying ballet at the relatively late age of 13. **Nonetheless**, she has risen to the top of her field.

4 Iceland uses the same time all year and does not change the clocks in the summer. Because it is so far north, sunset and sunrise times change by many hours over the year. The effect of changing the clock by one hour would, **in comparison**, be very small.

5 The frequency of strong tornadoes has not significantly increased. The number of weak tornados, **on the other hand**, has increased over time.

6 Surprisingly, the company did not make most of its money from selling automobiles. **Instead**, it made money selling parts to other automakers.

7 The army officers didn't believe that the rainstorm would offer their own soldiers any protection. **On the contrary**, they knew that the clouds would provide cover for the enemy.

8 People can get the vitamin D they need from 10–15 minutes in the sun three times a week. **Alternatively**, they can eat foods high in the vitamin or take it in pill form.

Writers often use **linking adverbials** to focus a reader's attention on a contrast.

However is the most common linking adverbial. We can use it to signal most contrasts. Sometimes *however* signals concession—meaning that the previous sentence is true, but the contrasting idea is also true, as in **1**.

We can also use *nevertheless* and *nonetheless* for concession, as in **2 – 3**.

We can use *in comparison*, *in contrast*, *by contrast*, and *on the other hand* to contrast the features of different things, as in **4**, or to introduce a contrasting idea about one thing, as in **5**.

Notice: **However** could replace any of the linking adverbials in **2 – 5**.

We can use *instead* or *rather* to signal that an idea replaces another idea, as in **6**. The sentence before *instead* or *rather* is usually negative.

We can use *on the contrary* after a negative sentence, as in **7**. The negative sentence often describes an incorrect idea, and the next sentence (with *on the contrary*) provides the correct information (according to the writer).

We can use *alternatively* to introduce a different action or choice, as in **8**. We often use *alternatively* with *can* or *could*.

B

SHOWING SIMILARITY

9 Five hundred years ago, people rejected the "new model" of a round Earth because it was based on mathematical calculations that they could not understand. **Similarly**, Galileo was punished for his view that the Earth went around the sun, instead of the other way around.

10 Regular physical exercise is an effective way to enhance physical abilities. **In the same way**, mental activity can help develop mental ability.

Some **linking adverbials** introduce a similarity.

We can use *similarly*, *in the same way*, *in a similar way*, *in a similar vein*, *along the same lines*, and *likewise* to signal that ideas or features are similar, as in **9 – 10**.

WARNING! Do not use too many linking adverbials in your writing. They focus the reader's attention on important contrasts or transitions, but too many of them can make writing seem weak.

For more information on linking adverbials, see the Resources, pages R-34–R-36.

GO ONLINE For more practice with linking adverbials, go to the Online Practice.

4 | Noticing Linking Adverbials Circle the linking adverbial in parentheses that best completes each excerpt. `4.2 A–B`

EXCERPTS FROM ACADEMIC WRITING

1. In recent years, there has been more support for environmentally friendly vehicles. (However / On the contrary), there are at this point only about 5,000 hybrid[13] cars in the city.

2. Public opinion responds to events and changes from year to year. (Instead / Nevertheless), some trends in recent years seem clear.

3. A ringspot virus was destroying all of Hawaii's papayas[14] in the 1980s and 1990s. Researchers from Cornell University engineered a tree that could resist the virus. Now, more than 80 percent of Hawaiian papaya trees cannot get ringspot virus. (Similarly / In comparison), on farms throughout China, farmers have been engineering a cotton plant that can resist the cotton bollworm, a pest[15] that has been damaging many cotton plants.

4. For the Solar Decathlon program, architecture and engineering students designed 100 energy-saving homes. The program has been a valuable learning environment for the students, and it has taught thousands of visitors about the art and science of green homebuilding. (Alternatively / On the other hand), these same 100 or so houses account for a very large investment on the part of universities, local businesses, and taxpaying citizens.

a house designed by a Solar Decathlon team

5. When people in developed countries think about people who face the biggest health challenges in the developing world, they often imagine a small boy in a rural, dusty village who is suffering from an exotic disease. (Alternatively / Instead), the more accurate image in the twenty-first century really should be that of a working-age woman living in an urban environment, suffering from diabetes[16] or stroke[17], problems that once occurred only in wealthy nations.

6. People think that emotion interferes with decision making, but actually it is in many ways essential to the process. Emotion determines which elements of a problem we focus on, which helps us discover solutions. (In contrast / Along the same lines), emotion is necessary for making judgments or evaluations.

7. The ability to control one's own emotions is not automatic. (On the other hand / On the contrary), it is a skill, and like other skills, it can be learned.

8. Nuclear energy policy differs among European Union countries, and some have no active nuclear power stations. (Nevertheless / On the contrary), France has a large number of these plants.

9. When astronomers are looking at the sky, they often adjust the telescope in order to get better results. (In the same way / In comparison), some math problems are also easier to solve when they are transformed through close examination.

10. Programs for improving health in rural areas work in different ways. They might provide seeds, fertilizer[18], and training to people so that they can maintain kitchen gardens. (On the contrary / Alternatively), training may focus on health-related goals directly.

11. Archeologists have found some interesting items on the site of the ancient city of Himera. More study of the items is required before their importance can be determined. (Nonetheless / Rather), it is already clear that these recent discoveries will be of major importance for understanding the history of the area.

12. Investigators have found that talking about psychological trauma[19] can help to relieve[20] the effects of the trauma. (In a similar vein / On the other hand), participants in our study who wrote about their personal feelings and opinions were also able to reduce some of their anxiety.

Think about It Which linking adverbials in Activity 4 could be replaced by *however*?

5 | Usage Note: Placement of Linking Adverbials Read the note. Then do Activity 6.

The most common placement of **linking adverbials** is before the subject of the second sentence. This signals the relationship between the two sentences (for example, a relationship of contrast).

1 The agency is issuing new standards for vehicles. **However**, these new standards may not be effective until next year. (adverbial + clause)

Writers sometimes choose to place linking adverbials, especially *however*, in other parts of the sentence. This can help maintain the cohesion of the writing.

2 Most of the students that we interviewed were in their first year of college. Some students, **however**, were high school seniors. (new subject + adverbial + rest of clause)

3 Many animals occasionally wake up from winter sleep to eat food that they have stored ahead of time. Bears, **on the other hand**, usually sleep through the winter without waking. (new subject + adverbial + rest of clause)

We also sometimes use linking adverbials:

- after other phrases that link back to the previous sentence
- after pronoun + *be* or *there* + *be*

4 The French name *pomme de terre* translates as "apple of the earth," and usually refers to the potato. **In this case**, **however**, it refers to a similar vegetable common in Minnesota.

5 Rails are small birds that are generally weak fliers. **They are**, **nevertheless**, able to cover long distances.

6 | Noticing Placement of Linking Adverbials Underline the linking adverbial(s) in each passage.
`4.2 A–B`

NATURE VS. NURTURE[21]

1. Discussions about nature and nurture relate to the importance of the traits that an individual is born with (nature) versus[22] the traits that are acquired from experience (nurture). Many scientists feel that the distinction between nature and nurture is no longer useful because of recent discoveries in genetics[23]. Nevertheless, nature versus nurture debates are still quite common among the public.

2. At one extreme, some philosophers once believed that all children were born the same, and that all behavioral traits develop during life. This idea, however, is not taken seriously in the modern age. The extreme opposite view—that environment plays no role in a person's behavior—is equally unacceptable.

3. One major change in the nature versus nurture discussion has been the definition of *nurture*. At one time, *nurture* referred to[24] the influence of the home environment, especially the mother. In recent times, however, *nurture* often refers more generally to environment. It may include school or friends or cultural influences such as television.

4. Another complication[25] in the nature versus nurture issue is the definition of *nature*. Genes clearly influence both physical and behavioral traits, but genes themselves are influenced by changes in the body. This can be demonstrated by looking at a physical trait like height. A child may have tall parents and genes for above-average height, but that child cannot grow to full height without adequate nutrition. Similarly, genes for behavioral traits are influenced by the physical environment both before and after birth.

5. One way to look at the relative contribution of genes and environment is to study twins. There are several different kinds of twin studies. Some of them involve studying identical twins who have been raised in different homes. Identical twins have the same genes, so this kind of study should be very effective at separating the influence of genes and environment. There are, however, some problems with these studies. For one thing, it is preferable for scientific studies to include large numbers of people, but this has not been true of twin studies. Another problem with studies of identical twins is that the twins are sometimes raised in environments that are very similar. Many studies have shown that identical twins have similar intelligence even when they are raised apart. However, if both twins are raised by families with similar income and education levels, the role of genetics is less clear.

identical twins

6. Another way that scientists study twins is by looking at fraternal twins—these are twins who are *not* identical. Like all siblings, they share only half of their genes. But because they are the same age and raised in the same home, studying their differences provides important information about the influence of genes. These kinds of studies, however, will miss small but potentially important aspects of the individual's environment. Events such as illness, exposure[26] to chemicals, or experiences at school or in places where the twins are not together may all influence behavior in ways that the study will not catch.

7. It is important to remember that the relationship between genes and environment is extremely complicated. When scientists say that a trait is strongly genetic, they are talking about populations. They may describe the importance of genes with percentages, for example, by saying that personality is 60 percent inherited[27]. It is, nonetheless, not possible for *individuals* to conclude from this that 60 percent of their own personality comes from their genes. For any individual, environmental factors may strongly influence personality and behavior.

Talk about It Discuss these questions with a partner.

1. What is meant by *nature*? By *nurture*?

2. How do twin studies help scientists separate the effects of nature and nurture?

3. Do you have traits that you think are mostly part of your nature? What are they?

Think about It Write the sentences with linking adverbials from Activity 6 in this chart.

Linking adverbial	Clause

New subject	Linking adverbial	Rest of clause

Phrase	Linking adverbial	Subject + rest of clause

Pronoun + *be*	Linking adverbial	Rest of clause

There + be	Linking adverbial	Rest of clause

Look at each adverbial above that is not at the beginning of the sentence. Why do you think the writer chose this placement?

7 | Using Linking Adverbials Complete the sentences with a linking adverbial. (Different answers are possible.) `4.2 A–B`

PERSONALITY THEORIES

> GET READY TO READ
> You are going to read an article about William Sheldon's personality theory.

1. It's easy to confuse personality and temperament, but most psychologists do distinguish between them. A person's temperament is the qualities that he or she was born with, such as whether the person is shy or outgoing[28], active or inactive[29]. _____, personality refers to the traits that a person acquires during life. Education and upbringing can affect personality.

2. The Greek physician[30] Hippocrates (c. 460–c. 370 BCE) developed an early personality theory called humorism, which claimed that bodily fluids[31] caused four different personality types. Modern medical science has rejected the theory of the four temperaments. _____, some modern personality theories include similar categories.

3. In the twentieth century, with the growth of the new field of psychology, the number of personality theories exploded. Some psychologists, like Sigmund Freud, were interested in how a person's experiences shape[32] personality. Many scientists, _____, wanted to investigate the role of biology in personality.

4. Associating[33] appearance with personality traits has a long history. The ancient Greeks developed a pseudoscience[34] called phrenology, which argued that measurements of the skull[35] could provide information about the mind. _____, William Sheldon argued as recently as 1950 that body types are associated with temperament.

5. Sheldon's theory is controversial and his methods have been widely criticized. It is, _____, interesting for an individual to look at the theory and see how well it applies.

Think about It In which sentences in Activity 7 is more than one linking adverbial possible? Which adverbials are possible?

8 | Reading Read the article. Then do the tasks on page 129.

APPEARANCE AND PERSONALITY: SHELDON'S THEORY OF BODY TYPE AND TEMPERAMENT

by James and Tyra Arraj

1 In the 1940s, William Sheldon (1898–1977), an American psychologist, proposed a theory that particular body types are associated with particular personality characteristics. For his study of the human body, Dr. Sheldon looked at 4,000 photographs of college-age men in front, back, and side views. By carefully examining these photos, he determined that there are three basic components[36] of physical form. When mixed together in different combinations, the result is a set of seven possible body types.

2 Sheldon worked out ways to measure the three components of physical form and to express them numerically. Consequently, every human body could be described in terms of these numbers, and two independent observers[37] could arrive at very similar results when classifying[38] a person's body type. Sheldon named these three basic elements endomorphy, mesomorphy, and ectomorphy. He drew a triangular diagram on which he plotted the different extremes of body types.

3 Endomorphy is centered on the abdomen[39] and the whole digestive[40] system. Mesomorphy is focused on the muscles and the circulatory[41] system. Ectomorphy is related to the brain and the nervous system.

4 Every person has all three components in his/her physical makeup, however, just as we all have digestive, circulatory, and nervous systems. No one is endomorphic without also being to some degree[42] mesomorphic and ectomorphic. For example, Sheldon found that the large muscular person was quite common, as were the muscular thin person and the person who was spread out and round without being muscular at all. Sheldon created a scale to evaluate the extent to which[43] a person had each component. The scale ranges from 1 to 7—with 1 signifying[44] a minimum degree of a component and 7 signifying the maximum.

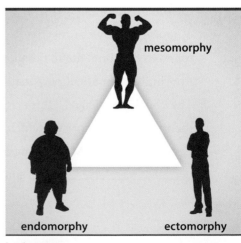

body types

5   The classification of body types was not Sheldon's ultimate goal. He wanted to resolve[45] the age-old question of whether our body type is connected with the way people behave. In short, he wanted to explore the link between body and temperament.

6   Sheldon used *temperament* to refer to personality and emotional makeup—the way people eat and sleep, laugh and cry, speak and walk. Sheldon's system for determining the basic components of temperament was much like the one he used for determining body types. He did in-depth interviews of several hundred people to find traits that he could use to describe the basic elements of behavior. He found three and named them similarly to their physical counterparts: endotonia, mesotonia, and ectotonia.

7   Endotonia is seen in the love of relaxation, comfort, food, and people. Mesotonia is centered on assertiveness[46] and a love of action. Ectotonia focuses on privacy, restraint[47], and a highly developed self-awareness.

8   Just as he had with physical traits, Sheldon created a way of numerically rating these personality traits. His system was based on a checklist of 60 characteristics. The extremes can also be plotted on a triangular diagram. The "7-1-1" person is extremely endotonic, the "1-7-1" person is extremely mesotonic, and the "1-1-7" person is extremely ectotonic.

9   As his terminology[48] implies, Sheldon found a strong correspondence[49] between the ectomorphic body type and the ectotonic temperament, between the mesomorphic body type and the mesotonic temperament, and between the endomorphic body type and the endotonic personality. But, just as a person's body type has all three elements, so, too, does a person's temperament.

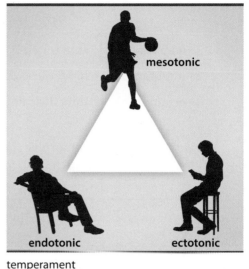

temperament

Talk about It Discuss these questions with a partner.

1. What was Sheldon's main goal?
2. Based on your experience, would you expect there to be any connection between body type and temperament? Why or why not?

Think about It Answer these questions about the article in Activity 8.

1. Circle *however* in the article (paragraph 4). What position did the writers choose for *however*? Could it have been put in a different position? Where?
2. Could the writers have used a different linking adverbial? If so, which ones?
3. Circle these words in the article. Check (✓) the part of speech for each.

	Noun	Adjective	Preposition	Adverb
different (paragraphs 1 and 2)	☐	☐	☐	☐
like (paragraph 6)	☐	☐	☐	☐
similarly (paragraph 6)	☐	☐	☐	☐
correspondence (paragraph 9)	☐	☐	☐	☐

4. Look at paragraph 3. The writers contrast three body types, but do not use any special language for contrasting. Instead, they use repeated forms. What forms are repeated in the three sentences?

9 | Using Linking Adverbials to Make Comparisons Complete the chart below with the personality traits in the box. Then write sentences comparing different kinds of people according to Sheldon. Use the linking adverbials in parentheses. **4.2 A**

PERSONALITY TRAITS

active	good-humored	relaxed
combative	introverted	sensitive
courageous	quiet	tolerant

Body type	Physical traits	Personality traits
1. endomorphic	soft, round body	
2. mesomorphic	hard, muscular body	
3. ectomorphic	thin, delicate build[50]	

4. endomorphic/mesomorphic (in contrast)

   According to Sheldon, an endomorphic person . . . _____

   _____

5. endomorphic/ectomorphic (in comparison)

   _____

   _____

6. mesomorphic/ectomorphic (on the other hand)

   _____

   _____

WRITING ASSIGNMENT I

Follow steps A–D to write a paragraph comparing information about yourself with Sheldon's expectations.

A | Planning Follow these steps to plan your paragraph.

1. Determine your body type based on Sheldon's ideas. Look at the Physical traits column in the chart in Activity 9. For each body type, rate yourself below. Give yourself a number from 1 (lowest degree present) to 7 (highest degree present) for each category.

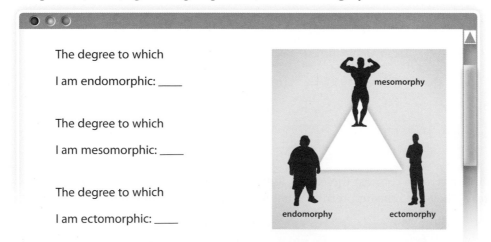

The degree to which

I am endomorphic: ____

The degree to which

I am mesomorphic: ____

The degree to which

I am ectomorphic: ____

2. Determine your personality type. Fill out this temperament profile for yourself. For each item in the chart, give a number from 1 (very little or no preference) to 7 (strong preference) for every possible answer.

SIMPLIFIED SCALE OF TEMPERAMENT					
	Endotonia 1–7		**Mesotonia 1–7**		**Ectotonia 1–7**	
1. When troubled, I seek out . . .	people.	____	action.	____	solitude[51].	____
2. I prefer . . .	physical comfort.	____	physical adventure.	____	privacy.	____
3. The time in my life that I favor is . . .	childhood.	____	early adulthood.	____	later years.	____
4. What would bother me most would be . . .	being cut off from other people.	____	being closed off in small places.	____	being exposed to endless noise.	____
5. When in a group, I like to . . .	mingle[52].	____	take charge[53].	____	take off[54].	____
6. I prefer to . . .	let things take their course[55].	____	do things.	____	observe what is going on.	____
7. The thing I like most is . . .	eating.	____	exercise.	____	time to myself.	____
Total		____		____		____

Talk about It Look at your total numbers in the chart above. Divide each number by 7 to figure out your average scores for endotonia, mesotonia, and ectotonia. Write these scores below. Compare and discuss your results with a partner.

The degree to which I am endotonic: ____

The degree to which I am mesotonic: ____

The degree to which I am ectotonic: ____

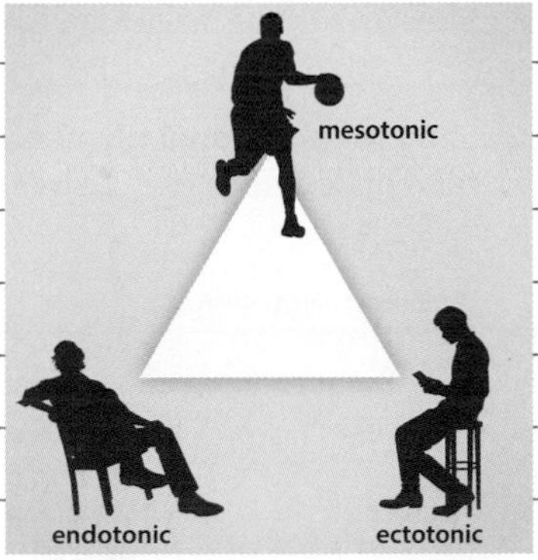

mesotonic

endotonic   ectotonic

B | Writing Look again at the scores you gave yourself in Activity A for body type and temperament. According to Sheldon, most people would get similar numbers for endomorphic and endotonic, for mesomorphic and mesotonic, and for ecotomorphic and ectotonic. Is this true for you? Write a paragraph comparing your results to Sheldon's expectations. Include a linking adverbial (such as *on the other hand* or *similarly*) to show the relationship between two of your ideas.

> *According to Sheldon's system, my body type falls somewhere between endomorphic (soft and round) and mesomorphic (hard and muscular). I don't think anyone would describe me as thin and delicate, so I have a very low ectomorphic score. This means that Sheldon would expect me to be relaxed, tolerant, and good-humored, but also somewhat active or possibly combative. However, my results on the Simplified Scale of Temperament do not fit with this prediction....*

C | Peer Reviewing Share your writing with a partner. Answer these questions about your partner's paragraph.

1. Did your partner clearly compare his or her results with Sheldon's expectations?
2. Did your partner use a linking adverbial to show a contrast or a similarity?

D | Revising Follow these steps to revise your paragraph.

1. Using your partner's feedback, rewrite your paragraph.
2. Check your writing for mistakes and clarity. Did you use a linking adverbial to show the relationship between two of your ideas? Make any final corrections necessary.

4.3 Making Comparisons with Adverb Clauses and Prepositional Phrases

A

1 The author believes that wanting to be happy is not enough. **Just as people must do certain things to become physically stronger, they must do certain things to become happier.**

2 **While our public education system has improved in recent decades, it is** still far behind those in other states.

3 **Calculus is the mathematical study of change, in the same way that** geometry is the study of shape.

We can use **adverb clauses**, as in **1 – 3**, to make comparisons within sentences. The adverb clause begins with a subordinator and can come before the **main clause**, as in **1 – 2**, or after the main clause, as in **3**.

ADVERB CLAUSE		
	subordinator	
SIMILARITY	just as in the same way that	+ rest of clause
CONTRAST	while though whereas despite the fact that although	+ rest of clause

For more information on adverb clauses, see the Resources, pages R-37–R-39.

B

4 Some say that Cobble Tunnel was the world's first subway tunnel. However, **unlike modern subway systems, it had no stations.**

5 The country suffered from wars, political changes, and social problems. **Despite the difficulties, learning and culture continued to grow.**

6 To create opportunities for growth, **the state has introduced a variety of businesses** rather than relying on just one industry.

We can also compare using **prepositional phrases**, as in **4 – 6**. Prepositional phrases can come before the **main clause**, as in **4 – 5**, or after the main clause, as in **6**.

PREPOSITIONAL PHRASE		
	preposition	
SIMILARITY	similar to like	+ noun phrase
CONTRAST	in contrast to unlike despite in spite of rather than instead of	+ noun phrase

GO ONLINE For more practice with prepositional phrases, go to the Online Practice.

10 | Making Comparisons with Adverb Clauses Complete the sentences below with a subordinator from the box. Then compare answers with a partner. (Different answers are possible.) `4.3 A`

| although | despite the fact that | in the same way that | just as | though | whereas | while |

EXCERPTS FROM RESEARCH PAPERS

1. This study examines educational tourism. _____ we understand that many people travel for educational reasons, we believe that there is a need to define this particular form of tourism, which is still relatively under-researched. We refer to organized, commercial[56] tours that offer a structured learning experience. _____ other companies promote relaxation or adventure as a feature of their product, educational tour operators promote learning.

2. This paper investigates the strategies that blind people use to orient[57] themselves in an environment. _____ sighted persons can use visual signs in order to orient themselves, a blind person moving in an unfamiliar environment cannot.

3. The basis of Suzuki's method of learning music is the belief that children who experience music as a natural part of their culture become natural musicians _____ children become natural speakers by hearing language spoken.

4. Our findings[58] show that companies all over the world are developing new genetically engineered drugs to fight cancer. Some will prevent forms of cancer completely, _____ others will help stop cancers from growing.

5. There is a need for future studies which examine mathematical thinking among children with learning difficulties. _____ difficulty with reading comprehension[59] can signal different learning problems, difficulty with mathematics can also be caused by a variety of issues.

6. In a recent survey of their buying habits, college students were asked why they purchased several specific products. _____ the majority of these products are rarely advertised, 44 out of 109 individuals said that they regularly saw advertisements for them.

7. The study suggests that a physical education class should not be a "one size fits all" environment. Students of different skill levels may have very different needs and interests, and it would benefit physical educators to understand them. _____ all the students who were subjects in this study liked physical education, there were some differences among them. Subjects didn't all like the same types and levels of physical activity.

8. Much of children's academic success during the school-age years is based on the ability to acquire new vocabulary. _____ some vocabulary learning is gained through formal teaching, most is accomplished[60] though simple contact with language.

Think about It Can you restate any of the contrasts or comparisons above using different subordinators or expressions? Which ones?

11 | Making Comparisons with Prepositional Phrases Circle the word or phrase in parentheses that best completes the sentence. 4.3 B

Personality Tests

1. The first modern personality test was used in 1919 by the U.S. Army. Its purpose was to identify soldiers who might have problems during a fight. (Like / Despite) most personality tests, it included a series of questions for the subjects to respond to.

2. For the Rorschach inkblot test, developed in 1921, a subject looks at abstract shapes and interprets their meaning. The person giving the test uses these responses to make judgments about the subject's personality. (Rather than / Unlike) most personality tests, the Rorschach test does not involve written questions or statements.

3. The Thematic Apperception Test is (similar to / in contrast to) the Rorschach test because the subject responds to an image (rather than / unlike) answering questions. In this test, however, the images represent recognizable[61] things and situations.

4. In 1942, the Minnesota Multiphasic Personality Inventory[62] was published as a way of learning if a subject had psychological problems. This test has been adapted many times and is still widely used. (Despite / Rather than) its origins as a test for abnormal[63] psychology, it is not often used as a way to understand personality in general.

5. The True Colors personality test was developed in 1978. It was based on other personality tests, like the Myers-Briggs personality index, but (despite / instead of) describing personality types with labels, it uses four colors—blue, orange, gold, and green.

6. The Personality and Preference Inventory was developed in the early 1960s. (In contrast to / Instead of) other, more general personality tests, it focuses on the aspects of personality that are important in the workplace.

7. The DISC personality test is widely used in businesses to evaluate how employees will interact with others and whether they have leadership potential. (In spite of / Like) this common use of the test now, it was originally intended as a tool for self-understanding.

8. Many personality tests are based on the Five-Factor Model (FFM), originating from the idea that there are five basic personality traits in humans. Traditionally, FFM tests have been developed primarily for adults. However, in 2008 an FFM test was developed for use with children (rather than / unlike) adults.

FYI

Despite (the fact that), in spite of, instead of, (in) the same way that, just as, rather than, whereas, and *while* are often followed by a **gerund**.

Rather than **settling** the larger issue themselves, the parties agreed to wait.

Rather than is also sometimes followed by the base form of a verb.

Rather than **abolish** the old structures, the new government minimized conflict by financing them while establishing replacements.

Rorschach inkblot

12 | Comparisons with Adverb Clauses and Prepositional Phrases Complete each statement with a subordinator or preposition. Compare answers with a partner. (Different answers are possible.)

4.3 A–B

MYERS-BRIGGS PERSONALITY TYPES

1. _____ correlating[64] body type with personality as Sheldon does, Myers and Briggs examine only personality types.

2. _____ Sheldon and Myers-Briggs both developed their theories in the 1940s, only the Myers-Briggs Type Indicator (MBTI) is still well known today.

3. _____ the Sheldon scale called for people to classify their own personality traits, the Myers-Briggs Type Indicator also calls for self-analysis.

4. _____ people closer to the "judgment" side of the scale prefer to arrange their lives according to the calendar, people on the "perception" side prefer to wait and see what happens.

5. _____ introverts, extroverts are energized by social activity.

6. *Intuition* means relying on your "inner voice" to make judgments and decisions, _____ *sensing* means relying on your observations.

GET READY TO READ

You are going to read an article about the Myers-Briggs method of personality typing.

Think about It Which statements above required subordinators? Which required prepositions? Why?

13 | Reading Read the article. Then do the tasks on page 136.

Personality Analysis: The Myers-Briggs Type Indicator

One of the most popular personality tests is the Myers-Briggs Type Indicator (MBTI), first published by Isabel Briggs Myers and her mother, Katharine Cook Briggs, during the 1960s.

The MBTI is based on the idea that there are four pairs of personality traits, or "functions":

- **Extroversion–Introversion:** Do you recharge[65] your energy via external contact and activity (extroversion) or by spending time in your inner space (introversion)?
- **Intuition–Sensing:** Do you rely on your inner voice (intuition) or observation (sensing)?
- **Thinking–Feeling:** When making decisions, what do you rely on most—your thoughts or your feelings?
- **Judgment–Perception:** Do you tend to set schedules and organize your life (judgment) or do you tend to leave options open and see what happens (perception)?

People respond to a series of statements or questions to determine the degree of each trait in their personalities.

The first function defines the source and direction of a person's energy expression. The *extrovert* prefers action and gets energy from being active and from interacting with the outside world, while the *introvert* prefers thought and needs to take a break from action in order to maintain a high energy level. No one is only introverted or extroverted, but one side is usually dominant[66].

The second function defines how a person perceives information. *Sensing* means that a person believes mainly in information he/she receives from the outside world. *Intuition* means that a person believes mainly in information he/she receives from the internal or imaginative world. The short quiz on sensation and intuition on page 136 illustrates the differences.

	Intuition	Sensation
I tend to . . .	a. get excited about the future.	b. enjoy the present moment.
When I have definite plans, . . .	a. I feel somewhat tied down.	b. I am comfortable with them.
If I worked for a manufacturer, I would prefer to do…	a. research and design.	b. production and distribution.
I am likely to . . .	a. get involved in many projects at once.	b. do one thing at a time.
If people were to complain about me, they would say . . .	a. I have my head in the clouds[67].	b. I am in a rut[68].
People would call me . . .	a. imaginative.	b. realistic.
When I find myself in a new situation, I am more interested in . . .	a. what could happen.	b. what is happening.

The third function defines how a person processes information. *Thinking* means that a person makes decisions mainly through logic. *Feeling* means that, as a rule, the person makes a decision based on emotion.

The fourth category defines how a person implements or uses information that he/she has processed. *Judging* means that a person organizes all his/her life events and acts strictly according to personal plans. *Perceiving* means that the person is inclined to improvise[69] and seek alternatives.

The different combinations of the traits determine a type. There are 16 possible types. Every type has a name (or formula). Letters stand for each trait. For example, ISTJ is Introvert Sensing Thinking Judging, or ENFP is Extrovert Intuitive (N) Feeling Perceiving.

A type formula can be determined using the type inventory and then described, as shown below.

> **ENFP:** ENFPs take their energy from the outer world of actions and spoken words. When they are down, they seek out the company of others to lift their spirits. Preferring to lead a flexible life, they follow new insights[70] and possibilities as they arise. They are creative and insightful, often seeking to try new ideas that can be of benefit to people. Although sometimes neglectful[71] of details and planning, they can work toward a general goal. They enjoy work that involves experimentation and variety.

Think about It Look at this sentence from the article in Activity 13. Then answer the questions below.

> The *extrovert* prefers action and gets energy from being active and from interacting with the outside world, while the *introvert* prefers thought and needs to take a break from action in order to maintain a high energy level.

1. How does the author show contrast between introverts and extroverts?
2. Is there another connecting word you could use?
3. Would it make sense to use a linking adverbial? Why or why not?
4. Would the sentence work as well with the clauses reversed? Why or why not?

14 | Replacing Linking Adverbials with Adverb Clauses and Prepositional Phrases

Combine the pairs of sentences below using an expression from the box instead of the linking adverbial used in each sentence. You may need to rewrite or change the order of words. (Different answers are possible.) **4.3 A–B**

in contrast to	just as	similar to	whereas
in the same way that	rather than	unlike	while

SHELDON AND MYERS-BRIGGS

1. Sheldon's theory uses self-reporting as an assessment tool. In the same way, the MBTI depends on an individual's honest answers to a series of questions.

   In the same way that Sheldon's theory uses self-reporting as an assessment tool, the MBTI depends on an individual's honest answers to a series of questions.

2. Sheldon's endomorphs are lively, social people who enjoy group activities. Similarly, Myers-Briggs' extroverts enjoy human contact and social situations.

3. Sheldon claims to examine personality based on a relationship between body type and temperament. Myers and Briggs, on the other hand, make no claims about physical appearance.

4. Sheldon's theory includes three basic personality types. Myers-Briggs' theory, on the other hand, looks at four pairs of traits.

5. Sheldon's theory is of historical interest, but not widely known or used today. In comparison, the Myers-Briggs scale is still the basis for many personality profiles.

6. In Sheldon's theory, you determine the degree to which you fit each personality type. However, in the Myers-Briggs Type Indicator, you combine eight different traits to determine your type.

7. Sheldon incorporates[72] love of comfort and food into his personality types. In comparison, Myers-Briggs focuses on ways of understanding.

8. Sheldon's ectotonics seek solitude in times of trouble. Similarly, Myers-Briggs' introverts choose "private" over "social" to describe themselves.

Think about It Compare the sentences you wrote above with a partner. Did you choose the same connecting words? If not, do the choices work equally well?

15 | Usage Note: Comparisons and Writing Cohesion Read the note. Then do Activity 16.

Writers try to maintain cohesion in their writing so that it is easy for readers to follow. The placement of adverb clauses and other comparisons can affect cohesion.

We often place **adverb clauses** before the main clause when they refer to information from a previous sentence or information that is already known by the reader.

Lion populations have decreased by as much as 50 percent during the last 20 years. **Although the reason for the decrease is not completely understood**, it was certainly caused by humans.

We often place adverb clauses after the main clause when they are very long.

The Technical University of Madrid was founded in 1971, **although the majority of its centers are hundreds of years old and were founded in the eighteenth and nineteenth centuries.**

PSYCHOLOGY AND PERSONALITY

1. Sigmund Freud and Carl Jung were both pioneers[73] in the field of psychology in the early 1900s. Although they lived and worked at the same time, Jung was about 20 years younger than Freud.

2. Freud developed the theory of the unconscious—the idea that a person's behavior is caused by things they are unaware of, especially experiences from childhood. While Freud's theories were more widely accepted than Jung's, Jung was the first person to identify the personality traits of extroversion and introversion, which had an important influence on later personality theories.

Sigmund Freud

3. The concepts of introversion and extroversion are important in personality theory today, although they are not always viewed in the same way. Carl Jung (and Myers-Briggs after him) suggested that most people are sometimes introverted and sometimes extroverted, whereas many others see the two traits as a continuum[74], meaning that the more introverted a person is, the less extroverted he or she is.

4. One of the most widely used personality models today is the Five-Factor Model (FFM). Whereas the Myers-Briggs model looks at eight personality traits, this model includes five.

Carl Jung

5. Like Myers-Briggs and most other personality models, the FFM includes extroversion as one of the important personality traits. Extroverts are seen as outgoing and social, while introverts are considered to be quieter and not as social.

6. Another personality trait in the FFM is openness to experience. "Openness" is used to describe people who are open to new experiences, curious, and willing to try new things. Whereas open people like change and new experiences, "closed" people do not like change and prefer familiar experiences.

7. The FFM also includes the personality trait of conscientiousness. A person who is conscientious is very efficient and well organized. They are dependable[75] and usually follow the rules. Although conscientiousness is viewed as a personality trait, research shows that it can change with age.

8. The fourth of the "Big Five" personality traits is agreeableness. An agreeable person likes to get along well with others. They may be described as generous or kind. Employers often look for a high agreeableness score because they believe that agreeable people make better leaders. While some studies have supported this idea, others have not.

9. The last trait in the FFM is neuroticism. People with high scores on this trait often experience negative emotions, such as anger or depression. They are often in a bad mood. However, just as conscientiousness can change with age, a person's level of neuroticism may change with life events. Having a large number of bad experiences may cause a person to score higher on the neuroticism scale. It is important to note that people with low scores on neuroticism are not necessarily happy. Although they are less likely to frequently feel angry or sad, that doesn't mean that they often feel good.

Talk about It Look again at the Big Five FFM traits discussed in Activity 16: extroversion, openness to experience, conscientiousness, agreeableness, and neuroticism. Would you score high or low on measures of each of these traits? Discuss with a partner.

WRITING ASSIGNMENT II

Follow steps A–D to write a paragraph comparing information about yourself with the Myers-Briggs system.

A | Planning Review the Myers-Briggs Type Indicator article in Activity 13. Look at the four groups of words in the chart below. In the first column, label each group according to which pair of personality traits, or function, it describes. Then label the second and third columns according to the individual traits. Add one word or phrase describing each trait.

Pairs of personality traits (functions)	Individual traits	Individual traits
Group 1: _E I_	_E_ social expressive interaction action before thought _unpredictable_	_I_ private quiet concentration thought before action _stable_
Group 2: ___	___ analyzing objective logical criticism ___	___ sympathizing subjective personal appreciation ___
Group 3: ___	___ decide organize firmness control ___	___ explore inquire flexibility spontaneity[76] ___
Group 4: ___	___ facts experience present realism ___	___ possibilities novelty future idealism ___

> **PAIRS OF PERSONALITY TRAITS (FUNCTIONS)**
> **E I** = extroversion–introversion
> **N S** = intuition–sensing
> **T F** = thinking–feeling
> **J P** = judgment–perception

Talk about It Discuss the words or phrases you added in Activity A with a classmate. Then look at the personality traits or functions and decide which ones apply to you. Discuss these questions with a partner.

1. What is your type formula? (See the article in Activity 13 for an explanation of "type formula.")
2. Do your results in the Sheldon system (see Writing Assignment I on pages 130–132) match your results in the Myers-Briggs system?
3. If not, what could explain the difference?

B | Writing Write a paragraph comparing your results in the Sheldon system with your results in the Myers-Briggs system. Include at least one adverb clause or prepositional phrase for comparison.

On Sheldon's Scale of Temperament, my highest scores are in mesotonia and endotonia, and on the MBTI, my personality type is ENFP—extroversion, intuition, feeling, and perception. While there are some similarities between the two, there are also important differences. The Sheldon results show that I'm active and I like to do things, and also that I care about people and would not like to be cut off from others. Both of these are similar to extroversion on the MBTI. Another result from Sheldon is that I "prefer to let things take their course," which is like the perception part of my MBTI score. People on the perception side enjoy flexibility and spontaneity. However, there are several traits that are described by one scale but not the other. My Sheldon scores also suggest that I like eating and exercise, and neither of these things is included on the MBTI, and my MBTI results include "intuition," which is not similar to anything on Sheldon's scale.

C | Peer Reviewing Share your writing with a partner. Answer these questions about your partner's paragraph.

1. Did your partner clearly explain how his or her results were similar or different for Sheldon and Myers-Briggs?
2. Did your partner use any adverb clauses or prepositional phrases for comparison? Do you agree with the placement (before or after the main clause)?

D | Revising Follow these steps to revise your paragraph.

1. Using your partner's feedback, rewrite your paragraph.
2. Check your writing for mistakes and clarity. Did you use at least one adverb clause or prepositional phrase for comparison? Make any final corrections necessary.

4.4 Paired Connectors and Clauses with Negative Connectors

A

PAIRED CONNECTORS

1 Tree kangaroos are known to be able to live in **both mountainous regions and lowland locations.** (noun phrase . . . noun phrase)

2 One possible conclusion about this book is that the characters are **neither brave nor clever.** (adjective . . . adjective)

3 Turing **not only achieved outstanding academic performance, but also made a significant contribution to the life of his school.** (verb phrase . . . verb phrase)

4 **Either by chance or by design**, islands of forest are left amidst a sea of non-forest habitat. (prepositional phrase . . . prepositional phrase)

5 **Either the law should be changed or a new law should be enacted.** (clause . . . clause)

Writers often make comparisons using **paired connectors** such as:

- **both . . . and**
- **neither . . . nor**
- **not only . . . but also**
- **either . . . or**

Paired connectors should combine items with the same grammatical form (verb + verb, noun phrase + noun phrase, etc.), as in **1 – 5**. We call this **parallelism (parallel structure)**.

GRAMMAR TERM: Paired conjunctions are also called **correlative conjunctions**.

B

CLAUSES WITH NEGATIVE CONNECTORS

6 **Not only** has she suggested that much research remains to be done, **but she has also** provided encouragement as well as a number of useful suggestions.

7 The men had not spent much time in the area. **Neither had they acquired** any military training before their arrival. (helping verb + subject + main verb)

8 Most of the changes we seek cannot be achieved through law alone, but **neither can they be achieved** without law. (helping verb + subject + main verb)

9 The neighborhood was not particularly wealthy, **nor was it** especially poor. (be + subject)

10 Many of the students do not have the capabilities at home to practice with technology. **Nor do they have** the necessary background knowledge to be successful with technology in school. (do + subject + main verb)

Not only . . . but also is commonly used to combine clauses, as in **6**. The **subject** and **helping verb** of the second clause usually come between *but* and *also*.

We can also use **neither** and **nor** to connect one negative clause to a previous negative clause. Sometimes *neither* begins a new sentence, as in **7**. Sometimes it is connected with *but* or *and*, as in **8**.

We can separate short *nor* clauses with a comma, as in **9**. We separate longer clauses with a period, as in **10**.

The subject-verb word order is reversed in clauses beginning with negative connectors like *not only*, *neither*, and *nor*. Notice:

- We place the first helping verb before the subject, as in **6 – 8**.
- In sentences with *be*, we place *be* before the subject, as in **9**.
- In sentences without *be* or a helping verb, we add *do / did* before the subject, as in **10**.

17 | Noticing Connectors Underline and label the structures (verb phrase, noun phrase, or clause) that are being compared or contrasted. `4.4 A–B`

Wind Power and Solar Power

1. Solar power not only <u>produces a nearly limitless[77] supply of energy</u>,
   verb phrase
   but also <u>accomplishes this during the day when people use the
   most electricity</u>.
   verb phrase

2. Wind power requires both large structures
   and large amounts of land.

3. Not only is solar power easily distributed by
   placing panels[78] on streetlights and rooftops,
   but it is also getting more affordable as the
   price of panels comes down.

4. Both wind energy and solar energy offer big
   advantages over fossil fuels[79].

5. Wind and sunshine are clean, producing
   neither the pollutants[80] that cause smog[81] nor
   the carbon dioxide that contributes to climate change.

6. Solar panels are not difficult to install. Neither are they as expensive as
   many people think.

7. In areas without access to fossil fuels, either wind or solar power can
   be an affordable alternative.

8. Not only can solar power be used to generate electricity for cities,
   but it can also be used to power devices like calculators, and even
   experimental cars.

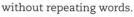

FYI

Paired connectors allow writers to combine ideas without repeating words.

The new procedures are **not only** incorrect, **but also** dangerous.
(Subject and verb are not repeated.)

Negative connectors allow writers to emphasize important ideas. Compare:

The new procedures are both incorrect and dangerous.

Not only are the new procedures incorrect, **but** they are **also** dangerous.
(*Dangerous* is emphasized.)

Think about It Answer these questions with a partner.

1. Which sentences above have reversed subject-verb word order?

2. Rewrite sentence 8. Use *not only* and *but also* to connect the *to-* infinitive forms.
   What happens to the subject-verb word order?

---

18 | Combining Sentences with Paired Connectors Combine the sentences with the paired connectors in parentheses. (Different answers are possible.) `4.4 A–B`

1. Tasman had not found a promising area for trade. He had not found a
   useful new shipping route. (neither . . . nor)
   Tasman had found neither a promising area for trade nor a useful new shipping route.

2. A Japanese robotics lab has developed a robot that can change its
   expression. It can also move its hands and feet and twist[82] its body.
   (not only . . . but also) _____

   _____

Japanese robot

3. The accident and the events that came after it were documented[83] widely by local media. They were also documented by foreign media. (both . . . and) _____

_____

_____

4. He was raised in an extended family in a shack[84] that didn't have electricity. The shack didn't have plumbing[85]. (neither . . . nor)

_____

_____

5. Several important documents were completed during the review period. Several important documents were revised during the review period. (either . . . or) _____

_____

6. There is no cure for this disease. There is not a standard course of treatment for this disease. (neither . . . nor)

_____

_____

7. The visual system includes structures in the eyes. The visual system includes structures in the brain. (both . . . and)

_____

8. The Romans agreed to return the prisoners. They agreed to double their previous payment of 350 Roman pounds. (not only . . . but also) _____

_____

9. The social environment affects a person's health by influencing behavior. It also influences health by means of other mechanisms[86] that are still poorly understood. (not only . . . but also) _____

_____

_____

10. The new program will provide better medical care for patients. The new program will also address the concerns of physicians. (not only . . . but also) _____

_____

Think about It Discuss these questions with a partner.

1. Connectors allow writers to avoid repeating information. Which of these structures did you "cut" from the second sentence when you combined each pair of sentences above?

subject	complete verb	main verb	helping verb	object	prepositional phrase

"In number 1, we cut the subject and the complete verb."

2. What is another way to combine the pairs of sentences in numbers 8, 9, and 10 in Activity 18 with *not only* and *but also*?

19 | Connecting Clauses Combine the clauses with the connectors in parentheses. Reverse the order of subjects and (helping) verbs where necessary. 4.4 B

MAKING CONNECTIONS

1. The most creative individuals will be allowed to develop their skills. The more typical students will gain a clearer understanding of the subject. (not only . . . but also)

   Not only will the most creative individuals be

   allowed to develop their skills, but the more typical students will also gain a clearer

   understanding of the subject.

2. Long meetings are time consuming. Long meetings take employees away from important work that they should be doing. (not only . . . but also)

   _____

   _____

3. The final agreement was not a formal decision by the committee. The final agreement was not approved by management. (nor)

   _____

   _____

4. Posters do not stay up for very long. They are covered by other posters. Or, cleaning crews are ordered to remove them. (either . . . or)

   _____

   _____

5. Mosquitoes can carry diseases that harm humans. Mosquitoes can transmit[87] several diseases to other animals. (not only . . . but also)

   _____

   _____

6. The market does not provide the right kind of community for evaluating scientific work. The market does not provide the right kind of criteria[88] for this purpose. (neither)

   _____

   _____

7. Teachers cannot be considered highly qualified and effective if they are limited to only knowledge in their subject area. Teachers cannot be considered highly qualified and effective if they do not possess good communication skills. (nor)

   _____

   _____

   _____

8. We need to develop new technology. We need to train employees on how to use it. (not only . . . but also)

   _____

   _____

9. The changes should not be adopted too quickly. We cannot delay for much longer. (but neither)

_____

_____

10. Most earlier studies have not examined the relationship between unemployment and mental health. Most earlier studies have not addressed whether gaining employment improves psychological well-being. (neither)

_____

_____

_____

20 | Error Correction Correct any errors in these sentences. (Some sentences may not have any errors.)

1. Not only ~~the prices are~~ *are the prices* higher in the downtown area, but the environment can also be unpleasant.

2. Robinson does not reject Martin's argument. Neither he provides any evidence to support it.

3. Some employees felt that the new furniture wasn't useful nor attractive.

4. The instructions were both difficult to understand and also they were very long.

5. The king does not appoint[89] the government, nor any public official acts in his name.

6. The program helped them not only in economic terms but also their quality of life was better.

7. The subjects were neither working full time nor attending school.

8. Four hundred books were either recycled or they sent them to another library.

9. We can't afford seeds or equipment for farms, nor we can buy shoes or clothes.

10. The first calculators became not only a status symbol[90] in France but also in other parts of Europe.

FINAL WRITING ASSIGNMENT
Write a Comparison Essay

Your Task
Write a multi-paragraph essay about the similarities and differences between William Sheldon's body type and personality assessment and the Myers-Briggs Type Indicator. Include the following in your essay: how the theory was developed, the number of possible personality types, the range and method of application, and the credibility[91] of the theory.

Alternative Task
Write a multi-paragraph essay about the similarities and differences between one other theory of personality and either the Sheldon body type and personality assessment or the Myers-Briggs index. For example, do research on a theory such as Type A/Type B personalities, handwriting analysis, or birth order personality types. Include the following in your essay: how the theory was developed, the number of possible categories, the range and method of application, and the credibility of the theory.

GO ONLINE Go to the Online Writing Tutor for a writing model and to write your assignment.

A | Gathering Ideas Complete the charts for the theories you will be writing about.

1. Review the article about Sheldon on pages 128–129 and the chart in Activity 9 on page 130. Complete the chart below.

BODY TYPES AND PERSONALITY	
Methodology used in determining body types	> *examined 4,000 photos of college-age men* > *determined 3 components that make up body types and designed system of measuring them*
BODY TYPES AND PERSONALITY	
Name and primary characteristics of each body type	
Method used to link body and personality types	
Number of personality types	
Name and primary characteristics of each personality type	

2. Review the article about Myers-Briggs on pages 135–136 and complete this chart.

MYERS-BRIGGS THEORY	
Basis of theory	*the idea that there are 4 pairs of personality traits, or functions*
Methodology used in determining personality type	
Number of personality traits/ functions	
Names of personality traits/functions	
Total number of personality types that can be described using this theory	
How results are obtained	

3. For the Alternative Task, create and complete a similar chart for your other theory.

B | Planning Follow these steps to plan your essay.

1. Fill in the typology questionnaire. Write the names of the theories you are comparing at the top of each column. Answer yes or no for each theory based on your understanding of the readings.

TYPOLOGY QUESTIONNAIRE		
	Theory 1	**Theory 2**
1. Are the results the same every time the theory is applied?	*no*	*no*
2. Can it be applied to the general population?		
3. Does it work for different cultural backgrounds?		
4. Are the results based on scientific experiments?		
5. Are the results based on self-reports?		
6. Are the results based on the observations of the theorist(s)?		
7. Is the theory useful for hiring suitable personnel[92] for a job?		
8. Is the theory useful for helping people find business partners, friends, or love interests?		
9. Is the theory useful for helping people understand themselves better?		
10. Do you think two independent researchers using this theory would always come up with the same results?		

2. Compare and contrast the two theories. Do a point-by-point comparison by filling in the chart with the similarities and differences for each point of comparison.

Points of comparison	Similarities	Differences
Method of development		
Number of categories		
Method of application (e.g., self-reporting survey; observation)		
Credibility		

C | Writing Note: Introductory Paragraphs for Comparison Essays Read the note. Then do Activity D.

A comparison essay is not just a list of similarities and differences. The comparison is used to make a larger point. For example:

an evaluation of the two things (for example, Theory A is more useful than Theory B)   OR   an argument that the similarities and differences reveal important information or a wider truth (such as demonstrating the effect of having a particular personality type on one's health or chances for success)

The purpose and approach of your essay should be clear in the introductory paragraph.

D | Focus on Introductory Paragraphs Read this introductory paragraph comparing Sheldon's theory with the Myers-Briggs theory. Then answer the questions below.

Why do we do the things we do? William Sheldon's body type and temperament theory and the Myers-Briggs Type Indicator (MBTI) are two attempts to answer this question. These two theories are very similar in their origins. Neither of them is based on controlled scientific studies. Sheldon hoped to show that there is a link between people's personalities and their physical appearance. The MBTI, on the other hand, is based on the idea that people's personalities are not physical but psychological. Both Sheldon's theory and MBTI claim that assumptions and predictions can be made about a person based on his or her personality type. Although each system is different, their common assertion[93] that their own system can predict behavior is fundamentally[94] flawed[95] and potentially harmful.

QUESTIONS

1. Does this introduction have a hook? If so, what is it?
2. What is the thesis statement?
3. What is the writer's attitude toward these theories?
4. What words in the paragraph help the writer explain similarities? What words highlight differences?
5. How does the thesis statement point to similarities and contrasts at the same time?

E | Writing Note: Essay Organization Study the diagrams of possible ways to organize a comparison essay. Then do Activity F.

Comparison essays are often organized following one of these two methods.

METHOD 1	METHOD 2
INTRODUCTION origins of both theories	**INTRODUCTION**
BODY ¶ 1 similarities and differences of one aspect of the theories	**BODY ¶ 1** explanation of theory 1
BODY ¶ 2, ¶ 3, ¶ 4, ETC. similarities and differences of other aspects of the theories	**BODY ¶ 2** explanation of theory 2, with comparison to theory 1, as appropriate
BODY ¶ 3 criticism or commentary	**BODY ¶ 3, ¶ 4, ¶ 5, ETC.** criticisms or commentary
CONCLUSION your opinion or connection back to thesis	**CONCLUSION** your opinion or connection back to thesis

Personality Tests and Human Nature

Personality tests identify specific characteristics of human behavior and are beneficial in several ways. They can be used by an individual to help understand his or her own strengths and weaknesses. They can also be valuable to employers in helping them understand what types of personalities their employees have in order to better interact with them. Likewise, psychologists can use personality tests to understand and explain human actions and behavior. Today there are many different personality tests, each one based on its own unique theory of personality. Some of these tests, including Eysenck's Personality Questionnaire (EPQ), were originally based on the theory of the four temperaments, which was developed over 2,000 years ago. The similarities between a modern personality test like the EPQ and an ancient theory may seem surprising, but they are explained by history and by human nature.

The four temperaments personality test is the oldest known personality assessment. About 2,500 years ago, the ancient Greeks believed that in order to maintain health, people needed an even balance of four body fluids: blood, phlegm[96], yellow bile[97], and black bile. These four body fluids were linked to certain organs[98] and illnesses and represented the four temperaments of personality (Chapman). Hippocrates (c. 460–c. 370 BCE) connected these bodily fluids to personality types, which were later interpreted by the philosopher and physician Claudius Galen (129 CE–c. 216 CE) into the four temperaments categories:

- **sanguine**—cheerful, optimistic, and comfortable with one's work
- **phlegmatic**—slow, lazy, and dull
- **choleric**—quick, hot-tempered, and often aggressive
- **melancholic**—sad, depressed, and pessimistic

These ideas dominated Western thinking about human behavior and the treatment of diseases until the mid-1800s.

The four temperaments influenced several later personality tests, and inspired the British psychologist Hans Jürgen Eysenck to develop his Personality Questionnaire in 1964. Eysenck extensively researched Galen's four temperaments. While the four temperaments classify an individual into one of four personality types, the EPQ measures personality using two variables[99]: introverted versus extroverted and stable[100] versus unstable. The EPQ has a series of questions that test-takers respond to with yes or no answers. Those answers are then tabulated[101] to determine one's personality type. Eysenck's method produced four main types of personality classifications with two scales evident within each type:

- **Stable–extroverted** is defined as sociable, outgoing, talkative, responsive[102], easygoing, lively, carefree[103], and having leadership skills. This personality type corresponds to Galen's sanguine temperament.
- **Unstable–introverted** is described as moody[104], anxious, rigid[105], sober[106], pessimistic, reserved[107], unsociable, and quiet. Eysenck linked it to the four temperaments melancholic category.
- **Unstable–extroverted** is defined as touchy[108], restless[109], aggressive, excitable, changeable, impulsive[110], optimistic, and active. It corresponds with the choleric category in the four temperaments.
- **Stable–introverted** is described as calm, even-tempered, reliable, controlled, peaceful, thoughtful, careful, and passive. This category was linked to phlegmatic in Galen's four temperaments.

Comparing the two personality tests shows that the EPQ allows for a more descriptive assessment of an individual's personality. This more accurate result can assist individuals, employers, and psychologists alike to gain a better understanding of how one's personality affects one's behavior. The EPQ is based on a modern understanding that personality is influenced by genetics rather than ancient ideas about blood, phlegm, and bile. And yet there are clear similarities between the EPQ and the four temperaments theory. Both describe personality in similar ways, and both are based on the idea that each individual is born with his or her personality. This idea is only partially accepted today—psychologists now believe that many aspects of personality are adaptable[111] and influenced by environmental factors. Nevertheless, talk to any parent with multiple children and you might hear them say something like "My son is so different from my daughter. He was just born that way," and they may describe their children as "naturally cheerful," or "hot-tempered," just as parents must have described their children in ancient times.

Modern psychologists would never dream of using bodily fluids as the basis for personality evaluation, and it is still unclear exactly how environment influences our personalities or how much they can change over time. Nevertheless, the ancient four temperaments theory has not been forgotten. It is clear that however much our understanding of what drives human behavior has changed over time, humans themselves have not changed very much.

Works Cited

Boeree, C. George. "Hans Eysenck (and Other Temperament Theorists)." *Personality Theories*. Web. 1 Dec. 2014. <http://webspace.ship.edu/cgboer/eysenck.html>

Chapman, Alan. "Personality Theories, Types, and Tests." Self/Personal Development. *Businessballs.com*. Web. 1 Dec. 2014. <http://www.businessballs.com/personalitystylesmodels.htm>

"The Eysenck Personality Questionnaire (EPQ)." *Trans4mind*. Web. 1 Dec. 2014. <http://www.trans4mind.com/personality/EPQ.html>

QUESTIONS

1. Which method of organization from the Writing Note on page 148 did the writer use?

2. Find and copy an example of these structures used to discuss similarities and differences in the model essay.

Paragraph 1

linking adverbial _____

adjective _____

comparative adverb _____

noun _____

Paragraph 2

superlative adjective _____

Paragraph 3

subordinator _____

Paragraph 4

-*ing* verb form _____

preposition _____

noun _____

adjective _____

linking adverbial _____

subordinator _____

H | Writing a First Draft Using information from your diagram in Activity F, write a first draft of your essay. Try to use some of the structures that you have practiced in this unit.

I | Peer Reviewing When you have finished writing your first draft, share it with a partner. After discussing your essay, you may want to reorganize your ideas, add more support, and make other changes to strengthen your essay.

Checklist for revising the first draft

When you review your partner's essay and discuss your own, keep these questions in mind.
1. Does the introduction clearly state the two theories being compared?
2. Does the introduction give the reader an idea of the approach to the topic that the writer is going to take?
3. Does each body paragraph focus on one element of the comparison?
4. Does the writer use a variety of expressions to show similarities and differences?
5. Is the writer's opinion in the conclusion? Is this opinion supported by the body paragraphs?

J | Writing the Second Draft Using your partner's feedback, write a second draft that includes all of your changes.

K | Proofreading Check your essay for the forms in Chart 4.5. Make any final corrections necessary.

4.5 Summary Chart for Proofreading

EXPRESSIONS FOR SIMILARITY AND CONTRAST	PROOFREADING QUESTIONS	EXAMPLES
LINKING ADVERBIALS however nevertheless nonetheless instead rather in comparison in contrast by contrast on the other hand on the contrary alternatively similarly in the same way in a similar way in a similar vein along the same lines likewise	Do the **linking adverbials** signal the correct meanings (contrast, concession, similarity)? Are they in the best position to maintain the flow of ideas (for example, after a phrase that refers back to the previous sentence, as in **1**)?	**1** There have been relatively few institutions of higher education involved in **recent efforts to measure and improve quality. These efforts**, **however**, have led to major policy changes.
SUBORDINATORS just as in the same way that although though while whereas despite the fact that	Do the **subordinators** signal the correct meanings (contrast, concession, similarity)? Do they begin an adverb clause that is attached to a main clause, as in **2**?	**2** The troops were composed primarily of militia members, but they also included volunteers who responded to a call from a local captain. **While** militia members could only serve in their local area for six months at a time, volunteers could serve as long as 12 months and across state lines.
PREPOSITIONS similar to like in contrast to unlike despite in spite of instead of rather than	Do the **prepositions** signal the correct meanings (difference or similarity)? Are they followed by a **noun phrase**, as in **3**?	**3** The creative arts are often divided into more specific categories, each related to its technique, such as decorative arts, performing arts, or literature. **Unlike scientific fields**, art is one of the few subjects that is academically organized according to technique.

PAIRED CONNECTORS

Are you linking parallel grammatical forms (for example, noun phrases, adjectives, or clauses)?

4 They may enjoy both **being in social settings** and **being alone.** (similar noun phrases)

5 The strategy is not only **effective** but also **economical.** (adjectives)

6 The introvert would rather **work through problems alone** than **seek the advice of a group.** (verb phrases)

CLAUSES WITH NEGATIVE CONNECTORS

If you used negative connecting words to join clauses, did you reverse the subject-verb word order?

7 The author doesn't mention children with learning difficulties, **nor does he explain** how his theory will apply to adults.

8 Not only **can researchers learn** about specific events, but they can also collect information about a subject's emotions.

5

Softening and Strengthening Statements

Don't raise your voice;
improve your argument.

—DESMOND TUTU,
SOUTH AFRICAN LEADER
(1931–)

Talk about It What does the quotation above mean? Do you agree or disagree?

WARM-UP

A | Read the two versions of each statement, and look especially at the words in blue. Which version of the statement is stronger? Check (✓) the stronger version. Then compare answers with a partner.

Technologies

1. ☐ a. Video games for children are educational.

   ☐ b. Video games for children **can** be educational.

2. ☐ a. It is **sometimes** acceptable to download music without paying for it.

   ☐ b. It is acceptable to download music without paying for it.

3. ☐ a. **Some** college courses are more educationally effective in a face-to-face format than in an online format.

   ☐ b. College courses are more educationally effective in a face-to-face format than in an online format.

4. ☐ a. Computers and the Internet were **clearly** the most important technological developments of the twentieth century.

   ☐ b. Computers and the Internet were **possibly** the most important technological developments of the twentieth century.

5. ☐ a. In the next decade, increasing use of social media **will** make people feel more isolated from each other, rather than more connected.

   ☐ b. In the next decade, increasing use of social media **may** make people feel more isolated from each other, rather than more connected.

6. ☐ a. It is **likely** that neither technology nor laws will ever be able to guarantee privacy of personal information online.

   ☐ b. It is **certain** that neither technology nor laws will ever be able to guarantee privacy of personal information online.

B | Discuss the pairs of statements as a class. Which version of each statement do you agree with more? What is the difference between the versions? Does this difference affect which version you agree with?

5.1 Overview of Softening and Strengthening Statements

USING HEDGES TO SOFTEN A STATEMENT

In academic writing, accuracy is important. We therefore use **hedges** (as in **1b**)—words and phrases that soften or limit statements—to help make sure that our statements are not inaccurate. Hedges help us avoid being too general or broad and in this way enable us to express our claims more precisely. Compare:

1a "Individualistic" cultures emphasize personal responsibility. (statement without a hedge)
1b "Individualistic" cultures **tend to** emphasize personal responsibility. (statement with a hedge)

A

2 The test **appears** to be **somewhat** too difficult for students at that level. Of the 137 students who took the test, 36 (or 26 percent) failed.

3 Rock formations that **seem** to have been shaped by flowing water **suggest** that Mars **may** once have been much warmer than it is today.

4 **In some studies**, chemicals in the water were linked to bee deaths.

5 It is **often** a good thing that people say exactly what they think online, especially about injustice that they see around them.

6 **Most** patients with severe depression have responded to psychotherapy.

Hedges can soften statements in various ways, including by:

- using words that express possibility (rather than certainty), such as *appears* in **2** and *seem, suggest,* and *may* in **3**.
- saying that our evidence is in some way limited, as in **4**.
- saying that the situation is not true all the time, as in **5**.
- saying that the situation is not true for everyone or everything, as in **6**.

Notice: We can use several hedges in a sentence, as in **2** (two hedges) and **3** (three hedges).

USING BOOSTERS TO STRENGTHEN A STATEMENT

In academic writing, we sometimes use **boosters** (as in **7b**)—words and phrases that show our certainty about what we are saying and that help emphasize the points that we are making. Boosters can be an important tool, especially when we argue for a position. Compare:

7a The study's conclusions are incorrect. (statement without a booster)
7b The study's conclusions are obviously incorrect. (statement with a booster)

B

8 Studies have clearly shown that these medications help patients live longer.

9 Organic crops contain significantly more vitamins and minerals than conventionally grown crops.

10 Lack of sleep has serious effects on the body's ability to fight disease.

11 All young people experience learning losses when they do not engage in educational activities during the summer.

12 According to nutritionists, certain studies clearly show why children need breakfast.

13a (original source) The study shows that 60 percent of patients with depression improve with therapy and 57 percent improve with medication.

13b (statement about 13a) In the study, **more patients** improved with therapy than with medication.
(NOT: ~~In the study, significantly more patients improved with therapy than with medication.~~)

Boosters can strengthen statements in various ways, including by:

- expressing certainty about the situation in the statement, as in **8**. (Notice that this example contains two boosters: *clearly* and *shown*.)
- expressing the importance or extreme degree of the situation, as in **9** and **10**.
- emphasizing a situation as always true or true for everyone or everything, as in **11**.

Notice: We can use a **hedge** and a **booster** together in a sentence, as in **12**.

WARNING! Do not use boosters where they could make a statement inaccurate, as in **13b**.

1 | Noticing Hedges and Boosters Read each statement. Do the words in **bold** make the statement softer or stronger? Check (✓) the correct column. Then compare answers with a partner. **5.1 A–B**

	SOFTER	STRONGER
1. We **suggest** that the Internet **can** help improve the quality of your life and the lives of people everywhere.	☐	☐
2. With the technological advancements[1] that we enjoy today comes the **possibility** of an invasion[2] of our privacy.	☐	☐
3. Their position is that software ownership should not be allowed; **all** information should be free, and **all** programs should be available for copying.	☐	☐
4. Occupational prestige[3] is **strongly** correlated[4] with education.	☐	☐
5. These requirements **could** cause job dissatisfaction and lead to high staff turnover[5].	☐	☐
6. Studies of workplaces **prove** there is a **highly significant** relationship between employees' morale[6] and employees' productivity.	☐	☐
7. Psychotherapy **appears** to be as effective as medication in treating episodes of depression, even if severe.	☐	☐
8. A study of twins **shows convincingly** that genes are influential in shaping our political views.	☐	☐
9. Indeed, **some researchers feel** the research argues for a connection between the two theories.	☐	☐
10. The fossil[7] remains have been found in Scotland, Germany, Argentina, and the U.S., but these creatures **most certainly** had a worldwide distribution.	☐	☐

Think about It What kinds of words do we use to hedge or boost our statements—that is, what parts of speech are these words? Can you think of any other words that could be hedges or boosters?

2 | Identifying Hedges and Boosters Read this passage. Are the **bold** words and phrases used as hedges or boosters? What function does each serve? With a partner, write the number of each **bold** word or phrase in the chart on page 156. **5.1 A–B**

The Twentieth Century

How did the world of the 1990s compare with the world of 1914? It contained five or six billion people, **perhaps** three times as many people as at the start of the First World War. . . . **Most** people
                  1   2
in the 1990s were taller and heavier than their parents, better fed, and **far** longer-lived, though the
                                                                                            3
catastrophes[8] of the 1980s and 1990s in Africa, Latin America, and the ex-U.S.S.R. **may** make this
                                                                                                        4
difficult to believe. The world was **incomparably**[9] richer than ever before in its capacity to produce
                                                  5
goods and services in **endless** variety. . . . **Most** people until the 1980s lived better than their parents,
                          6   7
and in the advanced economies, better than they had ever expected to live or even imagined it
possible to live.

   For some decades in the middle of the century it even looked as though ways had been found of
                                          8
distributing **at least some** of this **enormous** wealth with **a degree of** fairness to the working people of
                  9   10   11

¹ See page V-9 for the Vocabulary Endnotes for this unit.

the richer countries, but at the end of the century, inequality[10] once again had the upper hand[11]. . . .

Humanity was **far** better educated than in 1914. Indeed, **probably** for the first time in history **most**
12   13   14
human beings could be described as literate[12], **at least in official statistics**. . . .
15

   Perhaps the **most dramatic** practical consequence of the rapid development of technology was a
16   17
revolution in transportation and communication, which **virtually** eliminated[13] time and distance. . . .
18

It let people speak to one another across oceans and continents at the touch of a few buttons, and

for most practical purposes, abolished the cultural advantages of city over countryside.
19

   Why, then, . . . did so many reflective[14] minds look back upon the century without satisfaction and

certainly without confidence in the future?
20

—Eric Hobsbawm, *The Age of Extremes*

These words hedge a statement by . . .	
• expressing possibility, rather than certainty.	_1_
• saying the evidence is limited.	
• saying something is not true all the time.	
• saying something is not true for everyone or everything; not completely.	

These words boost a statement by . . .	
• expressing certainty.	
• expressing great degree.	

RESEARCH SAYS...

Hedges are much more common than boosters in academic writing, especially in the humanities (e.g., literature, history) and social sciences (e.g., psychology, economics).

CORPUS

3 | Noticing Hedges and Boosters Read these sentences from student papers. Find five sentences with hedges(s) and four sentences with booster(s). Underline the hedges once; underline the boosters twice.

5.1 A–B

1. Tourism <u>clearly</u> matters to the economies of coastal nations.
2. However, development of coasts for tourism has seriously damaged coastal reefs[15].
3. Improving the area's beaches may cause some damage to reefs.
4. Some of the problems in coastal development appear to have arisen in part from a lack of planning.

5. International law can be defined as a system of rules and principles that govern the relations between nations.
6. Nevertheless, there is no doubt that nations remain the most important subject of international law.
7. It is clear that the nature of international law is different from that of national law.
8. In many but not all cases, international law is taken into account by states and obeyed.
9. Perhaps the main reason international law suffers from a lack of effectiveness is that it lacks a formal legislative[16] body to respond rapidly to new situations.

Talk about It With a partner, try restating the sentences without the hedges or boosters. What is the difference in meaning between the two versions?

5.2 Hedging with Modals

Modals are a very common type of hedge in academic writing. They are useful as hedges because they can express different degrees of belief, probability, and possibility.

A

MAY, MIGHT, CAN, COULD

We often use **may (not)**, **might (not)**, **can**, and **could** to express the idea that a situation is only probable or possible, as in **1 – 11**.

may, might, can, could	**1** Prekindergarten programs **may be** especially beneficial for children from low-income families.
	2 In the future, education **might be valued** for its own sake.
	3 These early childhood factors **might explain** the children's later difficulties.
	4 When blood is prevented from reaching the heart, a heart attack **can result**.
	5 These new technologies **could increase** health-care costs without significantly improving the quality of care.
may not, might not	**6** The fight for an ethical Internet **may not** yet **be** a lost cause.
	7 The increased number of applicants **might not result** in higher enrollments.

We can use **may have**, **might have**, or **could have** + a **past participle** as hedges, as in **8 – 11**. These structures express possibility in the past. They can be used in **past real conditional** statements, as in **9**, and in **past unreal conditional** statements, as in **10 – 11**.

may have, might have, could have	**8** The twentieth century **may have been** the bloodiest century in history.
	9 If different species of early humans used the same kinds of tools, they **could have used** them in different ways.
	10 If the Archduke Franz Ferdinand had not been assassinated in 1914, World War I **might have been avoided**. . . . The Austro-Hungarian Empire **might not have collapsed**.
	11 If he had not gotten medical treatment in time, he **could have lost** his eyesight.

For more information on modals, see the Resources, pages R-9–R-11. For more information on real and unreal conditionals, see pages R-41–R-42.

B

SHOULD AND WOULD

SHOULD

12 In late October, when the comet makes its closest approach to Earth, it **should be** visible to the naked eye in regions away from cities.

13 The study **should show** that compared to non-certified nurses, certified nurses have better results in managing patients' symptoms.

We can use **should** as a hedge when we want to express a strong expectation about a desirable general or future outcome, as in **12** and **13** (the outcome is highly possible but not certain).

WOULD

14 A lesson on energy **would be** a great opportunity to clarify some basic science concepts.

COMPARE

15a To solve this problem of risky development, one option **would be** to require property developers in potential flood areas to purchase flood insurance.

15b To solve this problem of risky development, one option **might be** to require . . .

Because **would** is often used in hypothetical (unreal) situations, we can use it as a hedge in statements about possible plans and actions for general and future time, as in **14** and **15a**.

May, might, can, and *could* can be used for a similar purpose, but they indicate a stronger hedge (more uncertainty) than *would*. (**15b** is slightly more hedged than **15a**.)

GO ONLINE For more practice with modals and conditionals, go to the Online Practice.

4 | Understanding Modals in Past Conditionals
Underline the modal + main verb in these sentences. Does the modal express a real past possibility or an unreal past possibility? Check (✓) the correct answer. `5.2 A`

	REAL PAST POSSIBILITY	UNREAL PAST POSSIBILITY
SCIENTIFIC SPECULATIONS		
1. If the dangerous effects of global warming had been widely recognized 50 years ago, governments <u>might have cooperated</u> better to reduce the harm.	☐	☑
2. If birds evolved from dinosaurs, some dinosaurs might have had feathers.	☐	☐
3. It might not have been easy to change the way electricity is delivered to homes and businesses, even if cheaper, cleaner, and more efficient ways of generating electricity had been developed.	☐	☐
4. What if planets formed around most stars and many of those planets had atmospheres, mild temperatures, and water? Life could have become common throughout the universe.	☐	☐
5. Geography, climate, and mineral resources are clearly important factors in how civilizations grow and develop. If these factors had been more uniform throughout the world, what other factors might have acquired similar historical importance?	☐	☐
6. Critics of the food industry argued that many diseases might have been much less common if the industry had been more concerned with health than with profits.	☐	☐
7. If the fake fossil known as Piltdown man—an ape's jawbone that had been attached to the skull[17] of a modern human—fooled many scientists, the reason could have been that they were too eager to find a clear evolutionary link between apes and humans.	☐	☐
8. If the oldest evidence of human presence in North America had been found in Alaska, that could have supported the theory that humans from Siberia first entered this continent by a land bridge across the Bering Strait.	☐	☐

5 | Noticing Hedging with Modals
Underline the modal hedges (modal + main verb) in these passages. `5.2 A-B`

1. A wild grizzly bear[18] was spotted in the Bitterroot area of Montana and Idaho, suggesting that a viable[19] population of grizzlies <u>might</u> still <u>exist</u> there. If confirmed, this discovery would mean a lot more protection for the area under the Endangered Species Act.

2. In the Guanajuato region of Mexico, an increase in soil erosion[20] in the second half of the eighteenth century could have been directly associated with an expansion of agriculture. It could be, then, that an increase in flooding at this time was an indirect result of the increased population in the area. Silver mining activities also may have contributed to flooding. Indeed, the devastating[21] 1760 flood in Guanajuato may have been associated with intense mining around that city, though it appears that a severe storm event may have been a direct cause of this flood.

> **RESEARCH SAYS...**
>
> The modals *may, could, might,* and *would* are among the most common hedges in academic writing.
>
> **C**ORPUS

3. On Captain Cook's voyages, the carpenter was responsible for keeping the wooden parts of the ship in good shape. The carpenter on Cook's ship the *Endeavour* had a very important role. When in 1770 the *Endeavour* was wrecked on the Great Barrier Reef in Australia, if Cook and his men had not had a good ship's carpenter on board, they might not have been able to repair the ship and get safely home.

4. A number of people believe that Titan, Saturn's largest moon, might have an environment that is suitable for life but where life has not yet started. So Titan can give us a glimpse of what our planet might have looked like a few billion years ago before life began. In that sense, it might even tell us what our roots are and how we came about.

Titan revolving around Saturn

5. Following recent advice from judges and members of all the main family law[22] professional organizations, the British government is considering measures which would offer divorcing couples greater certainty and clarity. This should lead to less litigation[23] and therefore should reduce costs both for the couple themselves and for the taxpayer. We are considering the benefits of changing the law to add a set of guiding principles which could make clear the process a judge now follows in determining the allocation[24] of property on divorce. This could provide greater certainty and clarity but unlike, for example, a rigid[25] formula, could be flexible enough to take account of individual circumstances.

6 | Hedging with Modals Rewrite these statements, using the modals in parentheses to hedge the statements. Make any necessary changes. 5.2 A–B

ILLEGAL DOWNLOADING OF INTELLECTUAL PROPERTY[26] (MUSIC, MOVIES, BOOKS, ETC.)

1. Technology is advancing far too quickly for intellectual property law to keep up. (might)

2. According to pessimists[27], the idea of intellectual property has come to an end because of new technologies and near-universal Internet access. (may)

3. The introduction of peer-to-peer[28] file sharing—for example, with Napster in 1999—has been a particularly important technological change. (might)

4. For young people today, file sharing seems like simply a usual way of obtaining movies, music, books, and other materials. (can)

5. Many young people—and others—don't see it as wrong to download a movie for free rather than pay for it on Netflix. (might)

6. We are not able to clearly analyze the effects of technological changes so far. (may)

7. As a result of illegal downloading, musicians have experienced a decrease in income. (may)

8. Now that the technology of streaming is more common, the frequency of illegal downloading has declined. (might)

9. Illegal downloading actually helps musicians by giving them more exposure. (could)

10. To combat[29] illegal downloading, one option is to establish educational programs in the field of ethics[30] and intellectual property. (would)

11. By discussing ethical issues, students will gain an awareness of the consequences of illegal downloading. (should)

12. However, the ethical issues, like the effects of the changes, are not as clear as some believe. (might)

GET READY TO READ

You are going to read an article about the ethics of illegal downloading.

Peer-to-Peer File Sharing[31]: Harmful Piracy[32] or Helpful Sharing?

by Aram Sinnreich

Few issues in the world of media and technology are as divisive[33], and as misunderstood, as peer-to-peer (P2P) file sharing. On the face of it[34], the issue seems simple: Hundreds of millions of consumers, using their Internet-connected devices like laptops, phones, and tablets, log on to networks and services like BitTorrent, isoHunt, and the Pirate Bay or share files with one another via cloud[35]

services like Mega, Dropbox, and Google Drive. Businesses that make money from producing and distributing the media consumers share, like record labels[36], movie studios, and software companies, try to stop them, by any means necessary[37]. Some people get caught and have to pay the price[38], while most just shrug their shoulders[39] and keep on doing it. This has been going on since the twentieth century, so today's young people have never known a world without P2P; it's just a normal part of being online. Yet many questions remain: How damaging is this technology, and to whom? Are there potential benefits, as well? And finally, perhaps the most frequently asked but most difficult question of all: Is it wrong?

From the perspective of many companies in the music, film, and software industries, the answers to these questions are straightforward. P2P is digital piracy. Yes, it is damaging, and of course it's wrong. After all, why would a consumer choose to spend money for a movie, game, or album if he or she can simply download it for free? Each time someone downloads a file in this way, they argue, the industry loses the ability to sell it to them. Fewer sales means lower profits, which means that the companies can't make as many products. This, in turn, hurts three different groups:

- *Artists* won't be able to sell as much work or receive as many royalties[40]. For example, global music sales fell by more than a third between 2000 and 2011, according to music industry trade group IFPI.
- *Workers* might lose their jobs. For example, supporters of stronger copyright[41] laws in the U.S. claim that online piracy has cost 750,000 jobs in America alone.
- *Consumers* won't get to enjoy as many movies, albums, and games.

On the other side of the debate stand a range of consumer advocates[42], digital media innovators[43], scholars, and activists, who argue that the media industry's concerns are not based on the facts or are exaggerated. They express concern that the remedies the industry proposes, such as stronger laws, steeper penalties, and heavier policing, will cause more damage than they prevent. For evidence, they point to several sources, including economic analysis by the U.S. government, which has established that the claims of job losses by the media industries cannot be verified, and research by Harvard's Felix Oberholzer-Gee, which shows that "file sharing does not hurt sales at all," in part because it inspires consumers to buy more, rather than less. They also cite[44] examples of popular culture[45] that have thrived either despite or because of their popularity on file-sharing networks, such as HBO's *Game of Thrones*, which was the most popular television show on BitTorrent in 2012, a year during which HBO added 2 million new paying subscribers[46]. Finally, critics argue that the main effects of new copyright laws and international treaties designed to combat digital piracy will actually be to help governments and corporations to spy on private citizens and allow established businesses to collude[47] against innovative newcomers.

Nearly everyone on both sides of the debate can agree that the record labels, movie studios, and software companies face a challenge when it comes to file sharing: specifically, that new technologies create new expectations in the minds of consumers and require new business models to achieve profitability. Most would also agree that the challenge has not yet been met. Though exciting new business models like streaming[48] and cloud storage[49] have emerged in recent years, there are still considerable difficulties in developing legal and economic models that benefit artists, industries, and consumers.

A significant part of the problem could be that it took over a decade for the movie studios and record labels to admit that this challenge existed. If these companies had embraced[50] P2P and used it as a platform to market and distribute their content (rather than demonizing[51] it) when the technology was first introduced, they might have been able to develop and introduce newer business models much sooner and saved everyone both money and trouble.

Finally, as to the question of whether it's wrong for consumers to share files with one another via the Internet: You'll have to decide for yourself.

Talk about It Discuss these questions with a partner.

1. What is peer-to-peer file sharing? Explain it in your own words.

2. Have you ever done P2P file sharing? How? What kinds of file sharing might be legal?

3. What is intellectual property (in your own words)? Why do many countries have intellectual property laws? In way way(s) might P2P file sharing threaten intellectual property?

4. What are some other ways of violating intellectual property laws besides illegal downloading?

Think about It Consider these statements from the reading in Activity 7. Check (✓) the sentences in which the modals help to hedge statements.

1. ☐ Why would a consumer choose to spend money for a movie, game, or album if he or she can simply download it for free?

2. ☐ Nearly everyone on both sides of the debate can agree that the record labels, movie studios, and software companies face a challenge.

3. ☐ A significant part of the problem could be that it took over a decade for the movie studios and record labels to admit that this challenge existed.

4. ☐ If these companies had embraced P2P . . . when the technology was first introduced, they might have been able to develop and introduce newer business models much sooner.

8 | Using Modals in Arguments Complete this chart with information from the reading. Use your own words, and use modals to hedge the arguments you include. (Different answers are possible.) `5.2 A`

ARGUMENTS FOR AND AGAINST PEER-TO-PEER FILE SHARING	
Arguments against P2P file sharing	**Evidence and sources supporting the arguments**
	Who takes this position: many companies in music, film, and software industries
1. P2P file sharing may hurt several groups.	Global music sales fell 1/3+ from 2000 to 2011, according to IFPI (music industry trade group).
2. Artists might not earn as much money.	
3. Workers _____.	750,000 U.S. jobs might have been lost, according to supporters of stronger copyright laws.
4. Consumers _____ _____.	
Arguments for P2P file sharing	**Evidence and sources supporting the arguments**
	Who takes this position: _____ _____ _____
1. Media industry concerns might be false or exaggerated.	
a. Claims about job losses may not be accurate, as they can't be proven true.	_____ _____ _____
b. _____ _____	Research by Oberholzer-Gee of Harvard; research showing that pirating of *Game of Thrones* might have helped HBO
2. Stronger laws and other remedies against digital piracy could do more harm than good.	
a. _____ _____	
b. They could help companies work together to hurt innovative new companies.	
3. The media industry's problems might be its own fault because it did not come up with ways to meet the challenge of file sharing.	

Talk about It The author tells readers they will need to decide for themselves if peer-to-peer file sharing is wrong. Often, authors may not directly state an opinion but their writing may reflect a position. Do you think this author is taking a position on whether peer-to-peer file sharing is wrong? If so, which position do you think he is taking? What makes you think this? Discuss your ideas with your classmates.

Talk about It Do you think file sharing is wrong? Discuss your opinion with a partner.

WRITING ASSIGNMENT I

Follow steps A–D to write a paragraph exploring your opinion of illegal downloading.

A | Planning Follow these steps to plan your paragraph.

1. Make two lists—one of possible points to support an argument for illegal downloading and the other of possible points to support an argument against it. The points can be from the reading and from your own ideas. Then think about these points. Which do you find convincing? Do you have questions about any of them? Add notes to your lists.

<table>
<tr><td align="center">Against illegal downloading</td><td align="center">For illegal downloading</td></tr>
<tr>
<td>• artists might lose money (this would be a problem—artists already don't make much money—or would consumers buy more, like the reading says?)</td>
<td>• people could share ideas, music, etc. more easily (this would be great!)</td>
</tr>
<tr>
<td>• the fact that it's illegal (this seems to me like a very important point)</td>
<td>• it's hard to know when something is wrong (this is important, because it seems like now it's easy to get in trouble without realizing it)</td>
</tr>
</table>

2. Discuss your lists with a partner. Compare lists, and ask for your partner's thoughts about the items in your lists. Add further ideas to your lists.

B | Writing Based on your lists and your discussion with your partner, write a paragraph in which you explore your opinion about illegal downloading of music and other copyrighted material. Do you think it is acceptable or wrong? Acceptable or wrong in all situations or just in some situations? Explore your reasons for your opinion. You may reach a definite conclusion, but you do not have to. Include at least two modals to hedge your ideas.

> *Unlike most of my peers, I am not a big consumer of digital media. I'm more interested in getting together with my friends face to face than by phone, and staring at a screen while pressing buttons doesn't feel like a fun thing to do with another person. That might be why I think it's easy to answer the question of whether illegal downloading is wrong: it's wrong because it's against the law. After all, the law against illegal downloading isn't an obviously bad law with terrible consequences like people dying or losing their homes. Maybe if I were a bigger consumer I would feel more "damaged" by not being able to download music or movies. Most of my peers aren't rich, and they might feel very damaged—shut out from things that are highly important to them—if they couldn't engage in peer-to-peer file sharing. Unfortunately, it seems like almost no one cares that it's illegal, and so many people do it that it's impossible to enforce the law. In my opinion, the only real solution would be to change the law.*

C | Peer Reviewing Share your writing with a partner. Answer these questions about your partner's paragraph.

1. Does your partner explore the points he or she mentions? Are there any important ideas related to these points that are missing and that should be included?
2. If your partner reaches a conclusion, do you feel the points in the paragraph support this conclusion?

D | Revising Follow these steps to revise your paragraph.

1. Using your partner's feedback, rewrite your paragraph.
2. Check your writing for mistakes and clarity. Did you use at least two modal hedges? Make any final corrections necessary.

5.3 Hedging or Boosting with Other Structures

A

HEDGES

1 We worry about what our children see online, and filtering and/or monitoring **seems** like the easy way out.

2 We **think** that this is a **possible** solution to the problem of student learning loss during the summer vacation months.

3 Viewing violence **tends** to correlate with willingness to engage in violence. Children **often** behave differently after they have been watching violent programs on TV. **Sometimes** watching a single violent program can increase aggressiveness.

4 **Perhaps** the task is too difficult for students at that level.

5 On the equator, the day and night stay **approximately** the same length all year.

6 **A number of** universities are now looking at a wider range of factors when considering applicants.

7 In **some** studies, nearly 80 percent of women overestimated their size.

8 There is a **possibility** that people who have come in contact with the patient are at risk.

9 Internet monitoring of employees will have negative results **if it lowers employee morale**.

10 **If my proposal were adopted**, medical students **would be trained** to engage meaningfully with the wide range of people who will be their patients. (NOT: ~~If my proposal was adopted . . .~~)

COMPARE

11a There seems to be some evidence to suggest that cultural differences may explain the communication problems.
(too many hedges)

11b Evidence suggests that cultural differences explain the communication problems.

In addition to modals, there are other structures we can use to **hedge** our statements. These include:

- **main verbs** such as *seem, suggest, appear, tend, assume, believe,* and *think,* as in **1 – 3**
- **adjectives** such as *possible, probable, likely,* or *potential,* as in **2**
- **adverbs***: **frequency adverbs** such as *sometimes* and *often;* **stance adverbs** such as *possibly, perhaps, likely,* and *typically;* and **degree adverbs** such as *somewhat* and *approximately,* as in **3 – 5**
- **quantifiers** such as *some, a number of, many,* or *most,* as in **6 – 7**
- **nouns** such as *possibility* or *likelihood,* as in **8**
- **conditional adverb clauses**, as in **9** (real conditional) and **10** (unreal conditional with *would / would have*)

Remember: For the present unreal conditional of the verb *be,* as in **10**, we use *were* for all subjects. This is a **subjunctive** form.

WARNING! Be careful not to use too many hedges together, as this can make your writing seem weak, as in **11a**.

*For more information on adverbs and adverbials, see the Resources, page R-36.

B

BOOSTERS

12 Facilitating a culture of trust **will result** in employees' conforming to certain rules as a result of mutual respect.

13 Both sides **must be required** to come to the table to work out a solution that benefits everyone.

14 We have a **clear** responsibility to adopt practices that will spare future generations significant harm.

15 Overcrowding in the classroom is a **serious** issue that needs to be addressed.

16 The data indicates with **certainty** that the new law has prevented some people from voting.

17 Privacy has become a major problem today because of **the fact that social media dominates our lives**.

18 **Obviously**, **all** information should be free, and **all** programs should be available for copying.

19 Scientists have **clearly demonstrated** that the fuel cell electric drive is ready for the road.

20 America **urgently needs** a new approach that gives both businesses and workers flexibility.

21 These studies **document** that several sources contributed to the contamination of the drinking water.

Structures we can use to boost statements include:

- the **modals** *will* and *must,* as in **12 – 13**
- **adjectives** such as *obvious, clear, definite, significant,* and *serious,* as in **14 – 15**
- **nouns** such as *certainty, evidence,* and *fact,* and **noun clauses beginning with *the fact that*,** as in **16 – 17**
- **quantifiers** such as *all* or *no,* as in **18**
- **adverbs** such as *obviously, certainly, surely, clearly, always, never, actually, indeed,* and *urgently,* as in **18 – 20**
- **main verbs** such as *demonstrate, show, know, require, document,* and *need,* as in **19 – 21**

WARNING! Use boosters only with great care and only to make a very strong statement. Make sure they do not affect the accuracy of your statements. Overuse of boosters can affect your credibility with readers.

9 | Identifying Hedges Underline the hedges in these passages. Look for the different types of hedges shown in Chart 5.3 A. (Different answers are possible.) `5.3 A`

SCIENTIFIC RESEARCH

1. Research proposals must <u>sometimes</u> be reviewed quickly to meet funding deadlines. Timing is <u>probably</u> the main factor to consider in designing proposals.

2. In our clinical trial on mouth and throat cancer, it looked as though beta carotene[52] might have significantly lowered the risk of a recurrence[53] of cancer if the study had been larger.

3. It seems that we like people who are somewhat masculine or feminine, but not too much. The reasoning is that maybe women want men who can be somewhat sensitive and gentle, and good providers, while men want women who have some spunk[54]. Again, this is guesswork; there could be another explanation entirely.

4. Government agencies in Japan and Europe are already playing a central role in robotics[55]. If we fail to think about proper policy now, robotics could be the first significant technology since steam in which America has not played a role.

5. A study conducted by a research team from the University of Oxford revealed data that suggests a possible relationship between obesity[56] and dementia[57]. According to the team, the risk tends to be higher for people who were obese when younger. Various factors appear to reinforce this possible link between obesity in early life and dementia. However, further research may be necessary.

engineer working on a robot

6. New research suggests that a faltering[58] sense of smell might signal the early stages of Alzheimer's disease[59] and that an inexpensive, low-tech smell test could spot who needs more extensive screening for dementia. According to Dr. Kenneth Heilman, a professor at the University of Florida College of Medicine in Gainesville, "A loss of sense of smell does not mean you have Alzheimer's disease. But if [it occurs together with other symptoms], Alzheimer's is a possibility."

7. Global warming could send North America and Western Europe into a deep freeze, possibly within only a few decades. The thawing[60] of sea ice covering the Arctic could disturb or even halt[61] large currents[62] in the Atlantic Ocean. Without the vast heat that these ocean currents deliver, Europe's average temperature would likely drop 5 to 10 degrees Celsius. . . . Some scientists believe this shift in ocean currents could come surprisingly soon.

Talk about It Compare and discuss your answers above with a partner. Did you and your partner identify different words as hedges?

Think about It Write the hedges (without the clauses) that you underlined above in this chart. Based on Activity 9, which kinds of words seem to be especially common as hedges?

Main verb	Modal	Quantifier	Adverb	Adjective	Noun

10 | Using Different Structures to Hedge Rewrite the statements below to include hedges using the structure in parentheses. Use the words in the box or your own words. Add and change words in the sentences as needed. (Different answers are possible.) **5.3 A**

likely (adj)	may	seem	sometimes
main	often	some	suggest

1. The reason that students fail to meet deadlines is poor time management skills. (adjective)

   The main reason that students fail to meet deadlines is poor time management skills.

2. Babies get an uncomfortable condition called *colic*[63]. (quantifier)

3. Infants'[64] cries relate to discomfort of some sort. (adverb)

4. It is the case that all our emotions develop from two basic emotions in infancy. (modal)

5. The best way to make our writing clear is to use simple sentence structures. (adverb)

6. The evidence shows that relatively advanced civilizations existed in ancient times in the Ohio and Mississippi valleys. (verb)

7. Cultural assimilation[65] was the outcome for Native Americans who survived contact with Europeans. (adjective)

8. Obesity rates in American children and teenagers are slowing down and even dropping. (verb)

a colicky baby

Write about It Rewrite four of the sentences you wrote above with a different type of hedge for a different hedged sentence with a similar meaning. Then compare answers with a partner.

11 | Identifying Boosters Underline the boosters in these passages. Look for the different types of boosters shown in Chart 5.3 B. (Different answers are possible.) **5.3 B**

1. The tobacco industry is raising numerous issues which may distract the public from the fact that secondhand smoke[66] poses a real and preventable health risk.

2. A new study shows that eating trans-fats[67]—used in many packaged cookies and crackers—may damage memory. . . . The benefits of reducing or eliminating trans-fats are obvious, said a scientist who was interviewed. "Heart disease is declining more rapidly in areas where trans-fats have been banned and trans-fat reduction is almost surely contributing to recent declines in diabetes rates in the U.S."

3. All these contaminants wind up in storm drains[68], where they usually travel untreated[69] into the nearest river or lake. Polluted runoff[70] has serious consequences for the health of our waterways, wildlife, and ourselves. Moreover, in the absence of new measures to control runoff, the problems will certainly increase.

4. People who argue that sexism[71] does not exist in science are wrong. The data in this study shows they are wrong. And if you encounter them, you can now use this study to inform them they're wrong. You can say that a study found that absolutely all other factors held equal, females are discriminated against in science. Sexism exists. It's real.

> **RESEARCH SAYS...**
>
> Common boosters in academic writing include *will*, *the fact that*, *show*, *clear*, *clearly*, *obvious*, *actually*, *indeed*, *always*, and *of course*.
>
> **C**ORPUS

Talk about It Compare and discuss your answers in Activity 11 with a partner. Did you and your partner identify different words as boosters?

Think about It Write the boosters (without the clause) that you underlined in Activity 11 in this chart.

Main verb	Modal	Quantifier	Adverb	Adjective

Think about It Notice that passage 2 of Activity 11 also has hedges. Why do you think the writer of this passage used boosters and hedges together?

12 | Noticing the Effects of Boosters
Read the two passages, and identify words and phrases that you feel serve as boosters. Compare answers with a partner. (Different answers are possible.) **5.3 B**

TWO ETHICAL AND PRACTICAL CALLS FOR ECOLOGICAL[72] ACTION

1. The climate crisis is, <u>indeed</u>, <u>extremely</u> dangerous. <u>In fact</u>, it is a <u>true</u> planetary[73] emergency. Two thousand scientists, in a hundred countries, working for more than twenty years in the most elaborate[74] and well-organized scientific collaboration in the history of humankind, have forged[75] an exceptionally strong consensus[76] that all the nations on Earth must work together to solve the crisis of global warming.

   The voluminous[77] evidence now strongly suggests that unless we act boldly and quickly to deal with the underlying[78] causes of global warming, our world will undergo a string of terrible catastrophes, including more and stronger storms like Hurricane Katrina, in both the Atlantic and the Pacific. We are melting the North Polar ice cap and virtually all of the mountain glaciers[79] in the world. We are destabilizing[80] the massive mound[81] of ice on Greenland and the equally enormous mass of ice propped up[82] on top of islands in West Antarctica, threatening a worldwide increase in sea levels of as much as twenty feet.

   —from Al Gore, *An Inconvenient Truth*

2. While there's little agreement as to what's going to happen ecologically due to human activity, there's no doubt that we've made drastic changes to just about every natural habitat[83] on the planet. Our oceans and natural water sources are polluted, the composition of our soil has been chemically altered, the atmosphere has been heavily influenced by emissions[84], our forests have been dramatically reduced, and on and on.

   One area of particular importance is biodiversity[85]. Beyond the fact that biodiversity itself protects humans from the effects of agricultural catastrophes like the Irish potato famine[86], the loss of a species results in significant changes in natural habitats that can hurt us badly down the road[87].

   —from Brian Clark, "The Butterfly Effect and the Environment"

RESEARCH SAYS...

Some words—including *often, usually, frequently, likely, many, most,* and *typically*—can be either **hedges** or **boosters**, depending on the context. Compare:

Although it's too soon to say, the outcome of the election will **likely** be a conservative shift.

Successful change is not only possible but the **likely** outcome.

CORPUS

the Briksdal Glacier in Norway

Think about It In each passage above, can you find a hedge used along with a booster?

Write about It Rewrite one of the passages in Activity 12, omitting the boosters you identified or replacing them with words and phrases that do not boost. Make any other changes necessary to keep the sentences grammatical. Read your rewritten passage, and compare it to the original passage. What differences do the boosters make?

Think about It In addition to using boosters, the authors of the passages in Activity 12 strengthen the language of their argument by choosing some words that are stronger than other possible choices. For example, in the first passage, the author describes the situation as a "planetary emergency," rather than as just a "problem." Read the passages again, and write down other words like these that you find. Compare answers with a partner.

13 | Hedging and Boosting Sentences Hedge or boost the **bold** words in the sentences below by using the words in the box to replace and/or add to the **bold** words. Make any other changes necessary. (Different answers are possible.) Compare answers with a partner. `5.3 A–B`

can	important	most	significantly
considerable	many	show	

ETHICS

1. Ethics, a branch of philosophy, **is defined** as the study of right and wrong behavior and of the right way to live. (hedge)
2. **People** learn ethical principles at home, at school, and in the community. (hedge)
3. Ethics play **a role** in **our daily-life decisions**. (booster; hedge)
4. There are **differences** among people when it comes to ethical principles and decision making. (booster)
5. Studies **suggest** that different people look at the same issue from different ethical perspectives. (booster)
6. Indeed, over the centuries philosophers have developed **different** theories of ethics. (booster)

> **GET READY TO READ**
>
> You are going to read summaries of the theories of three important thinkers in the history of the philosophy of ethics.

14 | Reading Read the article. Then do the tasks on page 169.

Theories of Ethics
by Joseph Chuman

Immanuel Kant

Immanuel Kant

Immanuel Kant proposed that when you make a moral decision, you should ask yourself a question: What if everyone acted this way? Kant advocated the use of maxims, personal rules that you use to make a moral decision. He said that you must never act in a way that contradicts[88] a maxim. For Kant, there is no concept of "sometimes." He was an absolutist.

One of Kant's maxims is that we must never lie. He once said that he would tell a murderer where his intended victim was hiding. Because we cannot predict consequences, we must ignore them and be consistent[89].

According to Kant, people must respect all other people and their freedom because human beings possess dignity[90]. We should never use people as tools, as we do chairs or a pen. Lying is a form of manipulation[91], a way of using someone as a tool.

John Stuart Mill

John Stuart Mill

John Stuart Mill believed that if you want to act morally, you have to look at consequences. He said that you must use your imagination and try to predict the results of your actions. For Mill, you are acting morally if the consequences of your action bring happiness to the greatest number of people, including yourself. If people will suffer because of your action, then you shouldn't do it.

Because Mill's ideas only deal with consequences, his philosophy of ethics is called utilitarianism. In Mill's view, you should weigh the morality of an action in terms of its utility, or usefulness.

Aristotle

Aristotle

For Aristotle, those things that help us grow and flourish[92] are good, and those things that stifle[93] or stunt[94] our growth are bad. Aristotle's concept of growth includes those physical and social things that are necessary for human development. The physical things include clean air and water and good food. The social things include friendship, supportive social relationships, and education.

If you are attempting to live an ethical life, Aristotle said you should ask yourself what kind of person you want to become. Then you can make moral choices based on whether an action will help you become that person. Also crucial to living an ethical life is the development of virtue[95], by acting in a way that reflects practical wisdom, moderation[96], courage, and justice. Justice involves treating other people in a way that is fair and appropriate.

Think about It Although the words *should* and *must* occur various times in the description of Kant's ideas in Activity 14, their use cannot really be considered hedging or boosting. Why not? More generally, Chuman does not use hedges and boosters in his descriptions of Kant, Mill, and Aristotle. Why do you think he does not?

Think about It Discuss these questions with a partner.

1. The theories of Kant, Mill, and Aristotle each represent one of the three main types of ethical theories. Ethics relates to situations where a person performs an action, which has consequences. Which one of the three philosophers focused on the action itself? Which one focused on the consequences of the action? Which one focused on the person?

2. Summarize each of the three theories of ethics in your own words. Which of the three theories do you most agree with? Which of the theories do you least agree with? How would you describe your own theory of ethics?

15 | Hedging or Boosting Ideas Read the scenarios. Check (✓) *Yes* or *No* to answer each question based on your understanding of the reading on pages 168–169. `5.3 A–B`

Ethical Dilemmas

		YES	NO
1.	A friend invites you to his house for dinner. You don't want to go, but you don't want to hurt his feelings, so you tell a "white lie" (a small, harmless lie): you have to study for a test. Would Kant approve of telling this white lie?	☐	☑
2.	A medical test reveals bad news about a patient. Her doctor decides to keep this bad news from the patient in order to give her hope. Would Kant approve of this?	☐	☐
3.	You are walking on the beach and you see someone drowning. There's no lifeguard[97] on the beach, and no time to get help. You can swim, but you're not a great swimmer. Although it makes you terribly upset, you decide you had better not try to save the person. Would Mill approve of this?	☐	☐
4.	Medical researchers decide to test an experimental drug on some patients. The patients are terminally[98] ill and cannot be helped by the drug. Would Mill approve of this?	☐	☐
5.	A graduate student is applying for a summer internship[99] that would be extremely useful for her professional development and credentials[100]. To have a realistic chance of getting the internship, she needs a slightly higher GPA (grade point average). She decides to "round up" her GPA on her application. Would Aristotle approve of this?	☐	☐
6.	A student has become a computer and video game addict. He spends hours developing his computer skills. His contacts with people are almost entirely through social media. Would Aristotle approve of this?	☐	☐

Write about It Write each answer above as a sentence. Some answers are clearer from the readings than others are. Hedge or boost your answers accordingly.

Kant definitely would not approve of telling a white lie to protect a friend's feelings.

Talk about It Compare your answers above with a partner. Are your answers the same? Did you hedge and boost the same answers? Discuss any differences, supporting your opinions with ideas from the reading.

Think about It Why do we use the word *would* in the question for each scenario and in our answers? What does the use of *would* signal to a reader or listener?

Follow steps A–D to write a paragraph about one of the scenarios in Activity 15. You will write about the philosopher's response to the scenario and about whether you agree or disagree.

A | Planning Follow these steps to plan your paragraph.

1. Make a list of three scenarios from Activity 15 that interest you. Think about your own response to each scenario and about the reasons for your response. Do you agree with the philosopher? Make notes next to the scenario.

   • *lying to a friend: I don't agree with Kant that this is wrong—people often tell lies like this so their friends won't feel bad.*

   • *bad news on a medical test: Again, I don't agree with Kant—people are different, and what to do here might depend on the person.*

   • *not trying to rescue a person who is drowning: I'm not really sure what Mill would say (?), but I wouldn't approve of not trying to save the person.*

2. Discuss your list with a partner. Does your partner agree with your responses and reasons? Why or why not? If this discussion gives you further ideas about the scenarios, add these ideas to your notes.

B | Writing Choose one of the scenarios from your list. Write a paragraph in which you discuss the ethics of the scenario. Give the philosopher's response and reasons; then indicate whether you agree with the philosopher's response, and give your own response and reasons. Include hedges and boosters where you think softening or strengthening your statements is appropriate.

Clearly, Kant would never approve of lying to a patient about the result of a medical test, even if the test showed that the patient had a terrible, painful disease and didn't have long to live. Kant would probably say that we couldn't know for sure that the test result was correct and that lying would be taking away the patient's freedom to decide how to use her remaining time. I mostly agree with Kant, but I would not say never. For example, what if the patient was terrified of dying and unable to keep from becoming hysterical and falling apart? What if the person was young, like 17 or 18, and her parents wanted the test results kept secret from her? I think Kant is wrong not to see that there might be valid exceptions to such an absolute rule, not just in this scenario but in a lot of other cases too. In fact, it's probably impossible to think of an ethical rule that would apply in every possible situation.

C | Peer Reviewing Share your writing with a partner. Answer these questions about your partner's paragraph.

1. Does your partner clearly explain the philosopher's response and reasons and his or her own response and reasons? Could your partner add anything to make this discussion of responses and reasons clearer?
2. Find the hedges and boosters in the paragraph. Does your partner use them appropriately?

D | Revising Follow these steps to revise your paragraph.

1. Using your partner's feedback, rewrite your paragraph.
2. Check your writing for mistakes and clarity. Did you include hedges and boosters? Are there any other statements in your paragraph that you want to hedge or boost? Make any final corrections necessary.

5.4 Using the Passive in Complex Sentences

THE PASSIVE

Remember: The **passive** lets us highlight the receiver of the action by reordering information in sentences. In academic writing, we often use passive verb forms (rather than **active** verb forms) when the agent is obvious or unimportant.

COMPARE

1a Scientists have gained major insights into the birth of stars and planets and into the origin of the universe.
1b Major insights have been gained into the birth of stars and planets and into the origin of the universe.

For more information on using the passive, see the Usage Note on page 174 and the Resources, pages R-12–R-16.

A

USING THE PASSIVE IN A *THAT* CLAUSE OR *TO*- INFINITIVE CLAUSE **2a** Archeologists believe that an early artist made the statue about 25,000 BCE. (*The statue* is the object of the *that* clause.) **2b** Archeologists believe that the statue was made about 25,000 BCE. (*The statue* is the subject of the *that* clause.) **3a** Police believe unknown persons to have started the fire deliberately. **3b** Police believe the fire to have been started deliberately.	We can use the passive in a *that* clause or *to*- infinitive clause, as in **2b** and **3b**. The **object** of an **active** clause becomes the **subject** of the **passive** clause, as in **2a** – **2b** and **3a** – **3b**. The use of the passive puts the emphasis on the receiver of the action (*the statue*; *the fire*), rather than on the agent (*an early artist*; *unknown persons*).
USING THE PASSIVE IN THE MAIN CLAUSE **4a** Scientists now assume that REM sleep is necessary for infant brain development. **4b** It is now assumed that REM sleep is necessary for infant brain development. **4c** That REM sleep is necessary for infant brain development is now assumed. (less common) **5a** Investigators assume the remains to be those of Miguel de Cervantes, the famed author of *Don Quixote*. **5b** The remains are assumed to be those of Miguel de Cervantes, the famed author of *Don Quixote*.	We can use **active** or **passive** forms in the main clause of a complex sentence (a sentence with two or more clauses), as in **4a** – **4c** (with a *that* clause) and **5a** – **5b** (with a *to*- infinitive clause). In sentences with a *that* clause, we can use an **empty it** as the subject of the passive main clause, as in **4b**. The empty *it* subject is common with verbs such as *believe*, *think*, *say*, *argue*, and *know* (verbs that describe speech, thought, or belief). The empty *it* lets us put a long element (new information) at the end of a sentence. NOTE: Instead of using the empty *it* structure, we can make the entire *that* clause the subject, as in **4c**. However, the empty *it* structure is more common and often creates better cohesion.
USING THE PASSIVE IN BOTH CLAUSES **6** Alpacas are a member of the Camelid family. It is believed that they were created through selective breeding. **7** All the issues with the car were thought to have been addressed.	We can also use the passive both in the main clause and in the *that* clause or *to*- infinitive clause, as in **6** – **7**.

GO ONLINE For more practice with the passive with empty *it*, go to the Online Practice.

16 | Identifying the Passive
Underline the passive verb forms in these passages. (The passive forms may appear in the main clause, *that* clause, or *to-* infinitive clause.) Then follow the instructions below. `5.4 A`

Dawenkou pottery

1. A study <u>was conducted</u> by Kirby (1996) with the aim of investigating mood changes associated with the cognitive[101] processes of an elite[102] runner during a 48-hour race. Cognitive processes were assessed by asking the running athlete what she was thinking immediately before, during, and after the run.

2. At the Dawenkou and Taixi sites in China, no pottery signs with numerals[103] have been discovered. However, it cannot be concluded that numerals had not been used by inhabitants at that time. The sample is too small to allow for such a conclusion. Comparing the pottery signs from these two sites with pottery signs from other sites before and after that time, it has been shown that numerals had been understood and used by people at that time.

3. During the 1950s, a theory was proposed concerning "pole[104] shift," a periodic shift of the earth's crust[105], which moved the poles. The main reason for this was the buildup of ice at the poles. It was theorized that the weight from the increase in ice and snow would, over a long period of time, become too heavy and make the crust slip. Again, an asteroid[106] hitting the earth was thought to possibly be a cause for this. The earth slip theory was proved to be wrong.

4. In Armenia, women are considered to be the transmitters[107] of culture, customs, and tradition and are seen as responsible for child rearing[108]. Children are highly valued and they occupy the center of attention in households until they reach puberty[109]. At puberty they are disciplined[110] and are expected to take on responsibilities.

5. Estimates of the risks associated with exposure to dangerous types of radiation[111] are based mainly on studies of people exposed to high levels of radiation. The most important study is that of the survivors of the atom bomb attacks on Japan. The health of these survivors has been studied over several decades.

6. No other plant species has been found to be susceptible[112] to the brown spot fungus[113]. While brown spot fungus does not usually affect soybean yield[114] in Nebraska, it does become increasingly more severe with the continuous growth of soybeans in a field.

INSTRUCTIONS

1. Of the sentences in which you underlined the passive verb forms above, which three sentences include an empty *it* subject and a *that* clause? Write a checkmark (✓) above those sentences.

2. Of the sentences in which you underlined the passive verb forms above, which five sentences include a *to-* infinitive clause? Write an *X* in front of those sentences.

Think about It Can you find two sentences above that have a passive form in both clauses—in the main clause and in the *that* or *to-* infinitive clause?

Write about It Work with a partner. Rewrite passage 4 above using active sentences instead of passive sentences. Compare your passage to the original passage. What difference does the passive make? Why did the writer of the original passage use the passive?

17 | Usage Note: Functions of the Passive in Academic Writing Read the note. Then do Activity 18.

In academic and other informational texts, writers may favor the **passive** in some contexts because the passive has several important uses.

1 The procedures **must be performed** in the same sequence in each repetition (by experimenters).	The passive allows writers to:
2 Jackie Robinson **was chosen** by Branch Rickey to break baseball's color barrier because Rickey knew he had the strength of character to overcome the taunts that would come. Robinson won the Rookie of the Year award in 1947 and helped lead the Dodgers to seven pennants in the ten years he played for them. He **was elected** to the Baseball Hall of Fame in 1962.	• de-emphasize an unimportant, obvious, or unknown agent by moving it out of the subject position, either by deleting it or by moving it to a later position in the sentence (in a *by* phrase), as in **1**.
3 The accurate but cumbersome method of DNA fingerprinting of the 1990s **was replaced** by a new method. This new method . . . (The writer was discussing the 1990s method. Now he introduces and will discuss the new method.)	• establish or continue the focus on the topic of a passage by putting the topic in the subject position, as in **2**. This makes the topic more noticeable or closer to the preceding discussion of it. In example **2**, Jackie Robinson, not Branch Rickey, is the topic.
4 Statistics vary, but **it is thought** that viral meningitis causes between 25,000 and 50,000 hospital visits each year in the U.S. (hedge)	• put new information later in the sentence (in a *by* phrase), while putting old information, often the topic, in the subject position, as in **3**.
5 **It is known** that water quality is an issue of public concern. (boost)	• hedge or boost sentences with verbs of thinking / believing followed by a *that* clause or *to*- infinitive clause. Using **empty it** + verb + *that* clause, as in **4** and **5**, draws readers' attention to the hedging or boosting verb and to the claim that follows in the *that* clause.
	In these ways, the passive can help make writing more cohesive.

18 | Identifying Functions of the Passive Read the beginning of the article below about a famous psychology experiment. Look at the passive forms in **bold**. Why is the passive used in each instance? Consider the reasons listed in the word box and write *1*, *2*, and/or *3* above each passive form. (You may list more than one reason for each example.) **5.4 A**

> REASONS TO USE THE PASSIVE
> 1. to move or omit an unimportant, obvious, or unknown agent
> 2. to keep the focus on a noun phrase that is the topic by using it in the subject position
> 3. to put new information later in the sentence

The Stanford Prison Experiment

The Stanford prison experiment was a study of the psychological effects of becoming a prisoner or a prison guard. The experiment **was conducted** at Stanford University during August 14–20, 1971 by a team of researchers led by psychology professor Philip Zimbardo. It **was funded** by the U.S. Office of Naval Research and was of interest to both the U.S. Navy and the U.S. Marine

RESEARCH SAYS...

In passive sentences, we omit active agents far more often than we move them (85 percent versus 15 percent of the time).

CORPUS

Corps as an investigation into the causes of conflict between military guards and prisoners.

Twenty-four male students **were selected** to take on randomly assigned roles of prisoners and guards in a mock[115] prison situated in the basement of the Stanford psychology building. . . .

19 | Using the Passive in Writing Rewrite the **bold** sentences or clauses in the passive to improve cohesion. (Different answers are possible.) `5.4 A`

1. Paris clearly demanded a republic. Thus, **on 21 September, the members of the assembly[116] laid the foundation of the new constitution. The members of the assembly abolished monarchy[117] in France.**

   Thus, on 21 September, the foundation of the new constitution was laid.

2. At what point would the expansion of the citizenship affect the basic categories and distinctions on which Greek culture was based—and in this way encourage revolution[118]? **People and politicians had raised this complex set of questions in the very early days of Greek culture.**

3. It was an exciting time. **Scientists had proven that uranium[119] gives off radiation similar to X-rays.** In fact, **scientists had only just discovered X-rays**. Thomson built upon this work by demonstrating the existence of the electron[120].

4. Jane Goodall rocked the scientific world in the 1960s with the discovery that chimpanzees[121] make and use tools. **Previously, scientists had thought that only humans use tools.**

5. **Scientists have shown that most of the human genome[122] originated long before humans themselves. Consequently, scientists will use the genomes of the 11 non-mammalian[123] animals** to learn more about the human genome.

Jane Goodall

6. Parenting that is psychologically unavailable can seriously compromise[124] a child's development by punishing normal behaviors. **Psychologists have found effects of such parenting to include decreased academic performance and emotional instability.**

7. The main division of labor in Venezuela is between rural and urban populations. **By far, people consider rural occupations such as agriculture to be less sophisticated.**

8. On several occasions during the past years, astronomical images revealed faint[125] objects, seen near much brighter stars. **Astronomers have thought some of these images to be of orbiting[126] planets.**

9. So long as astronomers had the planets moving in perfect circles, **astronomers assumed their speed to be constant[127]**, so the predictions were never quite right. Kepler allowed the planets to move in ellipses[128], and at last the planets began to show up on time.

elliptical orbits

Talk about It Compare your answers above with a partner. If your answers to an item are different, read the different versions aloud. Does one version sound better? If so, why?

20 | Error Correction Read this student paragraph and think about how you can improve the writing by using active and passive sentences. Decide whether each sentence would be better as an active or a passive sentence. Write *A* over a sentence (passive or active) that you think should be active. Write *P* over a sentence (passive or active) that you think should be passive. Then edit the paragraph to show your decisions. (Different answers are possible.) **5.4 A**

GMO Foods

A

GMO foods are foods that are genetically modified organisms[129]—plants or other living things whose genes have been changed in some way. In the U.S. today, farmers plant GMOs on about half of the total land used for crops. People continue to debate the benefits and costs of GMOs. That GMO crops make possible higher crop yields is believed to be one benefit. Perhaps the most important benefit is that GMO crops make possible the use of fewer pesticides[130] and herbicides[131]. In the past, many environmental problems were caused by the use of pesticides and herbicides. However, GMOs may also have serious costs, including for human health. Scientific research has not yet fully determined the effects on human health. Also, the developers of GMOs do not always know the full range of effects of modifying genes. Unexpected—and harmful—effects are therefore a possibility. Moreover, if GMO plants cross-pollinate[132] with other plants, those other plants may be affected as well. For all these reasons, we need much more research into the possible effects of GMO plants.

Talk about It Compare your answers above with a partner. Discuss any differences between your edited paragraphs. For each sentence, explain why you preferred an active or a passive version.

5.5 Empty *It* Constructions in Active Sentences

In addition to its use in passive sentences with *that* clauses, we can use **empty it** in active sentences with a *that* clause or *to-* infinitive clause, as in **1 – 3**. In these sentences, the main clause has a **linking verb**, such as *be, seem,* or *appear*. Sometimes the linking verb is followed by an **adjective**.

A

1a It seems that the source of this "bird flu" is an animal other than a bird.

1b It seems **possible** that the source of this "bird flu" is an animal other than a bird.

2 It is **important** that the reader continually **ask** questions.

3 In order to understand the meaning of particular behaviors, **it is important** to have an understanding of what causes the behavior in the first place.

An **adjective** may or may not be used with *seem* or *appear* before a *that* clause, as in **1a – 1b**.

Following certain **adjectives** (usually with a meaning of necessity or requirement), we use the **subjunctive form of the verb**[*] (the base form) in the *that* clause, as in **2**. These adjectives include:

appropriate	essential	important	necessary
crucial	imperative	impossible	

Notice that the empty it can introduce a hedge, as in **1a – 1b** (with *seems* and *seems possible*) or a booster, as in **2 – 3** (with *important*).

*For more information on the subjunctive form, see the Resources, page R-25.

21 | Identifying Constructions with an Empty *It* Underline the constructions with an empty *it*.

5.5 A

1. By 1968 <u>it was estimated that 96 percent of black-footed ferret habitat had been eliminated from South Dakota</u>. In Meeteetse, Wyoming a population of black-footed ferrets was discovered in 1981, seven years after it was thought that black-footed ferrets went extinct[133].

2. In flying aphids it has been suggested that the primary function of color vision lies in distinguishing plants from the sky. Eastop suggested that the aphid's sensitivity to color may be related to the plants it feeds on. Our recent studies have shown for the first time that the flight activity of aphids in an environment without ultraviolet[134] light was dramatically reduced.

3. During the late nineteenth and early twentieth centuries, many valleys in the American West began to be covered with arroyos[135]. Theories of arroyo formation[136] involving climate changes have recently been proposed. It is known that arroyos existed before humans occupied the area, so it appears likely that arroyos can occur as a natural part of drainage[137] system development.

4. The influence of Welsh is strongest in the northern counties, where Welsh/English bilingualism is most commonly found. It is not certain when speakers of an English dialect arrived in Wales, but it seems probable that Mercian settlers[138] were in the Wye valley by the eighth century. In the winter of 1108–1109, Henry I established a group of Flemish settlers in Pembrokeshire, and it is likely that there were English speakers among that group.

5. To understand the genetic basis of tame[139] and aggressive behavior in the silver fox, it is first essential to have a genome map[140] of the fox. Fortunately, due to the evolutionary relationship between the dog and fox, the relationship between the dog and fox genomes is well understood.

6. Younger bears are not as efficient at catching seals, so many may rely on the remains of kills made by other bears. It is possible that if, with climate warming, polar bears' kills are reduced, a result may be less food for younger bears. How species of seals will be affected by climate warming is also uncertain, but it appears possible that habitat for ringed seals in particular may be reduced.

7. The cemetery served the community from around 1834 until its abandonment[141] in 1873. Before the excavations[142] of 1994, local tradition held that the grave contents at the Grafton Cemetery had been moved to the new Scenic Hill Cemetery. The tradition appears to be based entirely upon the fact that at least 29 grave markers from the old Grafton Cemetery were moved to the new one sometime after 1872. It was assumed that the contents of those graves were moved with them. Archeological[143] evidence, however, suggests otherwise[144].

F Y I

In addition to using *it* with **that** noun clauses, we also use it with **wh-** noun clauses (noun clauses beginning with *who, where,* etc.).

It is known **that** 60 percent of mice vaccinated with medicine are protected from a certain disease.

It is not known **what** was said, but one source said the remarks were inappropriate.

black-footed ferrets

aphids

arroyo

8. For many years the thymus gland[145] was held to be a nonfunctioning leftover[146] of evolution. We now understand the thymus gland's important function in the development of a normal immune system[147]. The tonsils, appendix, and pineal gland are further examples of organs that long were held to be leftovers from evolution but now are known to have important functions in the development and operation of our bodies. It would seem that evolution has been a hindrance[148] rather than a help in the practice of medicine.

Think about It Which passages in Activity 21 include an *it* construction . . .

1. in a passive sentence with a *that* clause? _____1_____
2. in an active sentence with a *that* clause? _____
3. in an active sentence with a *to-* infinitive clause? _____

Think about It Which passage in Activity 21 includes an *it* construction with a *wh-* noun clause?

22 | Usage Note: Special Uses of Modals in Arguments Read the note. Then do Activity 23.

In arguments, we sometimes use **modals**, especially *may*, *might*, and *could*, in a main clause that introduces an idea we will argue against, as in **1a**, **2a**, and **3a**. The idea (with which we disagree) is presented in a *that* clause. By using a modal hedge in this way, we soften the idea we will argue against.

We may introduce our argument in the next sentence, as in **1b**, **2b**, and **3b**. We may use a **connecting word of contrast** for this, as in **1b** and **3b**.

   1 [a] It **might** be thought that we are in the presence of something culturally unusual. [b] In fact, **however**, I would argue quite the contrary.

   2 [a] As everyone has smart devices, it **could** seem that people would have a pretty comprehensive knowledge of technology. [b] That isn't exactly the case.

   3 [a] One **may** assume that in poor countries, girls live harder lives than boys. [b] **However**, the data shows a more complex picture.

23 | Using Modals to Introduce and Argue Against an Idea Look at the arguments in the readings on pages 160–161 and 168–169. Find two arguments that you do not agree with, and for each argument, write a pair of sentences with the argument and an opposing argument. Use modals to introduce the ideas you will argue against.

It might be assumed that musicians lose money when people download their music without paying. I would argue, however, that these downloads help musicians make more money.

WRITING ASSIGNMENT III

Follow steps A–D to write a paragraph examining illegal downloading in terms of your views and the views of one of the philosophers discussed in "Theories of Ethics" on pages 168–169.

A | Planning Follow these steps to plan your paragraph.

1. Look back at the reading on pages 168–169. What do you think Kant, Mill, and Aristotle would have thought about the illegal downloading of music and movies from the Internet? In the chart on page 179, check (✓) *Ethical*, *Unethical*, or *Not sure* (if you think the philosopher would not have been sure). Then explain why.

ILLEGAL DOWNLOADING			
	Ethical	Unethical	Not sure	Reasons
Kant	☐	☐	☐	
Mill	☐	☐	☐	
Aristotle	☐	☐	☐	
My opinion	☐	☐	☐	

2. With a partner, discuss the philosophers' ideas and then your own ideas. Ask and answer the following questions: Do you and your partner agree about what the philosophers would think and why? Do you think illegal downloading is ethical or unethical or are you not sure? What are your reasons? Are they similar to any of the philosophers' reasons, or are they different reasons?

3. After the discussion, revise the chart above. Include any new ideas about the philosophers, and complete the last row to give your opinion and reasons.

B | Writing Choose one of the philosophers. Write a paragraph in which you discuss the ethics of illegal downloading in terms of the philosopher's likely opinion and reasons and your response to the philosopher based on your own opinion and reasons. Include hedges and boosters, as well as at least one passive verb form and at least one construction with an empty *it*.

I find myself unable to decide if it is ethical to illegally download files from the Internet. Similarly, I feel that Aristotle probably would have been unsure about it, if he had known about downloading and the Internet. Aristotle says that things that help us grow are good, such as education and friendship. He also says that being fair is important in being ethical. It is very possible that Aristotle would recognize that downloading files can be educational and can help us grow and can be a big part of friendships. However, he would probably think it is unfair to the companies and writers or artists who created the things being downloaded because it is like stealing from them. I agree with Aristotle that it seems unfair to download other people's files, and that makes it unethical. However, I don't agree that anything that helps us grow is good. What if you take food from someone because you need it—how could that be ethical? For me, the main reasons why downloading seems like it might be ethical are that everyone does it, a lot more people are benefited by it than hurt by it, and there's no way to stop it. Instead of having a society where millions of people are considered to be breaking the law, it would be much better to stop considering downloading illegal.

C | Peer Reviewing Share your writing with a partner. Answer these questions about your partner's paragraph.

1. Do you understand how your partner's views are similar to and/or different from the philosopher's views?

2. Can you understand all of the points your partner is making? Are the points made in the right order?

3. Are hedges and boosters used appropriately?

D | Revising Follow these steps to revise your paragraph.

1. Using your partner's feedback, rewrite your paragraph.

2. Check your writing for mistakes and clarity. Did you use hedges and boosters? Did you use at least one passive and at least one construction with an empty *it*? Make any final corrections necessary.

FINAL WRITING ASSIGNMENT
Write a Proposal Argument Essay

Your Task

Illegal downloading raises many issues, as you saw in the article on page 160, including the issues of being able to share materials on the Internet and of fair payment to artists and companies. What should be done to address illegal downloading generally or some issues that it raises? Ideas about a solution depend in part on your views on the ethics of illegal downloading. Write a multi-paragraph proposal argument essay. In your essay, argue that illegal downloading or some aspect of illegal downloading is right or wrong, and argue against the opposing position. Include the ideas of one or more of the philosophers (from the reading on pages 168–169) in your argument, either as support for your argument or as ideas that you are arguing against. Then, based on your argument about ethics, propose a solution to illegal downloading generally or to some issues it raises.

Alternative Task

Write a multi-paragraph proposal argument essay on an ethical issue and a possible solution for addressing the issue. You might write about an ethical issue involving the Internet or about any other ethical issue that interests you. In your essay, present your position on the ethical issue and at least one argument against an opposing position. Include the ideas of the philosophers, either as support for your position or as ideas you argue against. Then, based on your argument about ethics, propose a solution to the ethical issue in general or to some important aspects of the issue.

GO ONLINE Go to the Online Writing Tutor for a writing model and to write your assignment.

A | Planning Reread the paragraphs that you wrote for Writing Assignments I and III. Think about what your position on the ethics of illegal downloading is. Then complete this chart.

My position on the ethics of illegal downloading	
Reasons that I could give in support of my position (including philosophers' ideas)	
Reasons that someone else might give against my position (including philosophers' ideas)	
My possible arguments against this other position	
Based on my position on illegal downloading, some possible ideas for dealing with problems related to illegal downloading	

B | Writing Note: Proposal Argument Essays Read the note. Then read the proposal argument essay in Activity C.

> In a **proposal argument essay**, writers argue for their position regarding a problem and propose a solution to that problem. Because writers want to persuade readers to take their position, they attempt, through the organization and language of their essay, to:
> - interest and involve readers in the essay
> - show readers that they are fair
> - show readers that they have a strong argument

C | Reading a Model Read the model proposal argument essay. Then do Activity D.

How Much Is Your Data Worth?

How much did you get paid for your personal data last year? Whenever you go online, companies track you and collect data about which sites you visit and what you do there. They sell this personal data to other companies without paying you a cent. Buying and selling personal data has become big business. It is estimated that in 2012 the market for personal data was worth $39 billion (Kovacs). Companies should pay people for their personal data.

People should be paid for their personal data because their personal data belongs to them. It may be generated and recorded using technology and equipment belonging to corporations, but the valuable part of personal data is that it is unique and specific to the person who generated it. Personal data, in other words, is an original product of the creator, even if it is not the result of deliberate action, the way a book or movie is. This makes it similar to other forms of intellectual property and works to which copyright can apply. There is also the matter of fairness. Companies spend billions of dollars trading personal data, so they obviously think it is very valuable. It is not fair for them to be the only ones to profit. When people go online, they create value by creating data. They deserve to benefit when their data is bought and sold. In short, paying people for their data is both right—since it is theirs—and fair.

Companies that collect data might say that people are already paid for their personal data since the online services they are using are provided free of charge. For example, social network sites do not charge a fee but allow people to interact with one another in exchange for their personal data. Companies like Fitbit and Jawbone, which make personal health tracking devices, might say that the cost of their devices is low because of the data they collect and share. If companies had to pay people to use their personal data, they would have to charge more for their services and devices. They might argue that such an arrangement would not be economical for them. While there may be some truth to this argument, companies that collect data are making huge profits. According to Pam Dixon, executive director of the World Privacy Forum, the data buying and selling industry consists of more than 3,500 companies, some of which have made billions of dollars. It is hard to believe that individuals are getting fair value for their personal data, even if they are getting services and devices for little or no cost.

Once we accept the idea that people should have control over who can copy and use their data and the right to be paid for the data, as with other forms of intellectual property, we can figure out ways to develop a fair solution. Perhaps companies could license the rights to collect and use personal data in a way similar to how other creative works are licensed. If there were such a system, companies would have to pay for a license to use someone's personal data. There is already a copyright system to protect other kinds of data, like software, music, and movies. Why not use a similar system for personal data? Another way to implement a copyright system for personal data might be data lockers. Data lockers are services that allow the creators to deposit their personal data online and give businesses access to it (Oram). This is a new idea that start-up companies are now looking at. People would receive something in exchange for their personal data. For example, they could receive credits toward groceries or a discount at their favorite restaurant.

People should have a copyright on their personal data so that they can control how it is used. It is important to remember that personal data belongs to the person who created it. While companies may provide services where people can interact with their data, clearly these services do not adequately reflect the true value of personal data. People should be paid for their personal data or receive something of value in exchange for it. In the last ten years, computers and online social networking have made it possible for us to create and collect personal information in revolutionary ways. We do not know what the consequence will be, so we must be cautious. We must make sure that the individual people who are creating that data have their rights respected.

Works Cited

Dixon, Pam. "Congressional Testimony: What Information Do Data Brokers Have on Consumers?" *World Privacy Forum*. 8 Dec. 2013. Web. 21 Jan. 2015. <https://www.worldprivacyforum.org/2013/12/testimony-what-information-do-data-brokers-have-on-consumers/>

Kovacs, Gary. "Tracking Our Online Trackers." *TED*. Feb. 2012. Web. 19 Jan. 2015. <http://www.ted.com/talks/gary_kovacs_tracking_the_trackers>

Oram, Paul. "Would You Like to Make Money from the Personal Data You Share Online?" *Freshminds*. 28 Feb. 2013. Web. 4 Feb. 2015. <http://www.freshminds.net/2013/02/would-you-like-to-make-money-from-the-personal-data-you-share-online/>

D | Analyzing Argument Structure Look again at the model proposal argument essay in Activity C and answer these questions. Discuss your answers with a partner.

1. In the introduction of a proposal argument essay, the writer often includes:
   - a hook, to interest readers in the essay
   - general background information, to help readers understand the issue
   - a clear thesis statement, mentioning the problem and solution, to make clear to readers what will be argued

   a. Does the model essay have a hook? If so, what is it?

   b. Does the introduction offer any background information on the issue? If so, what is it?

   c. What is the thesis statement? Does it make clear to readers what the writer will argue?

2. In one or more body paragraphs, the writer presents the **argument** by giving the main points and, to make the argument strong, supporting each point with evidence—reasons, examples, statistics, expert opinions, and so on.

   a. What is the topic sentence of body paragraph 1? Does it state the main points of the argument?

   b. How many main points does body paragraph 1 make? What are these points?

   c. What kind of evidence does the writer give to support these points? Is this evidence effective? Why or why not?

3. In one or more body paragraphs, the writer presents the **counterargument**: the writer mentions objections to the argument that have been made or that could be made, and responds to these objections with a **concession**—saying that people making the objection have a point—or a **refutation**—explaining why the objection is in some way weak or wrong. Usually, writers concede minor points and refute major points.

   a. In body paragraph 2, what objection to his or her argument does the writer mention?

   b. In the counterargument, the writer makes a small concession while mainly refuting the objection. What is the concession? Concessions often strengthen an argument by showing it as being fair. Do you think this concession works that way?

   c. What is the refutation in this paragraph? What evidence does the writer give for the refutation? Do you find the refutation convincing?

   d. What is the topic sentence of body paragraph 2?

4. In one or more body paragraphs, the writer presents a **proposal** to solve the problem, showing how this proposed solution can in fact solve the problem.

   a. What is the writer's proposal?

   b. What support does the writer offer for this proposal?

   c. What is the topic sentence of body paragraph 3?

   d. In your opinion, does the writer make a convincing case in this paragraph that the proposal will solve the problem discussed in the previous paragraphs? Instead of suggesting one specific way of carrying out his or her proposal, the writer has two different suggestions. In your opinion, does this strengthen or weaken the proposal?

5. In the conclusion, the writer often restates the thesis, summarizes main points, and/or gives some concluding thoughts.

   a. Does the conclusion restate the thesis? If so, what is this restatement?

   b. What, if anything, is the summary of main points?

   c. What are the writer's concluding thoughts? In your opinion, are they an effective way of ending the argument? Why or why not?

E | Writing Note: The Language of Argument Read the note. Then do Activity F.

> Language that is common in strong argument essays includes the following:
> - **Hedges** (See Charts 5.2–5.3.) Hedges help writers to show readers that they are being accurate and that they are expressing the strength of their claims appropriately.
> - **Boosters** (See Chart 5.3.) Through boosters, writers strengthen their arguments by, for example, making clear to readers that the writer's points are important or that the writer holds a position strongly.
> - **Signposting words and phrases that involve readers** By using imperatives and other words that address the reader, writers can keep readers engaged in their argument.
>   Examples: *note that, consider, think about*
> - **Signposting words and phrases that show the argument structure** These words help readers to follow your argument by showing them how you have organized it.
>   Examples: *first, second, finally, one reason, another reason, for example, to summarize, in conclusion*
>   - **Introducing a source** By connecting your claims to particular experts or research evidence, these phrases serve to both boost and hedge.
>   Examples: *according to ____, as ____ says, ____ argues that*
>   - **Introducing a concession**
>   Examples: *it is true that, it is highly likely that, I agree that, I would acknowledge that*
>   - **Introducing a point you will refute and your refutation**
>   Examples: *it has been said that, it might be thought that, however, although it has been said that ____, I would argue that*
>   - **Repeating key words** also helps show argument structure and increase coherence.

F | Analyzing Argument Language Look again at the model proposal argument essay in Activity C and answer these questions. Discuss your answers with a partner.

1. In the introductory paragraph, what word does the writer use repeatedly to engage the reader? Why does the writer use it in the introductory paragraph?

2. The writer uses some modal hedges and other hedges, especially in body paragraph 2, where the writer presents an objection and his or her counterargument, and in body paragraph 3, where the writer presents his or her proposal. Circle the hedges in these two paragraphs. What specific purposes(s) do the hedges serve in paragraph 2? What specific purposes(s) do they serve in paragraph 3?

3. The writer uses several boosters in the concluding paragraph. Circle the boosters in this paragraph. Why do you think the writer uses boosters in the conclusion?

4. What language does the writer use to present the concession and introduce the refutation?

5. Although the writer includes two sources just as citations in parentheses, he or she introduces one source with a signposting phrase. What is the phrase? Why might the writer have chosen to signpost this source?

6. Where could the writer have included words to show the structure of his or her argument?

G | Writing Note: Essay Organization Study the diagram for organizing a multi-paragraph proposal argument essay. Then do Activity H.

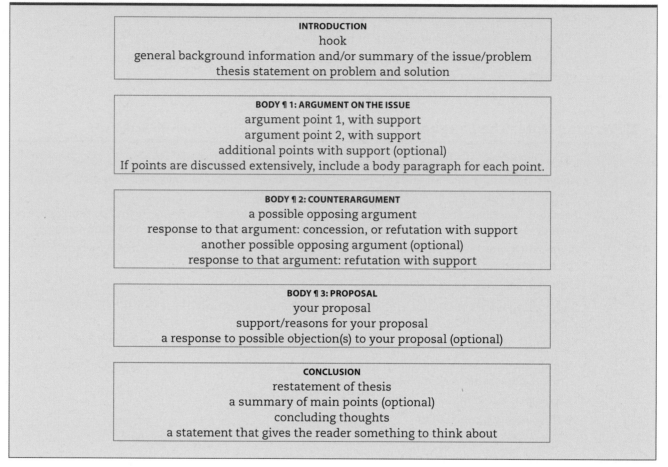

INTRODUCTION
hook
general background information and/or summary of the issue/problem
thesis statement on problem and solution

BODY ¶ 1: ARGUMENT ON THE ISSUE
argument point 1, with support
argument point 2, with support
additional points with support (optional)
If points are discussed extensively, include a body paragraph for each point.

BODY ¶ 2: COUNTERARGUMENT
a possible opposing argument
response to that argument: concession, or refutation with support
another possible opposing argument (optional)
response to that argument: refutation with support

BODY ¶ 3: PROPOSAL
your proposal
support/reasons for your proposal
a response to possible objection(s) to your proposal (optional)

CONCLUSION
restatement of thesis
a summary of main points (optional)
concluding thoughts
a statement that gives the reader something to think about

H | Organizing Your Essay Draw your own diagram like the one above. Write your ideas in each section.

I | Writing a First Draft Using information from your diagram, write a first draft of your essay. Try to use some of the structures that you have practiced in this unit.

J | Peer Reviewing When you have finished writing your first draft, share it with a partner. After discussing your essay, you may want to reorganize your ideas, add more support, and make other changes to strengthen your essay.

Checklist for revising the first draft

When you review your partner's essay and discuss your own, keep these questions in mind.

1. Does the thesis statement clearly express the argument that the writer will make?
2. Does the introduction capture the reader's interest and give the reader any basic background information needed on the problem that the essay discusses?
3. In the body paragraph(s) presenting the argument, does the writer make clear points in support of the argument and give convincing evidence in support of each point?
4. In the body paragraph presenting the counterargument, does the writer give one or more opposing arguments and convincingly concede or refute those arguments?
5. In the body paragraph presenting the proposal, does the writer propose a logical solution to the problem and give support for this proposal?
6. Does the conclusion effectively restate the writer's argument and leave the reader with something to think about?

K | Writing the Second Draft Using your partner's feedback, write a second draft that includes all of your changes.

L | Proofreading Check your essay for the forms in Chart 5.6. Make any final corrections necessary.

5.6 Summary Chart for Proofreading

SOME COMMON HEDGES	PROOFREADING QUESTIONS	EXAMPLES
may, might, could suggest, tend seem, appear think, assume some, many sometimes possible, possibly possibility	Are **hedges** and **boosters** used where appropriate and not overused? Do **hedges** make your claims more precise and accurate? Do **boosters** express certainty and help emphasize important points?	**1** Calculations of the costs of illegal downloading that don't also consider the benefits will **probably** be inaccurate. Furthermore, a policy of labeling as criminal an entire generation of young Internet users **may** itself have **significant** costs in the long run. **2** While downloading one song **may** not feel like that serious a crime, the cumulative impact of millions of songs downloaded illegally—and **without any** compensation to **all** the people who helped to create that song and bring it to fans—is **devastating**.
SOME COMMON BOOSTERS will, must show all, no always certain, certainly clear, clearly obvious, obviously actually the fact that		
	Do you use the **passive** and **empty it** to improve cohesion, to focus and emphasize elements, and to move long clauses to the end of sentences?	**3** Regular participation in aerobic exercise **has been shown** to decrease overall levels of tension, elevate and stabilize mood, improve sleep, and improve self-esteem. **4** Social scientists can promote this policy by addressing several specific issues. First, **it** is important to identify individuals most at risk.

Vocabulary Endnotes

Unit 1

WARM-UP (page 3)

[1] **boatman** (n) a man who earns money from small boats, either by carrying passengers or goods on them, or by renting them out

[2] **steamboat** (n) a boat driven by steam, used especially in the past on rivers and along coasts

[3] **acre** (n) a unit for measuring an area of land; about 4,050 square meters

[4] **countless** (adj) very many

Activity 1 (pages 4–5)

[5] **crossword (crossword puzzle)** (n) a game in which you have to fit words across and downward into spaces with numbers in a square diagram; you find the words by solving clues

[6] **insert** (n) a thing that is put into something else

[7] **uncluttered** (adj) not containing too many objects, details, or unnecessary items

[8] **restless** (adj) not able to stay still or relax because you are bored or nervous

[9] **spontaneity** (n) the quality of not planning but doing something because you suddenly want to do it

  ▸ **spontaneous** (adj)

[10] **contemplate** (v) to think carefully about something or the possibility of doing something

[11] **reminder** (n) something that makes you remember something

Activity 2 (page 7)

[12] **consist of** (v) to be made from two or more things; to have things as parts

[13] **clock in** (v) to begin work by punching a time card

[14] **busser** (n) a person who works at a restaurant setting and cleaning tables

[15] **pioneer** (n) a person who goes somewhere or does something before other people

Activity 3 (page 8)

[16] **seizure** (n) a sudden strong attack of an illness, especially one affecting the brain

[17] **paralyze** (v) to make someone unable to feel or move all or part of their body

[18] **gesture** (n) a movement of your head or hand to show how you feel or what you want

[19] **troublemaker** (n) a person who deliberately causes trouble

[20] **remittance** (n) a sum of money that is sent to somebody in order to pay for something

Activity 4 (page 9)

[21] **steamer** (n) a ship that is driven by steam

[22] **outlaw** (v) to make something illegal

[23] **colony** (n) a country or an area that is ruled by another country

[24] **settlement** (n) a group of homes in a place where no people have lived before

[25] **land rush** (n) the process of people making their home in a place

Activity 6 (page 10)

[26] **disorder** (n) an illness in which the mind or part of the body is not working properly

[27] **mound** (n) a small hill; a large pile of earth

[28] **distinctive** (adj) clearly different from others and therefore easy to recognize

[29] **diameter** (n) a straight line across a circle, through the center

[30] **astronomer** (n) a scientist who studies the sun, moon, stars, planets, etc.

  ▸ **astronomical** (adj)

Activity 7 (page 11)

[31] **nanny** (n) a woman whose job is to look after the children of a family

[32] **leftover** (n) food that has not been eaten at the end of a meal

Activity 10 (page 12)

[33] **brew** (v) to make a drink of tea or coffee by adding hot water

[34] **naan** (n) a round, flat bread

[35] **marmalade** (n) a type of soft, sweet food (called jam) made from oranges or lemons

Activity 11 (page 13)

[36] **rebirth** (n) a period of new life, growth, or activity

[37] **summit** (n) the top of a mountain

[38] **momentarily** (adv) for a very short time

[39] **communal** (adj) shared by a group of people

Activity 12 (page 14)

[40] **relate to** (v) to connect to

[41] **palm** (n) the flat part of the front of your hand

Activity 13 (page 16)

[42] **algae** (n) very simple plants that grow mainly in water

[43] **lifeboat** (n) a boat that goes to help people who are in danger at sea

[44] **tilt** (v) to have one side higher than the other; to move something so that it has one side higher than the other

[45] **suspend** (v) to hang something from something else

[46] **plaster** (v) to cover a wall with plaster to make it smooth

[47] **scrub** (v) to rub something hard to clean it, usually with a brush and soap and water

Activity 14 (page 17)

[48] **modernism** (n) a style and movement in art, architecture, and literature popular in the middle of the twentieth century in which modern ideas, methods, and materials were used rather than traditional ones

[49] **maid** (n) a woman whose job is to clean in a hotel or a large house

[50] **faculty** (n) one department in a university, college, etc.

[51] **author** (v) to write books or stories

Activity 16 (pages 18–19)

[52] **carousel** (n) a moving belt at an airport that carries luggage for passengers to collect

[53] **inspect** (v) to look at something carefully

[54] **easel** (n) a frame that an artist uses to hold a picture while it is being painted

[55] **shoo** (v) to make somebody or something go away by saying "shoo" and waving your hands

[56] **dim** (v) to become less bright

[57] **stride** (v) to walk with long steps

[58] **glance** (v) to look quickly at somebody or something

Activity 17 (pages 19–20)

[59] **barren** (adj) not good enough for plants to grow on

[60] **fertile** (adj) If soil is fertile, plants grow well in it.

[61] **negotiate** (v) to reach an agreement by talking with other people

[62] **treaty** (n) a written agreement between countries

[63] **weather** (v) to survive difficult times

[64] **census** (n) an official count of the people who live in a country, including information about their ages, jobs, etc.

[65] **ministry** (n) a part of the government that controls one special thing

[66] **revenue** (n) money regularly received by a government, company, etc.

[67] **suffrage** (n) the right to vote in political elections

[68] **glow** (v) to send out soft light or heat without flames or smoke

[69] **impoverished** (adj) very poor; without money

[70] **aid** (n) money, food, etc. that is sent to a country or to people in order to help them

Activity 18 (Reading, page 20)

[71] **tuft** (n) a small amount of something such as hair or grass growing together

[72] **drift** (v) to move slowly in the air or on water

[73] **bundle up** (v) to put on warm clothes or coverings

[74] **wreak havoc** (v) to cause chaos or confusion

⁷⁵**cluck** (v) to make a noise with the tongue

⁷⁶**trademark** (n) a special way of behaving or dressing that is typical of someone and that makes them easily recognized

⁷⁷**horde** (n) a very large number of people

⁷⁸**gust** (n) a sudden strong wind

⁷⁹**intoxicating** (adj) making you feel excited so that you cannot think clearly

⁸⁰**taut** (adj) (used about rope, wire, etc.) stretched very tight; not loose

⁸¹**tug** (v) to pull something hard and quickly

⁸²**blast** (v) to make a loud noise

⁸³**mantu** (n) a type of dumpling (a small ball of steamed or fried dough)

⁸⁴**pakora** (n) a flat piece of spicy South Asian food consisting of meat or vegetables fried in batter

⁸⁵**thudding** (n) the sound that a heavy thing makes when it hits something

WRITING ASSIGNMENT I

Activity B (page 21)

⁸⁶**tow truck** (n) a truck used to pick up vehicles that aren't working

Activity 19 (page 23)

⁸⁷**eminent** (adj) famous and respected, especially in a particular profession

⁸⁸**prompt** (v) to cause somebody to do something

⁸⁹**eclipse** (n) an occasion when the moon passes between the earth and the sun or the earth's shadow falls on the moon, so you cannot see all or part of the sun or moon

Activity 20 (pages 24–25)

⁹⁰**crown** (n) the king and/or queen

⁹¹**verify** (v) to check or state that something is true

Activity 22 (pages 25–26)

⁹²**apt** (adj) often likely to do something

⁹³**liable** (adj) likely to do something

⁹⁴**prone** (adj) likely to suffer from something or to do something bad

⁹⁵**drowsiness** (n) the state of being tired and almost asleep

⁹⁶**eligible** (adj) having the right to do or have something

⁹⁷**hesitant** (adj) slow to speak or act because you are not sure if you should or not

⁹⁸**inclined** (adj) wanting or likely to do something

Activity 24 (pages 26–27)

⁹⁹**smokestack** (n) a metal chimney, for example on a ship or an engine, through which smoke comes out

¹⁰⁰**trench** (n) a long, narrow hole that is dug in the ground, for example to put pipes or wires in

¹⁰¹**petition** (v) to make a formal request to someone in authority

¹⁰²**legislator** (n) a member of a group of people that has the power to make laws

WRITING ASSIGNMENT II

Activity A (page 27)

¹⁰³**skylight** (n) a window in a roof

Activity B (page 27)

¹⁰⁴**refuge** (n) a place where you are safe from somebody or something

Activity 25 (Reading, pages 28–29)

¹⁰⁵**welfare** (n) financial support from the government

¹⁰⁶**strain** (v) to try to make something do more than it is able to do

¹⁰⁷**stem from** (phr v) to result from

¹⁰⁸**impeccable** (adj) without any mistakes or faults; perfect

¹⁰⁹**dignity** (n) calm and serious behavior that makes other people respect you

¹¹⁰**take for granted** (phr) to not appreciate

¹¹¹**materialism** (n) the belief that money and possessions are the most important things in life

¹¹²**indulge** (v) to allow yourself to have or do something for pleasure

¹¹³**vice** (n) weakness; evil or immoral behavior

¹¹⁴**have a fit** (v - phr) (informal) to get very angry

¹¹⁵**crate** (n) a big box for carrying bottles or other things

¹¹⁶**make out** (phr v) used to ask if someone managed well or was successful in a particular situation

FINAL WRITING ASSIGNMENT

Activity B (pages 30–31)

¹¹⁷**in recognition of** (phr) in praise of; showing appreciation for

Activity C (pages 31–32)

¹¹⁸**drought** (n) a long time when there is not enough rain

¹¹⁹**microfinance** (n) financial services for small businesses that are too small or too poor to get help from large banks

¹²⁰**advocate** (v) to recommend or say that you support a particular plan or action

Activity M (page 35)

¹²¹**shallow** (adj) not concerned with anything serious or important and lacking any depth of understanding or feeling

¹²²**special education** (n) the education of children who have physical or learning problems

¹²³**mentor** (n) an experienced person who advises and helps somebody with less experience over a period of time

Unit 2

Activity 1 (page 39)

¹**outbreak** (n) the sudden start of something bad

²**epidemic** (n) a disease that many people in a place have at the same time

³**pandemic** (n) a disease that spreads over a whole country or the whole world

⁴**pinpoint** (v) to find the exact position of something

⁵**emergence** (n) starting to exist; appearing or becoming known

⁶**laborer** (n) a person whose job involves hard physical work, especially work done outdoors

⁷**unearthed** (adj) discovered

⁸**mobilization** (n) organizing or arranging for a group of soldiers or other workers especially for the purpose of carrying out war efforts

⁹**hypothesis** (n) an idea that is suggested as the possible explanation for something but has not yet been found to be true or correct

¹⁰**viral** (adj) related to a virus

¹¹**smoking gun** (n) something that seems to prove an idea, for example, about who or what did something

¹²**plague** (n) any infectious disease that kills a lot of people

¹³**ancestral** (adj) being an earlier form of something

¹⁴**virulent** (adj) (used about a disease) very strong and dangerous

¹⁵**immune system** (n) the system in your body that produces substances to help it fight against infection and disease

¹⁶**catastrophic** (adj) having huge and terrible effects
  ► **catastrophe** (n)

¹⁷**follow in the tracks** (phr) to move along the same path

Activity 2 (page 41)

¹⁸**provocative** (adj) intended to cause an argument

¹⁹**soap opera** (n) a story about the lives and problems of a group of people that is broadcast every day or several times a week on television

²⁰**editorial** (n) an article in a newspaper or magazine that expresses the editor's opinion about an item of news or an issue

²¹**black-and-white** (adj) making people and things seem completely one way or another

²²**exaggerated** (adj) made to seem larger, better, worse, or more important than it really is or needs to be

²³**overly** (adv) too

²⁴**screenwriter** (n) a person who writes screenplays for films

²⁵**fulfillment** (n) the achievement of something

²⁶**broad** (adj) having a great variety
  ► **breadth** (n)

²⁷**virtue** (n) behavior or attitudes that show high moral standards

²⁸**excess** (n) more than is necessary, reasonable, or acceptable

²⁹**obstacle** (n) a situation, an event, etc. that makes it difficult for you to do or achieve something

³⁰**increased odds** (phr) a higher chance of something happening

³¹**respiratory** (adj) connected with breathing

Activity 3 (pages 42–43)

³² **caffeine** (n) the substance in coffee and tea that makes you feel more active and awake

³³ **brewed** (adj) of coffee or tea, made by mixing with hot water

³⁴ **adolescent** (n) a young person who is developing from a child into an adult

³⁵ **deliver** (v) to do what you promised to do or are expected to do; to produce or provide what people expect

Activity 4 (pages 44–45)

³⁶ **indivisible** (adj) that cannot be divided into smaller parts

³⁷ **linguist** (n) a person who is involved in the scientific study of language

³⁸ **definable** (adj) possible to show what the meaning is

³⁹ **phenomenon** (n) a fact or an event in nature or society, especially one that is not fully understood

⁴⁰ **engagement** (n) involvement with and interest in something

⁴¹ **comprehensive** (adj) including all, or almost all, the items, details, facts, information, etc. that may be concerned

⁴² **chameleon** (n) a small lizard that can change color according to its surroundings, or a person who can change their behavior, etc. according to the situation

Activity 5 (pages 46–47)

⁴³ **elevate** (v) to move to a higher level, e.g., a higher moral or intellectual level

Activity 8 (page 50)

⁴⁴ **interagency** (adj) between agencies or organizations

⁴⁵ **privatization** (n) the process of taking organizations and functions out of the control of the government and into the control of private businesses

⁴⁶ **dead end** (n) a situation that cannot lead to further progress

Activity 9 (page 51)

⁴⁷ **organism** (n) a living thing

⁴⁸ **GMO** (n) = genetically modified organism
  ▶ **GM** = genetically modified; **GE** = genetically engineered

⁴⁹ **hysteria** (n) an extremely excited and exaggerated way of behaving or reacting to an event

⁵⁰ **insecticide** (n) a substance that is used for killing insects

Activity 10 (Reading, pages 52–53)

⁵¹ **trial** (n) a test; the process of testing the ability, quality, or performance of someone or something, especially before you make a final decision about them

⁵² **malnourished** (adj) in bad health because of a lack of food or a lack of the right type of food

⁵³ **ploy** (n) words or actions that are carefully planned to get an advantage over someone else

⁵⁴ **echo** (v) to express an opinion or attitude that agrees with or repeats one already expressed or thought

⁵⁵ **activist** (n) a person who works to achieve political or social change, especially as a member of an organization with particular aims

⁵⁶ **contaminate** (v) to make a substance or place dirty or no longer pure by adding a substance that is dangerous or carries disease

⁵⁷ **pollen** (n) a fine powder, usually yellow, that is formed in flowers and carried to other flowers of the same kind by the wind or by insects, to make those flowers produce seeds

⁵⁸ **fertilize** (v) to put pollen into a plant so that a seed develops

⁵⁹ **consumption** (n) the act of using energy, food, or materials

⁶⁰ **portray** (v) to describe or show someone or something in a particular way, especially when this does not give a complete or accurate impression of what they are like

⁶¹ **biotechnology** (n) the use of living cells and bacteria in industrial and scientific processes
  ▶ = biotech (n)

⁶² **patent** (v) to obtain a patent, an official right to be the only person to make, use, or sell a product or an invention

⁶³ **yield** (n) the total amount of crops that are produced

⁶⁴ **soybean** (n) a type of bean, used for oil or instead of meat or animal protein in some foods

⁶⁵ **herbicide** (n) a chemical substance that farmers use to kill plants that are growing where they are not wanted

⁶⁶ **weed** (n) a wild plant growing where it is not wanted, especially among crops or garden plants

⁶⁷ **till** (v) to prepare and use land for growing crops

⁶⁸ **humanitarian** (adj) concerned with reducing suffering and improving the conditions that people live in

⁶⁹ **subsistence farmer** (n) someone who grows food to feed himself and his family so that there is little or none left over to be marketed

⁷⁰ **exploitation** (n) a situation in which someone treats someone else in an unfair way, especially in order to make money from their work

⁷¹ **compelling** (adj) that makes you pay attention to it because it is so interesting and exciting

⁷² **greenhouse gas** (n) any of the gases that are thought to cause the greenhouse effect, especially carbon dioxide

⁷³ **lump together** (v) to combine items and treat them as one unit

⁷⁴ **sabotaged** (adj) deliberately damaged (equipment, transportation, machines, etc.) to prevent an enemy from using them, or to protest about something

Activity 13 (page 56)

⁷⁵ **commission** (n) an official group of people who are asked to find out about something

⁷⁶ **industrial relations** (n) relations between employers and employees

⁷⁷ **unrest** (n) a political situation in which people are angry and likely to protest or fight

⁷⁸ **hearing** (n) an official meeting at which facts about a situation are presented to a group of people who will decide what action to take

⁷⁹ **testimony** (n) a formal statement of what you know to be true, especially in a court of law
  ▶ **testify** (v)

⁸⁰ **urge** (v) to advise or try hard to persuade someone to do something

⁸¹ **handicap** (v) to make something more difficult for someone

⁸² **finding** (n) information that is discovered as the result of research into something

⁸³ **set (something) in motion** (phr) to start something moving, including figuratively

Activity 14 (pages 57–58)

⁸⁴ **far from (something)** (phr) almost the opposite of something

Activity 15 (page 59)

⁸⁵ **blood relative** (n) a person related to someone by birth

⁸⁶ **longevity** (n) long life

⁸⁷ **secondhand smoke** (n) smoke that is breathed in from other people's cigarettes

⁸⁸ **compensation** (n) money given in exchange for something

⁸⁹ **amount to** (v) to make a certain amount when you add everything together

Activity 16 (page 60)

⁹⁰ **underdog** (n) a person, etc. thought to be in a weaker position than others

⁹¹ **intolerance** (n) a lack of willingness to tolerate ideas or people who are different

⁹² **lone** (adj) only; without other people

⁹³ **vaccine** (n) a substance that is put into the blood and protects the body from disease
  ▶ **vaccination** (n)

Activity 17 (pages 61–62)

⁹⁴ **altruism** (n) feelings and behavior based on caring about the needs of others rather than one's own needs

⁹⁵ **hacking** (n) the action of secretly finding a way of looking at and/or changing information on somebody else's computer system without permission

Activity 18 (pages 62–63)

⁹⁶ **originate** (v) to create something new

⁹⁷ **cognitive** (adj) connected with the mental processes of understanding

⁹⁸ **point of view** (n) a particular way of considering a situation

⁹⁹ **violate** (v) to break a rule, etc.

Activity 19 (pages 63–64)

¹⁰⁰ **habitable** (adj) suitable to be lived in

¹⁰¹ **consumerism** (n) the buying and using of goods and services; the belief that it is good for a society or an individual to buy and use a large quantity of goods and services

¹⁰² **intruder** (n) a person who enters a place without permission

¹⁰³ **feminism** (n) the belief that women should have the same rights and opportunities as men
  ▸ **feminist** (adj)

Activity 20 (pages 65–66)

¹⁰⁴ **commentator** (n) a person who gives a commentary, for example, on radio or television

¹⁰⁵ **consensus** (n) an opinion that all members of a group agree with

¹⁰⁶ **output** (n) the amount of something that is made or done

¹⁰⁷ **arsenal** (n) a collection of weapons

¹⁰⁸ **founder** (n) a person who starts an organization

¹⁰⁹ **field-testing**, or **field trial** (n) testing something in an actual situation

¹¹⁰ **sustain** (v) to keep alive and healthy

¹¹¹ **hard to swallow** (phr) hard for people to believe or accept as true

Activity 21 (Reading, pages 67–68)

¹¹² **resistant** (adj) not harmed or affected by something (e.g., herbicide-resistant = not harmed or affected by herbicides)
  ▸ **resistance** (n)

¹¹³ **devastating** (adj) causing a lot of damage and destruction

¹¹⁴ **staple** (n) a basic type of food that is used a lot

¹¹⁵ **nutrient** (n) a substance that is needed to keep a living thing alive and to help it grow

¹¹⁶ **application** (n) a practical use of something, especially of a theory, discovery, etc.

¹¹⁷ **agroecology** (n) an approach to agriculture that looks at areas with agriculture as ecological systems and at how agriculture affects the environment

¹¹⁸ **sustainability** (n) involving the use of natural products and energy in a way that does not harm the environment

¹¹⁹ **ecosystem** (n) the relation of plants and living creatures in an area to each other and to their environment
  ▸ **ecologist** (n)

¹²⁰ **stabilize** (v) to make something stable and unlikely to change

¹²¹ **acreage** (n) an area of land measured in acres

¹²² **trait** (n) a quality, especially a genetic characteristic

¹²³ **be on the brink of** (phr) to be about to

¹²⁴ **fertilizer** (n) food for plants

¹²⁵ **peek into** (v) to take a quick look at something

¹²⁶ **pipeline** (n) something that is in the pipeline is being planned or prepared and will happen soon.

¹²⁷ **dispiriting** (adj) making someone lose their hope or enthusiasm

¹²⁸ **confer** (v) to give an advantage

Activity 23 (pages 71–72)

¹²⁹ **green** (adj) protecting the environment

¹³⁰ **prey on** (v) of an animal or bird, to hunt or kill another animal or bird for food

¹³¹ **poplar** (n) a tall straight tree with soft wood

¹³² **starchy** (adj) containing a lot of starch (e.g., foods such as potatoes, flour, and rice)

¹³³ **antibody** (n) a substance that the body produces in the blood to fight disease, or as a reaction when certain substances are put in the body

¹³⁴ **inactivate** (v) to make something no longer active

Activity 24 (page 72)

¹³⁵ **slimy** (adj) as if covered by an unpleasant thick liquid substance

¹³⁶ **unexplored** (adj) not yet examined or discussed thoroughly

¹³⁷ **phobia** (n) a very strong fear or hatred that you cannot explain

¹³⁸ **indulge** (v) to allow yourself to have or do something for pleasure

¹³⁹ **vulnerable** (adj) likely to be hurt or damaged

¹⁴⁰ **crunch** (n) a situation in which there is not enough of something

¹⁴¹ **intake** (n) the amount of food, drink, etc. that you take into your body

Activity 26 (pages 73–74)

¹⁴² **expel** (v) to force air or liquid out of something

¹⁴³ **droplet** (n) a small amount of liquid that forms a round shape

¹⁴⁴ **contagious** (adj) A contagious disease spreads by people touching each other.

Unit 3

WARM-UP (page 81)

¹ **reliance** (n) the state of needing someone or something in order to survive, be successful, etc.; the fact of being able to rely on someone or something

² **productivity** (n) the rate at which a worker, company, or country produces goods and the amount produced, compared with how much time, work, and money is needed to produce them

³ **misconduct** (n) unacceptable behavior, especially by a professional person

Activity 1 (pages 83–84)

⁴ **irrelevant** (adj) not connected with something and not important

⁵ **prospective** (adj) likely to be or to happen; possible

⁶ **bias** (n) a strong feeling of favor toward or against one group of people, or on one side in an argument, often not based on fair judgment or facts

⁷ **discrimination** (n) the practice of treating someone or a particular group in society less fairly than others

⁸ **third party** (n) a person who is involved in a situation in addition to the two main people involved

⁹ **lawsuit** (n) a claim or complaint against someone that a person or an organization can make in court

Activity 2 (page 84)

¹⁰ **applicant** (n) a person who asks for (applies for) a job or a place at a university, for example

¹¹ **seeker** (n) a person who is trying to find or get something

¹² **invasion of privacy** (phr) the unwelcomed arrival of someone into another person's state of being alone and undisturbed

¹³ **publicly** (adv) to everybody; not secretly

¹⁴ **stability** (n) the state or quality of being steady and not changing

¹⁵ **transcript** (n) a written or printed copy of what someone has said

¹⁶ **predictor** (n) something that can show what will happen in the future

Activity 3 (page 85)

¹⁷ **resistance** (n) when people try to stop something that is happening; fighting against somebody or something

Activity 5 (page 86)

¹⁸ **abundant** (adj) existing in very large quantities; more than enough Activity 6 (page 88)

¹⁹ **radiometric** (adj) relating to a measurement of radioactivity

²⁰ **eclipse (lunar)** (n) an occasion when the earth passes between the moon and the sun, so you cannot see part or all of the moon

²¹ **track** (v) to use information to help find something or someone

²² **hesitant** (adj) slow to speak or act because you are not sure if you should or not

Activity 7 (page 89)

²³ **collide** (v) to move fast toward somebody or something and hit them hard

²⁴ **crater** (n) a large hole in the ground caused by something large hitting it

²⁵ **observer** (n) a person who watches someone or something

²⁶ **hypothesis** (n) an idea that is suggested as the possible explanation for something but has not yet been found to be true or correct

²⁷ **radiation** (n) powerful and very dangerous rays that are sent out from radioactive substances

Activity 8 (pages 89–90)

²⁸ **predecessor** (n) something or someone that comes before another; a thing such as a machine that has been followed by something else

²⁹ **Mars rover** (phr) a small vehicle made by NASA (National Aeronautics and Space Administration) and sent to explore the surface of the planet Mars

³⁰ **spacecraft** (n) a vehicle that travels in space

³¹ **navigation** (n) deciding which way a ship or other vehicle should go by using a map, etc.

³² **diameter** (n) a straight line across a circle, through the center

Activity 9 (pages 90–91)

[33] **surveillance** (n) the careful watching of someone who may have done something wrong

[34] **sue** (v) to go to a court of law and ask for money from a person who has done something bad to you

[35] **dissuade** (v) to persuade someone not to do something

Activity 10 (page 91)

[36] **caution** (n) great care, because of possible danger

[37] **participant** (n) a person who does something together with other people

Activity 11 (page 92)

[38] **peek** (v) to look at something quickly and secretly because you should not be looking at it

Activity 12 (page 95)

[39] **workforce** (n) the total number of people who work in a company, factory, etc.

[40] **satire** (n) the use of humor to attack somebody or something that you think is bad or silly

[41] **journal** (n) a magazine about one particular thing

[42] **format** (n) the way something is arranged or produced

[43] **precision** (n) the quality of being exact, accurate, and careful

[44] **eliminate** (v) to remove something that is not needed or wanted

Activity 13 (page 96)

[45] **taxation** (n) money that has to be paid as taxes

[46] **mammoth** (n) an animal like a large elephant covered with hair that lived thousands of years ago and is now extinct

[47] **enforce** (v) to make people obey a law or rule or do something that they do not want to

Activity 15 (page 97)

[48] **finding** (n) information that is discovered as the result of research into something

[49] **prescribe** (v) to say that somebody must take a medicine

[50] **effectiveness** (n) how well something can produce the result that is wanted or intended

[51] **stroke** (n) a sudden serious illness in which the brain stops working properly

[52] **canoe** (n) a narrow boat

Activity 16 (pages 97–98)

[53] **detect** (v) to discover or notice something that is difficult to see

[54] **motivate** (v) to make somebody want to do something

[55] **appetizer** (n) a small amount of food or a drink that you have before a meal

Activity 17 (page 99)

[56] **humanitarian** (adj) concerned with reducing suffering and improving the conditions that people live in

[57] **defect** (n) something that is wrong with or missing from someone or something

[58] **violation** (n) a refusal to obey a law, an agreement, etc.

[59] **exceed** (v) to be greater than a particular number or amount

Activity 18 (pages 99–100)

[60] **variability** (n) the fact of something being likely to vary or change

[61] **dietary supplement** (n) a product, like a pill or liquid, that adds nutritional value to the diet

Activity 19 (page 100)

[62] **peninsula** (n) an area of land that is almost surrounded by water

Activity 20 (pages 100–101)

[63] **labor union** (n) a workers' organization

[64] **opposition** (n) disagreeing with something and trying to stop it

[65] **complementary** (adj) going together well with someone or something

[66] **troublesome** (adj) causing trouble, pain, etc. over a long period of time

Activity 21 (page 101)

[67] **acronym** (n) a word formed from the first letters of other words in a name or title. For example, NASA is an acronym for National Aeronautics and Space Administration.

[68] **physician** (n) a doctor

[69] **carpenter** (n) a person whose job is to make things from wood

[70] **pioneer** (v) to be one of the first people to do, discover, or use something new

[71] **reform** (n) a change to something to make it better

Activity 22 (page 102)

[72] **sensor** (n) a device, often electronic, that can sense or show something that is hidden or difficult to sense

[73] **determine** (v) to discover the facts about something

[74] **posture** (n) the way that a person sits, stands, walks, etc.

[75] **collaboration** (n) the act of working with another person or group of people to create or produce something

Activity 24 (pages 103–104)

[76] **innovation** (n) a new idea or way of doing something

[77] **watermill** (n) a mill next to a river in which the machinery for grinding grain into flour is driven by the power of the water turning a wheel

[78] **labor** (n) hard work that you do with your hands and body

[79] **bead** (n) a small ball of wood, glass, or plastic with a hole in the middle. Beads are put on a string to make jewelry.

[80] **millennium** (n) a period of a thousand years

[81] **ignite** (v) to start burning or to make something start burning

[82] **conquest** (n) an act of conquering something

[83] **assertion** (n) a statement that says you strongly believe that something is true

[84] **mule** (n) an animal whose parents are a horse and a donkey (an animal like a small horse with long ears)

[85] **prior to** (prep) before

Activity 25 (page 106)

[86] **globalization** (n) the fact that different cultures and economic systems around the world are becoming connected and similar to each other

[87] **outweigh** (v) to be more in amount or importance than something else

[88] **retreat** (n) a movement away from a place

[89] **glacier** (n) a large mass of ice that moves slowly down a mountain

[90] **exclude** (v) to deliberately not include something

[91] **assumption** (n) something that you accept is true even though you have no proof

[92] **launch** (v) to send something such as a spacecraft, weapon, etc. into space or into the sky

[93] **equation** (n) a statement showing that two amounts or values are equal

[94] **iceberg** (n) an extremely large mass of ice floating in the ocean

Activity 26 (pages 106–107)

[95] **consistent** (adj) always the same

[96] **ultimately** (adv) in the end

[97] **interest rate** (n) a measurement of the amount of extra money that you pay back when you borrow money

[98] **observatory** (n) a building from which scientists can watch the stars, the weather, etc.

[99] **tendency** (n) something that a person or thing usually does

Activity 28 (Reading, pages 107–108)

[100] **browse** (v) to look for or to look at information on a computer, especially on the Internet or a specific website

[101] **recipient** (n) a person who receives something

[102] **correspondence** (n) the letters/messages a person sends and receives

[103] **soar** (v) If the value, amount, or level of something soars, it rises very quickly.

[104] **be on the lookout for (someone or something)** (v) to pay attention in order to see, find, or avoid someone or something

[105] **clog** (v) to block or become blocked

[106] **ethical** (adj) connected with beliefs of what is right or wrong

[107] **jeopardize** (v) to risk harming or destroying something or someone

[108] **deterrent** (n) a thing that makes someone less likely to do something

[109] **bandwidth** (n) a measurement of the amount of information that a particular computer network or Internet connection can send in a particular time. It is often measured in bits per second.

¹¹⁰**scroll** (v) to move what you can see on a computer screen up or down so that you can look at different parts of it

¹¹¹**wiretap** (n) a listening device, sometimes used illegally to listen to people's telephone conversations

¹¹²**entrust** (v) to make someone responsible for something

¹¹³**take offense** (phr) to feel upset because of something someone said to you that was rude or embarrassing

Activity 29 (page 111)

¹¹⁴**cell differentiation** (n) change in cells (the smallest units of life) as they grow and reproduce

¹¹⁵**intervention** (n) an involvement in a situation in order to improve or help it

¹¹⁶**multicultural** (adj) for or including people from many different countries and cultures

¹¹⁷**respondent** (n) a person who answers questions, for example, in a survey

¹¹⁸**defensive measures** (n) acts to protect someone or something against attack

¹¹⁹**pest** (n) an insect or animal that damages plants or food

¹²⁰**invader** (n) an unwelcome species that enters an area

¹²¹**untreated** (adj) not made safe by chemical or other treatment

¹²²**severity** (n) the extreme badness or seriousness of something

¹²³**adolescent** (n) a young person who is developing from a child into an adult

¹²⁴**recreational** (adj) connected with activities that people do for enjoyment when they are not working

¹²⁵**consistent with** (phr) in agreement with something; not contradicting something

¹²⁶**comply** (v) to obey an order or request

¹²⁷**fund** (n) money that will be used for something special

Activity 30 (pages 112–113)

¹²⁸**advancement** (n) the process of helping something to make progress or succeed; the progress that is made

¹²⁹**hacking** (n) the action of secretly finding a way of looking at and/or changing information on someone else's computer system without permission

¹³⁰**anonymous** (adj) If a person is anonymous, other people do not know their name.

FINAL WRITING ASSIGNMENT
Activity D (pages 114–115)

¹³¹**assert** (v) to say something clearly and firmly

¹³²**momentum** (n) the ability to keep increasing or developing; the force that makes something move faster and faster

¹³³**arise** (v) If a problem or difficult situation arises, it happens or starts to exist.

¹³⁴**capitalize on (something)** (v) to use something to your advantage

Unit 4

WARM-UP (page 119)

¹**extroverted** (adj) confident; preferring to be with other people rather than alone

> ▸ **extrovert** (n) a person who is extroverted

> ▸ **extroversion** (n) the quality of being extroverted

²**introverted** (adj) more interested in your own thoughts and feelings than in spending time with other people

> ▸ **introvert** (n) a person who is introverted

> ▸ **introversion** (n) the quality of being introverted

³**trait** (n) a quality that forms part of your character or personality; can also refer to part of the body, as in "physical trait"

⁴**pursue** (v) to try to make (something) happen

Activity 1 (page 120)

⁵**affluent** (adj) having a lot of money and a good standard of living; wealthy

⁶**characterize** (v) to be typical of someone or something

Activity 3 (pages 121–122)

⁷**diversity** (n) the wide variety of something

⁸**applicant** (n) a person who asks for (applies for) a job or a place at a university, for example

⁹**nutritional** (adj) (used about food) providing substances necessary for your body to grow and be healthy

> ▸ **nutritious** (adj) (used about food) good for your health; containing substances that help your body grow and remain healthy

> ▸ **nutrition** (n) the food that you eat and the way that it affects your health

¹⁰**square kilometer** (n) a unit for measuring distance; 1,000,000 square meters

¹¹**flute** (n) a metal musical instrument shaped like a thin pipe

¹²**trombone** (n) a large brass musical instrument. You play it by blowing and moving a long tube up and down.

Activity 4 (pages 124–125)

¹³**hybrid** (n) a vehicle that uses two different types of power, especially gas or diesel and electricity

¹⁴**papaya** (n) a large tropical fruit which is sweet and orange inside and has small black seeds

¹⁵**pest** (n) an insect or animal that damages plants or food

¹⁶**diabetes** (n) a disease that makes it difficult for your body to control the level of sugar in your blood

¹⁷**stroke** (n) a sudden serious illness in which the brain stops working properly

¹⁸**fertilizer** (n) food for plants

¹⁹**trauma** (n) (an event that causes) a state of great shock or sadness

²⁰**relieve** (v) to make a bad feeling or a pain stop or get better

Activity 6 (pages 125–126)

²¹**nurture** (n) care, encouragement, and support for someone or something while it is growing and developing

²²**versus** (prep) used to compare two different ideas, choices, etc.

²³**genetics** (n) the scientific study of the ways in which different characteristics are passed from each generation of living things to the next

> ▸ **gene** (n) one of the parts inside a cell that control what a living thing will be like. Genes are passed from parents to children.

> ▸ **genetic** (adj) connected with genes that control what a person, animal, or plant will be like

²⁴**refer to** (v) to talk about; to mean

²⁵**complication** (n) something that makes a situation more difficult

²⁶**exposure** (n) the state of being unprotected from something

²⁷**inherited** (adj) passed down genetically from one's parents

Activity 7 (pages 127–128)

²⁸**outgoing** (adj) friendly and interested in other people and new experiences

²⁹**inactive** (adj) doing nothing; not active

³⁰**physician** (n) a doctor

³¹**fluid** (n) a liquid

³²**shape** (v) to give form to something

³³**associating** (n) making a connection between people or things in your mind

³⁴**pseudoscience** (n) a set of beliefs or practices that are falsely based on scientific principles

³⁵**skull** (n) the bone structure that forms the head and surrounds and protects the brain

Activity 8 (Reading, pages 128–129)

³⁶**component** (n) one of several parts of which something is made

³⁷**observer** (n) a person who watches someone or something

³⁸**classify** (v) to decide which type or group somebody or something belongs to

³⁹**abdomen** (n) the front middle part of your body, which contains your stomach

⁴⁰**digestive** (adj) connected with the digestion of food

> ▸ **digest** (v) When you digest food, it is changed into substances that your body can use.

> ▸ **digestion** (n) the process of digesting food

⁴¹**circulatory** (adj) connected with the movement of blood around the body

⁴² **to some degree** (phr) to an extent of something

⁴³ **extent to which** (idm) how much something has happened

⁴⁴ **signify** (v) to be a sign of something; to mean

⁴⁵ **resolve** (v) to find an acceptable solution to a problem or difficulty

⁴⁶ **assertiveness** (n) the quality of expressing opinions or desires in a strong and confident way, so that people take notice

⁴⁷ **restraint** (n) self-control

⁴⁸ **terminology** (n) the special words and expressions that are used in a particular profession, subject, or activity

⁴⁹ **correspondence** (n) connection

Activity 9 (page 130)

⁵⁰ **build** (n) the proportions of a body

WRITING ASSIGNMENT I
Activity A (pages 130–131)

⁵¹ **solitude** (n) privacy; the state of being alone

⁵² **mingle** (v) to combine or make one thing combine with another

⁵³ **take charge** (phr) to assume control of something

⁵⁴ **take off** (phr v) to leave a place, especially in a hurry

⁵⁵ **take their course** (idm) to develop in the usual way and come to the usual end

Activity 10 (page 133)

⁵⁶ **commercial** (adj) connected with the buying and selling of goods and services

⁵⁷ **orient** (v) to figure out where you are; to become familiar with a place

⁵⁸ **finding** (n) information that is discovered as the result of research into something

⁵⁹ **comprehension** (n) understanding

⁶⁰ **accomplish** (v) to succeed in doing something; to achieve

Activity 11 (page 134)

⁶¹ **recognizable** (adj) easy to know or identify

⁶² **inventory** (n) a detailed list

⁶³ **abnormal** (adj) different from what is normal or usual, in a way that worries you or that is unpleasant

Activity 12 (page 135)

⁶⁴ **correlate** (v) to have or to show a relationship or connection between two or more things

Activity 13 (Reading, pages 135–136)

⁶⁵ **recharge** (v) to get back your strength and energy by resting for a time

⁶⁶ **dominant** (adj) more important, powerful, or noticeable than other things

⁶⁷ **have (your) head in the clouds** (idm) to be thinking about something that is not connected with what you are doing

⁶⁸ **be in a rut** (phr) to be stuck in a boring way of life that does not change

⁶⁹ **improvise** (v) to make or do something using whatever is available, usually because you do not have what you really need

⁷⁰ **insight** (n) an understanding of a person or situation

  ▸ **insightful** (adj) showing a clear understanding of a person or situation

⁷¹ **neglectful** (adj) not giving enough care or attention to someone or something

Activity 14 (page 137)

⁷² **incorporate** (v) to make something a part of something else; to have something as a part

Activity 16 (page 138)

⁷³ **pioneer** (n) a person who goes somewhere or does something before other people

⁷⁴ **continuum** (n) a continuous series of things, in which each one is only slightly different from the things next to it, but the last is very different from the first

⁷⁵ **dependable** (adj) that can be trusted; reliable

WRITING ASSIGNMENT II
Activity A (page 139)

⁷⁶ **spontaneity** (n) the quality of not planning but doing something because you suddenly want to do it

Activity 17 (page 142)

⁷⁷ **limitless** (adj) without a limit; very great

⁷⁸ **(solar) panel** (n) a piece of equipment on a roof that uses light and heat energy from the sun to produce electricity or heating

⁷⁹ **fossil fuel** (n) fuel from a dead plant or animal that has been in the ground for thousands of years

⁸⁰ **pollutant** (n) a substance that pollutes air, rivers, etc.

⁸¹ **smog** (n) dirty poisonous air that can cover a whole city

Activity 18 (pages 142–143)

⁸² **twist** (v) to turn in many directions

⁸³ **document** (v) to write about or film

⁸⁴ **shack** (n) a small building, usually made of wood or metal, that has not been built well

⁸⁵ **plumbing** (n) the pipes that carry water into and around a building

⁸⁶ **mechanism** (n) the way in which something works or is done

Activity 19 (pages 144–145)

⁸⁷ **transmit** (v) to send or pass something from one person or place to another

⁸⁸ **criterion** (n) the standard that you use when you make a decision or form an opinion about someone or something (pl: criteria)

Activity 20 (page 145)

⁸⁹ **appoint** (v) to choose somebody for a job or position

⁹⁰ **status symbol** (n) something that a person owns that shows that they have a high position in society and a lot of money

FINAL WRITING ASSIGNMENT
Your Task (page 145)

⁹¹ **credibility** (n) the quality that something has that makes people believe or trust it

Activity B (page 147)

⁹² **personnel** (n) the people who work for an organization

Activity D (page 148)

⁹³ **common assertion** (phr) a statement made frequently and believed to be true

⁹⁴ **fundamentally** (adv) in every way that is important; completely

⁹⁵ **flawed** (adj) damaged or spoiled

Activity G (pages 149–150)

⁹⁶ **phlegm** (n) the thick substance that is produced in your nose and throat when you have a cold

⁹⁷ **bile** (n) the greenish-brown liquid with a bitter, unpleasant taste that comes into your mouth when you vomit with an empty stomach

⁹⁸ **organ** (n) a part of your body that has a special purpose; for example, your heart

⁹⁹ **variable** (n) a predictor; a situation, number, or quantity that can vary or be varied

¹⁰⁰ **stable** (adj) not likely to move, fall, or change

  ▸ **unstable** (adj) Something that is unstable may fall, move, or change.

¹⁰¹ **tabulate** (v) to arrange facts or figures in columns, lists, or tables so that they can be read easily

¹⁰² **responsive** (adj) paying attention to someone or something and reacting in a suitable or positive way

¹⁰³ **carefree** (adj) with no problems or worries

¹⁰⁴ **moody** (adj) If you are moody, you often change and become angry or unhappy without warning.

¹⁰⁵ **rigid** (adj) not able or not wanting to be changed

¹⁰⁶ **sober** (adj) serious

¹⁰⁷ **reserved** (adj) (of a person or their character) slow or unwilling to show feelings or express opinions

¹⁰⁸ **touchy** (adj) easily upset or made angry

¹⁰⁹ **restless** (adj) not able to stay still or relax because you are bored or nervous

¹¹⁰ **impulsive** (adj) doing things suddenly and without thinking carefully

¹¹¹ **adaptable** (adj) able to change in a new situation

Unit 5

Activity 1 (page 155)

¹ **advancement** (n) the process of helping something to make progress or succeed; the progress that is made

² **invasion** (n) the unwelcomed act of someone entering something by force in order to take control of it

³ **prestige** (n) the respect and admiration that someone or something has because of their social position or what they have done

⁴ **correlate** (v) to have or to show a relationship or connection between two or more things

⁵ **turnover** (n) the rate at which employees leave a company and are replaced by other people

⁶ **morale** (n) how happy, sad, confident, etc. a group of people feels at a particular time

⁷ **fossil** (n) a part of a dead plant or an animal that has been in the ground for a very long time and has turned into rock

Activity 2 (pages 155–156)

⁸ **catastrophe** (n) a sudden disaster that causes great suffering or damage

⁹ **incomparably** (adv) greater than any comparison could suggest

¹⁰ **inequality** (n) difference between groups in society because one has more money, advantages, etc. than the other

¹¹ **have the upper hand** (phr) to get the advantage and be in control of a situation

¹² **literate** (adj) able to read and write

¹³ **eliminate** (v) to remove or get rid of something or someone

¹⁴ **reflective** (adj) (used about a person, mood, etc.) thinking deeply about things

Activity 3 (page 156)

¹⁵ **reef** (n) a long line of rocks or plants just below or above the surface of the sea

¹⁶ **legislative** (adj) connected with the act of making laws

Activity 4 (page 158)

¹⁷ **skull** (n) the bone structure that forms the head and surrounds and protects the brain

Activity 5 (pages 158–159)

¹⁸ **grizzly bear** (n) a large aggressive brown bear that lives in North America and parts of Russia

¹⁹ **viable** (adj) that can be done; that will be successful

²⁰ **erosion** (n) the process by which the surface of something is gradually destroyed through the action of wind, rain, etc.

²¹ **devastating** (adj) causing a lot of damage and destruction

²² **family law** (n) the system of rules that pertain to subjects dealing with divorce and domestic violence

²³ **litigation** (n) the process of taking legal action in a court of law

²⁴ **allocation** (n) an amount of money, space, etc. that is given to somebody for a particular purpose

²⁵ **rigid** (adj) not able to be changed; not flexible

Activity 6 (page 159)

²⁶ **intellectual property** (n) an idea, a design, a literary or other artistic work, etc. that someone has created and that the law prevents other people from copying

²⁷ **pessimist** (n) a person who always thinks that bad things will happen or that something will not be successful

²⁸ **peer-to-peer** (adj) in a computer system, data sharing without the need for a central server, as each computer can act as a server for the others

²⁹ **combat** (v) to fight against something; to try to stop or defeat something

³⁰ **ethics** (n) the branch of philosophy that deals with moral principles

Activity 7 (Reading, pages 160–161)

³¹ **peer-to-peer file sharing** (phr) sharing digital files, often illegally, between two or more people

³² **piracy** (n) the illegal copying of books, videotapes, etc.; also, the crime of attacking ships in order to steal from them

³³ **divisive** (adj) likely to cause disagreements or arguments between people

³⁴ **on the face of it** (phr) used to say that something seems true but that this opinion may need to be changed when you know more

³⁵ **cloud** (n) a server where files are located that is not in the same place as the computer that created the files

³⁶ **label** (n) a company that produces and sells recorded music

³⁷ **by any means necessary** (phr) to get something accomplished in any way possible or to any extent

³⁸ **pay the price** (phr) to suffer because of bad luck or something you've done

³⁹ **shrug (one's) shoulders** (phr) to treat something as not important (**shrug** = to raise and then drop your shoulders to show that you don't know or care about something)

⁴⁰ **royalty** (n) a sum of money that is paid to someone who has written a book, piece of music, etc. each time that it is sold or performed

⁴¹ **copyright** (n) If a person or an organization holds the copyright on a piece of writing, music, etc., they are the only people who have the legal right to publish, broadcast, perform it, etc. and other people must ask their permission to use it or any part of it.

⁴² **advocate** (n) a person who supports or speaks in favor of somebody or of a public plan or action

⁴³ **innovator** (n) someone who introduces new things, ideas, or ways of doing something

▸ **innovative** (adj)

⁴⁴ **cite** (v) to mention something as a reason or an example, or in order to support what you are saying

⁴⁵ **popular culture** (phr) music, literature, etc. that is enjoyed by a lot of people

⁴⁶ **subscriber** (n) a person who pays to receive a newspaper or magazine regularly or to use a particular service

⁴⁷ **collude** (v) to work together secretly or illegally in order to trick other people

⁴⁸ **streaming** (n) a method of sending or receiving data, especially video, over a computer network

⁴⁹ **cloud storage** (n) a model of data storage in which data is maintained, managed, and backed up remotely and made available to users over a network (typically the Internet)

⁵⁰ **embrace** (v) to accept an idea, a proposal, a set of beliefs, etc., especially when it is done with enthusiasm

⁵¹ **demonize** (v) to describe somebody or something in a way that is intended to make other people think of them or it as evil or dangerous

Activity 9 (page 165)

⁵² **beta carotene** (n) a substance found in carrots and other plants, which is needed by humans

⁵³ **recurrence** (n) If there is a recurrence of something, it happens again.

⁵⁴ **spunk** (n) courage, determination, enthusiasm

⁵⁵ **robotics** (n) the science of designing and operating robots

⁵⁶ **obesity** (n) (of people) the condition of being very fat in a way that is not healthy

⁵⁷ **dementia** (n) a serious mental problem caused by brain disease or injury that affects the ability to think, remember, and behave normally

⁵⁸ **faltering** (adj) becoming weaker or less effective

⁵⁹ **Alzheimer's disease** (n) a kind of dementia, especially affecting older people

⁶⁰ **thawing** (n) the melting of snow and ice in warmer weather

⁶¹ **halt** (v) to make someone or something stop

⁶² **current** (n) water that is moving

Activity 10 (page 166)

⁶³ **colic** (n) pain in the stomach area, suffered especially by babies

⁶⁴ **infant** (n) baby

▸ **infancy** (n)

⁶⁵ **assimilation** (n) the act of becoming a part of a country or community rather than keeping a separate identity

Activity 11 (page 166)

66 **secondhand smoke** (n) smoke that is breathed in from other people's cigarettes

67 **trans-fat** (n) a type of fat produced when oils are changed by a chemical process into solids

68 **drain** (n) a pipe that carries away water
  ▸ **drainage** (n)

69 **untreated** (adj) not made safe by chemical or other treatment

70 **runoff** (n) rain, water, or other liquid that runs off land into streams and rivers

71 **sexism** (n) the unfair treatment of people, especially women, because of their sex; the attitude that causes this

Activity 12 (page 167)

72 **ecological** (adj) connected with the relation of plants and living creatures to each other and to their environment
  ▸ **ecologically** (adv)

73 **planetary** (adj) relating to a planet

74 **elaborate** (adj) not simple; with a lot of different parts

75 **forge** (v) to put a lot of effort into making something successful or strong so that it will last

76 **consensus** (n) an opinion that all members of a group agree with

77 **voluminous** (adj) very long and detailed; very large

78 **underlying** (adj) being the basis of something

79 **glacier** (n) a large mass of ice that moves slowly down a mountain

80 **destabilize** (v) to make a system become less safe and successful

81 **mound** (n) a small hill; a large pile of earth

82 **prop up** (v) to support something that would otherwise fall

83 **habitat** (n) the place where a particular type of animal or plant is normally found

84 **emission** (n) the production or sending out of light, heat, gas, etc.

85 **biodiversity** (n) the wide variety of animals and plants in a region which together make a good and healthy environment

86 **famine** (n) a lack of food during a long period of time in a region

87 **down the road** (phr) at some time in the future

Activity 14 (Reading, pages 168–169)

88 **contradict** (v) to say that something that someone else has said is wrong, and that the opposite is true

89 **consistent** (adj) always behaving in the same way, or having the same opinions, standards, etc.

90 **dignity** (n) a calm and serious manner that deserves respect

91 **manipulation** (n) the controlling or influencing of someone or something, often in a dishonest way so that it is not realized

92 **flourish** (v) to develop quickly and be successful or common

93 **stifle** (v) to stop something from happening, developing, or continuing

94 **stunt** (v) to prevent someone or something from growing or developing as much as they/it should

95 **virtue** (n) behavior or attitudes that show high moral standards

96 **moderation** (n) the quality of being reasonable and not being extreme

Activity 15 (page 170)

97 **lifeguard** (n) a person at a beach or swimming pool whose job is to help people who are in danger in the water

98 **terminally** (adv) (of an illness) that cannot be cured and will lead to death

99 **internship** (n) a job, for example, during the summer vacation, intended to give a student or new graduate practical experience in their area of interest

100 **credentials** (n) the experience, etc. that makes somebody suitable for something

Activity 16 (page 173)

101 **cognitive** (adj) connected with the mental processes of understanding

102 **elite** (adj) the best of a group

103 **numeral** (n) a sign or symbol that represents a quantity

104 **pole** (n) one of two places at the top and bottom of the earth

105 **crust** (n) a hard layer or surface

106 **asteroid** (n) one of the very large rocks or small planets that move around the sun

107 **transmitter** (n) a person or thing that transmits something from one person or thing to another

108 **(child) rearing** (n) the process of caring for children as they grow up, teaching them how to behave as members of society

109 **puberty** (n) the time when a child's body is changing and becoming physically like that of an adult

110 **discipline** (v) the practice of training people to obey rules and orders and punishing them if they do not; the controlled behavior or situation that results from this training

111 **radiation** (n) powerful and very dangerous rays that are sent out from radioactive substances

112 **susceptible** (adj) very likely to be influenced, harmed, or affected by somebody or something

113 **fungus** (n) any plant without leaves, flowers, or green coloring that grows on other plants or on other surfaces; for example, mushrooms

114 **yield** (n) the total amount of crops that are produced

Activity 18 (pages 174–175)

115 **mock** (adj) a copy of something; not real

Activity 19 (page 176)

116 **assembly** (n) a group of people who have been elected to meet together regularly and make decisions or laws for a particular region or country

117 **monarchy** (n) a system of government by a king or queen

118 **revolution** (n) an attempt, by a large number of people, to change the government of a country

119 **uranium** (n) a metal that can be used to produce nuclear energy

120 **electron** (n) one of the three types of particles that form all atoms

121 **chimpanzee** (n) a type of African ape

122 **genome** (n) the complete set of genes in a cell or living thing

123 **non-mammalian** (adj) any animal that does not give birth to live babies or feed its young on milk

124 **compromise** (n) an agreement made between two people or groups in which each side gives up some of the things they want so that both sides are happy at the end

125 **faint** (adj) that cannot be clearly seen

126 **orbiting** (adj) moving around another planet, star, etc. in a curved path

127 **constant** (adj) that does not change; fixed

128 **ellipse** (n) a regular oval shape, like a circle that has been pressed in from two sides

Activity 20 (page 176)

129 **organism** (n) a living thing

130 **pesticide** (n) a chemical substance that is used to kill insects and other creatures that eat food crops

131 **herbicide** (n) a chemical substance that is used to kill plants that are growing where they are not wanted

132 **cross-pollinate** (v) to move pollen from a flower or plant onto another flower or plant so that it produces seeds

Activity 21 (pages 177–178)

133 **extinct** (adj) no longer in existence

134 **ultraviolet** (adj) of electromagnetic waves that are just shorter than those of violet light in the spectrum and cannot be seen

135 **arroyo** (n) a narrow channel with steep sides cut by a river in a desert region

136 **formation** (n) the act of making or developing something

137 **drainage** (n) the process by which water or liquid waste is drained from an area

138 **settler** (n) a person who goes to live permanently in a place where not many people live

139 **tame** (adj) not wild

140 **genome map** (n) a method of determining the location of and distances between genes on a chromosome

141 **abandonment** (n) the act of leaving a person, thing, or place with no intention of returning

142 **excavation** (n) the activity of digging in the ground

143 **archeological** (adj) of or relating to the study of cultures of the past

144 **otherwise** (adv) used to state what the result would be if something did not happen or if the situation were different

145 **gland** (n) any of the small parts or organs inside your body that produce chemical substances for your body to use

146 **leftover** (n) an object that remains from an earlier time

147 **immune system** (n) the system in your body that produces substances to help it fight against infection and disease

148 **hindrance** (n) a thing that makes it difficult for you to do something

Resources

6.1 Useful Things to Remember about Verbs

A

VERBS

HELPING VERBS	MAIN VERBS
be, do, have, can, will, etc.	learn, change, disappear, etc.

1 Children **learn** languages easily.

2 Languages **are** always **changing**.

3 Many languages **have disappeared**.

4 How **can** I **improve** my language abilities?

The English language has **main verbs** and **helping verbs**. We describe states, actions, and events with main verbs, as in **1**. Helping verbs primarily give grammatical information. We use helping verbs together with main verbs, as in **2 – 4**.

For a list of irregular verbs, see page R-51.

B

COMPARE MAIN VERBS AND HELPING VERBS

5a No one **is** here.
5b No one **is coming** here.

6a Somebody **did** all the work.
6b **Did** you **do** anything yesterday?

7a We **have** plenty of time.
7b I **haven't seen** them all day.

We can use the verbs *be, do,* and *have* as either a main verb, as in **5a – 7a**, or a helping verb, as in **5b – 7b**.

GRAMMAR TERM: Helping verbs are also called **auxiliary verbs**. Main verbs are also called **lexical verbs**.

C

8 I **need** a new computer. (1 clause)

9 I **need** a new computer, but I **can't afford** it. (2 clauses)

10 When you **study**, you **should turn off** the TV. (2 clauses)

11 I **don't know** what she **wants**, but I'm going to **find out**.
(3 clauses)

A clause is a group of words with a subject and a complete verb. A sentence can have one or more clauses, but each clause needs a main verb, as in **8 – 11**.

D

12 How far can you **run**? (run = go quickly on foot)

13 He **runs** a restaurant. (run = manage)

14 This road **runs** south to Dover. (run = extend; reach)

Many main verbs have more than one meaning, as in **12 – 14**.

6.2 Non-Action Verbs

A

ACTION VERBS

1 He's leaving now.

2 Most people **don't get** enough exercise.

NON-ACTION VERBS

3 He **appears** to understand the problem.

4 She's sick.

5 I **know** him well. (NOT: I am knowing him well.)

6 I **own** this car now. (NOT: I am owning this car.)

Many verbs describe actions and activities, as in **1 – 2**. We call these verbs **action verbs**. Other verbs describe states or situations, as in **3 – 6**. We call these verbs **non-action verbs**.

With some non-action verbs, we rarely use the progressive form, as in **5 – 6**. Examples of these verbs include:

agree	belong	consist of	know	possess
believe	concern	exist	own	prefer

GRAMMAR TERM: Non-action verbs are also called **stative verbs**. For a list of non-action verbs, see page R-50.

B

NON-ACTIVE MEANING

7a He **has** a new computer. (has = owns)

8a She **looks** great. (looks = appears)

9a I **see** something in the distance. (see = view)

ACTIVE MEANING

7b I'm **having** trouble with my computer.
(having = experiencing)

8b Why are you **looking** at me? (looking – gazing)

9b My brother **is seeing** a new play tomorrow.
(seeing – viewing)

Some verbs have both an active meaning and a non-active meaning, as in **7a – 9b**. We sometimes use the progressive form with the active meaning of these verbs, as in **7b – 9b**.

Common verbs with both active and non-active meanings include:

appear	doubt	have	love	see	taste
be	feel	look	mind	smell	think

6.3 Transitive and Intransitive Verbs

Many verbs need a direct object in order to be complete, as in **1 – 2**. We call these verbs **transitive verbs**. Most (but not all) transitive verbs can be used with a passive form, as in **3 – 4**. Some verbs make sense without an object, as in **5 – 6**. These verbs, called **intransitive verbs**, cannot be used with a passive form.

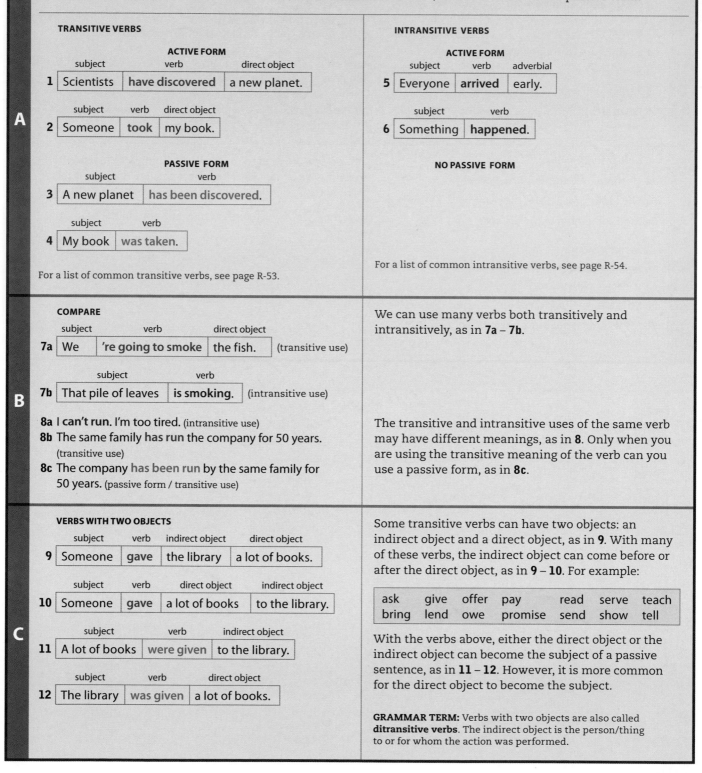

A

TRANSITIVE VERBS

ACTIVE FORM

subject	verb	direct object
1 Scientists	have discovered	a new planet.

subject	verb	direct object
2 Someone	took	my book.

PASSIVE FORM

subject	verb
3 A new planet	has been discovered.

subject	verb
4 My book	was taken.

For a list of common transitive verbs, see page R-53.

INTRANSITIVE VERBS

ACTIVE FORM

subject	verb	adverbial
5 Everyone	arrived	early.

subject	verb
6 Something	happened.

NO PASSIVE FORM

For a list of common intransitive verbs, see page R-54.

B

COMPARE

subject	verb	direct object	
7a We	're going to smoke	the fish.	(transitive use)

subject	verb	
7b That pile of leaves	is smoking.	(intransitive use)

8a I can't run. I'm too tired. (intransitive use)
8b The same family **has run** the company for 50 years. (transitive use)
8c The company **has been run** by the same family for 50 years. (passive form / transitive use)

We can use many verbs both transitively and intransitively, as in **7a – 7b**.

The transitive and intransitive uses of the same verb may have different meanings, as in **8**. Only when you are using the transitive meaning of the verb can you use a passive form, as in **8c**.

C

VERBS WITH TWO OBJECTS

subject	verb	indirect object	direct object
9 Someone	gave	the library	a lot of books.

subject	verb	direct object	indirect object
10 Someone	gave	a lot of books	to the library.

subject	verb	indirect object
11 A lot of books	were given	to the library.

subject	verb	direct object
12 The library	was given	a lot of books.

Some transitive verbs can have two objects: an indirect object and a direct object, as in **9**. With many of these verbs, the indirect object can come before or after the direct object, as in **9 – 10**. For example:

ask	give	offer	pay	read	serve	teach
bring	lend	owe	promise	send	show	tell

With the verbs above, either the direct object or the indirect object can become the subject of a passive sentence, as in **11 – 12**. However, it is more common for the direct object to become the subject.

GRAMMAR TERM: Verbs with two objects are also called **ditransitive verbs**. The indirect object is the person/thing to or for whom the action was performed.

6.4 Summary of Present, Past, and Future Forms

SIMPLE PRESENT / USES

I You We They	know. do not know. don't know.
He She It	knows. does not know. doesn't know.

We use the simple present to describe:
- current habitual behavior
- timeless truths
- general truths
- the state of something now
- scheduled events in the future

SIMPLE PAST / USES

I You We They He She It	knew. did not know. didn't know. arrived. did not arrive. didn't arrive.

We use the simple past to:
- signal an action, event, or state was completed at a definite time in the past
- indicate social or psychological distance

PRESENT PROGRESSIVE / USES

I	am listening. 'm listening. am not listening. 'm not listening.
He She It	is listening. 's listening. is not listening. 's not listening. isn't listening.
You We They	are listening. 're listening. are not listening. 're not listening. aren't listening.

We use the present progressive to:
- signal that a state or activity is temporary or in progress now
- talk about planned events in the future

PAST PROGRESSIVE / USES

I He She It	was listening. was not listening. wasn't listening.
You We They	were listening. were not listening. weren't listening.

We use the past progressive to:
- talk about something in progress at a particular time in the past
- describe a developing or changing situation in the past
- show social or psychological distance

FUTURE WITH *BE GOING TO* / USES

I	am going to help. 'm going to help. am not going to help. 'm not going to help.
He She It	is going to help. 's going to help. is not going to help. 's not going to help. isn't going to help.
You We They	are going to help. 're going to help. are not going to help. 're not going to help. aren't going to help.

We often use *be going to* to:
- talk about planned future events
- make predictions

FUTURE WITH *WILL* / USES

I He She It You We They	will do it. 'll do it. will not do it. won't do it.

We often use *will* to:
- make promises
- offer help and make requests
- talk about spontaneous plans
- make predictions

6.5 Summary of Perfect Forms

SIMPLE

PRESENT PERFECT

I You We They	have gone. 've gone.
	have not gone. haven't gone.
He She It	has gone. 's gone.
	has not gone. hasn't gone.

PAST PERFECT

| I You He She It We They | had left 'd left | by 6. |
| | had not left hadn't left | |

USES

We use the present perfect to describe something that:
- started in the past and continues to the present
- happened in the past but has an effect on the present

USES

We use the past perfect to show that one event in the past took place before another past time or event.

PROGRESSIVE

PRESENT PERFECT PROGRESSIVE

I You We They	have been waiting. 've been waiting.
	have not been waiting. haven't been waiting.
He She It	has been waiting. 's been waiting.
	has not been waiting. hasn't been waiting.

PAST PERFECT PROGRESSIVE

| I You He She It We They | had been waiting. 'd been waiting. |
| | had not been waiting. 'd not been waiting. hadn't been waiting. |

USES

We use the present perfect progressive to emphasize that something happened:
- repeatedly in the past and has an effect on the present
- continuously from a time in the past up until now

USES

We use the past perfect progressive to show that an earlier activity in the past was ongoing or repeated.

FUTURE

FUTURE PERFECT

| I You He She It We They | will have finished. 'll have finished. |
| | will not have finished. won't have finished. |

FUTURE PERFECT PROGRESSIVE

| I You He She It We They | will have been sleeping. 'll have been sleeping. |
| | will not have been sleeping. won't have been sleeping. |

USES

We use the future perfect to describe something that will be completed by or before a time in the future.

USES

We use the future perfect progressive to emphasize that something will be ongoing until a time in the future.

6.6 Overview of the Present Perfect

A

1 Life expectancy **has increased** since 1900. It's not uncommon for people to live into their eighties now.

2 Technology **has helped** people in many ways, but too much technology isn't healthy.

3 I**'ve watched** that movie too many times. I think I know it by heart.

4 Many roads here **have become** crowded, and this causes frequent traffic jams.

5 A: I need to talk to Barbara for a minute. Is she here?
B: No, she**'s gone** to the library.
(= She went to the library. She isn't here now.)

6 A: Are you hungry?
B: No, I**'ve already eaten.**
(= I ate something earlier so now I'm not hungry.)

When we want to show that a past action, event, or state is *connected to now* (the moment of speaking), we use the **present perfect** form of a verb, as in **1 – 6**. The past action, event, or state might be something that:

- started in the past and continues to the present, as in **1 – 2**
- happened repeatedly in the past and has an effect on something in the present, as in **3 – 4**
- started and ended in the past but has an effect on something in the present, as in **5 – 6**

REMEMBER: We form the present perfect with *have / has* (+ *not*) + the past participle (*-ed/-en* form) of the main verb. For a list of past participles of irregular verbs, see page R-51.

B

7 A: How's the movie?
B: It**'s been** great **so far.**

8 A: Is Uncle Bill here?
B: No, he **hasn't come** in **yet.**

9 We**'ve spoken** several times **in the past month**, and I think we are now ready to make a decision.

10 You**'ve always been** unhappy with your job. I think it's time to do something about it.

11 I**'ve just finished** my paper.

12 A: Sorry I'm late. How long **have** you **been** here?
B: Don't worry about it. I**'ve** only **been** here **for ten minutes.**

13 I **haven't worked since last December.** I really need to find a job soon.

We often use **adverbs** and **time expressions** with the present perfect, as in **7 – 13**. Some examples include:

already	just	never	yet
always	lately	so far	

in	+	the past few days / the last ten minutes
over	+	the past month / the last two years
for	+	a week / a year / the last two years
since	+	1980 / last year / January / then / my birthday

Notice: We can use some adverbs (such as *already, always, just,* and *never*) between *have / has* and the past participle, as in **10 – 11**.

We use *for* + a period of time, as in **12**. We use *since* + a specific time, as in **13**.

6.7 The Past Perfect and the Past Perfect Progressive

A

We use the **past perfect** to make the order of two past events clear. The past perfect signals the earlier event. The later event is often in the **simple past**, as in **1 – 2**. We can also use the past perfect in a sentence with a time phrase, as in **3**.

earlier event	later event
1	Somebody **had left** a newspaper on a chair,	so I **took** it and **sat** down.

later event	earlier event
2	By the time Thomas **arrived** in Phoenix,	his parents **had** already **left**.

later time	earlier event
3	**By the 1960s,**	the population of the world **had reached** 3 billion.

4 By the time we got there, they **had eaten** all the sandwiches and **drunk** all the juice.

Remember: We form the past perfect with *had* (+ *not*) + the past participle (*-ed /-en* form) of the main verb.

When we use two past perfect verbs together, it's not necessary to repeat the helping verb *had*, as in **4**.

B

5 She **was** angry **because** he **had forgotten** to call.

6 He **looked as though** he'd hardly **slept** at all.

7 When I **met** him, he **hadn't graduated** from college yet.

8 I **met** him **before** he **graduated** from college.

9 I **met** him **after** he **graduated** from college.

COMPARE

10a We **left** when he **got** there. (He got there and then we left.)

10b We'd **left** when he **got** there. (We left and then he got there.)

We often use the past perfect in sentences with *because, as though,* or *when.* The past perfect signals which past event happened first, as in **5 – 7**.

The words *before* and *after* make the order of events clear. We can use the simple past after these words, as in **8 – 9**. The past perfect is not necessary.

Notice the difference in meaning when we use the simple past compared to the past perfect, as in **10a – 10b**.

C

COMPARE

11a He was sure that someone **had used** his computer.
(Someone had used his computer at least one time.)

11b He was sure that someone **had been using** his computer.
(Someone had been using his computer repeatedly or for an ongoing period of time.)

We can use the **past perfect progressive** instead of the past perfect to emphasize that an earlier activity was ongoing or repeated, as in **11b**.

We form the past perfect progressive with *had* (+ *not*) + *been* + the *-ing* form of the main verb.

Modals and Modality

7.1 Summary of Modals

SIMPLE MODALS		PHRASAL MODALS
She **can speak** English well.	→	Many immigrants **are able to speak** English very well.
She **could speak** Chinese when she was a child.	→	She **was able to speak** Chinese when she was a child.
They say it **will rain** tomorrow.	→	They say it**'s going to rain** tomorrow.
They said it **would rain**, but it didn't.	→	They said it **was going to rain**, but it didn't.
Employees **must arrive** on time.	→	Employees **have to arrive** on time.
Employees **may take** two 15-minute breaks.	→	Employees **are permitted to take** two 15-minute breaks.
We **might finish** by 4:00, but I'm not sure.	→	—
He **should help** his mother.	→	He **is supposed to help** his mother.

SOCIAL PURPOSE MEANINGS

CAN(NOT)
Ability I **can swim**.
Permission We **can stay** for a few more hours.
Prohibition You **can't stay** any longer.
Offer **Can I help** you?

WILL
Offer I**'ll help** you with that.

MUST(NOT)
Obligation Employees **must sign in** when they arrive.

SHOULD(NOT)
Advice You **should take** Walker Boulevard.

MAY(NOT)
Permission **May I continue**?
Prohibition You **may not talk** during the test.
Offer **May I help** you?

MIGHT(NOT)
Suggestion You **might want to try** calling him again.

COULD
Permission **Could I sit** here?
Suggestion We **could try** that new restaurant downtown.
Request **Could you say** that again?

DEGREE OF CERTAINTY / LOGICAL PROBABILITY MEANINGS

CAN(NOT)
General possibility Honey **can make** your throat feel better.

very certain / very likely
strong probability

WILL / WON'T
They **will come** home soon.
They **won't be** out much longer.

MUST / CAN'T / COULDN'T
She has so many flowers. She **must love** to garden.
That **can't be** our train. It's too early.

SHOULD(NOT)
I **should be** home by 5:00. I **shouldn't be** late.

MAY(NOT)
I **may take** accounting next year. I haven't decided.

MIGHT(NOT) / COULD
They **might drop by** tomorrow, but I'm not sure.

The meeting **could last** for an hour.

not certain / not likely
weak probability

WOULD(NOT)
Counterfactual I **would help** you, but you haven't asked.

OTHER WAYS OF SHOWING PERMISSION / PROHIBITION / OBLIGATION

Permission On Fridays, we **were allowed to wear** casual clothing at work.
You **are permitted to turn** right on a red light here.

Prohibition Employees **are not allowed to eat** at their desks.

Obligation He **is required to take** a final exam for this class.
Children **are supposed to obey** their parents.

OTHER WAYS OF SHOWING CERTAINTY / UNCERTAINTY

ADVERBS
Strong certainty They are **certainly / definitely / clearly** going to enjoy this wonderful meal.
Moderate certainty He is **probably / most likely** going to come home tomorrow.
Weak certainty They are **possibly** going to get new uniforms.

PREPOSITIONAL PHRASES
In a way, this is the most difficult class I've ever taken.
In a sense, he is representing the class.
In some respects, nothing has changed.

7.2 Degrees of Certainty about the Present and Future

We can use **simple modals** and **phrasal modals** to show how certain we are that something is true or is likely to happen, as in **1 – 15**. We often provide evidence or a reason for what we are saying. Notice that some modals show different degrees of certainty in positive and negative sentences.

		POSITIVE	NEGATIVE
STRONGER CERTAINTY	*will/won't*	**1** She'**ll be** home at 6:00. Her schedule never changes.	**2** She **won't get** home early. She has too much work to do.
	be going to/ be (not) going to	**3** She's **going to be** home at 6:00. She told me so.	**4** She's **not going to come** home early.
	*must/ must not**	**5** She's not here, so she **must be** at work.	**6** She **must not be** at her desk— I called and she didn't answer.
	can't	—	**7** She **can't be** home already. I saw her at work five minutes ago.
	couldn't		**8** She **couldn't be** home already. I just saw her.
EXPECTATION	*should/ shouldn't*	**9** She **should be** at work by now. It usually takes her 30 minutes.	**10** She **shouldn't be** home yet. She usually works until 7:00.
WEAKER CERTAINTY	*may/ may not**	**11** She **may be** there already— she left before we did. **12** They **might visit** tomorrow. I have to call to find out. **13** I don't know him. He **could be** a new student, I guess.	**14** She didn't get paid. She **may not have** enough money to go out. **15** They **might not visit** tomorrow after all.
	*might/ might not**		
	could		—

*We don't usually contract *must not*, *may not*, and *might not*.

7.3 Past Certainty

We can use **modal** + *have* + the **past participle of a main verb** to express probability in the past, as in **1 – 8**. As with present and future modals, we often give evidence or a reason for our degree of certainty.

		POSITIVE	NEGATIVE
STRONGER CERTAINTY	*must have/ must not have**	**1** They **must have seen** us. We were only a few feet away from them.	**2** She's not up yet. She **must not have set** her alarm clock.
	couldn't have	—	**3** It was the first time you met her. You **couldn't have known** about her problems.
WEAKER CERTAINTY	*may have/ may not have**	**4** I'm not sure why he went home early. He **may have been** tired. **5** You **might have seen** him. Did you notice a guy in a blue jacket? **6** The temperature differences **could have affected** the data, but we're not sure if they did.	**7** She **may not have noticed** the stop sign. It was very dark. **8** They didn't do the project correctly. They **might not have understood** the directions.
	*might have/ might not have**		
	could have		—

*We don't usually contract *must not*, *may not*, and *might not*.

7.4 Other Ways to Express Modality

A

LOCATION OF ADVERBS OF CERTAINTY

POSITIVE STATEMENTS

	subject	*be* or first helping verb	adverb	main verb	
1	She	was	probably	—	frustrated.
2	This	will	most likely	change	later.
3	The people	can	certainly	decide	themselves.
4	He	—	definitely	knows	the answer.

NEGATIVE STATEMENTS

	subject	—	adverb	helping and main verbs	
5	Listeners	—	obviously	can't understand	her.
6	The phone	—	clearly	isn't working.	

We sometimes use **adverbs** to express degrees of certainty. We can place these adverbs:

- after a positive *be* verb, as in **1**, or the first helping verb, as in **2 – 3**
- before positive main verbs (besides *be*), as in **4**
- in negative sentences before any verb, including *be*, as in **5** and **6**

ADVERBS OF CERTAINTY		
STRONG CERTAINTY	certainly clearly definitely	evidently obviously
MODERATE CERTAINTY	most likely probably	
WEAK CERTAINTY	possibly	

B

PREPOSITIONAL PHRASES

7 **In a way**, I understand their decision. But I don't agree with it.

8 He has grown up a lot, but he has the same personality and character. **In a sense**, he hasn't changed at all.

9 Their jobs are different, but they both achieved success quickly. **In some respects**, their careers have followed the same path.

With some **prepositional phrases**, we can suggest that a statement is only partly true, as in **7 – 9**.

We often use these prepositional phrases at the beginning of a sentence.

The Passive

8.1 Summary of the Passive

USES

We sometimes use the passive:

- to focus a sentence on what happened and to what or whom
- because we can't or choose not to identify the performer of the action, or agent
- to avoid blaming someone for something
- to avoid taking responsibility for something
- to connect sentences in a paragraph by continuing the focus on a particular person or thing

SIMPLE PRESENT PASSIVE:
BE (AM, IS, ARE) + PAST PARTICIPLE

I	am	paid	twice a month.
He / She / It	is		
We / You / They	are		

SIMPLE PAST PASSIVE:
BE (WAS, WERE) + PAST PARTICIPLE

I / He / She / It	was	paid	last week.
We / You / They	were		

PRESENT PROGRESSIVE PASSIVE:
BE (AM, IS, ARE) + BEING + PAST PARTICIPLE

I	am	being helped.
He / She / It	is	
We / You / They	are	

PAST PROGRESSIVE PASSIVE:
BE (WAS, WERE) + BEING + PAST PARTICIPLE

I / He / She / It	was	being helped.
We / You / They	were	

PRESENT PERFECT PASSIVE:
HAVE / HAS + BEEN + PAST PARTICIPLE

I / We / You / They	have	been helped.
He / She / It	has	

PAST PERFECT PASSIVE:
HAD + BEEN + PAST PARTICIPLE

I / He / She / It	had been helped.
We / You / They	

MODALS:
MODAL + BE + PAST PARTICIPLE

The package	will should can must may might could would	be delivered	soon.

PHRASAL MODALS:
PHRASAL MODAL + BE + PAST PARTICIPLE

The package	is going to is supposed to has to is able to is allowed to	be sent	by air.

8.2 Using the Passive

Passive sentences are much less common than active sentences, but they are very useful when we want to focus on what happened and to what or whom. The first sentence in **1** below focuses on the agent or performer of the action (*My brother*) and uses an **active verb form**. The second sentence in **1** focuses on what happened (*was designed*) and to what/whom (the *house*) and uses **passive verb forms**.

1 My brother just **bought** an unusual house. It **was designed** and **built** in the 1950s.

A

2 Their car **was stolen**. (by someone unknown)

3 Dr. Henry, one of our most prominent scientists, **was honored** with an award last night. (We aren't interested in who gave the award.)

4 What **is** this **called** in English? (by everyone)

5 Sam Edwards, 32, **was arrested** at his home last night. (by the police)

We often use the passive because the agent:
- is unknown, as in **2**
- is unimportant in a particular context, as in **3**
- refers to people in general, as in **4**
- is obvious from the context, as in **5**

B

COMPARE

6a David didn't notify anyone about the meeting.
6b No one **was notified** about the meeting.

7a We have made many mistakes in this war.
7b Many mistakes **have been made** in this war.

We sometimes use the passive:
- to avoid blaming someone for something, as in **6b**
- to avoid taking responsibility for something, as in **7b**

C

8 Ega is an endangered language. It **is spoken** in Ivory Coast **by only 300 people**.

9 The engine **is started by an electric device**.

Because the focus of a passive sentence is on what happens and to what / whom, we rarely mention the agent. The few times that we do, it is because the agent is worth noticing. This might be because the agent is:
- new, unique, or unexpected, as in **8**
- nonhuman, as in **9** (We expect agents to be human.)

8.3 Comparing Active and Passive Sentences

A

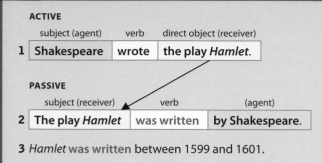

ACTIVE

subject (agent)	verb	direct object (receiver)

1 | Shakespeare | wrote | the play *Hamlet*.

PASSIVE

subject (receiver)	verb	(agent)

2 | The play *Hamlet* | was written | by Shakespeare.

3 *Hamlet* **was written** between 1599 and 1601.

In most sentences, the subject is the performer of the action, or agent, as in **1**. When the subject performs the action, we call the sentence an **active sentence**. The direct object is the receiver of the action.

A **passive sentence** lets us change the focus to what happened or who received the action, as in **2**.

- The receiver of the action becomes the subject of the sentence.
- When the agent is included, it follows the word *by*.

In passive sentences, however, the agent is usually omitted, as in **3**.

B

We form the passive with *be* + the **past participle of the main verb**. The form of *be* signals the time frame we are talking about.

			first helping verb (*be* or *have*)	*been*	*being*	past participle main verb
SIMPLE PRESENT	Active	The waiters serve the food quickly.				
	Passive	The food **is served** quickly.	= am / is / are →			
SIMPLE PAST	Active	The waiters served the food.				
	Passive	The food **was served**.	= was / were →			
PRESENT PROGRESSIVE	Active	The waiters are serving the food now.				
	Passive	The food **is being served** now.	= am / is / are →		being	served
PAST PROGRESSIVE	Active	The waiters were serving the food.				
	Passive	The food **was being served**.	= was / were →			
PRESENT PERFECT	Active	The waiters have already served the food.				
	Passive	The food **has already been served**.	= has / have	been →		
PAST PERFECT	Active	The waiters had just served the food.				
	Passive	The food **had just been served**.	= had			

For a list of past participles of irregular verbs, see page R-51.

8.4 The Passive with Modals

We often use the passive with modal and phrasal modal forms, as in **1b – 13b**.

MODAL + *BE* + PAST PARTICIPLE

WILL	Active	**1a** The organizers **will hold** the meeting tomorrow at 10:00.
	Passive	**1b** The meeting **will be held** tomorrow at 10:00.
SHOULD	Active	**2a** Somebody **should deliver** the package in two weeks.
	Passive	**2b** The package **should be delivered** in two weeks.
MUST	Active	**3a** Somebody **must tell** him soon.
	Passive	**3b** He **must be told** soon.
CAN	Active	**4a** We **can prevent** heart disease.
	Passive	**4b** Heart disease **can be prevented**.
MAY	Active	**5a** No one **may copy** any part of this publication.
	Passive	**5b** No part of this publication **may be copied**.
MIGHT	Active	**6a** They **might make** this offer again.
	Passive	**6b** This offer **might be made** again.
COULD	Active	**7a** The writer **could improve** this essay.
	Passive	**7b** This essay **could be improved**.
WOULD	Active	**8a** They said they **would hold** the election as promised.
	Passive	**8b** They said the election **would be held** as promised.

PHRASAL MODAL + *BE* + PAST PARTICIPLE

BE GOING TO	Active	**9a** They **are going to give** us another chance to play.
	Passive	**9b** We're going **to be given** another chance to play.
BE SUPPOSED TO	Active	**10a** We **are supposed to keep** this outside.
	Passive	**10b** This is supposed **to be kept** outside.
HAVE TO	Active	**11a** Somebody **has to do** something.
	Passive	**11b** Something **has to be done**.
BE ABLE TO	Active	**12a** Teachers **are** easily **able to use** this method in all schools.
	Passive	**12b** This method **is able to be used** easily in all schools.
BE ALLOWED TO	Active	**13a** No one **is allowed to take** photographs.
	Passive	**13b** No photographs **are allowed to be taken**.

A

Overview of Active and Passive Verb Forms

	ACTIVE FORMS					PASSIVE FORMS				
	—	*have*	*be*	*be*	*verb*	—	*have*	*be*	*be*	*verb*
SIMPLE FORMS										
Simple present	—	—	—	—	considers	—	—	is	—	considered
Simple past	—	—	—	—	considered	—	—	was	—	considered
Future with *will*	will	—	—	—	consider	will	—	be	—	considered
Simple modal	could	—	—	—	consider	could	—	be	—	considered
Simple *to-* infinitive	to	—	—	—	consider	to	—	be	—	considered
PROGRESSIVE FORMS										
Present progressive	—	—	is	—	considering	—	—	is	being	considered
Past progressive	—	—	was	—	considering	—	—	was	being	considered
Future progressive	will	—	be	—	considering	will	—	be	being	considered
Modal progressive	could	—	be	—	considering	could	—	be	being	considered
To- infinitive progressive	to	—	be	—	considering	to	—	be	being	considered
PERFECT FORMS										
Present perfect	—	has	—	—	considered	—	has	been	—	considered
Past perfect	—	had	—	—	considered	—	had	been	—	considered
Future perfect	will	have	—	—	considered	will	have	been	—	considered
Modal perfect	could	have	—	—	considered	could	have	been	—	considered
To- infinitive perfect	to	have	—	—	considered	to	have	been	—	considered
PERFECT PROGRESSIVE FORMS										
Present perfect progressive	—	has	been	—	considering	—	has	been	being	considered
Past perfect progressive	—	had	been	—	considering	—	had	been	being	considered
Future perfect progressive	will	have	been	—	considering	will	have	been	being	considered
Modal perfect progressive	could	have	been	—	considering	could	have	been	being	considered
To- infinitive perfect progressive	to	have	been	—	considering	to	have	been	being	considered
PARTICIPLE FORMS										
Present participle	—	—	—	—	considering	—	—	being	—	considered
Past participle	—	having	—	—	considered	—	having	been	—	considered
Past progressive participle	—	having	been	—	considering	—	having	been	being	considered

A

Nouns and Noun Phrases

9.1 Summary of Nouns and Pronouns

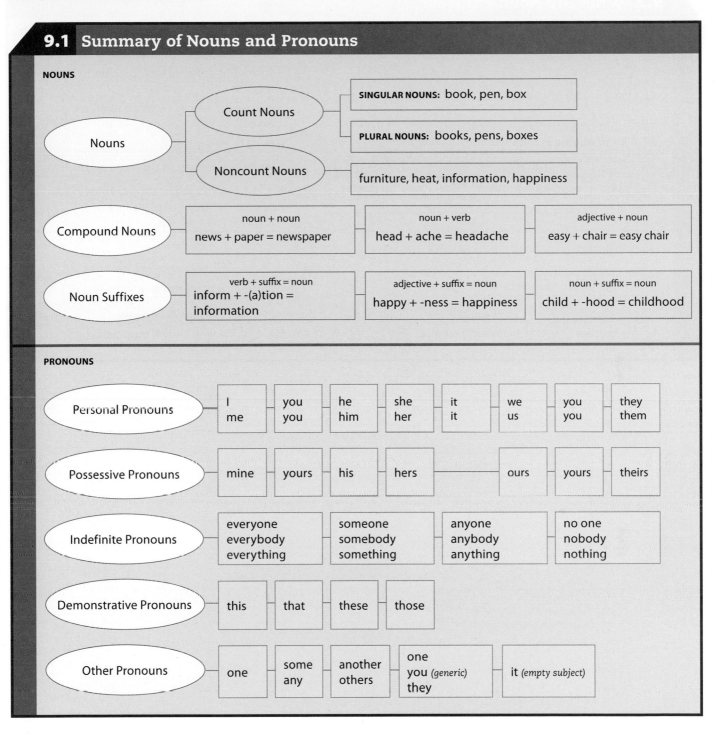

NOUNS

Nouns

Count Nouns

SINGULAR NOUNS: book, pen, box

PLURAL NOUNS: books, pens, boxes

Noncount Nouns

furniture, heat, information, happiness

Compound Nouns

noun + noun	noun + verb	adjective + noun
news + paper = newspaper	head + ache = headache	easy + chair = easy chair

Noun Suffixes

verb + suffix = noun	adjective + suffix = noun	noun + suffix = noun
inform + -(a)tion = information	happy + -ness = happiness	child + -hood = childhood

PRONOUNS

Personal Pronouns

I me	you you	he him	she her	it it	we us	you you	they them

Possessive Pronouns

mine	yours	his	hers		ours	yours	theirs

Indefinite Pronouns

everyone everybody everything	someone somebody something	anyone anybody anything	no one nobody nothing

Demonstrative Pronouns

this	that	these	those

Other Pronouns

one	some any	another others	one you (generic) they	it (empty subject)

9.2 What Are Noun Phrases?

A

noun phrase | noun phrase

1 | Money | isn't important to | me.

noun phrase

2 | I have | a lot of good friends.

noun phrase

3 | A lot of people in their twenties | work here.

noun phrase | noun phrase

4 | Debt is | a common problem | for | new graduates.
long noun phrase

A noun phrase can be:

- a single **noun** or **pronoun**, as in **1**
- a word or group of words + a **main noun**, as in **2**
- a group of words + a **main noun** + a group of words, as in **3**

Other words in a noun phrase add important information (details) to the main noun.

Notice: A long noun phrase can contain two or more short noun phrases, as in **4**.

B

We use noun phrases in different ways in a sentence, as in **5 – 8**.

subject

5 | A good boss | should be well organized.

subject | object of a preposition

7 | I | grew up in | a small town.

subject | object of a verb

6 | My brother | sent | many long emails.

subject | subject complement

8 | Yo-Yo Ma | is | a well-known musician.

9.3 Summary of Noun Phrases

Information before a Main Noun	Main Noun	Information after a Main Noun

DETERMINERS

Articles
(*a, an, the, some, Ø*)

| Honesty is | the best **policy.** |
| A house is not | a **home.** |

Possessives
(*my, your, her, etc.*)

| You can't have | your **cake** | and eat it. |
| A fool and | his **money** | are soon parted. |

Quantifiers
(*several, a few, many, etc.*)

| Many **hands** | make light work. |
| Every **picture** | tells a story. |

NUMBERS

| Don't put all your eggs in | one **basket.** |
| Every stick has | two **ends.** |

ADJECTIVES

| Honesty is | the **best** policy. |
| Bad **news** | travels fast. |

NOUNS

| Don't look | a **gift** horse | in the mouth. |
| Don't throw the baby out with | the **bath** water. |

APPOSITIVES

| Proverbs, short popular sayings, |
| usually state general and practical truths. |

PREPOSITIONAL PHRASES

| A **thing of beauty** | is a joy forever. |
| The best **things in life** | are free. |

ADJECTIVE CLAUSES

| Don't bite | the **hand that feeds you.** |
| A **man who is his own lawyer** | has a fool for a client. |
| People who live in glass houses |
| shouldn't throw stones. |

WE COMBINE INFORMATION BEFORE AND AFTER A MAIN NOUN IN MANY WAYS.

	Pictures		tell stories.
A	picture		tells a story.
My	picture		tells a story.
Every	picture	in the world	tells a story.
My family	pictures		tell wonderful stories.
Every motion	picture	that I have ever seen	tells a different story.
My favorite family	pictures		tell wonderful stories.

9.4 Adding Information to a Main Noun

We can give more information about a main noun by adding words before or after it.

The information **before** a **main noun** usually comes in a particular order, as in **1 – 5**.

A

NOUN PHRASE

		determiner	number	adjective	noun	main noun	
1	This is	a	-	thorough	research	project.	-
2	What are	your	two	favorite	childhood	memories?	-
3	Is there	any	-	new	-	information	on this?
4	Look at	the	first	-	-	chart	on page 30.
5	There are	a few		-	-	problems	that I can't solve.

B

Notice the kind of information that comes **after** a **main noun** in a noun phrase, as in **6 – 9**.

NOUN PHRASE

			main noun	appositive	prepositional phrase	adjective clause
6	We just met	our new	boss,	Mr. Wilson.	-	-
7	I answered	all the	questions	-	on the test.	-
8	The U.N. is	an international	organization	-	-	that works for peace.
9	There were	so many	people	-	in my past	who helped me.

C

10	I didn't know	anyone at the meeting.
11	We are looking for	those who are responsible.
12	This essay is clearer than	the one that I wrote.

We can also add more information to certain **pronouns**, such as:

- indefinite pronouns, as in **10**
- *these* or *those*, as in **11**
- *one*, as in **12**

This information usually comes after the pronoun.

9.5 Summary of Determiners

ARTICLES

	NOUNS		
	singular count	plural count	noncount
a / an	✓		
some		✓	✓
Ø		✓	✓
the	✓	✓	✓

(ARTICLES + NOUNS)

POSSESSIVES

	singular count	plural count	noncount
my your his her its our your their	✓	✓	✓

POSSESSIVE NOUNS

	singular count	plural count	noncount
singular noun + 's — the **plan's** success / irregular plural noun + 's — the **children's** tests / noncount noun + 's — **life's** challenges	✓	✓	✓
name ending in -s + ' — **Chris'** success / regular plural noun + ' — the **students'** tests / -	✓	✓	✓

QUANTIFIERS

	singular count	plural count	noncount
each every either neither	✓		
many several both a few few fewer		✓	
much a little little less			✓
all a lot of plenty of some more most		✓	✓
any no	✓	✓	✓

QUANTIFIERS WITH OF

	singular count	plural count	noncount
each of every one of either of neither of		✓	
many of several of both of a few of few of fewer of		✓	
much of a little of little of less of			✓
all (of) a lot of plenty of some of more of most of		✓	✓
any of none of		✓	✓

OTHER

	singular count	plural count	noncount
another	✓		
(Ø / some / most / many / both / etc.) other		✓	
(Ø / some / most / much / little / etc.) other			✓
the other	✓	✓	✓

DEMONSTRATIVES

	singular count	plural count	noncount
this that	✓		✓
these those		✓	

9.6 Prepositional Phrases

A

We can use a **prepositional phrase** to add more information to a noun phrase, as in **1 – 4**. The prepositional phrase often answers the question *what kind* or *which one*.

1 | New Zealand | has | **a population** of four million people. | (What kind of population?)

2 | What are | **the most important qualities** of a good boss? | (What kind of qualities?)

3 | He has written | **several papers** on climate change. | (What kind of papers?)

4 | Does | **anyone** in the class | have a car? | (Which person or people?)

For a list of common prepositions, see page R-56.

B

Sometimes we use several prepositional phrases in a noun phrase. Each prepositional phrase adds information to the noun phrase before it, as in **5 – 7**.

5 | Here you will find | news | about the Museum | of the City | of New York.

6 | We will discuss | reasons | for the increase | in health-care costs.

7 | We will meet at | the embassy | of the People's Republic | of China | in London.

C

COMPARE

8a **The box on the table** is mine. (Which box?)
8b Please put the box **on the table**. (Where do I put the box?)

9a Don't be late for **the meeting on Friday**. (Which meeting?)
9b Our meeting is **on Friday**. (When is the meeting?)

WARNING! A prepositional phrase can function in different ways. It can add more information to:

- a **noun phrase**, as in **8a** and **9a**.

- a verb or a whole sentence, as in **8b** and **9b**. In this case, it is not part of a noun phrase. (It functions like an adverb.)

Noun Clauses

10.1 Overview of Noun Clauses

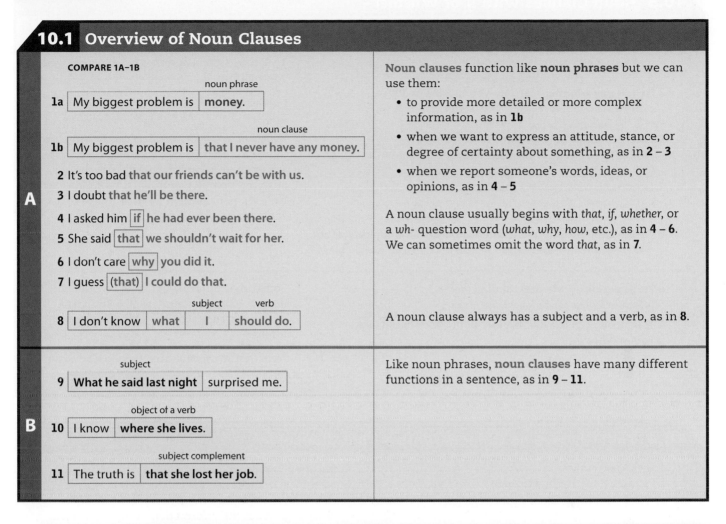

COMPARE 1A–1B

1a | My biggest problem is | **money.** ← *noun phrase*

1b | My biggest problem is | **that I never have any money.** ← *noun clause*

A

2 It's too bad **that our friends can't be with us.**

3 I doubt **that he'll be there.**

4 I asked him | **if** | he had ever been there.

5 She said | **that** | we shouldn't wait for her.

6 I don't care | **why** | you did it.

7 I guess | **(that)** | I could do that.

8 | I don't know | **what** (subject) | **I** | **should do.** (verb)

B

9 | **What he said last night** (subject) | surprised me.

10 | I know | **where she lives.** (object of a verb)

11 | The truth is | **that she lost her job.** (subject complement)

Noun clauses function like **noun phrases** but we can use them:

- to provide more detailed or more complex information, as in **1b**
- when we want to express an attitude, stance, or degree of certainty about something, as in **2 – 3**
- when we report someone's words, ideas, or opinions, as in **4 – 5**

A noun clause usually begins with *that*, *if*, *whether*, or a *wh-* question word (*what*, *why*, *how*, etc.), as in **4 – 6**. We can sometimes omit the word *that*, as in **7**.

A noun clause always has a subject and a verb, as in **8**.

Like noun phrases, **noun clauses** have many different functions in a sentence, as in **9 – 11**.

10.2 *Wh-* Noun Clauses

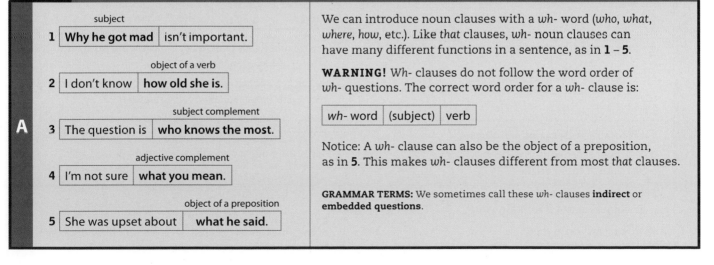

A

1 | **Why he got mad** (subject) | isn't important.

2 | I don't know | **how old she is.** (object of a verb)

3 | The question is | **who knows the most.** (subject complement)

4 | I'm not sure | **what you mean.** (adjective complement)

5 | She was upset about | **what he said.** (object of a preposition)

We can introduce noun clauses with a *wh-* word (*who*, *what*, *where*, *how*, etc.). Like *that* clauses, *wh-* noun clauses can have many different functions in a sentence, as in **1 – 5**.

WARNING! *Wh-* clauses do not follow the word order of *wh-* questions. The correct word order for a *wh-* clause is:

| *wh-* word | (subject) | verb |

Notice: A *wh-* clause can also be the object of a preposition, as in **5**. This makes *wh-* clauses different from most *that* clauses.

GRAMMAR TERMS: We sometimes call these *wh-* clauses **indirect** or **embedded questions**.

10.3 Noun Clauses with *If* or *Whether*

A

object of a verb
1 We don't know **if she's right or wrong.**
(= Maybe she's right; maybe she's wrong.)

adjective complement
2 I'm not sure **whether I can join you tonight or not.**
(= Maybe I can join you tonight; maybe I can't.)

subject
3 **Whether or not he will come** isn't certain.
(NOT COMMON: If he will come isn't certain.)

subject complement
4 The question is **whether I should stay or go.**
(NOT COMMON: The question is if I should stay or go.)

object of a preposition
5 We talked about **whether animals can truly communicate or not.**
(NOT COMMON: We talked about if animals can truly communicate or not.)

We use noun clauses with *if* or *whether* to show a choice between two options, as in **1 – 2**. The second option is often negative or contrasting.

Clauses with *whether* can have many different functions in a sentence, as in **1 – 5**.

If clauses are not used in as many different places as other kinds of noun clauses. We often use them as objects of verbs or adjective complements, as in **1 – 2**. However, they are not common in other places in a sentence, as in **3 – 5**.

B

6 I can't decide **if / whether I should move.**
(= Maybe I should; maybe I shouldn't.)

7 Your doctor can tell you **whether or not you should take your medication.**
(NOT: Your doctor can tell you if or not you should take your medication.)

Sometimes only one option is mentioned in an *if / whether* clause, as in **6**. In these sentences, the second option (*or not*) is implied.

Note that *or not* can directly follow *whether*, but not *if*, as in **7**.

10.4 *That* Clauses as Objects (Verb + *That* Clause)

A

VERB + *THAT* CLAUSE

verb	*that* clause
1 **I can see**	(that) we're going to be late.

2 **I couldn't believe** (that) I said it.

3 **I guess** (that) no one is at home.

4 **I told** her (that) I had to work late.

We often use a **that clause** as the object of a verb, as in **1 – 3**. In these sentences, the verb in the main clause often expresses thoughts, beliefs, attitudes, or feelings about the information in the *that* clause. Some common verbs we use in this way are:

believe	find	imagine	suppose
feel	guess	know	think

We also use *that* clauses to report what someone said, wrote, or asked, as in **4**.

GRAMMAR TERMS: *That* clauses used as the object of a verb are called **verb complements** or **verb completers**.

B

THAT CLAUSES IN SPEAKING AND WRITING

5 A: Somebody needs to clean this room.
B: I **guess** I could do it.

6 A: Hi, Jim. Come on in.
B: I **hope** I'm not bothering you.

7 A: You can't go in there.
B: I **know** I can't. (= I know that I can't go in there.)

8 Scientists **believe** that the animal is extinct.

9 He **explained** that the answers were not in the book.

10 She **argued** that she couldn't afford to pay the fine.

In speaking, we often omit the word *that* at the beginning of a noun clause, as in **5 – 6**.

Sometimes in a short answer, we do not include the full form of the verb in a *that* clause, as in **7**.

In writing, we often use the word *that* because it can make the writing easier to understand, as in **8**.

WARNING! In both conversation and writing, it is usually necessary to include *that* after the verbs *answer, argue, explain, reply,* and *understand,* as in **9 – 10**.

10.5 Subjunctive in *That* Clauses

A

VERB + *THAT* CLAUSE WITH BASE FORM VERB

1 She **demanded** that her employees | be | on time for work.

2 I **insist** that he | see | a doctor.
(NOT: I insist that he ~~sees~~ a doctor.)

3 We **recommend** that you | not go out | after dark.

After verbs that express urgency or a requirement, we usually use the base form of the verb in a *that* clause, even with third-person singular verbs, as in **1 – 2**. We form the negative with *not* + the base form of the verb, as in **3**.

Common verbs we use this way include *advise*, *ask*, *demand*, *insist*, *propose*, *recommend*, *request*, and *suggest*.

IT + *BE* + ADJECTIVE + *THAT* CLAUSE WITH BASE FORM VERB

4 It is **essential** that she | start | the work this week.

5 It is **important** that my brother | not hear | about this from you.

Sometimes we also need to use the base form of a verb in a *that* clause after *it* + *be* + adjective to express urgency or requirement, as in **4 – 5**. Common adjectives we use this way include *critical*, *crucial*, *essential*, *imperative*, *important*, and *vital*.

GRAMMAR TERM: When we use the base form of the verb with verbs and adjectives of requirement or importance, we call it a **subjunctive** form of the verb.

10.6 *That* Clauses as Complements

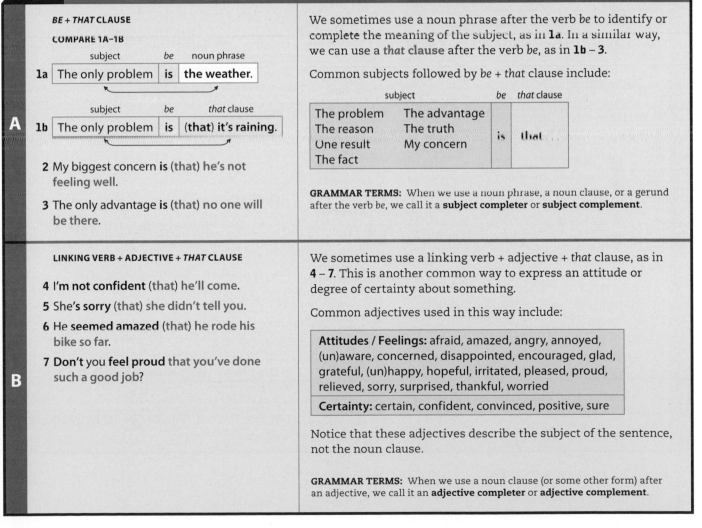

A

BE + *THAT* CLAUSE

COMPARE 1A–1B

subject	*be*	noun phrase
1a The only problem	is	the weather.

subject	*be*	*that* clause
1b The only problem	is	(that) it's raining.

2 My biggest concern **is** (that) he's not feeling well.

3 The only advantage **is** (that) no one will be there.

We sometimes use a noun phrase after the verb *be* to identify or complete the meaning of the subject, as in **1a**. In a similar way, we can use a *that* clause after the verb *be*, as in **1b – 3**.

Common subjects followed by *be* + *that* clause include:

subject		*be*	*that* clause
The problem	The advantage		
The reason	The truth	is	that …
One result	My concern		
The fact			

GRAMMAR TERMS: When we use a noun phrase, a noun clause, or a gerund after the verb *be*, we call it a **subject completer** or **subject complement**.

B

LINKING VERB + ADJECTIVE + *THAT* CLAUSE

4 I'm **not confident** (that) he'll come.

5 She's **sorry** (that) she didn't tell you.

6 He **seemed amazed** (that) he rode his bike so far.

7 Don't you **feel proud** that you've done such a good job?

We sometimes use a linking verb + adjective + *that* clause, as in **4 – 7**. This is another common way to express an attitude or degree of certainty about something.

Common adjectives used in this way include:

Attitudes / Feelings: afraid, amazed, angry, annoyed, (un)aware, concerned, disappointed, encouraged, glad, grateful, (un)happy, hopeful, irritated, pleased, proud, relieved, sorry, surprised, thankful, worried

Certainty: certain, confident, convinced, positive, sure

Notice that these adjectives describe the subject of the sentence, not the noun clause.

GRAMMAR TERMS: When we use a noun clause (or some other form) after an adjective, we call it an **adjective completer** or **adjective complement**.

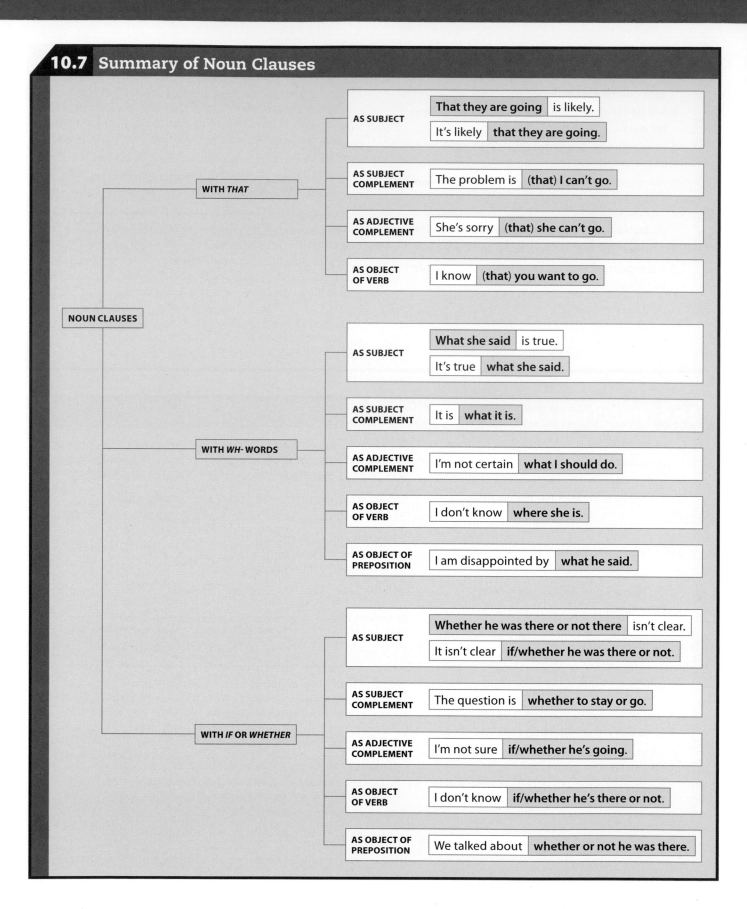

Adjective Clauses

11.1 Summary of Adjective Clauses

DEFINING SUBJECT ADJECTIVE CLAUSE

	noun	relative pronoun (subject)	verb + rest of adjective clause	
	The **children**	who	spoke two languages at home	did well on the test.
Do you have	a **knife**	that	has a sharper edge?	
He said	**something**	that	sounded very strange.	
I talked to	a **man**	whose son	had climbed Mount Everest.	

NON-DEFINING SUBJECT ADJECTIVE CLAUSE

	The **governor,**	who brought up this issue in the first place,	wasn't at the meeting.
They stayed in	**Majorca,**	which is an island off the coast of Spain.	

REDUCED ADJECTIVE CLAUSE

	Foods	containing a lot of salt	are not recommended.
We bought	**rice**	grown in Japan.	

DEFINING OBJECT ADJECTIVE CLAUSE

	noun	relative pronoun (subject)	subject + verb + rest of adjective clause	
	The **man**	(that / whom)	we met at the barbecue	was friendly.
Do you have	the **knife**	(that)	I lent you last month?	
I talked to	a **man**	whose son	I had met in China.	
	The **goal**	which	she had worked so hard for	was still out of reach.

		preposition + relative pronoun (object)	subject + verb + rest of adjective clause	
He talked about	the **teacher**	to whom	he was most grateful.	
	The **goal**	for which	she had worked so hard	was still out of reach.

NON-DEFINING OBJECT ADJECTIVE CLAUSE

	Tina,	whom we have known all of our lives,	is a unique person.
We went to	**Bolivia,**	which we have never visited before.	

11.2 Subjects and Objects in Adjective Clauses

A

RELATIVE PRONOUN = SUBJECT

	noun	subject	verb + rest of adjective clause	
1	My sister is the only **person**	who	has met the neighbors.	
2	The driver of the **car**	that	hit me last week	wasn't hurt.

↑ relative pronoun

RELATIVE PRONOUN = OBJECT

	noun	object	subject	verb + rest of adjective clause	
3	My sister is the only **person**	who*	they	have met.	
4	The driver of the **car**	that	I	hit last week	wasn't hurt.

↑ relative pronoun

*You may see the relative pronoun *whom* used in these adjective clauses. See Charts 11.3 and 11.4.

Different adjective clauses can have different word orders.

In many adjective clauses, the relative pronoun is the **subject**, as in **1 – 2**, so the verb agrees with the noun that the adjective clause describes.

In some other adjective clauses, the relative pronoun is the **object**, as in **3 – 4**. In this case, the verb agrees with the subject in the adjective clause (not the noun that the adjective clause describes).

B

OMITTING OBJECT RELATIVE PRONOUNS

		noun		subject + verb + rest of adjective clause
5	He mentioned	several **names**		I didn't know.
6	Do you remember	the **girl**	(that)	we met last week?
7	It was really cold	the **year**		we moved here.
8	It's	one of those **parks**		no one ever goes to.

9	The **birds**	that sit in that tree	are really noisy.

(NOT: ~~The birds sit in that tree are really noisy.~~)

We often omit object relative pronouns, as in **5 – 8**. This is common in speaking, especially when the subject of the adjective clause is a pronoun.

WARNING! We do not omit subject relative pronouns, as in **9**.

11.3 Adjective Clauses with Prepositions

A

COMMON IN SPEAKING

1 The **woman** (that / who) David spoke to said the first month would be free.
(David spoke to the woman.)

2 Someone bought the **house** (that) I used to live in.
(I used to live in the house.)

COMMON IN WRITING

3 This was one of the **victims for whom he sought justice.**
(He wanted justice for the victims.)

4 Sarah composed a long **letter, in which she described everything she had witnessed.**
(Sarah described everything she had witnessed in a long letter.)

If the verb in an **adjective clause** requires a preposition, we can include it in two ways:

- In conversation, we often use the preposition after the verb even though it is not followed by an object, as in **1 – 2**. We usually omit the relative pronoun, but we may also use *who* or *that*.
- Some people consider it unacceptable to use a preposition without an object after a verb. In formal writing, we often begin the adjective clause with the preposition + *which* or *whom*, as in **3 – 4**.

These adjective clauses can also be **non-defining**, as in **4**.

> In adjective clauses with prepositions, the relative pronoun is the object of the preposition.

B

5 She asked quite a few **questions, most of which we answered without any problem.**
(most of which = most of the questions)

6 The software has been used by hundreds of **people, all of whom were satisfied.**
(all of whom = all of the hundreds of people)

We often use quantity words and expressions with *of whom* and *of which* in non-defining adjective clauses, as in **5 – 6**. Some examples include:

five of which / whom	some of which / whom
all of which / whom	each of which / whom
many of which / whom	none of which / whom
most of which / whom	

11.4 Defining and Non-defining Adjective Clauses

A

DEFINING ADJECTIVE CLAUSES

1 The **ideas that the artist gave us** are going to be very useful in the future. (the ideas that the artist gave us = which ideas)

2 A gardener is a person **who takes care of plants.**
(a person who takes care of plants = definition of gardener)

Defining adjective clauses, as in **1 – 2**, help us identify the noun we are describing. Without the adjective clause, the meaning of the sentence would not be complete.

B

NON-DEFINING ADJECTIVE CLAUSES

3 The artist's **ideas, which rely more on imagination than logic,** are going to be useful in the future.

4 Let me introduce you to **Tom Jordan, who is the best gardener I know.**

5 The **principal, whom I had met several times before,** sat across the table from me.

6 My **parents, who came to this country 30 years ago,** had four children. (NOT: ~~My parents, that came to . . .~~)

7 The **cup, which I received from my grandmother as a child,** had a small crack. (NOT: ~~The cup, I received from . . .~~)

Another type of adjective clause gives additional information about the noun we are describing. We call this type of adjective clause **non-defining**. We usually use commas before and after non-defining adjective clauses.

We introduce most non-defining adjective clauses with:

- *which* to refer back to things, as in **3**
- *who* to refer back to people, as in **4**

We can also use the object relative pronoun *whom* (especially in writing) to refer back to people, as in **5**. However, this usually sounds more formal.

WARNING! In non-defining adjective clauses, we do not usually omit relative pronouns or use the relative pronoun *that*, as in **6 – 7**.

11.5 Using Adjective Clauses in Academic Writing

In academic writing, we often choose a more formal style of adjective clause.

A

LESS COMMON IN WRITING	MORE COMMON IN WRITING
1a It's hard to explain these ideas to **someone** [that] grew up in a different era.	**1b** It's hard to explain these ideas to **someone** [who] grew up in a different era.
2a The **experiments** [ ] **they did** provided some useful information.	**2b** The **experiments** [that] **they did** provided some useful information.
3a A **study** [that] came out several years ago showed a completely different result.	**3b** A **study** [which] came out several years ago showed a completely different result.
4a This was the first **group** [that] **we had complete data** [for].	**4b** This was the first **group** [for which] **we had complete data.**
5a The **subjects** [ ] **we spoke** [to] had already completed the trial.	**5b** The **subjects** [to whom] **we spoke** had already completed the trial.
6a They compared newcomers with [people] **who had lived in the country for more than three years.**	**6b** They compared newcomers with [those] **who had lived in the country for more than three years.**
7a The most successful programs are [the ones] **that offer a variety of ways for people to participate.**	**7b** The most successful programs are [those] **which offer a variety of ways for people to participate.**
	8 Systems [ ] **using the new software** were found to be much more effective.
	9 Decisions [ ] **based on these findings** will waste time and effort.

IN ACADEMIC WRITING

- In subject adjective clauses, we usually use *who* for people instead of *that*, as in **1a – 1b**.
- We usually use *that* for things, as in **2a – 2b**. We don't usually omit the relative pronoun.
- We sometimes choose *which* for things instead of *that*, as in **3a – 3b**.
- We often use a preposition + *whom* or *which*, as in **4a – 4b** and **5a – 5b**.
- Instead of using general nouns like *people* or *thing*, we often use the pronoun *those* + *who* or *which* to refer to a person or noun with a defining adjective clause, as in **6a – 6b** and **7a – 7b**.
- Reduced adjective clauses are very common, as in **8** and **9**.

B

COMPARE	
10a The wheat plant was developed thousands of years ago. It provided communities with a stable food source. It could be grown in large quantities.	In writing, we often use full and reduced adjective clauses to include a lot of information in one sentence. It is not unusual for a sentence to have more than one adjective clause, as in **10b**.
10b The wheat plant, developed thousands of years ago, provided communities with a stable food source which could be grown in large quantities.	

11.6 Reduced Adjective Clauses

We can sometimes reduce (or shorten) an **adjective clause** when the relative pronoun is the subject. We call this a **reduced adjective clause**.

A

COMPARE

1a The first **word** that was spoken on the moon was "OK."
1b The first **word** spoken on the moon was "OK."

2a The first **thing** that was mentioned at the meeting was the new tax law.
2b The first **thing** mentioned at the meeting was the new tax law.

3a There are a lot of **movies** that are based on books.
3b There are a lot of **movies** based on books.

We can reduce adjective clauses that have passive verb forms. We omit the relative pronoun and the verb *be*, as in **1 – 3**.

Remember: We form the passive with:

a form of *be*	+	the past participle of the main verb

Like a full adjective clause, the reduced adjective clause usually comes directly after the noun it describes.

Some past participles commonly used in reduced adjective clauses include:

based on	given	taken
caused	made	used
concerned with	produced	

B

COMPARE

4a The **boy** who was sitting in front saw everything.
4b The **boy** sitting in front saw everything.

5a I don't know the **woman** who is talking to Maria.
5b I don't know the **woman** talking to Maria.

6a The table was set with large **vases** that contained yellow flowers.
6b The table was set with large **vases** containing yellow flowers.

7a There are a number of **questions** that concern the company's finances.
7b There are a number of **questions** concerning the company's finances.

8 The cake that they're eating looks delicious.
(NOT: ~~The cake eating looks delicious.~~)

We can reduce adjective clauses that have present or past progressive verb forms by omitting the relative pronoun and the verb *be*, as in **4 – 5**.

We can reduce adjective clauses that have simple present or past verb forms by:

- omitting the relative pronoun
- replacing the verb with an *-ing* form, as in **6 – 7**

We can use the *-ing* verb form to reduce adjective clauses with many verbs that are not normally continuous. The most common examples are *concerning, containing, having, involving, requiring, resulting in,* and *using.*

WARNING! Because we cannot omit the subject of an adjective clause, we cannot reduce adjective clauses with object relative pronouns, as in **8**.

11.7 Appositives

A

appositive

1 | Mr. Adrian, my lawyer, | can answer this question.

appositive

2 | Mount Everest, the world's highest mountain, | is 60 million years old.

appositive

3 | There is little water on | Jupiter, the largest planet in the solar system.

We can add information after a main noun with an **appositive**, as in **1** – **3**. An appositive describes or gives another name to a main noun.

GRAMMAR TERM: An **appositive** is usually also a noun phrase. *Apposition* means that two noun phrases are set side by side.

B

4 *Flat Earth*, a fascinating book, was published in 2008.

5 Part of this exam (Section 2) focuses on vocabulary.

6 Mount Everest—Mount Chomolungma in Tibetan—is 8,848 meters high.

We usually use a comma before and after an appositive, as in **4**.

We sometimes use a dash—like this—or parentheses ( ) instead, as in **5** – **6**.

C

COMPARE

7a Mount Everest is the world's highest mountain. Climbing it can be very expensive.

7b Climbing **Mount Everest**, **the world's highest mountain**, can be very expensive.

Using an appositive is a useful way of combining information from several clauses or sentences into one sentence, as in **7b**. This is a short way to give a lot of information.

Adverbials

12.1 Using Adverbials to Explain *When*, *Where*, *How*, and *Why*

A

TIME ADVERBIALS

1 **Now** it's my turn. (when)

2 Reports in the natural sciences **often** begin with the results. (how often)

3 She arrived **this morning**. (when)

4 They're going to stay **for a while**. (how long)

We use some **adverbials** as time expressions. Time adverbials answer the question *when, how often,* or *how long,* as in **1 – 4**. The adverbial may be:

- an adverb or adverb phrase, as in **1 – 2**
- a noun phrase, as in **3**
- a prepositional phrase, as in **4**

B

PLACE ADVERBIALS

5 Everyone's **here**. (where)

6 Could I see you **in my office**? (where)

7 He's gone **to England**. (where)

8 They live **ten miles away**. (how far)

Some adverbials indicate location or distance. These place adverbials answer the question *where* or *how far,* as in **5 – 8**. The adverbial may be:

- an adverb or adverb phrase, as in **5**
- a prepositional phrase, as in **6 – 7**
- a noun phrase, as in **8**

C

MANNER ADVERBIALS

9 You need to do something **quickly**. (how)

10 Please handle this **with care**. (how)

11 She talks **like a businessperson**. (in what way / manner)

12 Did you come **by car**? (by what means)

Some adverbials answer the question *how, in what way / manner,* or *by what means,* as in **9 – 12**. We call them manner adverbials. The adverbial may be:

- an adverb or adverb phrase, as in **9**
- a prepositional phrase, as in **10 – 12**

D

REASON/PURPOSE ADVERBIALS

13 Classes were canceled **because of the weather**. (why)

14 **As a result of changing trends**, automobile sales have decreased. (why)

15 There were 50,000 deaths last year **due to car crashes**. (why)

16 **On account of the snow**, he hadn't even gone outside. (why)

17 We called **to invite them to dinner**. (for what purpose / reason)

18 I'm waiting **to finally have some free time**. (why)

We can also use adverbials to answer the question *why* or *for what purpose / reason,* as in **13 – 18**.

- In **13 – 16**, the adverbials are multi-word prepositional phrases.
- In **17 – 18**, the adverbials are *to-* infinitive phrases.

12.2 Sentence Patterns with Linking Adverbials

Linking adverbials have a special function. We use them to link or connect ideas within and across sentences, most often in academic writing. We can connect ideas in a number of different ways. For example:

A

PATTERN 1

independent clause / period (.) + linking adverbial / comma (,) + independent clause

1 | We haven't received the information. | Therefore, | we won't be able to comment on it. | (two sentences)

PATTERN 2

independent clause / semicolon (;) + linking adverbial / comma (,) + independent clause

2 | We haven't received the information; | therefore, | we won't be able to comment on it. | (one sentence)

PATTERN 3

independent clause / semicolon (;) + part of independent clause / comma (,) + linking adverbial / comma (,) + rest of clause

3 | We haven't received the information; | we won't, | therefore, | be able to comment on it. | (one sentence)

WARNING! Not all linking adverbials can be used with each pattern.

GRAMMAR TERMS: Linking adverbials are also called **transition words**, **connecting words**, or **conjunctive adverbials**.

12.3 Linking Adverbials That Signal a Result or Contrast

A

SIGNALING A RESULT OR CONSEQUENCE

1 There is twice as much hydrogen as oxygen in water. **Therefore**, its chemical formula is written as H_2O.

2 The author points out that we value some abilities over others; **as a result**, we often fail to develop our children's potential.

3 My father was born in Italy, but he grew up in California. **Consequently**, he feels more American than Italian.

We use **linking adverbials** to show a connection between two sentences or clauses. Different linking adverbials signal different kinds of connections. Some linking adverbials signal that a result or consequence of something in the first clause or sentence is coming in the second clause or sentence, as in **1 – 3**.

as a result	consequently	therefore	thus

B

SIGNALING A CONTRAST

4 A few years ago it seemed likely that computers would replace books. Now, **however**, most experts think that books are here to stay.

5 A professional cyclist can cover 30 miles in one hour. **In contrast**, the average cyclist covers only 16.

6 Cities are generally noisy, dirty, and expensive. **In spite of that**, the number of people moving to cities is increasing.

7 Many cities are dirty, noisy, and dangerous. **Nonetheless**, many people prefer cities because of the job opportunities and the excitement.

Some linking adverbials signal a contrast between two clauses, as in **4 – 5**.

however	in contrast	on the contrary
in comparison	instead	on the other hand

Certain other linking adverbials signal a contrast that is surprising or unexpected, as in **6 – 7**.

after all	besides	nevertheless
anyhow	in any case	nonetheless
at any rate	in spite of that	still

C

OTHER WAYS TO EXPRESS A RESULT OR CONTRAST

independent clause / comma (,) + *so* + independent clause

8 I'm going to graduate soon, **so** I'll probably relocate.

independent clause / comma (,) + (*and*) *yet* + independent clause

9 Everything was going wrong, **and yet** I was still happy.

independent clause / comma (,) + *but* + independent clause

10 Televisions were expensive at first, **but** they eventually became much cheaper.

12.4 Linking Adverbials That Signal Additional Information

A

SIGNALING AN EXAMPLE

1 Not all plants are gentle on the environment. Cotton plants, **for instance**, are often covered with chemicals.

2 Skilled public speakers use hand gestures for emphasis. **For example**, a speaker may point a finger or use a chopping motion.

We use some **linking adverbials** to signal that an example is coming next, as in **1 – 2**.

for example	for instance

B

SIGNALING NEW RELATED INFORMATION

3 Biking is a good way to get around Berlin because many parts of the city are hard to get to via public transportation. **Moreover**, the city is almost entirely flat, so it is easy to use a bike.

4 The study found that healthy employees are more productive during work hours. **In addition**, they take fewer sick days.

5 Diabetes rates are rising quickly and an increase in heart disease cannot be far behind. **Furthermore**, new evidence suggests that sitting all day is bad for your health.

Some linking adverbials signal that we are adding new information that is related to what we said before, as in **3 – 5**.

furthermore	likewise
in addition	moreover

C

OTHER WAYS TO SIGNAL ADDITIONAL INFORMATION

such as + noun phrase
6 In some countries, activities **such as bullfighting** are part of the culture.

besides + noun phrase
7 **Besides being the largest city in Canada**, Toronto has a multicultural population.

in addition to + noun phrase
8 **In addition to self-discipline**, a self-employed person needs to have a lot of motivation.

12.5 Linking Adverbials That Signal a List or Summary

A

SIGNALING A LIST

1 The popularity of Arabic coffee is due to several of its characteristics. **First**, it is easy to grow. More importantly, however, Arabic coffee has the best flavor.

2 It was not a typical lunch. **For one thing**, I was in a small boat. **For another**, my boat was tied to 16 other boats.

Some **linking adverbials** signal that a list or sequence of ideas is coming next, as in **1 – 2**.

first	first of all	to begin with
second	second of all	next
firstly	for one (thing)	lastly
secondly	for another (thing)	finally

B

SIGNALING A SUMMARY OF PREVIOUS INFORMATION

3 ... **In conclusion**, something must be done to ensure that children's toys are safe.

4 ... **All in all**, it has been a good year.

We can also use certain linking adverbials to signal that a summary of previous information is coming, as in **3 – 4**.

in sum	in conclusion	all in all
in summary	to conclude	overall
ultimately	to summarize	

12.6 Summary of Adverbials

TYPES OF ADVERBIALS	PURPOSE	COMMON EXAMPLES			
TIME ADVERBIALS	Explain *when, how often,* or *how long*	then always already usually	now still ever this morning	never today sometimes	again yesterday often
PLACE ADVERBIALS	Explain *where* or *how far*	here	there	outside	upstairs
ADVERBIALS OF MANNER	Explain *how, in what way, in what manner,* or *by what means*	fast	significantly	together	well
ADVERBIALS OF PURPOSE	Explain *why, for what purpose,* or *for what reason*	as a result of because of	due to on account of	to let everyone know *to* + base form of verb (*to-* infinitive)	
DEGREE ADVERBIALS	Explain *to what degree*	absolutely quite rather truly significantly about fairly somewhat	completely incredibly pretty perfectly much almost slightly	entirely extremely really reasonably approximately less	considerably highly so very nearly a (little) bit
FOCUSING ADVERBIALS	Focus attention on a word or a phrase	especially particularly	even	just	only
STANCE ADVERBIALS	Express an attitude about or comment on the information in a clause or sentence	hopefully fortunately of course undoubtedly perhaps actually	luckily certainly obviously clearly maybe really	surprisingly definitely very likely probably honestly in fact	thankfully no doubt without a doubt possibly seriously technically speaking to tell you the truth
LINKING ADVERBIALS	Connect ideas within and across sentences	**Result/Consequence** as a result **Contrast** however instead anyhow still **Additional information** for example in addition **List** first first of all to begin with **Summary** in sum in summary ultimately	 consequently in contrast though nevertheless nonetheless for instance likewise second secondly second of all in conclusion to conclude to summarize	 therefore in comparison on the contrary at any rate in any case furthermore firstly lastly finally all in all overall	 thus on the other hand besides in spite of that moreover for one thing for another thing next

Adverb Clauses

13.1 Overview of Adverb Clauses

We use an **adverb clause** to add information to a main clause. The adverb clause explains *why*, *when*, *where*, *how*, or *under what conditions* something happens. There are several important things to remember about adverb clauses:

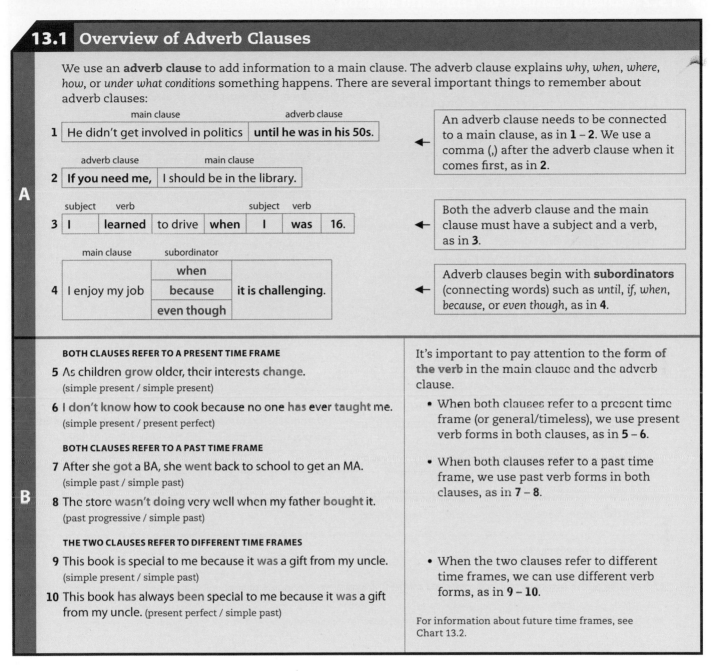

A

     main clause   adverb clause

1 | He didn't get involved in politics | until he was in his 50s.

     adverb clause   main clause

2 | If you need me, | I should be in the library.

An adverb clause needs to be connected to a main clause, as in **1 – 2**. We use a comma (,) after the adverb clause when it comes first, as in **2**.

  subject   verb   subject   verb

3 | I | learned | to drive | when | I | was | 16.

Both the adverb clause and the main clause must have a subject and a verb, as in **3**.

   main clause   subordinator

4 | I enjoy my job | when / because / even though | it is challenging.

Adverb clauses begin with **subordinators** (connecting words) such as *until*, *if*, *when*, *because*, or *even though*, as in **4**.

B

BOTH CLAUSES REFER TO A PRESENT TIME FRAME

5 As children **grow** older, their interests **change**.
(simple present / simple present)

6 I **don't know** how to cook because no one **has** ever **taught** me.
(simple present / present perfect)

BOTH CLAUSES REFER TO A PAST TIME FRAME

7 After she **got** a BA, she **went** back to school to get an MA.
(simple past / simple past)

8 The store **wasn't doing** very well when my father **bought** it.
(past progressive / simple past)

THE TWO CLAUSES REFER TO DIFFERENT TIME FRAMES

9 This book **is** special to me because it **was** a gift from my uncle.
(simple present / simple past)

10 This book **has** always **been** special to me because it **was** a gift from my uncle. (present perfect / simple past)

It's important to pay attention to the **form of the verb** in the main clause and the adverb clause.

- When both clauses refer to a present time frame (or general/timeless), we use present verb forms in both clauses, as in **5 – 6**.

- When both clauses refer to a past time frame, we use past verb forms in both clauses, as in **7 – 8**.

- When the two clauses refer to different time frames, we can use different verb forms, as in **9 – 10**.

For information about future time frames, see Chart 13.2.

13.2 Adverb Clauses of Time and Reason

A

ADVERB CLAUSES OF TIME

1 One study shows that babies can learn **before they are born.**

2 **Once the process began,** it was irreversible.

3 The lights automatically turn off **when people leave the room.**

4 **As plastic bags break down,** they release poisonous material into the water.

An **adverb clause of time** tells when one event happens in relation to another event in the main clause, as in **1 – 4.**

- We use some subordinators to show that one event happens before or after another event:

after	before	once	until
as soon as	by the time	since	when

- We use some subordinators to show that two events happen at the same time:

as	when	whenever	while

B

FUTURE ADVERB CLAUSES OF TIME

5 Nobody **will care when you get there tomorrow.**
(NOT: Nobody will care when you will get there tomorrow.)

6 What **are** you **going to do while we're away?**
(NOT: What are you going to do while we will be away?)

7 **After you read this,** you**'ll** probably **have** some questions.

8 We **aren't going to leave until you get back.**

When we make a prediction or talk about a future plan, we usually use a future verb form in the main clause but a present (not future) verb form in the adverb clause, as in **5 – 8.**

C

ADVERB CLAUSES OF REASON

9 My watch is important to me because it was a gift from my father.

10 Since we have some new people here today, let's start with introductions.

11 The meeting was canceled as no one could get there.

12 Now that prices have gone up, we can't afford to travel.

We can also use an adverb clause to give a reason for something in the main clause. **Adverb clauses of reason** usually begin with the subordinator *because,* *since, as,* or *now that,* as in **9 – 12.**

D

OTHER WAYS TO GIVE REASONS

because of + noun phrase
13 **Because of the increase in prices,** we can't afford to travel now. (*because of* = phrasal preposition)

independent clause + *so* + independent clause
14 **Prices have increased, so** we can't afford to travel now. (*so* = conjunction)

two separate sentences
15 We can't afford to travel now. **Prices have increased too much.**

13.3 Adverb Clauses of Contrast

An **adverb clause of contrast** adds unexpected, surprising, or contrasting information to a main clause, as in **1 – 2**.

A

main clause | adverb clause

1 | My grandfather still works | even though he's in his eighties. | (= unexpected or surprising information)

adverb clause | main clause

2 | Though cell phones have solved some problems, | they have created many others. | (= contrasting information)

B

SHOWING CONTRAST

3 **Although she's been teaching for ten years,** she still feels nervous at the beginning of the school year.
(= She's been teaching for ten years, but she still feels . . .)

4 **Though she said she wanted to help,** she didn't do anything. (= She said she wanted to help, but she . . .)

5 He wouldn't eat anything **even though he was hungry.**
(= He was hungry but he wouldn't eat anything.)

Adverb clauses of contrast often begin with the subordinator *although*, *though*, or *even though*, as in **3 – 5**. These subordinators usually include a meaning of concession or "but . . ."

Although, *though*, and *even though* are similar in meaning. However:
- *although* is more formal
- *even though* expresses a stronger contrast or emphasis

C

CONTRASTING ASPECTS OF THE SAME THING

6 **While smokeless tobacco may be safer than cigarettes,** it is not safe enough. (= Smokeless tobacco may be safer than cigarettes, but it is not safe enough.)

7 **While a college education is useful,** it doesn't guarantee a job after graduation. (= A college education is useful but it doesn't guarantee a job.)

CONTRASTING TWO DIFFERENT THINGS

8 Hawaii is warm **while Alaska is cold.**

9 My mother was an artist and very high-strung **while my father was quite calm.**

We can also use *while* to introduce an adverb clause of contrast.

- When we use *while* to contrast two aspects of the same thing, it usually includes a meaning of concession or "but . . ." as in **6 – 7**. With this use of *while*, the adverb clause usually comes before the main clause.

- We can also use *while* to make a direct contrast between two different things, as in **8 – 9**. With this use of *while*, the adverb clause usually comes after the main clause.

D

COMPARE: OTHER WAYS TO SHOW CONTRAST

independent clause + *but* + independent clause
10 My grandfather is in his eighties, but he still works. (*but* = conjunction)

11 Cell phones have solved some problems, but they have created many others.

despite + noun phrase
12 Despite **his age,** he has never had a job. (*despite* = preposition)

13 Despite **being hungry,** he wouldn't eat anything.

in spite of + noun phrase
14 In spite of **his age,** he has never worked. (*in spite of* = preposition)

13.4 Reduced Adverb Clauses of Time and Contrast

A

COMPARE FULL AND REDUCED ADVERB CLAUSES

same subjects

1a Although **the house** is small, **it** has lots of closets.

1b Although small, the house has lots of closets.

different subjects

2 Although **the house** is small, I still like it.

(NOT: Although small, I still like it.)

We can sometimes shorten an adverb clause of time or contrast when the subject of the adverb clause and the subject of the main clause are the same, as in **1a**. We call this a **reduced adverb clause**, as in **1b**.

When the subjects are different, the adverb clause cannot be reduced, as in **2**.

B

REDUCED ADVERB CLAUSES WITH THE VERB *BE*

3a While I **was** in school, I played a lot of football.

3b While in school, I played a lot of football.

4a Although my father **was** bothered by the news, he did his best to ignore it.

4b Although bothered by the news, my father did his best to ignore it.

5a When you**'re** looking for a job, you should be sure to keep your resume up to date.

5b When looking for a job, you should be sure to keep your resume up to date.

REDUCED ADVERB CLAUSES WITH OTHER VERBS

6a The train stopped several times before it finally **arrived**.

6b The train stopped several times before finally arriving.

7a Since David **graduated** from college, he's worked in three different banks.

7b Since graduating from college, David has worked in three different banks.

The way we reduce an adverb clause depends on the verb in the clause:

- When the adverb clause has a form of the verb *be* (as a helping verb or a main verb), we drop the subject and the form of the verb *be*, as in **3 – 5**.

- When the adverb clause has a verb other than *be*, we drop the subject and any helping verb, and we use the *-ing* form of the main verb, as in **6 – 7**.

WARNING! When you use a reduced adverb clause, make sure the subject in the main clause is clear, as in **4b** and **7b**.

We use these subordinators in reduced adverb clauses:

after	when	since	although
before	while		though

13.5 Conditional Adverb Clauses (Real Conditionals)

A

condition — result

1 | If I'm not too tired, | (then) I usually go out in the evening.

condition — result

2 | If you mix red, green, and blue light, | you get white light.

result — condition

3 | I can come over | if you need some help.

A **conditional adverb clause** shows what must happen first (the condition) so that another thing (the result) can happen, as in **1 – 3**.

A conditional clause:

- usually begins with the subordinator *if*
- can come before or after the main clause

B

PRESENT REAL CONDITIONALS

4 If eggs aren't properly cooked, they can make you sick.

5 If we want to go downtown, we usually take the bus.

6 If you don't know the meaning of a word, look it up in your dictionary.

PAST REAL CONDITIONALS

7 When I was a child, if my father wasn't working, we usually did something outdoors.

8 Our teachers were very strict. **If you didn't do all your homework, you failed the course.**

We often use conditional adverb clauses to talk about real situations or events. These could be:

- facts or general truths, as in **4**
- events that happen regularly, as in **5**
- commands or advice, as in **6**
- events that happened regularly in the past, as in **7 – 8**

In these clauses, it is possible to use *when* or *whenever* in place of *if*.

GRAMMAR TERM: The present and past real conditionals are sometimes called the **zero conditional**.

C

FUTURE REAL CONDITIONALS

9 If he's had a bad day, he probably **won't come** over.

10 This hypothesis **will need** to be tested to determine if it is accurate.

11 If I can get home early, **I will call** you.

12 We **might cancel** the meeting if they can't come.

13 If you need some help tomorrow, **call** me.

14 If I take two classes next summer, **I'll** graduate early.
(NOT: ~~If I will take two classes next summer, I'll graduate early.~~)

We sometimes use a conditional adverb clause when we make a prediction or talk about future events. In these sentences, we usually use a present verb form in the *if-* clause, as in **9 – 14**.

IF- CLAUSE	RESULT (MAIN) CLAUSE
present verb form *can* + base form *must* + base form	modal + base form imperative

Notice that we use a present form in the *if-* clause even when it has a future time expression, as in **14**.

GRAMMAR TERMS: This use of the future real conditional is sometimes called the **future-possible conditional** or **first conditional**.

13.6 Conditional Adverb Clauses (Unreal Conditionals)

A

1 It's too bad that my brothers are away. **If they were here**, I know they would help me. (They aren't here.)

2 You'd feel better **if you exercised**. (You don't exercise.)

3 I wouldn't have met my wife **if I had moved to London**. (I didn't move to London.)

4 **If you had studied harder**, you would have passed the test. (You didn't study hard enough.)

5 **If there were no air**, sound could not travel. (There is air.)

We can use some **conditional adverb clauses** to describe unreal, imaginary, unlikely, or impossible situations, as in **1 – 5**. We might use an unreal conditional:

- when we wish the situation were true, as in **1**
- to give advice, as in **2**
- to express cause and effect, as in **3**
- to criticize, as in **4**
- to give surprising information, as in **5**

GRAMMAR TERM: This use of the unreal conditional is sometimes called the **third conditional**.

B

PRESENT UNREAL CONDITIONALS

6 If it **weren't** raining, **I'd go** for a walk. (= It is raining.)

7 If my sister **were** here now, she **would know** what to do. (= She's not here now.)

8 If I **didn't have** to work today, I **could go** hiking. (= I do have to work today.)

9 If I **could do** anything I wanted, **I'd move** to Japan.

FUTURE UNREAL CONDITIONALS

10 If I **had** time next month, **I'd go** to Hawaii. (= I don't have time next month.)

11 If I **had to work** next week, I **wouldn't be able to go** with you. (= I don't have to work next week.)

To show that we are talking about an unreal or imaginary situation, we use special verb forms.

When both the condition and the result refer to a present or future time frame, as in **6 – 11**, we use:

UNREAL CONDITION IN PRESENT OR FUTURE	UNREAL RESULT IN PRESENT OR FUTURE
if + a past verb form	*would* + base form
	could + base form

WARNING! When we use the verb *be* in the *if-* clause, we usually use *were* instead of *was*, as in **6 – 7**.

PAST UNREAL CONDITIONALS

12 If I **hadn't eaten** earlier, I **would have gone** to lunch with you. (= I did eat earlier.)

13 If I **had had** any vacation days last month, I **could have gone** to Hawaii. (= I didn't have any vacation days last month.)

When both the condition and the result refer to past time, as in **12 – 13**, we use:

UNREAL CONDITION IN PAST	UNREAL RESULT IN PAST
if + a past perfect verb	*would have* + past participle
	could have + past participle

C

THE TWO CLAUSES REFER TO DIFFERENT TIME FRAMES

14 If we **had left** earlier, I **would be** home by now. (unreal past condition + present result)

15 If he **hadn't been helping** me, I **would** still **be living** an hour away from school. (unreal past condition + present result)

As with other adverb clauses, the time in an *if-* clause may be different from the time in a result clause, as in **14 – 15**.

13.7 Summary of Adverb Clauses

TYPE OF ADVERB CLAUSE	COMMON SUBORDINATORS	EXAMPLES
Time *When?*	*after, as, as soon as, before, by the time, once, since, until, when, whenever, while*	As soon as he graduates, he'll get a job. Whenever I see her, I feel happy. Once you travel the world, you're never the same again.
Reason *Why?*	*as, because, now that, since*	Since none of the students were ready, the test was postponed. Now that all the results are in, I'll announce the winners.
Contrast	*as though, even though, though, while*	Even though it was very cold, we decided to go ahead with the hike. I was determined to become a doctor although my parents didn't want me to.
Manner *How?* *In what way?*	*as, like*	Please check your spelling as directed in the instructions.
	as if, as though	He looks as though he has a bad cold.
Result	*so + adjective or adverb + that* *so many/few + plural noun + that* *so much/little + noncount noun + that* *such + (a/an) + adjective + noun*	She was so beautiful that people stared at her. There were so many people in the audience that we could hardly see the stage. It was such a funny movie that I couldn't stop laughing.
Purpose *For what purpose?* *Why?*	*so that*	I closed the blinds so that I wouldn't wake up too early.
Real Conditional	*if, unless, when, whenever*	If it rains, we'll change our plans. Don't go to Arizona unless you love hot climates. Whenever I exercise, I feel great.
Unreal Conditional	*if*	If I weren't working next week, I'd go to the beach.
	as if, as though	She felt as if she had been running a marathon.

Gerunds and *To-* Infinitives

14.1 Summary of Gerunds and To- Infinitives

Gerund as Subject	• **Reading** is to the mind what exercise is to the body. (Joseph Addison)
Gerund as Subject Completer	• The ony thing better than singing is **more singing.** (Ella Fitzgerald)
Gerund as Object of a Verb	• If we stop **loving animals**, aren't we bound to stop **loving humans** too? (Aleksandr Solzhenitsyn)
Gerund as Object of a Preposition	• Let no one come to you without **leaving better and happier.** (Mother Teresa)
Passive Form of a Gerund	• He who fears **being conquered** is sure of defeat. (Napoleon Bonaparte)

To- Infinitive as Subject (*It* + *Be* + Adjective + *To-* Infinitive)	• **To teach** is to learn twice over. (Joseph Joubert) • It's better **to be alone** than in bad company. (George Washington)
To- Infinitive as Subject Completer	• The only way to have a friend is **to be one.** (Ralph Waldo Emerson)
To- Infinitive as Object of a Verb	• Everyone wants **to share in a man's success**, but no one wants **to share in his misfortunes.** • Expect the most wonderful things **to happen**, not in the future but right now. (Eileen Caddy)
Wh- Word + *To-* Infinitive	• Never tell people **how to do things.** Tell them **what to do** and they will surprise you with their ingenuity. (George Patton)
Bare Infinitive	• No one can make you **feel** inferior without your consent. (Eleanor Roosevelt)
Linking Verb + Adjective + *To-* Infinitive	• Create the kind of self that you will be happy **to live with all your life.** (Golda Meir)
Noun + *To-* Infinitive	• For every good reason there is to lie, there is a better reason **to tell the truth.** (Bo Bennett)
To- Infinitive of Purpose	• **In order to excel**, you must be completely dedicated to your chosen sport. (Willie Mays)
Progressive Form of a *To-* Infinitive	• **To be doing good deeds** is man's most glorious task. (Sophocles)
Perfect Form of a *To-* Infinitive	• In my view you cannot claim **to have seen something** until you have photographed it. (Emile Zola)
Passive Form of a *To-* Infinitive	• I would like **to be called an inspiration to people**, not a role model—because I make mistakes like everybody else. (Britney Spears)

14.2 Verb + Gerund or To- Infinitive

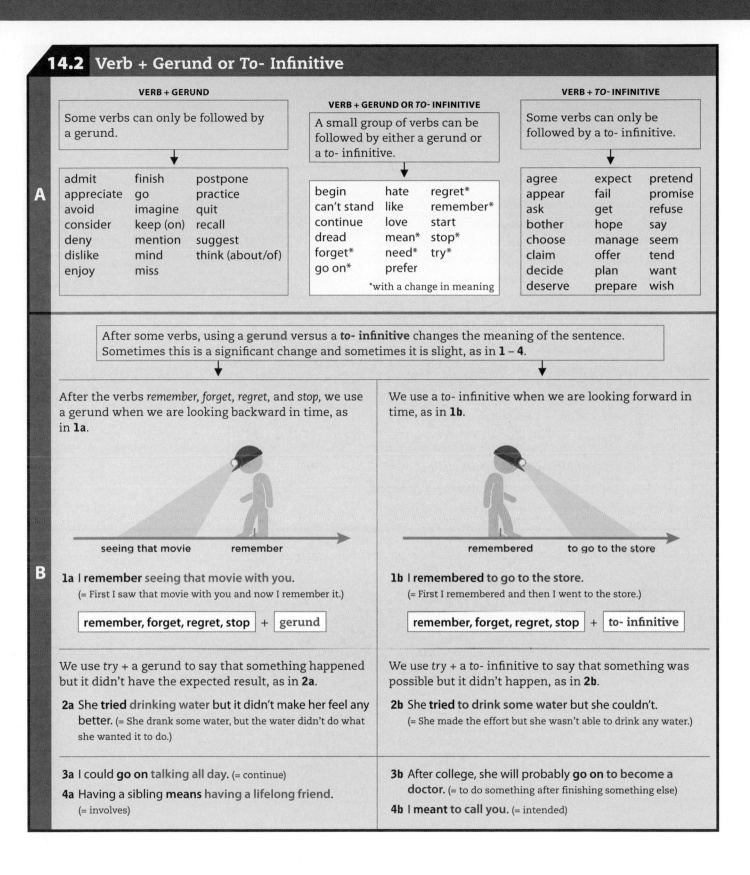

A

| VERB + GERUND | | | VERB + GERUND OR *TO-* INFINITIVE | | | VERB + *TO-* INFINITIVE | | |

VERB + GERUND

Some verbs can only be followed by a gerund.

admit	finish	postpone
appreciate	go	practice
avoid	imagine	quit
consider	keep (on)	recall
deny	mention	suggest
dislike	mind	think (about/of)
enjoy	miss	

VERB + GERUND OR *TO-* INFINITIVE

A small group of verbs can be followed by either a gerund or a *to-* infinitive.

begin	hate	regret*
can't stand	like	remember*
continue	love	start
dread	mean*	stop*
forget*	need*	try*
go on*	prefer	

*with a change in meaning

VERB + *TO-* INFINITIVE

Some verbs can only be followed by a *to-* infinitive.

agree	expect	pretend
appear	fail	promise
ask	get	refuse
bother	hope	say
choose	manage	seem
claim	offer	tend
decide	plan	want
deserve	prepare	wish

B

After some verbs, using a **gerund** versus a **to- infinitive** changes the meaning of the sentence. Sometimes this is a significant change and sometimes it is slight, as in **1 – 4**.

After the verbs *remember, forget, regret,* and *stop,* we use a gerund when we are looking backward in time, as in **1a**.

We use a to- infinitive when we are looking forward in time, as in **1b**.

seeing that movie   remember

remembered   to go to the store

1a I **remember** seeing that movie with you.
(= First I saw that movie with you and now I remember it.)

| remember, forget, regret, stop | + | gerund |

1b I **remembered** to go to the store.
(= First I remembered and then I went to the store.)

| remember, forget, regret, stop | + | to- infinitive |

We use *try* + a gerund to say that something happened but it didn't have the expected result, as in **2a**.

2a She **tried** drinking water but it didn't make her feel any better. (= She drank some water, but the water didn't do what she wanted it to do.)

We use *try* + a to- infinitive to say that something was possible but it didn't happen, as in **2b**.

2b She **tried** to drink some water but she couldn't. (= She made the effort but she wasn't able to drink any water.)

3a I could **go on** talking all day. (= continue)

4a Having a sibling **means** having a lifelong friend. (= involves)

3b After college, she will probably **go on** to become a doctor. (= to do something after finishing something else)

4b I **meant** to call you. (= intended)

14.3 Gerunds as Objects of Verbs and Prepositions

A

COMPARE 1A–1B

	verb	noun phrase as object
1a	I just **started**	that book.

	verb	gerund as object
1b	I just **started**	reading that book.

2 My boss never **stopped** talking. (Stopped what?)

3 I **miss** seeing my family. (Miss what?)

4 My generation is probably the last one that **remembers not having the Internet in high school.** (Remembers what?)

We can use a noun phrase as the object of a verb, as in **1a**. Like a noun phrase, a **gerund** can also function as the object of certain verbs, as in **1b**.

GRAMMAR TERM: A gerund used as an object of a verb is also called a **verb completer** or a **verb complement**.

The gerund answers the question *what*, as in **2 – 4**. Common one-word verbs followed by gerunds include:

begin	dislike	keep	quit	start
continue	finish	miss	remember	stop

For a list of common verbs followed by gerunds, see page R-54.

B

COMPARE 5A–5B

	preposition	noun phrase
5a	I left home	without	any money.

	preposition	gerund
5b	I left home	without	eating breakfast.

6 I'm angry with her **for** leaving **without** saying goodbye.

7 I decided **on** not getting a Facebook account.

8 Videoconferencing is a useful way **of** holding a meeting.

9 The president is responsible **for** preparing the budget.

Like a noun phrase, a gerund can also be used as the object of a preposition, as in **5**.

The gerund answers the question *what*, as in **6 – 9**.

14.4 Overview of To- Infinitives

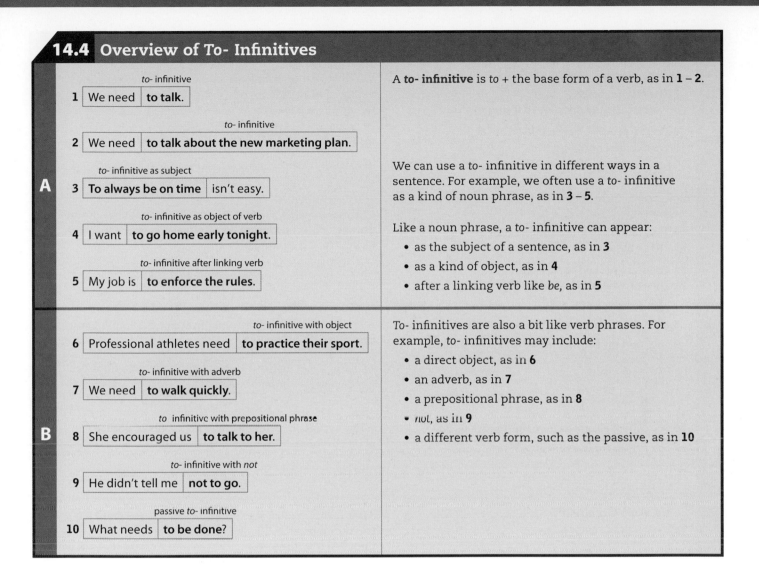

A

to- infinitive

1 We need | **to talk.**

to- infinitive

2 We need | **to talk about the new marketing plan.**

to- infinitive as subject

3 **To always be on time** | isn't easy.

to- infinitive as object of verb

4 I want | **to go home early tonight.**

to- infinitive after linking verb

5 My job is | **to enforce the rules.**

A **to- infinitive** is *to* + the base form of a verb, as in **1 – 2**.

We can use a *to-* infinitive in different ways in a sentence. For example, we often use a *to-* infinitive as a kind of noun phrase, as in **3 – 5**.

Like a noun phrase, a *to-* infinitive can appear:

- as the subject of a sentence, as in **3**
- as a kind of object, as in **4**
- after a linking verb like *be,* as in **5**

B

to- infinitive with object

6 Professional athletes need | **to practice their sport.**

to- infinitive with adverb

7 We need | **to walk quickly.**

to infinitive with prepositional phrase

8 She encouraged us | **to talk to her.**

to- infinitive with *not*

9 He didn't tell me | **not to go.**

passive *to-* infinitive

10 What needs | **to be done?**

To- infinitives are also a bit like verb phrases. For example, to- infinitives may include:

- a direct object, as in **6**
- an adverb, as in **7**
- a prepositional phrase, as in **8**
- *not,* as in **9**
- a different verb form, such as the passive, as in **10**

14.5 To- Infinitives as Objects

A

1 I **need to speak** to you.	We can use a **to- infinitive** as the object after certain verbs, as in **1 – 3**. Remember: We use *not* to make a *to-* infinitive negative, as in **4 – 5**.
2 They **forgot to go**.	
3 Please close the door. We're **trying to study**.	
	For a list of common verbs followed by *to-* infinitives, see page R-56.
4 Do you **promise not to tell**?	
5 We **decided not to go**.	**GRAMMAR TERM:** An infinitive used as an object of a verb is also called a **verb completer** or a **verb complement**.

B

COMPARE

6a They **expect to visit**. (They are going to visit.)	With some verbs, we can (but don't have to) use a **noun phrase / object pronoun** before the *to-* infinitive, as in **6b** and **7b**. For example:
6b They **expect us to visit**. (We are going to visit.)	
7a The story **proved to be untrue**.	
7b They **proved his story to be untrue**.	

ask	expect	need	promise	want

| 8 My parents **encouraged me to become a doctor**. | A few verbs must use a noun phrase or pronoun before the *to-* infinitive, as in **8 – 9**. For example: |
| 9 I **warned my brother not to go** in the water. | |

advise	help	persuade	teach	urge
encourage	order	remind	tell	warn

10 The school **arranged for a bus to pick us up**.	A few verbs can be followed by *for* + a **noun phrase / object pronoun** + *to-* infinitive, as in **10 – 11**. For example:
11 I can't **wait for the concert to start**.	

arrange	ask	love	pay	wait	wish

C

WH- WORD + *TO-* INFINITIVE

12 I didn't **know what to do**.	After certain verbs, we sometimes use a ***wh-* word** + a **to- infinitive**, as in **12 – 14**. This is a shorter and more informal way to express phrases like *the thing that*, *the way that*, or *the place where*. Common verbs include:
(= I didn't know the thing that I should do.)	
13 He **explained how to get there**.	
(= He explained the way that we could get there.)	
14 Do you **know where to go**?	
(= Do you know the place where we should go?)	

ask	explain	know	remember	wonder
decide	forget	learn	understand	

| 15 Can you **show me how to use this**? | We can also use a **noun phrase / object pronoun** + a *wh-* word + a *to-*infinitive after certain verbs such as *ask, advise, show, teach,* and *tell*, as in **15 – 16**. |
| 16 Did she **tell the driver when to be there**? | |

14.6 Other Uses of To- Infinitives

A

LINKING VERB + ADJECTIVE + *TO*-INFINITIVE

	adjective	to-infinitive
1 She **was**	**happy**	**to help us.**

2 I **was surprised to find** that things weren't so different here.

3 He's **apt to be** late.

We sometimes use a **to-infinitive** after a **linking verb + adjective**, as in **1 – 3**. The *to*-infinitive gives more information about the adjective.

A few adjectives are almost always followed by a *to*-infinitive. These include *able, apt, due, inclined, likely, prepared, ready,* and *willing.*

B

NOUN PHRASE + *TO*-INFINITIVE

	noun phrase	to-infinitive
4 I don't have	**any reason**	**to go there.**

5 Her **ability to manage** the office surprised us.

6 There are **many sights to see** in London.

We can also use a **to-infinitive** after a **noun phrase**, as in **4 – 6**. The *to*-infinitive gives more information about the noun phrase.

C

EXPRESSING A PURPOSE

7 She exercises **to stay healthy.**

8 He's studying **to become a doctor.**

9 A company needs good management **in order not to fail.**

10 **To be a good manager,** a person must be very organized.

We can also use a *to*-infinitive to explain *why* or *for what purpose*, as in **7 – 8**. We sometimes include the words *in order* before a *to*-infinitive (especially before negative infinitives and in more formal writing), as in **9**.

Sometimes we use a purpose infinitive at the beginning of a sentence, as in **10**. This focuses attention on the purpose. We use a comma to separate the purpose infinitive from the main clause of the sentence.

14.7 To- Infinitive Clauses

A

1 We **hope** to focus on the economy at this meeting.

2 They were **pleased** to discover that the situation had changed very little.

3 Our analysis reveals one **way** to address the problem.

4 To create a work of this size is not easy.

5 It is impossible to ignore the similarity between the two texts.

6 To continue in this way, they will have to gather more resources.

7 Educators wanted to expand the opportunities for students at the school. (*educators* = understood subject of *to expand*)

8 The doctors advised **her** to remain in bed for a week. (*her* = understood subject of *to remain*)

To-infinitive clauses are used in many ways.

We use a *to*-infinitive clause as a complement:

- after certain verbs, as **1**
- after certain adjectives, as in **2**
- after certain nouns, as in **3**

We can also use a *to*-infinitive clause:

- as the subject of a sentence, as in **4**
- in sentences beginning with empty *it*, as in **5**
- as adverbials, as in **6**

The **subject** of a *to*-infinitive clause is usually not stated, but we can identify the subject from the subject of the main clause, as in **7**.

After certain verbs, the object of the verb is the understood subject of the *to*-infinitive clause, as in **8**.

GRAMMAR TERM: These forms are sometimes called **non-finite clauses** or **to-infinitive phrases** because they don't have a full, tensed verb and a stated subject.

GRAMMAR REFERENCE

I. Non-Action Verbs

agree	consist of	fear	include	mind	recognize	think
appear	contain	feel	involve	need	remember	understand
appreciate	cost	fit	know	owe	see	want
be	dislike	hate	like	own	seem	weigh
believe	doubt	have	look	possess	smell	wish
belong	envy	hear	love	prefer	suppose	
conclude	equal	imagine	mean	realize	taste	

Remember:

- A non-action verb describes a state (an unchanging condition).
- Non-action verbs are also called **stative verbs**.
- Some verbs have more than one meaning. They can function as a non-action verb in one context and an action verb in another.

II. Linking Verbs

appear	become	get*	look	seem	sound	turn*
be	feel	grow*	remain	smell	taste	

*with a meaning of *become*

Remember: A linking verb can have an adjective as a complement.

III. Reporting Verbs

VERB + *THAT*				VERB (+ NOUN PHRASE) + *TO*		VERB + *WH-*
acknowledge*	contend	note	reveal*	advise	intend**	ask
add	demand	persuade***	say*	ask	persuade*	consider
admit*	demonstrate*	point out*	show**	assume	promise**	discuss
advise**	deny	promise**	speculate*	believe	propose*	establish*
agree	emphasize*	propose*	state*	challenge	prove	examine
announce*	estimate	protest	suggest*	claim*	remind	explain*
answer	explain*	prove*	tell***	consider	show	indicate*
argue	find	realize	think	convince	suppose	inquire (about)
ask	hypothesize	recognize	urge	encourage*	tell	investigate
assert	imply*	recommend*	warn**	estimate	urge	look at
assume	indicate*	remark*	write	expect**	warn*	question
believe	inform***	remind***		find**		say*
claim*	insist*	reply*				show*
complain*	intend	report*				talk about
concede*	maintain	request				tell*
conclude	mention*	respond*				wonder

*can be followed by *to* + a noun phrase

**can be followed by a noun phrase

***must be followed by a noun phrase

*must be followed directly by *to*- infinitive

**can be followed directly by *to*- infinitive

*usually negative when followed by *whether*

IV. Irregular Verbs

BASE FORM	SIMPLE PAST	PAST PARTICIPLE
arise	arose	arisen
beat	beat	beaten
become	became	become
begin	began	begun
bend	bent	bent
bet	bet	bet
bite	bit	bitten
bleed	bled	bled
break	broke	broken
bring	brought	brought
build	built	built
buy	bought	bought
catch	caught	caught
choose	chose	chosen
come	came	come
cost	cost	cost
cut	cut	cut
deal	dealt	dealt
dig	dug	dug
draw	drew	drawn
drink	drank	drunk
drive	drove	driven
eat	ate	eaten
fall	fell	fallen
feed	fed	fed
feel	felt	felt
fight	fought	fought
find	found	found
fly	flew	flown
forbid	forbade	forbidden
forget	forgot	forgotten
forgive	forgave	forgiven
freeze	froze	frozen
get	got	gotten
give	gave	given
go	went	gone
grow	grew	grown
hear	heard	heard
hide	hid	hidden
hit	hit	hit
hold	held	held
hurt	hurt	hurt
keep	kept	kept
know	knew	known
lay	laid	laid
lead	led	led
leave	left	left
lend	lent	lent
let	let	let
light	lit/lighted	lit/lighted
lose	lost	lost
make	made	made
mean	meant	meant
meet	met	met

BASE FORM	SIMPLE PAST	PAST PARTICIPLE
pay	paid	paid
put	put	put
quit	quit	quit
read	read	read
ride	rode	ridden
ring	rang	rung
rise	rose	risen
run	ran	run
say	said	said
see	saw	seen
seek	sought	sought
sell	sold	sold
send	sent	sent
set	set	set
sew	sewed	sewn
shake	shook	shaken
shoot	shot	shot
show	showed	shown
shrink	shrank	shrunk
shut	shut	shut
sing	sang	sung
sink	sank	sunk
sit	sat	sat
sleep	slept	slept
slide	slid	slid
speak	spoke	spoken
speed	sped	sped
spend	spent	spent
spin	spun	spun
spread	spread	spread
spring	sprang	sprung
stand	stood	stood
steal	stole	stolen
sting	stung	stung
stink	stank	stunk
strike	struck	struck
strive	strove	striven
swear	swore	sworn
sweep	swept	swept
swim	swam	swum
swing	swung	swung
take	took	taken
teach	taught	taught
tear	tore	torn
tell	told	told
think	thought	thought
throw	threw	thrown
understand	understood	understood
wake	woke	woken
wear	wore	worn
weep	wept	wept
win	won	won
wind	wound	wound
write	wrote	written

V. Spelling Rules for the -s/-es Form of Verbs

To form the third-person singular (*he/she/it*) for the simple present:

1 Add -es to verbs that end in -sh, -ch, -ss, -s, -x, or -z.

| finish | finishes | touch | touches | pass | passes | relax | relaxes |

2 For verbs ending in a consonant + -y, change the -y to -i and add -es.

| study | studies | worry | worries | deny | denies | fly | flies |

3 Three verbs have a special spelling:

| go | goes | do | does | have | has |

4 For all other verbs, add -s.

| like | likes | buy | buys | see | sees | speak | speaks |

VI. Spelling Rules for the -ing Form of Verbs

1 The base form of the verb ends in a vowel + consonant sound + -e: →	Drop the -e and add -ing. **live**–living **cause**–causing be**come**–becoming **take**–taking
2 The base form is one syllable, and it ends in one vowel + one consonant (except -w, -x, or -y): →	Double the final consonant and add -ing. **put**–putting **win**–winning **drop**–dropping
3 The base form has more than one syllable, it ends in one vowel + one consonant (except -w, -x, or -y), and the last syllable is stressed: →	Double the final consonant and add -ing. for·**get**–forgetting be·**gin**–beginning com·**mit**–committing
4 The base form ends in -ie: →	Change the -ie to -y and add -ing. **die**–dying **tie**–tying **lie**–lying
5 For other verbs: →	Add -ing. **play**–playing **show**–showing **help**–helping

VII. Spelling Rules for the -ed Form of Verbs

SPELLING RULES	base form	simple past
When the base form of a regular verb ends in -**e**, **add** -**d**.	clos**e** refus**e**	closed refused
When the base form ends in a consonant + -**y,** change the -y to -i and add -**ed**.	stu**dy** wo**rry** identi**fy**	studied worried identified
When the base form has one syllable and ends in a **c**onsonant + **v**owel + **c**onsonant (CVC), **double the final consonant and add** -**ed**. (Warning! Do not double a final -w, -x, or -y: play / played, wax / waxed, row / rowed.)	pl**an** j**og** d**rop**	planned jogged dropped
When the base form of a two-syllable verb ends in a **c**onsonant + **v**owel + **c**onsonant (CVC) and the last syllable is stressed, **double the final consonant and add** -**ed**.	re•**fer** re•**gret**	referred regretted
For all other regular verbs, **add** -**ed**.	open destroy	opened destroyed

VIII. Common Transitive Verbs

VERB + DIRECT OBJECT

Examples: *develop a theory; include your name and address; consider several possibilities*

allow	complete	enjoy	introduce	meet*	refuse	take
ask*	consider	expect	invent	move*	remember*	teach
attempt	create	feel*	involve	need	save	tell
begin*	cut*	find	keep*	pass*	say	think*
believe*	describe	follow*	know*	pay*	see*	throw
bring	design	forgive	leave*	produce	send	use
build	destroy	hear*	lend	provide	serve	visit*
buy	develop*	help*	like	put	show	want
call*	discover	hold*	lose*	raise	speak*	wash*
carry	divide*	identify	love	read*	start*	watch*
cause	do	include	make	receive	study*	win*
close*	end*	intend	mean	recognize	surround	write*

*verbs that we can also use intransitively (without a direct object)

Remember: Transitive verbs need an object (a noun phrase or pronoun) to complete their meaning.

VERB + INDIRECT OBJECT + DIRECT OBJECT

Examples: *ask your professor a question; show her the answer*

ask	forgive	lend*	pay	save	teach*
bring	give*	make	promise*	send*	tell*
buy	hand*	offer*	read*	serve*	throw*
find	leave*	owe*	refuse	show*	wish*

*The indirect object can come before or after the direct object.

IX. Common Intransitive Verbs

Examples: *The movie begins at 8. She doesn't hear very well.*

agree	come	follow*	leave*	rain	sneeze	wait
appear	cough	freeze*	lie	read*	snow	walk*
arrive	cut*	go	live	remember*	speak*	wash*
begin*	decrease*	happen	look	ring*	stare	watch*
belong	die	hear*	lose*	rise	start*	win*
bleed	disappear	help*	matter	see*	stop*	work
break*	dream*	hide*	meet*	shake*	study*	write*
burn*	drown	hurt*	move*	sit	swim	
call*	end*	increase*	occur	sleep	think*	
close*	fall	laugh	pass*	smile	visit*	

*verbs that we can also use transitively (with a direct object)

Remember: Intransitive verbs make sense without an object.

X. Common Verbs Followed by Gerunds

VERB + GERUND

Examples: *appreciate having; avoid getting; denied knowing*

admit	continue*	enjoy	love*	prefer*	risk
advise	defend	finish	mean**	quit	start*
appreciate	delay	forget**	mention	recall	stop**
avoid	deny	hate*	mind	recommend	suggest
begin*	detest	imagine	miss	regret**	tolerate
can't help	discuss	involve	need**	remember**	try**
can't stand*	dislike	keep	postpone	resist	
consider	dread*	like*	practice	resume	

*can also be followed by a *to*- infinitive   **can be followed by a *to*- infinitive but with a change in meaning

VERB + OBJECT + GERUND

Examples: *hear him talking; saw my friends leaving; found them sitting*

discover	feel	find	hear	notice	see	watch

XI. Common Verbs + Prepositions Followed by Gerunds

Examples: *argue about going; apologize for being; cope with losing; dream of becoming*

VERB + *ABOUT*	VERB + *AT*	VERB + *FOR*	VERB + *IN*	VERB + *INTO*
argue about care about complain about forget about talk about think about worry about	aim at work at	apologize for blame for care for forgive for thank for use for	believe in result in specialize in succeed in	look into

VERB + *LIKE*	VERB + *OF*	VERB + *ON*	VERB + *TO*	VERB + *WITH*
feel like	accuse of approve of dream of hear of think of	concentrate on depend on go on insist on keep on plan on work on	admit to confess to object to	cope with deal with

XII. Common Adjectives + Prepositions Followed by Gerunds

Examples: *afraid of being; bad at making; excited about going*

ADJECTIVE + *OF* + GERUND	ADJECTIVE + *AT* + GERUND	ADJECTIVE + *ABOUT* + GERUND
afraid of aware of capable of fond of incapable of proud of tired of	bad at better at effective at good at great at successful at upset at	bad about concerned about enthusiastic about excited about happy about nervous about serious about sorry about worried about

ADJECTIVE + *FROM* + GERUND	ADJECTIVE + *IN* + GERUND	ADJECTIVE + *FOR* + GERUND
different from evident from exempt from free from obvious from safe from tired from	crucial in effective in important in interested in involved in useful in	available for crucial for famous for important for necessary for responsible for sorry for suitable for useful for

XIII. Common Nouns + *Of* That Can Be Followed by Gerunds

Examples: *chance of getting; possibility of using*

advantage of*	effect of*	idea of*	point of	prospect of	task of*
chance of*	experience of*	importance of	possibility of*	purpose of*	thought of
charge of	form of*	intention of	practice of*	result of*	way of*
cost of*	habit of	means of*	problem of*	risk of*	
danger of	hope of	method of*	process of*	system of*	

*common in academic writing

XIV. Common Verbs Followed by *To-* Infinitives

VERB + *TO-* INFINITIVE

Examples: *agree to go; asked to leave; decide to stay*

afford	bother	demand	hate*	manage	proceed	seek	volunteer
agree	can't stand*	deserve	help	mean**	promise	seem	vow
aim	claim	desire	hesitate	need**	prove	start*	wait
appear	consent	dread*	hope	offer	refuse	stop**	want
ask	continue*	fall	intend	plan	regret**	struggle	wish
attempt	dare	forbid	learn	prefer*	remember**	tend	
beg	decide	forget**	like*	prepare	request	threaten	
begin*	decline	get	love*	pretend	say	try**	

*can also be followed by a gerund   **can be followed by a gerund but with a change in meaning

VERB + OBJECT + *TO-* INFINITIVE

Examples: *advised me to go; reminded me to call; helped them to move*

advise**	beg*	encourage**	hate*	know**	permit**	teach**
allow**	believe**	expect*	help*	like*	persuade**	tell**
appoint**	challenge**	forbid**	imagine**	love*	prefer*	urge**
assume**	choose*	force**	instruct**	need*	promise*	want*
ask*	consider**	get*	judge**	order**	remind**	warn**

*object is optional   **object is required

XV. Common Prepositions

ONE-WORD PREPOSITIONS

about	as	besides	except	like	outside	throughout	until
above	at	between	for	near	over	to	up
across	before	beyond	from	of	past	toward	upon
after	behind	by	in	off	per	towards	with
against	below	despite	including	on	since	under	within
among	beneath	down	inside	onto	than	underneath	without
around	beside	during	into	opposite	through	unlike	

GROUPS OF WORDS THAT FUNCTION LIKE ONE-WORD PREPOSITIONS

according to	away from	in exchange for	instead of	owing to
ahead of	because of	in front of	near to	prior to
apart from	by means of	in place of	on account of	rather than
as for	due to	in spite of	on top of	such as
as of	except for	in terms of	out of	thanks to
as well as	in addition to	inside of	outside of	up to

QUOTATION AND CITATION GUIDE

A Quoted Speech

PUNCTUATING A SINGLE QUOTATION

1a The author says, "The debate of GMOs concerns the extent to which people should trust the corporations that control the GMOs."

1b "The debate of GMOs concerns the extent to which people should trust the corporations that control the GMOs," states the author.

1c According to the author, "The debate of GMOs concerns the extent to which people should trust the corporations that control the GMOs. Most of the GMOs currently used in agriculture were developed and patented by Monsanto and Dupont."

Introduce a quotation with a reporting verb or phrase followed by a comma, as in **1a**. Capitalize the first word of the quotation. Put quotation marks after the comma and after the period.

If the reporting verb comes after the quotation, put a comma before the final quotation mark, as in **1b**.

If there are two sentences in a quotation, place a period between them, as in **1c**.

PUNCTUATING A QUOTATION WITH *THAT*

2a The author claims that "the debate of GMOs concerns the extent to which people should trust the corporations that control the GMOs."

2b He believes that "more work by independent, nonprofit groups needs to be done."

When introducing a quotation with *that* and a reporting verb such as *says, states, claims, believes,* etc., put quotation marks before the quotation and after the period, as in **2a – 2b**. Do not capitalize the first word of the quotation.

PUNCTUATING A SPLIT QUOTATION

3a "The patents," for example, "often require farmers to purchase new seed every year."

3b "Most consumers don't see any personal benefit from Roundup Ready crops," says the author, "but by reducing tilling these crops may help make it possible to significantly reduce greenhouse gas emissions."

When splitting a quotation into two parts, separate them by phrases or clauses, as in **3a – 3b**.

Follow the same punctuation patterns for multi-clause sentences, as in **3b**.

PUNCTUATING A FRAGMENT

4 Companies who are "aggressive in enforcing the patents" want to protect their profits.

Place quotation marks before and after a fragment, as in **4**. Make sure the quoted fragment follows the natural grammar of the sentence. Do not use a capital letter.

When reporting an author's ideas in an essay or research paper, writers have to give credit to the author using in-text citations. Many writers use the *MLA Handbook for Writers of Research Papers*, which sets guidelines for referencing sources through parenthetical citation. It is available in most writing centers and libraries. The following guidelines are from the seventh edition of the *MLA Handbook*. MLA style is commonly used in the liberal arts and humanities.

See Charts B2 and B3 for MLA style Works Cited instructions.

PRINT SOURCE WITH ONE AUTHOR **1a** "There is relatively strong evidence of association between metropolitan development patterns and use of active travel modes such as walking and transit" (Ewing 74). **1b** According to Ewing, "There is relatively strong evidence of association between metropolitan development patterns and use of active travel modes such as walking and transit" (74).	For print sources, such as books, magazines, and scholarly journal articles, set the author's last name and page number(s) in parentheses after the quotation marks, as in **1a**. Place a period after the parentheses. Note that there is no punctuation at the end of the quotation. If the author's last name is mentioned in the essay or research paper, provide only the page number(s) in parentheses at the end of the quotation, as in **1b**.
PRINT SOURCE WITH AN ORGANIZATION **2a** "Mass media campaigns use paid and non-paid forms of media to increase knowledge and change attitudes and behaviors toward diet and physical activity" (WHO 13). **2b** The World Health Organization states that "mass media campaigns use paid and non-paid forms of media to increase knowledge and change attitudes and behaviors toward diet and physical activity" (13).	If the print source is an organization, set the organization's acronym and the page number(s) in parentheses after the quotation, as in **2a**. Place a period after the parentheses. If the organization's name is mentioned in the essay or research paper, provide only the page number(s) in parentheses at the end of the quotation, as in **2b**.
PRINT SOURCE WITH THREE OR MORE AUTHORS **3** "Physical activity has been shown to improve health and reduce the risk of developing many chronic diseases, including cardiovascular disease, diabetes, and some forms of cancer" (Huston et al. 58).	If there are three or more authors, set only the first author's last name followed by *et al.* and the page number(s) in parentheses, as in **3**.
ELECTRONIC SOURCE (ONLINE) **4a** "Physical activity has a myriad of benefits when it comes to our brain health" (Borreli). **4b** Borreli points out that "physical activity has a myriad of benefits when it comes to our brain health."	For electronic sources, such as an online magazine, newspaper, or scholarly journal, set the author's last name in parentheses after the quotation, as in **4a**. Do not include a page number. Place a period after the parentheses. Alternatively, the author's last name can be mentioned within the essay or research paper, as in **4b**.
SOURCE WITH NO AUTHOR **5** Researchers have determined that "prolonged periods of inactivity are bad regardless of how much time you also spend on officially approved high-impact stuff like jogging or pounding treadmills in the gym" ("Standing orders").	If there is no author for a print or electronic source, include the title of the source in parentheses, as in **5**. Place quotation marks around the title. For long titles, include only the first two or three words of the title.

MLA guidelines require writers to include a Works Cited page at the end of a research essay. The entries must match the sources cited in your paper.

Here are some basic guidelines:

- Put the Works Cited page on a separate page at the end of your essay.
- Title the page "Works Cited." Center the title at the top of the page.
- List all citations in alphabetical order by the first author's last name. If there is no author, alphabetize by the first word of the article. (See Chart B3 for specific style instructions for different kinds of sources.)
- Capitalize the main words of the title. Do not capitalize prepositions, articles, or other small words that are not the first word of the title.
- Indent the second and all following lines by 0.5 inch. *Italicize* the name of a book, magazine, or scholarly journal. Put the title of an article in quotation marks.

Works Cited

Borreli, Lizette. "Regular Exercise Boosts Brain Function, Reducing Stress, Improving Memory, and More." *Medical Daily*. 7 May 2015. Web. 25 May 2015. <http://www.medicaldaily.com>

Ewing, Reid. "Can the Physical Environment Determine Physical Activity Levels?" *Exercise and Sport Sciences Reviews* 33.2 (2005): 69-75. Print.

Huston, Sara, Kelly Evenson, Philip Bors, and Ziya Gizlice. "Neighborhood Environment, Access to Places for Activity, and Leisure-time Physical Activity in a Diverse North Carolina Population." *American Journal of Health Promotion* 18.1 (2003): 58-69. Print.

Kotecki, Jerome. *Physical Activity & Health. An Interactive Approach*. New York: Jones & Bartlett Learning, 2010. Print.

Lukits, Ann. "Exercise in Short Bursts Is Effective." *Wall Street Journal*. 8 Jan. 2013: 2-3. Print.

Pruss-Ustun, Annette, and Carlos Corvalan. *Preventing Disease through Healthy Environments*. Geneva: World Health Organization, 2006. Print.

"Standing Orders." *The Economist*. 10 Aug. 2013. Web. 26 May 2015. <http://www.theeconomist.com>

WHO. *Fuel for Life, Household Energy and Health*. Geneva: World Health Organization, 2006. Print.

B3 MLA Works Cited Style Guide

BOOK WITH ONE AUTHOR

Author. *Title of Book*. City of Publication: Publisher, Year of publication. Medium of publication.

Kotecki, Jerome. *Physical Activity & Health: An Interactive Approach*. New York: Jones & Bartlett Learning, 2010. Print.

BOOK WITH MORE THAN ONE AUTHOR

Authors. *Title of Book*. City of Publication: Publisher, Year of publication. Medium of publication.

Pruss-Ustun, Annette, and Carlos Corvalan. *Preventing Disease through Healthy Environments*. Geneva: World Health Organization, 2006. Print.

ARTICLE IN A MAGAZINE OR NEWSPAPER

Author. "Title of Article." *Title of Periodical*. Day Month Year: pages. Medium of publication.

Lukits, Ann. "Exercise in Short Bursts Is Effective." *Wall Street Journal*. 8 Jan. 2013: 2-3. Print.

ARTICLE IN A SCHOLARLY JOURNAL

Author. "Title of Article." *Title of Journal* Volume.Issue (Year): pages. Medium of publication.

Ewing, Reid. "Can the Physical Environment Determine Physical Activity Levels?" *Exercise and Sport Sciences Reviews* 33.2 (2005): 69-75. Print.

ONLINE ARTICLE

Author. "Title of Article." *Name of Website*. Day Month Year. Medium of publication. Date of access. <URL>*

Borreli, Lizette. "Regular Exercise Boosts Brain Function, Reducing Stress, Improving Memory, and More." *Medical Daily*. 7 May 2015. Web. 25 May 2015. <http://www.medicaldaily.com>

*Note: The seventh edition of the *MLA Handbook* does not require a URL. Check with your instructor to see if the URL is preferred.

ONLINE ARTICLE WITH NO AUTHOR

"Title of Article." *Title of Periodical*. Day Month Year. Medium of publication. Date of access. <URL>

"Standing Orders." *The Economist*. 10 Aug. 2013. Web. 26 May 2015. <http://www.theeconomist.com>

C APA Citations & Style Guide

APA citation style is typically used in the social sciences, including psychology and sociology. The following are APA citation and reference guidelines from the sixth edition of the *Publication Manual of the American Psychological Association*, available in most writing centers and libraries.

CITATIONS

1a "There is relatively strong evidence of association between metropolitan development patterns and use of active travel modes such as walking and transit" (Ewing, 2005, p. 74).

1b According to Ewing (2005), "There is relatively strong evidence of association between metropolitan development patterns and use of active travel modes such as walking and transit" (p. 74).

1c Researchers have determined that "prolonged periods of inactivity are bad regardless of how much time you also spend on officially approved high-impact stuff like jogging or pounding treadmills in the gym" ("Standing orders," 2013).

Set the author's last name, year of publication, and page number(s) for the reference in parentheses at the end of the quotation, as in **1a**. Place a period after the parentheses.

If the author's last name is mentioned in the essay, provide the date in parentheses after the author's last name, as in **1b**. Include the page number(s) in parentheses at the end of the quotation.

If there is no author or page number for a source, include the title and year of publication in parentheses, as in **1c**. Place quotation marks around the title. For long titles, include only the first two or three words of the title.

REFERENCES

- Put the references on a separate References page at the end of your essay.
- List all citations in alphabetical order by the first author's last name and first initial. If there is no author, alphabetize by the first word of the article.
- Put the date of publication in parentheses after the author's name.
- Put the main title in *italics*. Capitalize only the first word of the title and subtitle.

BOOKS WITH ONE AUTHOR

Author (Year). *Title of book*. City of Publication: Publisher.

Kotecki, J. (2010). *Physical activity & health: An interactive approach*. New York: Jones & Bartlett Learning.

BOOKS WITH MORE THAN ONE AUTHOR

Authors (Year). *Title of book*. City of Publication: Publisher.

Pruss-Ustun, A., & Corvalan, C. (2006). *Preventing disease through healthy environments*. Geneva: World Health Organization.

JOURNAL ARTICLES

Author (Year). Title of article. *Title of Journal* Volume (Issue), pages.

Ewing, R. (2005). Can the physical environment determine physical activity levels? *Exercise and Sport Sciences Reviews* 33 (2), 69-75.

ONLINE ARTICLES

Author (Year, Month Day). Title of article. *Name of Website*. Retrieved from [website]

Borreli, L. (2015, May 7). Regular exercise boosts brain function, reducing stress, improving memory, and more. *Medical Daily*. Retrieved from http://www.medicaldaily.com

D1 Chicago Style Citations

The *Chicago Manual of Style* (CMS) is often used for essays and research papers in literature, history, and the arts. It uses a system of footnote citations and an end-of-paper bibliography. The following are style guidelines from the sixteenth edition of the CMS.

FOOTNOTE CITATIONS

Chicago style uses a footnote system to cite sources:

- All quotations and paraphrases from other sources are numbered in superscript, as in the example below.

- Footnotes at the bottom of each page provide the full bibliographical information for each numbered source using the format shown below. (See Chart D2 for Chicago style bibliography instructions.)

- When a source is cited two or more times in a row, write *Ibid* instead of the full bibliographic information.

As Houston's population continues to grow due to increasing numbers of people attracted by its job opportunities in the healthcare and energy industries, the city must consider the importance of quality-of-life. Access to parks and walking trails is a critical factor in motivating newcomers to reside in Houston long term. The city has added many new trails, but access is often restricted by highways. According to Ewing, "There is relatively strong evidence of association between metropolitan development patterns and use of active travel modes such as walking and transit."[1] Thus, cities like Houston need to ensure that these new parks and trails are easily accessible to pedestrians so that they are actually used.

This will also have the added benefit of people improving their overall health and reducing the risk of diseases linked to inactivity.[2] Many Houstonians are at risk of obesity, which is directly tied to access to public parks and walking paths.[3] If residents have access to outdoor spaces and are able to stay healthy at the same time, they are more likely to stay in Houston longer.

---

1. Reid Ewing, "Can the Physical Environment Determine Physical Activity Levels?" *Exercise and Sport Sciences Reviews* 33, no. 2 (2005): 69-75.

2. Sara Huston et al., "Neighborhood Environment, Access to Places for Activity, and Leisure-time Physical Activity in a Diverse North Carolina Population," *American Journal of Health Promotion* 18, no. 1 (2003): 58-69.

3. Ibid.

D2 | Chicago Style Bibliography

Chicago style requires writers to include a bibliography. The entries must match the sources cited in your paper.

Here are some basic guidelines:

- Put the bibliography on a separate page at the end of your essay.
- Title the page "Bibliography." Center the title at the top of the page.
- List all citations in alphabetical order by the first author's last name and first name. If there is no author, alphabetize by the first word of the article.
- Capitalize all major words of titles. Do not capitalize prepositions, articles, or other small words that are not the first word of the title.
- Indent the second and all following lines by 0.5 inch. *Italicize* the name of a book, magazine, or scholarly journal. Put the title of an article in quotation marks.

BOOKS WITH ONE AUTHOR

Author. *Title of book*. City of Publication: Publisher, Year.

Kotecki, Jerome. *Physical Activity & Health: An Interactive Approach*. New York: Jones & Bartlett Learning, 2010.

BOOKS WITH MORE THAN ONE AUTHOR

Authors. *Title of Book*. City of Publication: Publisher, Year.

Pruss-Ustun, Annette and Carlos Corvalan. *Preventing Disease through Healthy Environments*. Geneva: World Health Organization, 2006.

JOURNAL ARTICLES

Author. "Title of Article." *Title of Journal* Volume, no. [issue number] (Year): pages.

Ewing, Reid. "Can the Physical Environment Determine Physical Activity Levels?" *Exercise and Sport Sciences Reviews* 33, no. 2 (2005): 69-75.

ONLINE ARTICLES

Author. "Title of Article." *Name of Website* (Year). Accessed [Month Day, Year]. [website].

Borreli, Lizette. "Regular Exercise Boosts Brain Function, Reducing Stress, Improving Memory, and More." *Medical Daily* (2015). Accessed May 25, 2015. http://www.medicaldaily.com.

Index

OXFORD
UNIVERSITY PRESS

198 Madison Avenue
New York, NY 10016 USA

Great Clarendon Street, Oxford, OX2 6DP, United Kingdom

Oxford University Press is a department of the University of Oxford.
It furthers the University's objective of excellence in research, scholarship,
and education by publishing worldwide. Oxford is a registered trade
mark of Oxford University Press in the UK and in certain other countries.

© Oxford University Press 2016

The moral rights of the author have been asserted.

First published in 2016

2020 2019 2018 2017 2016

10 9 8 7 6 5 4 3 2 1

Special thanks to Electra Jablons and Rima Ibrahim for assistance with
language data research.

ISBN: 978 0 19 402829 5 (Student Book 4 with Online Practice Pack)
ISBN: 978 0 19 402848 6 (Student Book 4 as pack component)
ISBN: 978 0 19 402879 0 Online Practice website

Printed in China

This book is printed on paper from certified and well-managed sources.

ACKNOWLEDGEMENTS

*The publisher is grateful to those who have given permission to reproduce the following extracts
and adaptations of copyright material:* pp. 12 and 20 from *The Kite Runner* by Khaled
Hosseini, copyright © 2003 by Khaled Hosseini. Used by permission of Riverhead,
an imprint of Penguin Publishing Group, a division of Penguin Random House LLC;
by permission of Doubleday Canada, a division of Penguin Random House Canada
Limited, a Penguin Random House Company; and by permission of Bloomsbury
Publishing Plc; p. 28 "Cherries for My Grandma" by Geoffrey Canada, *The New York
Times, Late Edition (East Coast)*, February 13, 1995. Reprinted by permission of the
author; p. 39 from "1918 Flu Pandemic That Killed 50 Million Originated in China,
Historians Say" by Dan Vergano, *National Geographic*, January 24, 2014. Copyright
© 1996–2015 National Geographic Society. Reprinted by permission of National
Geographic Creative; p. 42 from "Caffeine: How much is too much?" by Mayo Clinic
Staff. Copyright © 1998–2015 Mayo Foundation for Medical Education and Research.
Reprinted by permission; p. 65 from "Core Truths" by Brooke Borel, *Popular Science*,
July 2014. Reprinted by permission of the author; p. 65 from "Can GMOs Help
Feed a Hot and Hungry World?" by Madeline Ostrander, *The Nation*, September 1–8,
2014. Copyright © 2014 The Nation Company, LLC. All rights reserved. Used by
permission and protected by the Copyright Laws of the United States. The printing,
copying, redistribution, or retransmission of this Content without express written
permission is prohibited. www.thenation.com; p. 66 from "Science That Is Hard
to Swallow" by Fred Hiatt, *The Washington Post*, February 8, 2015. Copyright © 2015
Washington Post Company. All rights reserved. Used by permission and protected
under the Copyright Laws of the United States. The printing, copying, redistribution,
or retransmission of this Content without express written permission is prohibited.
www.washingtonpost.com; p. 67 from "Why the GMO Debate Misses the Point" by
Sasha Wright, October 29, 2013, http://www.popsci.com/. Reprinted by permission of
Dr. Alexandra J. Wright; pp. 67–68 from "Crop Flops: GMOs Lead Ag Down the Wrong
Path" by Tom Philpott, *Grist*, January 21, 2014. Reprinted by permission of Grist.org;
p. 81 from "Privacy in the Workplace," FindLaw.com. Copyright © 2013 FindLaw, a
Thomson Reuters business. All rights reserved. Reprinted by permission of Thomson
Reuters; pp. 107–108 from "You've Got Inappropriate Mail" by Lisa Guernsey, *The
New York Times*, April 5, 2000. Copyright © 2000 The New York Times. All rights reserved.
Used by permission and protected by the Copyright Laws of the United States. The
printing, copying, redistribution, or retransmission of this Content without express
written permission is prohibited. www.nytimes.com; pp. 128–129 from *Tracking the
Elusive Human, Volume 1*, by Tyra Arraj and James Arraj. Reprinted by permission of the
authors; pp. 155–156 from *The Age of Extremes: 1914–1991* by Eric Hobsbawm, copyright
© 1994 by Eric Hobsbawm. Used by permission of Pantheon Books, an imprint of the
Knopf Doubleday Publishing Group, a division of Penguin Random House LLC, and
by permission of David Higham Associates Limited. All rights reserved; pp. 168–169
from "Immanuel Kant," "John Stuart Mill," and "Aristotle," from lectures by Dr. Joseph
Chuman. Used by permission of Dr. Joseph Chuman.

Illustrations by: 5W Infographics: pp. 24, 122, 128, 129, 130, 131, and 178.

We would also like to thank the following for permission to reproduce the following photographs:
Cover: blinkblink/shutterstock; back cover: lvcandy/Getty Images; global: Rodin
Anton/shutterstock; p. 2 Gabe Palmer/Corbis; p. 5 Tetra Images/Getty Images; p.
7 AP Photo/Nils Jorgensen/REX; p. 9 GL Archive/Alamy; p. 10 Emilio Segre Visual
Archives/American Institute of Physics/Science Photo Library; p. 12 Dreamworks/
The Kobal Collection; p. 14 Photo by Notman/http://hdl.loc.gov/loc.pnp/cph.3a15420;
p. 17 Michael Tran/FilmMagic/Getty Images; p. 20 Mohammad Ismail/Reuters/
Corbis; p. 24 Leemage/Getty Images; p. 29 Sviatlana Shmialiova/shutterstock; p. 32
alexandrovskyi/shutterstock; p. 36 wavebreakmedia/shutterstock; p. 41 Terry Eggers/
Terry Eggers/Corbis; p. 52 Joel Nito/AFP/Getty Images; p. 57 Biosphoto/Superstock;
p. 63 Marmaduke St. John/Alamy; p. 67 Maks Narodenko/Shutterstock, Singkham/
Shutterstock, Kalavati/Shutterstock; p. 71 AP Photo/John Gress; p. 72 OUP/Photodisc,
OUP/Ingram (2); p. 73 Image Source/Getty Images; p. 80 Ollyy/shutterstock; p. 83
nicolas hansen/Getty Images; p. 84 YAY Media AS/Alamy; p. 86 Edd Westmacott/
Alamy; p. 88 frantisekhojdysz/shutterstock; p. 89 Ria Novosti/Science Photo Library;
p. 90 NASA/JPL/Space Science Institute, Rich Legg/Getty Images, Amble Design/
shutterstock, Caiaimage/Sam Edwards/Getty Images; p. 95 Pietro Canali/SOPA/Corbis;
p. 96 The Science Picture Company/Alamy; p. 97 Tomas Rodriguez/Corbis; p. 101
John Opie/Getty Images; p. 104 verityjohnson/shutterstock; p. 106 Torleif Svensson/
AGE fotostock; p. 108 PhotoAlto sas/Alamy; p. 118 Tim Pannell/Corbis; p. 124 Stefano
Paltera/U.S. Department of Energy Solar Decathlon; p. 126 Image Source/Getty Images;
p. 133 Huntstock/Getty Images; p. 134 belopoppa/shutterstock; p. 138 Leemage/Corbis,
akg-images/Newscom; p. 142 USAart studio/shutterstock, Issei Kato/Reuters/Corbis;
p. 144 Lev Dolgachov/Alamy; p. 152 C. Camarena/Image Source/Corbis; p. 159 NASA/
JPL-Caltech/Space Science Institute; p. 160 YAY Media AS/Alamy; p. 165 Echo/Getty
Images; p. 166 Blend Images/Alamy; p. 167 Tony Waltham/Robert Harding/Newscom;
p. 168 Stefano Bianchetti/Corbis; p. 169 Leemage/Getty Images; Mary Evans Picture
Library Ltd/AGE fotostock; p. 173 Seattle Art Museum/Corbis; p. 175 Everett Collection
Historical/Alamy, BSIP/UIG Via Getty Images; p. 177 FWS/Alamy, Nigel Cattlin/Visuals
Unlimited/Corbis, Michael Hubrich/Science Photo Library.

ELEMENTS *of* SUCCESS
Online Practice

Elements of Success Online Practice extends your learning beyond the classroom.

Activities include additional **practice** and **online tests** assigned by your teacher.

Progress reports show what you have learned and where you still need more practice.

Email your teacher and your classmates.

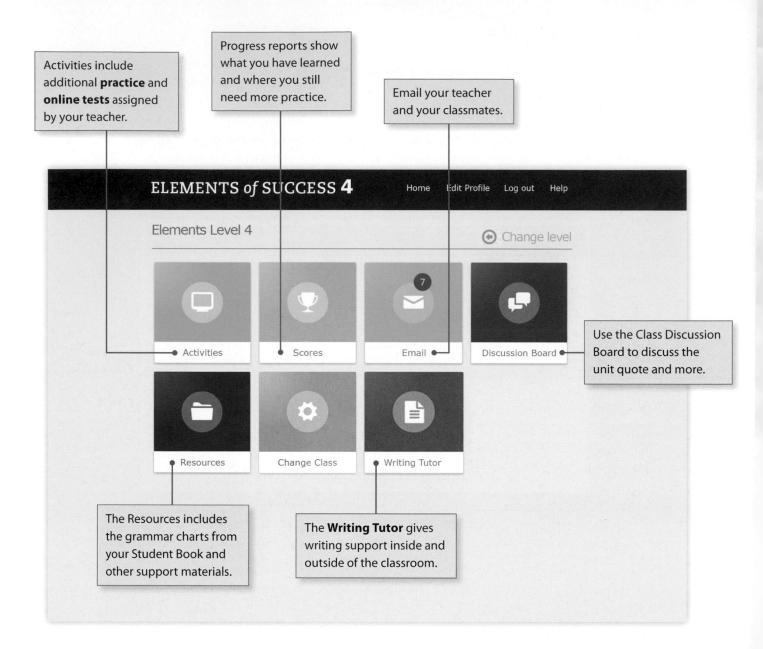

ELEMENTS *of* SUCCESS **4**

Home   Edit Profile   Log out   Help

Elements Level 4

Change level

Activities

Scores

7

Email

Discussion Board

Resources

Change Class

Writing Tutor

Use the Class Discussion Board to discuss the unit quote and more.

The Resources includes the grammar charts from your Student Book and other support materials.

The **Writing Tutor** gives writing support inside and outside of the classroom.